HISTORICAL ENCYCLOPEDIA OF
AMERICAN LABOR

HISTORICAL ENCYCLOPEDIA OF
AMERICAN LABOR

VOLUME 2
P–Z

Edited by
Robert E. Weir and James P. Hanlan

GREENWOOD PRESS
Westport, Connecticut • London

Library of Congress Cataloging-in-Publication Data

Historical encyclopedia of American labor / edited by Robert Weir and James P. Hanlan.
    p. cm.
    Includes bibliographical references and index.
    ISBN 0–313–31840–9 (set : alk. paper)—ISBN 0–313–32863–3 (vol. 1 : alk. paper)—
ISBN 0–313–32864–1 (vol. 2 : alk. paper)
    1. Labor—United States—History—Encyclopedias. 2. Labor movement—United
States—History—Encyclopedias. 3. Industrial relations—United
States—History—Encyclopedias. 4. Labor laws and legislation—United
States—History—Encyclopedias. I. Title: Encyclopedia of American labor. II. Weir,
Robert, E. 1952– III. Hanlan, James P.
    HD8066.H57   2004
    331.88'0973'03—dc21   2003052847

British Library Cataloguing in Publication Data is available.

Library of Congress Catalog Card Number: 2003052847

ISBN: 0–313–31840–9 (set)
       0–313–32863–3 (vol. 1)
       0–313–32864–1 (vol. 2)

First published in 2004

Greenwood Press, 88 Post Road West, Westport, CT 06881
An imprint of Greenwood Publishing Group, Inc.
www.greenwood.com

Printed in the United States of America

The paper used in this book complies with the
Permanent Paper Standard issued by the National
Information Standards Organization (Z39.48–1984).

10 9 8 7 6 5 4 3 2 1

Every reasonable effort has been made to track down the owners of copyright materials
in this book, but in some instances this has proven impossible. The editors and publisher
will be glad to receive information leading to more complete acknowledgments in
subsequent printings of the book and in the meantime extend their apologies for any
omissions.

Contents

Contents

Contents

Acknowledgments

The magnitude of this project makes it inevitable that small errors will occur. We take full responsibility for such slip-ups, although we have taken pains to ensure that the overall integrity of the historical record has not been compromised.

Our codicils aside, we are very proud of this work. That is in no small part due to the outstanding support we got from the labor history community and from Greenwood Press. When we put out a call for contributors to the H-Labor LISTSERV discussion group, we were overwhelmed by the number of those who responded, as well as by their generosity, knowledge, and desire to help. There are too many to list individually, but their names are listed with their entries and in the front matter, and we encourage readers to seek out their work. We thank each and every contributor.

Several individuals went above and beyond the call of duty in helping bring this project to fruition. Professor Weir's undergraduate labor history class at Bay Path College helped with some of the initial research in the fall of 2000. He wishes to thank Lisa Barber, Michele Bernier, Cheryl Conley, Yasmin Correa, Pauline Gladstone, Heather Hite, Shalynn Hunt, Leslie Juntunen, Maria Medina, Sara Pleva, Carina Reid, Maria Ruotolo, Aryu Sunyoto, and Teri Voight for their invaluable assistance. Professor Hanlan also drew upon the hard work of the students at Worcester Polytechnic Institute enrolled in his labor history seminar. They served as a sounding board and an inspiration. His colleagues Kent Ljungquist, Robert W. Thompson, Edmund Hayes, and Penny Rock provided companionship, counsel, and the best of friendship that any college faculty member could hope for. They showed me the joys of interdisciplinary and interdepartmental collegiality. I owe them much. Likewise I thank Provost John F. Carney for providing release time.

Our friend Scott Molloy, who directs the labor center at the University of Rhode Island, toiled long and hard on behalf of the project. Scott not only served on the advisory board, but he also enlisted his graduate students in the project and wrote numerous entries. A special thanks goes to another good friend and colleague, Bruce Cohen of Worcester State College. Other than our own names, Bruce's name appears more than any other in these volumes. Whenever we were stuck for coverage, we contacted Bruce and he took over our troublesome topics, to say nothing of the dozens of entries for which he actually volunteered. Bruce inspired both of us through his dedication to teaching and scholarship and especially through his genuine and heartfelt commitment to the well-being of the men and women who work and struggle to earn their livings.

The staff at the George Meany Memorial Archives at the National Labor College in Silver Spring, Maryland, were extremely generous in helping track down images and in providing support materials for the project. A special thank you goes to Lynda DeLoach at the archives and to Bob Reynolds, who edits the wonderful *Labor's Heritage* from the same location. They helped make Professor Weir's research and visit to the archives an absolute delight.

Greenwood Press could not have been more accommodating. Barbara Rader, the executive editor of the School and Public Library Reference division, got the ball rolling and showed great confidence in the editors' ability to get the job done. She then turned the editors over to the capable hands of Kevin Ohe and John Wagner, who shepherded the project to completion. Elizabeth Kincaid did a fine job of tracking down photos. The editors are indebted to Greenwood for their faith in them and for making this a quality work.

* * *

I would like to thank my wife, Emily, for her ongoing love and support. She is also the most affable research partner that one could hope to have. I am truly blessed to be able to share life's road with her.

In the middle of this project, I was fortunate enough to be a Fulbright scholar in New Zealand. I want to thank Jim Hanlan for taking up the slack while I was on the adventure of a lifetime. I had endless hours of fascinating discussions with Kiwi colleagues like Melanie Nolan and Pat Moloney at Victoria University, Jim McAloon at Lincoln University, Kerry Taylor at Massey University, Miles Fairburn and Graeme Dunstan at the University of Canterbury, and Tom Brooking and Erik Olssen at the University of Otago. My conversations with these individuals helped shape my words and thoughts in more ways than I can count. So too did my time at the Alexander Turnbull Library in Wellington, where I learned so much more not only about New Zealand labor history but also about American history. Many thanks to Frank Rogers, who came to one of my Turnbull talks and proceeded to share his wisdom with me, and to John Martin, the senior historian with the historical branch of the Department of the Interior and one of the most careful researchers I've ever met. A special thank you to Janet Horncy and Margaret Calder at the Turnbull Library, who gave me the freedom to pursue various research interests, but also made me feel like part of their extended families. And finally, a thank you to Jenny Gill and her staff at Fulbright New Zealand. You folks are simply the best!

I would like to dedicate my part of this work to my father, Archie Weir, a longtime union member, who died on April 11, 2002. His loss is deeply felt, but his fighting spirit lives on.

Robert E. Weir

I am indebted more than I can express to my wife, Gaye D. (Francis) Hanlan. She tolerated my distractions and absences and eased my burdens through this long project. Likewise, my children, George, Janet, and Jamo, served as promise for what the future can hold. I would like to express my thanks to the Lowell Central Labor Council, which, many years ago, provided a scholarship for my undergraduate education.

I dedicate my part of this work to the memory of my father and mother, George J. and Cecilia G. (Tynan) Hanlan. They knew what it was to endure a long and painful strike and to persevere. My father's pride in craftsmanship was exemplary. Together my parents inspired my life.

James P. Hanlan

Preface

Compiling the *Historical Encyclopedia of American Labor* has been a daunting task, to say the least. Like most historians, each of us is trained in a narrow specialty. Our long years of teaching experience have broadened us, but there were, invariably, gaps in our knowledge. Luckily, the labor history community is stocked with numerous bright and affable individuals who were ready to lend their expertise to the project. We thank them profusely and without them could not have finished these volumes.

The project was imposing because we knew from the outset that some professional labor educators were going to take umbrage with how we covered certain topics, what we covered, and what we left out. Our only defense is to say that this is *not* a collection for experts in the field. Ours is a guide for those starting research projects, writing school reports, or familiarizing themselves with hitherto unknown people, ideas, events, and organizations. It is designed primarily for public libraries, college and university library reference sections, high school libraries, and general repositories. Although we certainly hope that labor research centers, unions, and graduate schools find our efforts useful, we would be the last to say that the *Historical Encyclopedia* is the final word on *any* of the subjects it contains.

The *Historical Encyclopedia* offers almost 400 entries covering unions, union leaders, labor-related events, important statutes and court cases, and labor terminology. The entries are thoroughly cross-referenced, with mentions of other related entries highlighted upon their first appearance in the text of any particular entry. Entries conclude with a listing of suggested readings for those wishing to read in more detail on a particular subject. The *Historical Encyclopedia* is also illustrated with numerous photographs and includes an appendix containing excerpts from fifty-eight labor-related primary documents, including items such as statutes, interviews with workers, passages from the autobiographies of labor leaders, union documents, congressional testimony, and newspaper and magazine articles on labor topics and events. Finally, as a quick reference supplement to the entry readings, the *Historical Encyclopedia* offers a bibliography of important books and Web sites on labor-related topics and also includes a detailed subject index to provide quick, in-depth access to the information in the entries.

It is easy for experts immersed in the intricacies of research to forget that the general public knows little or nothing about American labor history. Most high school textbooks give scant attention to labor history, and our recent perusal of a half dozen popular college U.S. history survey texts reveals that among labor leaders only Terence Powderly, Samuel Gompers, A. Philip Randolph, Mary Jones, John L. Lewis, and Cesar Chavez are mentioned with any degree of regularity. Likewise, the only labor actions to warrant much coverage are the eight-hour-movement, the railroad strikes of 1877, the Pullman and Homestead strikes in the 1890s, the sit-down strikes of the 1930s, and the Professional Air Traffic Controllers Organization (PATCO) walkout of 1981. And even then, the operative word is "mentioned." Thorough discussions of the arc of labor history are noticeably absent. It has been more than four decades since the new social history admonished historians to consider race, class, and gender when writing history. Our observations reveal that class largely remains a junior partner within the troika.

When we began this project, we met with many people, scoured the indexes of numerous labor history textbooks, put out calls on the World Wide Web, and endlessly brainstormed. Our question was a basic one: *What would individuals with little or no background in labor history need to learn if they wished to begin studying the subject?* We tried to remember our own initial forays into the subject and Professor Weir recalled his high school teaching days. Experts may be dismayed to discover that cherished topics they've been researching for years are absent from this work. Our exclusion of topics is in no way a value judgment of their relative importance. Neither of us holds to elitist views of history that privilege some topics and individuals as more important than others. Our main criterion for choosing topics was simply the likelihood of a researcher to encounter it in the initial stages of a bigger project. We also endeavored to be as inclusive as possible on matters pertaining to race, gender, and ethnicity, but the fact is— and we decry it in numerous entries—the organized labor movement in the United States has been distressingly dominated by white males. Numerous entries on nonorganized labor made their way into the work as a way of partially addressing this imbalance.

Throughout the project, we remained cognizant that we were writing an encyclopedia. In that spirit, we opted to present general knowledge rather than specialized research, though we apologize in advance for what will seem to experts gross simplifications. We also opted, whenever possible, to avoid technical language, jargon, and arcane terminology. The staff at Greenwood continually reminded us that our target audience is a general one, and we tried our best to serve that readership. Those seeking to expand their understanding of American labor leaders not covered in these volumes are directed to another Greenwood publication, Gary Fink's superb *Biographical Dictionary of American*

Labor Leaders. We had to be very selective in choosing specific unions to include, but most labor unions past and present can be researched further on the World Wide Web, and several have outstanding Web sites that surpass any efforts on our part. The same is true for most of the events and terms we present. Good public, college, and university libraries are also filled with fine works from professional historians—many of whom we are proud to name as friends and colleagues—and we hope readers will consult them. Like all encyclopedias, this one is designed to make readers want to learn more. If it inspires novices to plumb depths we could not, our job will have been well done.

Robert E. Weir
Florence, Massachusetts

James P. Hanlan
Worcester, Massachusetts

Entry List

P

Part-Time Labor. Part-time labor is, according to the **Bureau of Labor Statistics,** any job in which an employee works fewer than thirty-five hours per week. Part-time work has been a feature of American labor from Colonial times, but it has taken on new urgency in recent years. As many as 25 percent of all jobs are now part-time, with critics charging that this trend impoverishes workers while enriching companies that could afford to hire workers on a full-time basis. Part-time jobs usually pay less than full-time jobs; benefits are often prorated or nonexistent.

Critics and defenders of contemporary hiring practices agree that as many as 80 percent of all part-time workers choose their status. Students, retirees, parents seeking flexible hours, and those making lifestyle choices make up the bulk of part-time workers. Their numbers are highest in the retail, food, and service industries, where over 30 percent of the workforce is part-time. They are also found in large numbers in manufacturing (18.7 percent) and farming (19 percent). Increasing numbers are also found in higher education; at some colleges and universities, more than half of all courses are taught by graduate students or adjunct faculty. Most part-time workers are younger than twenty-four or older than fifty-five. In 1998, 36.5 percent of women worked part-time, as did 21.2 percent of men.

Disagreements rage as to whether involuntary part-timers constitute a social problem. The Employment Policy Foundation claims that the percentage of involuntary part-time workers has remained around 18 percent of the total workforce since the 1970s, and that only one-fifth of these workers remain unwilling part-timers for more than a year. Feminists point to the gender discrepancies of part-time work and note that women are more likely to head single-parent households. Their critique has gained potency due to recent welfare reforms that require part-time "workfare" as a precondition for drawing benefits. Social reformers point to educational inequities; the less education a worker has, the more likely he or she is to be an involuntary part-time worker.

Unions note that full-time workers averaged $15.77 per hour in 1997, while part-timers earned only $8.89. In addition, many employers use part-time work as a way to avoid paying health care and other benefits. Unions also charge that part-time work is often used to discourage unionization; about 6.8 percent of part-time workers belong to unions, as opposed to nearly 15 percent of full-time employees.

Suggested Readings: Kathleen Barker and Kathleen Christensen, eds., *Contingent Work: American Employment Relations in Transition,* 1998; Employment Policy Foundation, "Part-Time Work: Not a Problem Requiring a Solution," http://www.epf.org/polpartwork.htm; "Share of Part-Time Workers by Industry."

Robert E. Weir

Paternalism. Paternalism is the principle or practice of administration in a fatherly manner. It can refer to the claim or attempt to provide, protect, and control a community as a father would his children. The *Chicago Times* coined the term in 1881 from the root *paternal* and applied it to industrial enterprises. Historians have applied the term to industries during the antebellum period as one dimension of the social relations of production, as well as to later businesses. The New England textile mill communities of Samuel Slater and the Lowell model provide two distinct examples. Slater built entire communities that included churches, shops, schools, and all other necessities for families in an attempt to obtain, retain, and control his workforce. The owners of the Lowell mills provided supervised dormitory accommodation for their largely

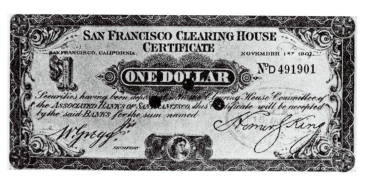

One aspect of the paternalistic practices of some nineteenth-century industries was the issuing of scrip, a privately printed form of "currency" that was redeemable only at the company store. Workers paid in scrip had no alternative but to purchase their necessities at company prices. © Bettmann/Corbis.

female workforce, maintained strict moral codes of behavior, and provided what the mill owners deemed to be suitable recreational activities. Other forms of paternalism are found in industrial communities, but all retain the basic principles of provision and control.

Theoretically, paternalism has also been applied to the southern slave communities, whereby a master provided all the physical needs for his slaves and regulated their behavior, as a father might his children. In the late nineteenth and into the early twentieth century, paternalism became less formal and took the form of a master-worker relationship. Employers might provide steady work, education for workers' children, and deflect immoral influences such as alcohol in exchange for workers' loyalty, certain levels of conduct on the shop floor, and employees' surrender to factory routines. During the first half of the twentieth century, paternalism evolved into corporate welfare schemes that were created to address labor-relations problems and that were characterized by new technology and routines within a more humane workplace. Thus, paternalism provided a distinct alternative to individualistic factory **capitalism**, despite the many forms it adopted over time in the various regions of America.

Suggested Readings: L. J. Alston and J. P. Ferrie, *Southern Paternalism and the American Welfare State: Economics, Politics, and Institutions in the South, 1865–1965*, 1998; Eugene Genovese, *Roll Jordan Roll: The World the Slaves Made*, 1972; Phillip Scranton, "Varieties of Paternalism: Industrial Structures and the Social Relations of Production in American Textiles," in *American Quarterly* 36, no. 2 (1984): 235–57.

Janet Greenlees

Paterson Silk Strike. The Paterson, New Jersey, silk mill strike began in January 1913, when the city's largest company, Doherty and Company, increased employee workloads by demanding each laborer tend four looms instead of two. This **stretch-out** meant faster, harder work. When Doherty fired members of a **grievance** committee seeking redress, 800 silk workers walked out. Strikers appealed to the **Industrial Workers of the World (IWW)** for help, and, flush with success from the **Lawrence textile strike**, the IWW sent organizers to Paterson. The IWW extended the **strike** to all of the city's 300 silk mills and virtually its entire workforce of 25,000 laborers, nearly a third of whom were Polish Jews.

Standing between two large American flags, Ann Burlak, secretary of the Textile Workers' Union, is shown addressing the large crowd of Silk Mill strikers, October 21st. © Bettmann/Corbis.

Using tactics honed in Lawrence, Massachusetts, the IWW set up soup kitchens and nationality committees, and organized mass rallies. Leaders like **William Haywood**, Patrick Quinlan, and **Carlo Tresca** took part in the strike, and **Elizabeth Gurley Flynn** organized women workers. Unlike Lawrence, however, Paterson officials avoided public-relations debacles whilst engaging in a brutal crackdown against strikers. Several strikers died, over 4,800 workers were arrested, and some 1,300 were jailed, including Flynn, Haywood, Quinlan, and Tresca. The opposition of the **American Federation of Labor**'s United Textile Workers union, which tried to **raid** IWW members and undermined its efforts, aided company efforts. In attempt to rally flagging support, journalist John Reed organized a strike pageant of over a thousand workers. The pageant was an artistic triumph but an economic boondoggle, despite selling out Madison Square Garden and attracting financial support from bohemian Greenwich Village socialites.

After a bitter twenty-two-week battle, oppression, hunger, and deprivation forced strikers to surrender and accept prestrike conditions. Paterson was the first of a series of post-Lawrence IWW setbacks in eastern industrial cities. Some of the events of Paterson in 1913 were dramatized in the 1981 film *Reds*, directed by and starring Warren Beatty.

Suggested Readings: Melvyn Dubofsky, *We Shall Be All*, 1969; David Goldberg, *A Tale of Three Cities*, 1989); Anne Trip, *The IWW and the Paterson Silk Strike of 1913*, 1987.

Don Binkowski

Pattern Bargaining. Pattern bargaining is the negotiation of a **contract** based on what has already happened to similarly situated firms in an industry and/or region. It is most often associated with the attempt to take **wages** out of competition in a particular field by examining other comparable contracts. The settlement of the first contract in the industry sets the terms for others to follow. Although the relationship between the companies is not formal, a trend becomes established due to the previous conduct of the parties. While pattern bargaining may eliminate some individual choice for businesses and unions, it does offer some advantages. Companies in highly regulated or monopolistic industries tend to like pattern bargaining because it stabilizes their workforce. If everyone is paying the same wage, they will be better able to retain their workforce, since the market has been set for workers' wages and they cannot go somewhere else for better remuneration. If all companies are paying the same compensation, then the firm with the best management or product will be the strongest.

Unions also favor pattern bargaining as it dissuades management from using regional wage differentials to undercut what all workers get paid. In addition, it mediates against rogue employers who pay substandard wages and thus unfairly compete against firms that employ union workers. The problem with this from a membership standpoint is that a local union may be unwilling to negotiate a better contract than the other locals for fear that it will cause disruption in the **international union**. An example occurred when the Canadian branch of the **United Auto Workers (UAW)** disaffiliated from the parent group in 1984 and created the Canadian Auto Workers when the UAW accepted a **profit sharing** plan that was not acceptable to the Canadian workers.

While pattern bargaining can work from the viewpoint of either side, it is most commonly sought by unions. The **International Brotherhood of Team-**

sters was quite successful in establishing pattern bargaining in the 1950s and 1960s. **Deregulation** of the trucking industry dealt a blow to Teamster pattern bargaining. In like fashion, many other unions lost pattern bargaining leverage with the onset of **globalization** in the 1970s. Wages in most industries have been put back into competition, making pattern bargaining difficult to achieve.

Suggested Readings: John W. Budd, "The Internal Union Political Imperative for UAW Pattern Bargaining," in *Journal of Labor Research*, Vol. 16: 1 (Winter 1995); Gary Samuels, "Bargaining in Detroit: One Size No Longer Fits All," in *Business Week* 30 (September 1996).

Joseph F. Rodgers

Pensions. Pensions are private plans, primarily employer-sponsored, intended to supplement the Social Security benefits a person receives upon retiring. They have come to be an extension of the government's minimalist approach in Social Security legislation. An employer makes the payments, usually a fixed amount, to retirees or their beneficiaries in consideration for the worker's years of service to the company. Normally the employee is entitled to collect these payments upon reaching a certain age, after working a number of years for the same employer, or a combination of both. The formula used to derive the compensation generally takes into consideration the years of service and the employee's previous compensation. There are several types of qualified pension plans that are allowed under the law, with a general restriction that the formulas cannot discriminate in favor of management.

The American Express Company established the first private pension plan in 1875. Five years later, the Baltimore and Ohio Railroad set up a plan; by 1930, some 400 pension plans were in place. Unions were often ambivalent about employer-managed pensions, with many voicing concern that they were little more than forms of **paternalism**. Labor organizations often offered their own pension plans; several railroad brotherhoods had modest plans in effect by the early twentieth century. Most unions embraced the 1935 Social Security Act, but soon realized that Social Security provided inadequate retirement benefits. In 1946, the **United Mine Workers of America (UMWA)** succeeded in negotiating the first employer-financed pension program that was jointly administered by employers and the UMWA. In 1948, the National Labor Relations Board ruled that unions could negotiate pensions in the **collective bargaining** process. That right was confirmed by the Supreme Court in the 1949 decision *Inland Steel v. the National Labor Relations Board*. Since then, pensions have become a standard negotiating item. Recent controversy centers on the rights of employers to move pension funds into other accounts, shifts that employees claim threaten the solvency of pension systems.

Suggested Readings: Everett Allen, *Pension Planning: Pensions, Profit Sharing, and Other Defined Compensation Plans*, 7th ed., 1992; Jay Conison, *Employment Benefit Plans in a Nutshell*, 1998.

Joseph F. Rodgers

Perkins, Frances Corlie (April 10, 1880–May 14, 1965). Frances Perkins was a reformer and the first female cabinet officer. Perkins was born in Boston, the only daughter of Frederick W. and Susan (Bean) Perkins. The family moved to Worcester, where Perkins attended Worcester Classical High before going on to Mount Holyoke College, where in 1902 she received a bachelor of arts in chemistry and physics.

A speech by Florence Kelly of the National Consumer's League (NCL) inspired Perkins toward social service. She taught at several New England girls' schools from 1902 through 1904, and then at Ferry Hall in Chicago from 1904 through 1907. While in Chicago, Perkins also worked for both Hull House and Chicago Commons, which were settlement houses. She then moved to Philadelphia, where she became the executive secretary of the city's Research and Protective Association, a social agency aimed at protecting immigrant women and recent African American arrivals from the South. She also studied economics and sociology at the Wharton School of Finance and won a Russell Sage Foundation fellowship that took her to the New York School of Philanthropy in 1909. She obtained her master of arts from Columbia, her thesis dealing with malnutrition among slum children.

In 1910, Perkins became NCL executive secretary and was mentored by Kelly. Perkins investigated safety and health conditions in **sweatshops** and bakeries and was profoundly affected by the **Triangle Factory Fire of 1911**. The tragedy led to the creation of the New York State Investigating Commission, for which Perkins served as executive secretary from 1912 through 1917. On September 26, 1913, Perkins married economist Paul C. Wilson; in 1916, the couple had a daughter, Suzanne.

Perkins's activities drew the attention of New York Governor Al Smith, whom Perkins advised on progressive factory legislation. Smith's successor, Franklin Delano Roosevelt, appointed her state industrial commissioner in 1929. When Roosevelt was elected president in 1932, he asked Perkins to serve as his secretary of labor, the first woman to hold a cabinet post. She advised the president during a chaotic period for organized labor that saw such events as the **sit-down strikes**, the birth of the **Congress of Industrial Organizations**, and the passage of the **National Labor Relations Act**. She was also instrumental in incorporating into the **Department of Labor** key New Deal programs like the Civilian Conservation Corps, the Civil Works Administration, **the Federal Emergency Relief Administration**, and the Public Works Administration. Perkins was at the forefront of advising Roosevelt on issues like the **minimum wage**, **child labor**, and public-works projects. She also reorganized both the Bureau of Immigration and the **Bureau of Labor Statistics**. Perkins pushed Roosevelt to sign both the Social Security Act of 1935 and the **Fair Labor Standards Act** of 1938.

During World War II, Perkins oversaw the Department of Labor's efforts to shift the economy from domestic to military production. She also thwarted FBI director J. Edgar Hoover's plan to keep dossiers on all American citizens.

Perkins resigned her post when Roosevelt died in 1945, but President Truman appointed her to the Social Security Commission in 1946, and asked her to attend the International Labor Organization's founding meeting in Paris. She also found time to pen *The Roosevelt I Knew*, a memoir of her service with the deceased president.

Perkins retired from government service in 1952, the same year her husband died. She taught at the University of Illinois until 1954, when she joined the industrial and labor relations faculty at Cornell. At the time of her death, she was working on a biography of Al Smith, which became the basis for a book by historians Hannah and Matthew Josephson.

Suggested Readings: George Martin, *Madame Secretary*, 1976; Lillian H. Mohr, *Frances Perkins*, 1979; Frances Perkins, *The Roosevelt I Knew*, 1946.

Robert E. Weir

Permit Cards. Permit cards establish a procedure whereby a union member can pre-pay **dues** and travel to a new area where another branch or local of their **international union** has **jurisdiction**. Presentation of one's card gains access to union hiring halls. The practice began in the late 1800s when union activists and strikers often found themselves on a blacklist that prevented them from obtaining local employment. Permit cards allowed blacklisted workers to relocate. Some unions, notably the **International Association of Machinists**, even gave card carriers shelter and meal money. Workers were expected to reimburse the union, and the names of deadbeats were published in union journals.

Albert V. Lannon

Pesotta, Rose (November 20, 1896–December 7, 1965). Rose Pesotta was an important activist in the **International Ladies' Garment Workers' Union (ILGWU)**. Her career illustrates both the militancy of Jewish women in organized labor and the problems encountered by **minority labor** within unions. Pesotta was born in Derazhyna, Ukraine (Russia), the daughter of grain dealers. She became an anarchist in her teens, and she fled Russia when she was sixteen to avoid an arranged marriage. She emigrated to New York City in 1913 and moved in with her older sister, Esther. Like many Jewish women, she found employment in the city's clothing industry and took a job sewing in a shirtwaist factory.

Despite a so-called protocol of peace negotiated between major employers and the ILGWU in 1911, industrial relations remained tense, with many employees remembering the **Uprising of the 20,000 (1909)**, smaller strikes in 1910, and the tragic **Triangle Factory Fire of 1911**. Pesotta joined a heavily Yiddish ILGWU local and quickly rose through the ranks, despite her involvement with the **anarchist** and free-love movements and her outspoken opposition to World War I. In 1920, she was elected to the ILGWU's executive board and also served as a national organizer. She was also active in the unsuccessful clemency campaign for **Sacco and Vanzetti**. The ILGWU sent Pesotta to Los

Angeles in the late 1920s, where she enjoyed success in bringing Latina members into the union. In 1933, new ILGWU president David Dubinsky promoted Pesotta to one of the union's vice presidencies, and he encouraged her work in Los Angeles.

Pesotta helped some 7,500 women spread among more than 200 **sweatshops** develop a Spanish/English bilingual newspaper and assisted them in a 1933 cloakmakers' strike that saw men break ranks and return to work. The fiery Pesotta used creative tactics to maintain **solidarity** among the women, including broadcasting strike messages from Mexico when a local station refused to air updates and holding a mock fashion show on a **picket** line outside a Los Angeles hotel where new spring fashions were being unveiled. Her tactics helped the women win a **contract** despite a lack of support from male cloakmakers.

From 1934 through 1942, Pesotta traveled across the continental United States, Puerto Rico, and Canada organizing women garment workers. Despite her successes, she was not comfortable inside the ILGWU, largely because of her political and personal views. She complained of sexism within the union, a charge made manifest by the fact that she was the sole woman officer for an organization whose membership was 85 percent female. Moreover, her advocacy of anarchism and free love made Dubinsky nervous, especially given his desire to purge the union of **communists** and other radicals.

In 1942, Pesotta helped Los Angeles workers win a contract against several important dress retailers, but her tactics and abrasive personality led to clashes with the ILGWU's male West Coast director, Louis Levy. When Dubinsky sided with Levy and removed Pesotta from the very local she founded, she abruptly resigned her ILGWU vice presidency and returned to work as a sewing-machine operator. In 1944, she also resigned from the ILGWU executive board. Although she continued to take part in some local activities, Pesotta's career within the ILGWU was over. After World War II, Pesotta toured Europe and took up the cause of refugees. The experience also enhanced Pesotta's Jewish identity. She won some acclaim for two autobiographical books, *Bread Upon the Waters* (1944), which recounted her union organizing efforts, and *Days of Our Lives* (1958), the story of her Ukranian childhood.

Pesotta's difficulties within the ILGWU underscored the sexism of much of the organized labor movement, an issue not fully addressed until feminists challenged unions in the 1960s and 1970s. Pesotta died in Miami in 1965, having retired from the dressmaker profession several years earlier.

Suggested Readings: Naomi Shepherd, *A Price Below Rubies: Jewish Women as Rebels and Radicals*, 1993; Ann Schofield, *"To Do & Be": Portraits of Four Women Activists, 1893-1986*, 1997; Elaine Leeder, *Gentle General: Rose Pesotta, Anarchist and Labor Leader*, 1993.

Bruce Cohen

James P. Hanlan

Phelps Dodge Strike. The Phelps Dodge strike was a brutal struggle against copper interests in Arizona during 1983 and 1984 that ended in a complete rout of over 2,000 strikers and the thirty local unions that represented them. The Phelps Dodge **strike** is viewed by many as one of the worst **downsizing, decertification**, and **concessions** strikes of the 1980s. Evidence suggests that the Phelps Dodge Corporation's intent from the start was to break its unions. The strike had a devastating effect on heavily Hispanic communities like Ajo, Clifton, and Morenci, Arizona.

Long before the 1983 strike, the Phelps Dodge Corporation was infamous for poor labor relations. In 1903, the company rounded up and deported Mexican activists attempting to unionize, and in 1917 a company-sponsored vigilante committee in Bisbee, Arizona, herded members of the **Industrial Workers of the World** into unventilated railroad boxcars and transported them to the desert. In 1941, the company was forced to rehire thirty-five members of the **International Union of Mine, Mill, and Smelter Workers (IUMMSW)** after Justice Felix Frankfurter blasted Phelps Dodge's union-busting record in his Supreme Court brief of *Phelps Dodge v. National Labor Relations Board.* Conditions remained tense, and in 1953 a strike broke out among largely Hispanic miners. It was immortalized in the documentary *Salt of the Earth,* a classic labor movie. The IUMMSW also had to endure red-baiting, as it contained communist members objectionable to both the company and the **Congress of Industrial Organizations**.

The IUMMSW was eventually forced to purge extreme left influences. In 1967, its remnants merged with the **United Steel Workers of America (USWA)**, which became the dominant union in the copper fields. Copper production was booming by 1970, and the USWA negotiated **pattern bargaining** agreements with most producers in the Southwest. Phelps Dodge was forced into pattern bargaining by a USWA-led strike in 1967. The next year, the company began relations with the University of Pennsylvania's Wharton School of Business, which was in the process of developing strategies for businesses wishing to break unions. (Today, the Wharton School's methods are considered the definitive way to defeat unions.)

Pattern bargaining held at Phelps Dodge into 1983, and the USWA and other unions had raised **wages** to an average of $12 per hour. Although copper-field wages were slightly below that of many other miners, a key element was the existence of provisions that granted periodic **cost-of-living adjustments (COLA)**. Company officials complained that high wages and COLAs made the firm uncompetitive against imported copper. It demanded concessions from various unions, including the right to pay new hires lower starting wages. When the **contract** with Phelps Dodge expired on June 30, 1983, and no progress emerged in negotiations, Phelps Dodge workers authorized a strike. The two locales most affected were the adjacent towns of Morenci and Clifton, the former a virtual **company town**, and the latter a union stronghold with a heavily Hispanic population.

It soon became apparent that Phelps Dodge intended to break the unions. It pulled out of pattern bargaining agreements with other producers, won injunctions to limit the number of **pickets**, threatened union workers, and began to recruit **scabs**. The company even tried to get courts to ban the word scab, though they were rebuffed in that effort. It did, however, take full advantage of the current political climate. In the wake of the Reagan administration's firing of **Professional Air Traffic Controllers Organization (PATCO)** workers, unions found themselves on the defensive. Court rulings that allowed firms to hire **replacement workers** during economic strikes gave Phelps Dodge the opening it wanted. Arizona's **right-to-work** laws allowed the firm to replenish its workforce quickly.

During the months that ensued, Phelps Dodge resorted to brutality seldom seen since the 1930s. Labor spies infiltrated union locals, and company **goons** precipitated violent clashes with strikers. That violence, in turn, was used to convince Arizona's Democratic Governor Bruce Babbitt to call in the National Guard on August 19, 1983. The Guard was also involved in violence, and several communities were transformed into armed camps, with tanks, helicopters, and camouflaged troops patrolling company property and town streets. Phelps Dodge also exerted influence on the media's reportage of the strike. All attempts at mediation were dismissed by company officials. It also played off ethnic and religious tensions by hiring mostly Protestant Anglos to take the places of Catholic Hispanics.

The affected towns suffered tremendously. Some strikers broke ranks and returned to work, raising tensions considerably. The Morenci Miners Women's Auxiliary set up food banks, day-care centers, clinics, and other community services, but faced inadequate capital and supplies. The women did, however, demonstrate more militancy than many of the men. They constantly harassed scabs, confronted police and guardsmen, and pressured local merchants and doctors to aid strikers. The unions seemed powerless to offer much more, however, and some strikers complained that leadership was out of touch. The USWA did bring in consultant Ray Rogers to launch a **corporate campaign** against Phelps Dodge. An attempt to pressure Manufacturers Hanover Investment Company—which dealt with Phelps Dodge and held union **pension** funds—yielded only minor results. Singer Bruce Springsteen donated $10,000 to strikers, but deprivation raged.

In the end, Babbitt's decision to use the National Guard doomed the strike. With strikers unable to disrupt production, there was little incentive for Phelps Dodge to negotiate. Unions filed several **unfair labor practices**, but given that the regional director of the National Labor Relations Board (NLRB), Milo Price, had once clashed with unions, they stood little chance of succeeding. For all intents and purposes, the strike was broken by September 1983. Production continued despite ongoing protests, and Phelps Dodge put into place all of its demands, including a two-tier wage system and an end to COLAs. Price called an October 9, 1984, union **decertification** vote. Strikers could not cast ballots, and the replacement workers voted out all thirty unions. Price announced the official results on January 24, 1985, and appeals lingered until February 19,

1986. As expected, the NLRB ruled against the unions, officially ending the strike.

One study calculated that Phelps Dodge invested about $92,000 per replacement worker rather than negotiate with union workers earning roughly $26,000 annually. The firm lost money during 1983, but copper prices quickly rebounded, and it began to post large profits. In 1988, it paid workers an $8,000 **bonus**, after posting a profit of over $420 million. The company could not buy goodwill, however, and it did not remain union-free. The USWA rebuilt some of its base, as did the International Brotherhood of Electrical Workers and the Office and Professional Employees International Union. In 1996, unionized workers in Chico, New Mexico, found themselves without a contract. Having learned a lesson in 1983, workers stayed on the job while their unions applied pressure through community groups, filed NLRB complaints, and exposed company environmental violations that stood to cost it tens of millions in fines. Phelps Dodge again tried to play hardball, threatening to lay off over 300 workers, but in the end was forced to capitulate. On November 19, 1998, the company signed a four-year contract with several unions.

The Phelps Dodge strike stands as a testament to corporate arrogance and to the unequal power relationship between capital and labor in the 1980s and beyond. Some observers draw more conclusions. The actions of Governor Babbitt led some to argue that labor's historic alliance with the Democratic Party is unwise. (President Clinton appointed Babbitt secretary of interior in 1993, further angering activists.) Moreover, NLRB actions suggest that the board has become a tool of partisan politics rather than industrial peace. Critics of **deregulation** see the Phelps Dodge struggle as emblematic of the abuse potential of laissez-faire economic policies. Still others argue that labor laws are tilted too far in favor of the business community. Optimists view strikes in the 1980s as a wake-up call for organized labor that showed a new generation needs to evolve new tactics. However one wishes to interpret it, the 1983–84 events devastated several small Arizona communities in ways that will take several more decades to repair.

Suggested Readings: Barbara Kingsolver, *Holding the Line: Women in the Great Arizona Mine Strike of 1983*, 1989; Jonathan Rosenblum, *Copper Crucible: How the Arizona Miners' Strike of 1983 Recast Labor-Management Relations in America*, 1996.

Robert E. Weir

Philadelphia Carpenters' Strike (1791). In one of the earliest **strikes** in the building industry, **journeymen** carpenters organized the first strike for a ten-hour workday in 1791. Following the American Revolution, wageworkers began to exercise independence in employment decisions. They became mobile and, in some instances, opened their own businesses in new locations. The pressures to earn a suitable living and find skilled and able laborers had already compelled masters to consolidate their efforts to control their trade. Philadelphia's master carpenters formed the Carpenters' Company in 1724 and created a book of prices to regulate their income and journeymen's **wages**. In 1786, masters drafted a new rule book, changing the measuring system that determined a journeyman's wage. It became practice to pay journeymen by the day instead of by the piece.

By the 1790s, journeymen carpenters who were concerned about meeting the cost and improving the quality of living formed a temporary union to confront what they perceived to be exploitation. Though they were disgruntled over their wages, the major issue of the strike was the length of the workday.

A membership certificate of the New York Mechanick Society dated 1791, the same year as the Philadelphia Carpenter's Strike. © George Meany Memorial Archives.

Their chief complaint was that they were made to "toil through the whole course of the longest summer's day" without having their "labour sweetened by the reviving hope of an immediate reward." The journeymen resolved that a day's work should "commence at six o'clock in the morning, and terminate, at six in the evening of each day." This included two hours for meals and compensation for **overtime**. Master carpenters argued that the strikers' complaints were unfounded, when in fact they shrewdly paid journeymen carpenters by piece wage during the shorter days of the winter months, and a flat wage during the longer summer days. Furthermore, since journeymen were denied access to their employers' rulebook, they could not estimate the value of their work. Recognizing the inequities of this arrangement, they demanded a standard workday regardless of the season. By specifying the hours they would spend at their occupation, workers were defining the limits an employer could place on their time. Unlike slaves or indentured servants, who were coerced into working whatever hours a master determined, wageworkers sequestered time for personal pursuits. In this way, they were asserting personal liberties and establishing a basis for the equality of all free citizens. Nevertheless, master carpenters did not acquiesce to the strikers' demands and depicted journeymen as lazy agitators and themselves as victims of an insecure trade. The journeymen lost the strike, but did not abandon the issue. From this point forward, the carpenters saw the expediency of establishing permanent labor organizations to address their needs. In 1827, Philadelphia's journeymen carpenters joined with other trade unions to form the Mechanics' Union of

Trade Associations. This citywide coalition of workers raised the ten-hour issue again in the 1820s and 1830s, and in 1835 they won the ten-hour strike plus increased wages for **piecework**. Thus, while the journeymen carpenters lost the 10-hour strike of 1791, they set in motion a chain of events that forever altered the relationship between laborers and employers. American workers began to distance themselves from a **paternalistic** system in which an employer controlled almost every aspect of a worker's life. Although the needs of a worker and his family were cared for, the system sustained a social hierarchy that prohibited upward mobility and stifled political equality. Because of the democratizing philosophies of the Revolution, workers no longer accepted the idea that employers were their natural superiors. Workers began to confront exploitation in the workplace and diligently press issues that would secure political equality and personal autonomy. In just a few years, Philadelphia's carpenters and other workers would establish a centralized, politically vital labor organization that ushered in the era of the modern labor movement.

Suggested Readings: David Brody, *In Labor's Cause: Main Themes on the History of the American Worker*, 1993; Philip S. Foner, *History of the Labor Movement in The United States, vol. 1: From Colonial Times to the Founding of the American Federation of Labor*, 1962; Sharon V. Salinger, "Artisans, Journeymen, and the Transformation of Labor in Late Eighteenth-Century Philadelphia," in *William and Mary Quarterly*, vol. 3 (January 1983): 62–84.

Dinah Mayo

Philadelphia Shoemakers' Strike (1805). The first case of an organized labor **strike** in the United States involved the **Federal Society of Journeymen Cordwainers** (shoemakers) of Philadelphia. Philadelphia's journeyman shoemakers began to organize as early as 1792 and formed the Federal Society of Journeymen Cordwainers (FSJC) in 1794. In 1805, the society organized a strike to protest low **wages**. Consequently, in 1806, George Pullis, head of the journeymen's society, along with seven others, was charged with conspiracy (*Commonwealth v. Pullis*). The cordwainers' trial was one of the first labor conspiracy trials in the United States. The strike and conspiracy trial revealed Americans' emerging notions of equality and independence, which encompassed both personal and political freedom as well as the right to govern the conditions of their labor. It also addressed the political contention over the place of British common law in the United States.

Before the eighteenth century, wages and prices were established through the English government by statute or ordinance. Often, workers' wages were decided by justices of the peace or local magistrates who consulted with prominent members of a craft. By the 1760s, revolutionary rhetoric encouraged master cordwainers to form an organization to control the trade. They established prices for their products, payment for themselves, and the wages of **journeymen**. Soon, the same notions of independence that motivated master cordwainers to organize also compelled journeymen to take control of their labor. By attempting to establish the value of their labor, the strikers were rejecting a social hierarchy that had dominated every phase of their lives. After the Revolution, the United States became a major exporter of shoes, exporting close to 50,000 pairs in the late 1790s. The earnings of master cordwainers rose and remained high throughout the decade, but the wages of journeyman cordwainers did not. Journeymen earned approximately £117 annually, while the yearly cost of living was £120. Thus, their income did not meet the cost of living. When master cordwainers attempted to reduce journeymen's wages during the slow winter months of 1805, the journeymen's frustrations led to a strike. In return, master artisans brought charges of conspiracy against the journeymen.

The conspiracy trial raised questions concerning the new nation's recognition of, and adherence to, English common law. In the eighteenth century, conspiracy, as defined in English law, prohibited workers from acting collectively, and although the range of offenses was not restricted to labor, it was interpreted to include restraint of trade. Thus, the FSJC itself was in defiance of common law, and their strike strengthened the claims against the union. The court found the journeymen cordwainers guilty of "a combination to raise their wages." Although none of the strikers was sentenced to jail, the fines imposed, which were between $1 and $10, equaled as much as seven-days' wages. The FSJC did not survive the strike, but workers continued to form labor organizations to address their concerns, monitor employer-employee relations, and stage strikes against unfair labor practices. The Philadelphia cordwainers' strike is significant for many reasons. The resulting trial tested the limits of individual freedom, the right of workers to organize, the role of the judicial system in labor disputes, and the contours of economic growth in the United States. While the conspiracy trial of 1806 was one of several involving American cordwainers, only in the Philadelphia trial would the court declare it illegal for workers to organize. Thus, issues raised over the rights of American workers probed the nation's commitment to equality and, by making demands of their employers, the cordwainers expanded the precincts of democracy into the workplace. Finally, although employers continued to charge striking workers with conspiracy as late as the twentieth century, the Philadelphia cordwainers' strike signaled the beginning of laborers' willingness to flout tradition, challenge social hierarchies, and exercise the prerogative to organize and strike for fair wages and acceptable working conditions.

Suggested Readings: John R. Commons, et al. *History of Labour in The United States,* 1961; E.E. Cummins, *The Labor Problem in The United States,* 1932; Billy G. Smith, *The Lower Sort: Philadelphia's Laboring People, 1750–1801,* 1990; Christopher L. Tomlins and Andrew J. King, eds. *Labor Law in America: Historical and Critical Essays,* 1992.

Dinah Mayo

Picketing. Picketing is a form of "speech" used by an individual or a group to publicize concerns by marching or protesting at a location where a perceived offense is being committed. Although characterized mostly by **strikes**, picketing can achieve social goals as well. Labor has long used picketing as a tool to publicize **grievances**, **contract** stalemates, or other issues affecting employer-employee relations. In these situations, workers try to exert pressure through peaceful means by informing the public about the controversies that exist in the workplace. The goal is to bring public pressure to bear and force employers to improve working conditions.

Section 7 of the **National Labor Relations Act** (NLRA) specifically protects the rights of striking workers to picket to gain public support, but this right does not extend to intimidating others, deliberately misinforming the public, or inflicting more economic harm on an employer than is necessary to achieve their goals. Although considered a form of free speech, a worker's right to picket is limited by the harm it may cause the public.

Chicago picketers in 1910. © George Meany Memorial Archives.

There are other forms of labor picketing that are not part of strikes or **lockouts**. Workers use informational picketing to educate the public about mutual concerns and place external pressure on employers. A union that attempts to get a company to recognize it as the representative of the workers is participating in organizational or recognition picketing. Prior to the enactment of the NLRA, this type of picketing was the only way most unions could achieve negotiations. It is illegal for a union to picket for recognition if there is already a certified union in place. Unions may also apply "force" to the struck employer by picketing businesses that have no direct dispute with the union, but whose relationship is important enough that the protest might encourage a third party to intercede. So-called secondary picketing was common in the nineteenth century, but is now legal only in a limited number of situations. Picketers may not enjoy job protection for such an activity, and thus unions tread very carefully in this contested legal terrain. It has proved useful in recent **corporate campaigns**.

Suggested Readings: Kenneth Jenero and Mark Spognardi, "Defending Against the Corporate Campaign; Selected Legal Responses to Common Union Tactics," in *Employee Relations Law Journal* 22 (Autumn 1996); Douglas Leslie, *Labor Law in a Nutshell*, 4th ed., 2000.

Joseph F. Rodgers

Piecework. Piecework—the practice of paying workers by the item produced, rather than by the hour or week—has been a familiar practice in many sectors of American manufacturing, although it is most commonly associated with the clothing industry. Other, more euphemistic terms for it include "working on commission" and "payment by results." Piecework has been favored by employers—and some employees—as a way of rewarding faster, more diligent workers, and has been allowed into some labor agreements. Over the course of the twentieth century, however, it has fallen out of favor among labor organizations on the basis that it leads to general **speedups** of work and decrease in pay. Piecework has been the subject of many significant labor disputes, especially in the garment trades from the 1890s through the 1930s. Even when this form of payment was generally accepted, the question of which side (or both) had the power to set piece rates was an ongoing struggle. In the clothing industry, piecework and piece rates were an especially lively issue, in part because changing fashions necessitated near-continuous renegotiations of piece rates. Efforts to make piecework less exploitative, and hence more acceptable, including the introduction of a base pay rate, were attempted during the early twentieth century with varying degrees of success. Piecework remained, and even increased in frequency, as a form of payment through the 1940s, and then went into decline in the 1950s.

Suggested Readings: International Labour Office. *Payment by Results*, 1984; Louis Levine, *The Women's Garment Workers: A History of the International Ladies' Garment Workers' Union*, 1924; Gus Tyler, *Look for the Union Label: A History of the International Ladies' Garment Workers' Union*, 1995.

Susan Roth Breitzer

Pink-Collar Workers. *See Blue-Collar Workers. See also Minority and Labor.*

Pinkertons. Pinkertons were agents employed by the Pinkerton Detective Agency, the most notorious of numerous private companies contracted by capital to sabotage the efforts of labor unions. The agency was founded by Scottish immigrant Allan Pinkerton in 1850 and is often considered the first modern American detective agency. Its earliest days were devoted to investigating counterfeit rings, train robberies, and outlaw gangs. Pinkerton detectives also proved effective spies for the Union cause during the American Civil War.

After railroad **strikes** associated with the **Great Labor Uprising** of 1877, and the passage of state laws giving corporations the power to hire private militias, the Pinkerton agency expanded its activities to include union-breaking. Between 1875 and 1877, Pinkerton spy James McParlan gave testimony at a series of trials that sent ten men to the gallows for allegedly belonging to the **Molly Maguires**. McParlan's exposure of this supposed Irish American terrorist group in Pennsylvania's anthracite coal region led to an increase in demand for Pinkerton services. Its industrial policies took two main forms: planting labor spies within unions to identify activists or expose their tactics, and providing private armies for employers engaging **scabs** or **locking-out** their employees.

Although other firms, including the Burns Detective Agency, also provided these services, the Pinkertons became synonymous with repression and corporate brutality in the minds of many workers. Groups like the **Knights of Labor** lobbied for the passage of laws to curtail the hiring of private industrial armies. The Pinkertons gained especial notoriety when they precipitated violence during the 1890 New York Central strike and when they engaged in shootouts with workers during the 1892 **Homestead Steel strike**, which left over a dozen people dead. It did not help the company's reputation that many of those it hired during labor disputes were little more than thugs. The firm's reputation was further tarnished when **William Haywood** and several associates were acquitted of murder charges stemming from the 1903–04 Colorado coal strikes when it was revealed that James McParlan blatantly lied and falsified evidence. (McParlan was so discredited that some historians have come to doubt his Molly Maguire revelations.)

The Pinkerton agency's role in industrial disputes began to diminish as a result of poor public relations, an outcry against private industrial armies, and the formation of federal agencies like the Federal Bureau of Investigation. The agency did provide information used to repress the **Industrial Workers of the World**, a campaign that employed future author Dashiell Hammett, but

The Pinkerton Detective Agency logo. © Library of Congress.

public outrage from the 1914 **Ludlow Massacre** eventually led to the passage of laws curtailing private armies, as did revelations from the 1937 La Follette Civil Liberties Committee. Many of the worst practices were expressly forbidden by the **National Labor Relations Act**.

Although the Pinkertons and similar agencies engaged in many worthy law-enforcement activities, they stand for many as veritable symbols of the oppression of working people, and Pinkerton was a term that aroused hatred and fear among workers from roughly 1875 to 1940. The Pinkerton agency still exists, though its 47,000 employees are mainly engaged in building security, conducting employee background checks, providing personal-protection services, and investigating fraud. Both it and the Burns agency—once its chief rival—are wholly owned subsidiaries of the Swedish firm Securitas.

Suggested Readings: Alan Axelrod and Charles Phillip, *Cops and Crooks and Criminologists*, 2000; Wayne Broehl, *The Molly Maguires*, 1964; Leon Wolff, *Lockout: The Story of the Homestead Steel Strike of 1892*, 1965.

Robert E. Weir

Pittston Coal Strike. The Pittston Coal strike was a successful 10-month **strike** during 1989–90 led by the **United Mine Workers of America (UMWA)** against the nation's second-largest coal exporter. It was an important victory for organized labor, coming after nearly a decade of lost **downsizing**, **decertification**, and **concessions** strikes. To many analysts, it also suggested that labor unions should engage in militant actions and ignore labor laws tilted in favor of employers.

The strike began on April 5, 1989, and involved miners employed by the Pittston Coal Group in Virginia, West Virginia, and Kentucky. Workers had already labored without a **contract** for fourteen months. At the heart of the dispute were working conditions and benefits. Pittston sought to operate its mines around-the-clock, abolish the eight-hour day, and require Sunday work. One company official even claimed that workers feigned interest in church to avoid work. Matters came to a head when the company announced plans to eliminate medical benefits for more than 1,800 individuals, including widows, disabled miners, and those on **pensions**. Company arrogance led 1,700 miners to walk out on April 5. Eventually nearly 9,000 miners took part in the strike. Because the National Labor Relations Board (NLRB) ruled Pittston guilty of **unfair labor practices**, the company could not hire permanent **replacement workers**, though it did import more than a thousand **scabs**.

Aside from the initial NLRB ruling, most other official actions went in favor of the company. Virginia state police were used to escort scabs, and company property was patrolled by Vance Security, a firm specializing in antiunion activity. Numerous court rulings went against the UMWA, including injunctions limiting **picketing**. At one point, strikers attempted to bottleneck roads in and out of Pittston mines by driving slowly. Slow driving was ruled a violation of federal injunctions, and drivers were arrested; several spent up to ninety days in jail, and the UMWA was slapped with fines.

Strikers and the UMWA responded with a variety of tactics. Some militants tossed jackrocks (a welded assemblage of spikes designed to flatten tires) on the roads, while others pelted scabs with rocks. The UMWA did not sanction acts of violence, but was nonetheless fined. (A decision was made early in the strike to engage in acts of nonviolent civil disobedience.) When UMWA officials told a Virginia judge, Don McGlothin, Jr., that the strike was a "class war," he slapped more than $30 million in fines on the union. The UMWA responded with roving pickets and public demonstrations. It also briefly sanctioned **wildcat** and **sympathy strikes**, which broke out in eleven states and idled 46,000 miners, calling them **memorial strikes**. The UMWA quickly retreated from this and withdrew its official sanction, though it did little to discourage acts of **solidarity**. It did, however, authorize a **corporate campaign** against Pittston that picketed Shawmut Bank in Boston and led the Boston City Council to remove funds from the bank. (Shawmut later went out of business.)

Key to winning the strike was the remarkable level of unity sustained. A sympathetic council in New Jersey petitioned the **American Federation of Labor-Congress of Industrial Organizations (AFL-CIO)** to call a one-day sympathy strike by all AFL-CIO members. That request was turned down, but more than 30,000 supporters went to the UMWA's Camp Solidarity in Virginia between June and September 1989, including the Reverend Jesse Jackson. Jackson's presence symbolized the unity of black and white miners during the strike. Strikers also received assistance from the International Confederation of Free Trade Unions, which convinced Secretary of Labor Elizabeth Dole to visit Camp Solidarity. In an evocation of the 1937 **General Motors sit-down strike**, ninety-nine individuals illegally occupied Pittston's Moss Number 3 mill between September 17 and September 20. Miners and the UMWA ignored an NLRB order to vacate Moss and the $13.5 million fine it levied; occupiers left after seventy-seven hours on their own accord, defiantly waiting until an NLRB-imposed deadline had passed.

Also key to the strike was the role of women. Wives, daughters, and sympathizers of the mostly male strikers formed the Daughters of **Mother Jones** (DMJ) to offer support. Unlike women's auxiliaries in previous eras, the DMJ went well beyond support that extended traditional domestic roles to strikers. In addition to supplying food and child care, women also helped plan and participate in militant tactics. Many of them were among the more than 4,000 individuals arrested for acts of civil disobedience, and they played the central role in planning public demonstrations and taking charge of public relations. Several newspapers and television stations gave positive coverage of the strike, a rarity in the 1980s. Women also helped get out the vote. The UMWA rejoiced when one of its members upset twenty-two-year incumbent Don McGlothin, Sr.—father of the judge who fined the union—for a seat in the Virginia state legislature after only a three-week write-in campaign.

Pittston lost over $25 million in the last quarter of 1989, and it was clear the company was losing the strike as well. Secretary Dole appointed a federal mediator, and West Virginia Senator Jay Rockefeller introduced successful legislation to protect miner pensions. An agreement was hammered out on December 31, 1989, that gave Pittston the right to operate its mines twenty-four hours per day, but which did not allow the company to make miners work during daylight hours on Sundays. The UMWA also won preservation of health and pension benefits, and a guarantee that laid-off miners would be offered jobs when openings occurred in Pittston's nonunion mines. Most of the fines levied against the UMWA were lifted. UMWA officials like **Richard Trumka** received praise from many **rank-and-file** members for their willingness to use militant tactics. The rank and file insisted on several minor changes in the December settlement before ratifying a new contract on February 19, 1990. Three days later, miners returned to work.

The Pittston strike was an important symbolic, as well as actual, victory for organized labor. After years of antiunion activity sanctioned by the Reagan administration, victory during successor George H. W. Bush's tenure signaled the possibility of reversing the downward trend. Many came away from Pittston convinced that militancy led to success. Some activists openly advocated ignoring U.S. labor laws in favor of **direct action** at the point of production. Few AFL-CIO officials shared such sympathies, but **John Sweeney** did make renewed militancy a component of his successful bid for the AFL-CIO presidency. In 1995, documentary filmmaker Anne Lewis recounted the strike in *Justice in the Coalfields*. It has proved a popular film among union advocates.

The strike contained notes of irony. By 1995, only about one-third of the strikers still had union jobs. Technological change and a declining demand for coal led to layoffs in the Pittston Group. In December 1997, the UMWA reopened a contract with the Bituminous Coal Operators Association nine months early and signed a new five-year agreement with operators, which included Pittston. Militants protested the UMWA's agreement to work rules that allow workers to be scheduled two Saturdays out of every three, as well as a requirement that they must continue operating equipment until relieved by the incoming shift. Some complained that Trumka had become a **business unionist** and had quashed rank-and-file militancy. Overall, UMWA strength declined from around 120,000 in 1982 to about 40,000 in 1998.

Suggested Readings: Adrienne Birecree, "The Importance of Women's Participation in the 1989–90 Pittston Coal Strike," in *Journal of Economic Issues* 30:1 (March 1996): 187–211; Jeremy Brecher, "Resisting Concessions," http://www.zmag.org/ZMag/brechermay98.htm; James Green, *Taking History to Heart: The Power of Building Social Movements*, 2000.

Robert E. Weir

Popular Front. The Popular Front was a loose alliance of politically and socially minded activists, which was active between 1935 and 1949 and dedicated to aggressive organizing and the establishment of a social democratic America. Its support from organized labor was almost entirely restricted to unions associated with the **Congress of Industrial Organizations (CIO)**. The Popular Front included relatively moderate voices, like CIO President **Philip Murray** and CIO Secretary-Treasurer **James B. Carey**, as well as **communists**, **socialists**, Trotskyites, and **anarchists**. Popular Front radicalism led enemies of labor to assert communist domination of individual unions and the CIO itself. Conservative backlash ultimately led to the demise of the Popular Front.

Before the 1930s, communists had some successes, but mostly endured a troubled relationship with American labor unions. Shifting tactics sometimes led communists to forge alliances with other groups, at others to denounce former friends. Abroad, hostility between the powerful socialist and communist parties in Germany contributed to the triumph of Nazism in 1933. In France in 1934, socialist and communist workers cooperated in physically battling and defeating an attempted fascist coup. During 1935 at the World Congress of Communist Parties in Moscow, Georgi Dmitrov proclaimed the new policy of the Popular Front as a bulwark to defeat fascism. In the United States, such a policy of left-wing cooperation was already operating informally in many locations as a means to combat the Great Depression and organize desperate, increasingly radicalized American workers.

The biggest boost to the Popular Front in the United States came with the surge of **industrial unionism**. **John L. Lewis** had actually banned communists from membership in the **United Mine Workers of America** in 1927. **Sidney Hillman** of the **Amalgamated Clothing Workers of America** fought his own battles with the communists during the 1920s. Yet both men embraced former opponents in their aggressive drive to organize America's production workers. Communists provided organizational expertise and dedication needed to galvanize industrial workers.

Though prominent, communists were hardly alone in labor's Popular Front. In addition to members of other organized political groups, individuals called "fellow travelers" were an important part of the CIO's success. At the national level, Lee Pressman, CIO general counsel, not only negotiated and drew up **contracts** with employers, but also brokered affairs between the differing factions. **Leonard De Caux**, editor of the *CIO News*, was also influential. Among national unions, Mike Quill of the Transport Workers Union and Joseph Curran of the National Maritime Union maintained alliances with the Popular Front that enabled their unions to make major gains.

At its most influential, American labor's Popular Front alliance provided a united, powerful, and more radical counterpart to the New Deal. During World War II, it supported the establishment of the new United Nations and brought American labor into the new, inclusive World Federation of Trade Unions (WFTU). However, pressures generated by the deepening Cold War and conservative backlash at home shattered the Popular Front. Beginning in the **United Auto Workers (UAW)** with the election of **Walter Reuther** as president, the balance of forces within the CIO decisively shifted.

As the external environment for labor grew more hostile, CIO leaders felt the need to become even more dependent on government largesse. The price was the exclusion of communists. The antiunion **Taft-Hartley Act** in 1947, congressional committees like the House Com-

Many union leaders, such as Mike Quill, president of the Transport Workers Union, maintained a close association between their organization and the Popular Front. © George Meany Memorial Archives.

mittee on Un-American Activities, and state investigating boards like California's Tunney Committee were intent on rolling back labor gains, which forced the CIO to retrench. By February 1948, markers of CIO loyalty included demands that unions support the Marshall Plan and renounce the presidential campaign of progressive candidate Henry Wallace. The following year, the CIO withdrew from the WFTU and began expelling unions it deemed unduly influenced by communists. Nearly one-third of the CIO's total membership was purged. The Popular Front among American labor was finished, and communist influence was eventually eradicated. But along with it, the progressive nature of American unions suffered, and militancy declined.

Suggested Readings: Michael Denning, *The Cultural Front: The Laboring of American Culture in the Twentieth Century,* 1996; Robert H. Zieger, *The CIO, 1935–1955,* 1995.

Stephen Burwood

Postal Strike of 1970. The Postal Strike of 1970 was the first nationwide strike of federal employees. It began in New York City on March 18, 1970, and quickly spread to over 200,000 letter carriers, clerks, and mail handlers nationwide. The **walkout** was prompted by the poor pay earned by urban postal workers and the difference in pay rates between the government and private sectors. Although the **strike** ended within one week, it was responsible for a dramatic overhaul of the relationship between the federal government and organized labor.

The strike had a long gestation period. As inflation and the cost of living rose throughout the 1960s, in part because of the war in Vietnam, post office employees' real **wages** fell drastically. Full-time postal employees earning the top pay rate after twenty-one years' service in New York City received only $8,400 per annum. Many full-time employees qualified for welfare benefits. The United Federation of Postal Clerks and the National Association of Letter Carriers (NALC), the two largest of seven national unions representing post office workers, deleted no-strike clauses from their constitutions in 1968. Both unions repeatedly warned of worker discontent and the impossibility of keeping their members on the job without significant improvements. Under prevailing federal law, however, strikes were illegal, unions could not bargain directly with post-office management, and they had to lobby Congress for pay increases. On March 12, 1970, the House of Representatives' Post Office and Civil Service Committee offered a pay raise that was rejected by the **rank and file**. New York City Letter Carriers Local 36 was especially angry over the congressional inactivity and timid union leadership. When President Richard Nixon announced that the next scheduled wage increase would be postponed for six months, workers responded. Rejecting pleas by their representatives—at one point they hanged NALC President James Rademacher in effigy—Local 36 voted to strike. They were joined by the Postal Clerks Union as well as other New York locals, and within two days postal workers in Buffalo, Boston, Pittsburgh, Detroit, and other locales walked off in **solidarity** with the New Yorkers.

At its peak, approximately 25 percent of the nation's postal employees were on strike, shutting down New York–based financial and business centers and halting national mail delivery. Rademacher claimed that radical students affiliated with Students for a Democratic Society had infiltrated the NALC and precipitated the strike. Although some younger workers were influenced by 1960s social movements, the strike was the product of the workers' desperation and government inaction, not outside agitators. The *New York Times* blamed Congress and the White House, and public sentiment was generally favorable toward the strikers. Nevertheless, the federal government obtained a court injunction requiring postal unions to compel their members to return to work. When the unions found Postmaster General Winton Blount unwilling to concede any issue that would encourage workers to abandon the strike, representatives from all seven postal unions asked Secretary of Labor George Shultz to intervene. Shultz pressured Blount into a secret meeting with union officials on March 20, the day the NALC met to decide whether to make the strike official. When union members rejected the secret meeting's modest compromise, President Nixon announced that if the strike did not end by March 23, he would move to ensure mail delivery. Ignored by the workers, Nixon declared a state of national emergency and ordered 25,000 soldiers and National Guardsmen to New York City to sort and move mail. Nixon did stipulate that troops be unarmed, dress in uniforms without battle gear, and that they avoid confrontations with strikers. There was no way that federal troops could hope to replace the 57,000 striking New Yorkers, thus they concentrated on moving mail vital to business interests and did not make home deliveries. The administration won additional injunctions that would have levied crushing fines on locals remaining on strike after March 25, and these forced most strikers back to work.

With the workers once again delivering the mail, public and political pressure shifted to post-office management. Both sides quickly reached agreement on a new contract that included an immediate 6 percent wage increase, with a slightly larger increase coming after congressional approval; reduction of length-of-service for top pay from twenty-one years to eight; withholding disciplinary action against individual strikers; and future **collective bargaining** with binding **arbitration**, which relieved Congress of the responsibility for post-office wage negotiations. Strikes remained illegal. Congress quickly approved the agreement, and President Nixon signed the bill into law on April 15, less than one month after the strike began. The strikers' gains reverberated among other federal workers, including truckers, who engaged in a **wildcat strike**, and air traffic controllers, who held a **sick-out** in the wake of the postal-workers strike. (The latter was successful, but during the **Professional Air Traffic Controllers Organization (PATCO) strike** of 1981, President Ronald Reagan fired striking air traffic controllers.)

On August 12, Nixon signed into law the Postal Reorganization Act, which changed the relationship between the post office and the federal government. For unions to bargain collectively, the post office was transformed into an autonomous and self-supporting government corporation. In exchange, postal employees gave up the right to strike and agreed to binding arbitration. The strike marked the beginning of a long process that brought a living wage to postal workers. Workplace issues related to work conditions and work-related chronic medical ailments are still unresolved.

Suggested Readings: Joseph Lowenberg and Michael Moskow, eds., *Collective Bargaining in Government: Readings and Cases*, 1972; Stephen Shannon, "Work Stoppage in Government: The Postal Strike of 1970," in *Monthly Labor Review* 101 (July 1978): 14–22; John Walsh and Garth Mangum, *Labor Struggle in the Post Office: From Selective Lobbying to Collective Bargaining*, 1992.

John Cashman
Robert Shaffer

Post–World War I Strikes. After the November 1918 armistice ending World War I, working people worldwide declared their own war against employers by

striking in record numbers. In the United States, the 1919 postwar strike wave included an unprecedented four million workers, who staged more than 3,500 strikes. These included national strikes of coal miners and steelworkers, a regional New England telephone operators' strike, the Seattle general strike, and the famed **Boston police strike**. Clothing workers in New York, textile workers in the East, copper miners in Montana, and streetcar workers in the Midwest also staged **walkouts**. In all cases, strikers faced intense opposition from employers, who used local police, state militia, and, in some cases, federal troops to force workers back on the job. Though the **steel strike of 1919** did not result in union recognition, others strikers succeeded. Clothing workers won shorter hours, coal miners won a **wage** increase, and telephone operators won a better **contract**.

The explosion of postwar strike activity had several causes. Most strikers responded to massive wartime inflation. Between 1914 and 1918, the cost of living rose an average of 17 percent a year. Even **working-class** families who managed to keep pace with inflation during the war through **overtime** and war **bonuses** could not make ends meet once war-production lapsed. Not only did workers face common hardships, but their wartime experience raised expectations of change. President Woodrow Wilson had pledged that the United States was fighting a "war to make the world safe for democracy," leading many workers to expect a measure of "industrial democracy" after the war. But when employers instead sought to lower wage rates, campaign for the antiunion **open shop**, and dismantle federal agencies such as the National War Labor Board, many working people felt betrayed. The strikes also took place in the shadow of the 1917 Bolshevik Revolution in Russia, which some early observers proclaimed the first workers' republic. This event was reflected in the radical demands of some strikers. A group of Illinois coal miners called for "mines to the miners," while workers in Seattle refused to load a shipment of arms destined for the anti-Bolshevik white armies in Russia. The event was reflected as well in the accusation by business and political leaders that the communists lurked behind every American striker. Though untrue, this charge paved the way for the red scare and Palmer Raids of 1920.

Suggested Readings: Jeremy Brecher, *Strike!*, 1997; Philip Foner, *History of the Labor Movement in the United States, Volume 8: Postwar Struggles, 1918–1920*, 1988; David Montgomery, *The Fall of the House of Labor: The Workplace, the State, and American Labor Activism, 1865–1925*, 1987.

Carl Weinberg

Powderly, Terence Vincent (January 22, 1849–June 24, 1924). Terence V. Powderly, the national leader of the **Knights of Labor (KOL)** from 1878 through 1893, later served as commissioner general of immigration and in the **Department of Labor**. Powderly was born in Carbondale, Pennsylvania, the son of Terence and Margery (Walsh) Powderly. He attended Carbondale schools until age thirteen, at which time he became a railroad worker. In 1866, he **apprenticed** as a machinist and worked at various shops in the greater

Scranton area until 1877. He married Hannah Dyer on September 19, 1872. The couple had a child that died in infancy.

In the early 1870s, Powderly got caught up in the various causes that defined his life: Irish nationalism, temperance, politics, and labor. As the son of an Irish immigrant father, Powderly was deeply interested in Irish politics. He was an active member of the Irish Land League, supported Irish independence, and was an outspoken critic of British policy towards the Irish. Powderly was also a teetotaler and an ardent supporter of temperance causes. During his tenure as leader of the KOL, the organization established a working relationship with the Women's Christian Temperance Union.

Terence Powderly. © George Meany Memorial Archives.

The exploitation of labor after the Civil War had a profound effect on young Powderly. Though he later denounced radicalism and supported the Republican Party, for a brief period he paid **dues** to the Socialist Labor Party. He was also caught up in the **Greenback** Labor Movement and in 1878 rode that ticket to victory as mayor of Scranton. He served three, two-year terms.

Powderly came to fame as a labor leader. He joined the Machinists and Blacksmiths Union in 1871. Like many unions, the machinists were badly hurt by the panic of 1873. He gravitated towards the ultrasecret Noble and Holy Order of the KOL and probably joined it in 1874. Appointed an organizer in 1876, he helped expand the KOL westward from its Philadelphia base. In that same year, he became president (master workman) of his local, then corresponding secretary for his district assembly.

In 1879, Powderly became the general master workman of the entire KOL when founder Uriah Stephens resigned. Powderly led the Knights from secrecy and obscurity to national prominence as an open organization. There were fewer than 10,000 members in 1878; by mid-1886, there were perhaps a million. Powderly lectured and organized tirelessly on behalf of the Knights and managed administrative affairs admirably given the KOL's inadequate bureaucratic development. He supported the organization of both women and African Americans into the KOL and oversaw the KOL's greatest triumph: its 1885 strike victory over Jay Gould's Southwest railway conglomerate. Powderly also called for an end to the **wage** system and its replacement by producer and distributor **cooperatives**. By the mid-1880s, Powderly was the nation's most famous labor leader. Politicians and reformers sought his advice, and local assemblies, retail products, and children were named for him.

Powderly's KOL tenure was controversial, however. Despite the victory over Gould, Powderly was bitterly opposed to **strikes** and called for mandatory **arbitration**, a position that angered many trade unionists and radicals. He was also lukewarm to the idea of independent labor parties and, after the **Haymarket bombing** of May 4, 1886, an outspoken critic of **anarchism**, **socialism**, and radicalism. Critics claimed he was vain, argumentative, petty, and self-serving. Some accused him of trying to make the KOL into a personal power machine, while others said he was part of an internal conspiracy that was opposed to trade unions. When the KOL began to decline in the wake of the **Great Upheaval**, Powderly often bore the brunt of criticism. A coalition of urban socialists and agrarian radicals removed Powderly from office in late 1893. He battled the KOL over **back pay** and other matters and was briefly expelled from the Knights.

He worked as a lawyer for several years until 1897, when President William McKinley appointed him U.S. commissioner general of immigration. But his xenophobic, anti-immigrant diatribes did little to distinguish him. He left his post in 1902 and served in several positions with the Department of Labor. His wife, Hannah, died in 1901, and on March 31, 1919, he married Emma Fickenscher, his former

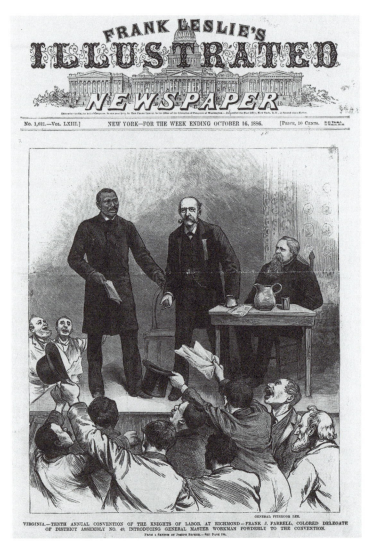

Tenth annual convention of the Knights of Labor, at Richmond. Frank J. Farrell, African American delegate, introducing General Master Workman Powderly to the convention. © Library of Congress.

secretary. He died in Washington, D.C., on June 24, 1924. At the time, he was nearly forgotten, but in many respects, Terence Powderly was the first prominent leader of an American labor federation. In January 2000, Powderly was inducted into the Labor Hall of Fame.

Suggested Readings: Harry Carman, Henry David, and Paul Guthrie, *The Path I Trod: The Autobiography of Terence V. Powderly*, 1960; Craig Phelan, *Grand Master Workman: Terence Powderly and the Knights of Labor*, 2000; Robert E. Weir, *Knights Unhorsed: Internal Conflict in a Gilded Age Labor Movement*, 2000.

Robert E. Weir

Preferential Shop. The preferential shop, also known as the preferential union shop, was one of the cornerstones of the Protocols of Peace, one of the earliest successful efforts to harmonize labor-management relations in New York's garment industry in the 1910s. The term, first coined by Louis Brandeis, was an attempt to compromise between the irreconcilable demands of management for an open shop, in which union membership was not required, and labor's demand for the **closed shop**, or union shop, in which employees must belong to the union, either upon hiring, or within a limited time thereafter. In the preferential shop, the employer was required to give preference to union over nonunion workers, provided that they were of equal competence. The preferential shop quickly became a compromise that pleased neither side, with the **International Ladies' Garment Workers' Union** initially rejecting the offer, and the **National Association of Manufacturers** later arguing that the preferential shop was little different from the union shop. Even when the protocols were accepted as a matter of industrial law, labor and management alike attempted to manipulate the preferential union shop to their own advantage. By the 1920s, with the effective demise of the protocol, the preferential union shop also declined in practice as shops became either open or closed, depending on union strength or weakness.

Suggested Readings: Louis Levine, *The Women Garment Workers: A History of the International Ladies' Garment Workers' Union*, 1925; National Association of Manufacturers, *Open Shop Encyclopedia for Debaters: A Reference Book for Use of Teachers, Students, and Public Speakers*, 1921; Gus Tyler, *A History of the International Ladies' Garment Workers' Union*, 1995.

Susan Roth Breitzer

Premium Pay. Premium pay is an adjustment made to the hourly **wage** in consideration for working outside of normal hours or job classification. Often, companies use premiums as an incentive to entice workers to accept undesirable conditions or schedules. Employees may earn extra compensation for night, weekend, or holiday work, or for working in uncommon situations with greater risk.

The most common form of premium is **overtime** pay, which is mandated by the **Fair Labor Standards Act**, which requires that nonsalaried, nonmanagerial employees receive one-and-a-half times their regular hourly wage for time worked in excess of forty hours per week, or past their normally scheduled day. (Unions may negotiate a higher premium in the **collective bargaining** process.)

Suggested Reading: Robert Covington and Kurt Decker, *Individual Employee Rights in a Nutshell*, 1995.

Joseph F. Rodgers

Prevailing Wage. Prevailing wage refers to the pay standards for construction workers within a given geographical territory. The thirty-one states that have prevailing-wage laws stipulate that an employer must pay **wages** in line with local custom on any job open to public bid or involving state or federal **contracts**. Employers must meet that minimum standard whether or not the workforce is unionized, though they may pay more. The prevailing wage is an outgrowth of the 1931 **Davis-Bacon Act**.

Prevailing-wage laws are designed to protect local wage structures. They apply mainly in the building industry where large public projects are usually put out for competitive bids. Prevailing-wage laws emerged to prevent nonlocal firms from gaining contracts funded by local taxpayers, then importing low-wage workers who would undercut local wage rates. Employers must pay prevailing wages if they accept a contract, even if their workers customarily work for lower rates. States publish the prevailing wage for various regions, and that information is available to contractors before they put in bids. The **Department of Labor** also maintains current data on prevailing wages. There are also nonprofit agencies, like the Prevailing Wage Contractors Association, that assist firms in complying with existing laws.

Some states establish thresholds that stipulate the total value of a contract before prevailing wages must be paid, though eight states have no minimum threshold whatsoever. This figure is usually low, though it is $400,000 for new construction in Connecticut and $500,000 in Maryland. With the exceptions of New Hampshire and Vermont, all of the states without prevailing wage laws are located in the South or west of the Mississippi River.

The construction and business communities are generally opposed to prevailing-wage laws and have funded expensive campaigns to overturn them. Since 1979, Colorado, Florida, Idaho, Louisiana, New Hampshire, and Utah have repealed prevailing-wage legislation. Studies reveal that those states experienced an immediate 2 to 4 percent decline in construction industry wages and about a 10 percent decline for unionized workers. In recent years, unions have done a better job of fending off attacks. No state has repealed a law since 1988, despite well-financed efforts to do so.

Suggested Readings: David Francis, "The Effect of Repealing Prevailing Wage Laws," National Bureau of Economic Research, http://www.nber.org/digest/amy00/w7454.html; Prevailing Wage Contractors Association Web site, http://www.pwca.net/; U.S. Department of Labor Web site, http://www.dol.gov/esa/programs.

Robert E. Weir

Professional Air Traffic Controllers Organization (PATCO) Strike. The Professional Air Traffic Controllers Organization (PATCO) strike was a pivotal 1981 battle between PATCO and the administration of President Ronald Reagan that ended in the complete rout of the union. Many observers see the crushing of PATCO as the event that legitimized organized capital's ongoing program to break the power of labor unions.

On August 3, 1981, roughly 13,000 air traffic controllers employed by the Federal Aviation Administration (FAA) refused to report for duty in airport control towers and in control centers which managed traffic between air hubs. This **walkout** of nearly 80 percent of the FAA's air traffic control personnel was organized by their union, PATCO. Staged in defiance of federal law, which forbids **strikes** by U.S. government employees, the job action crippled the flow of air traffic, prompting a showdown between PATCO and President Reagan. PATCO demanded a thirty-two-hour workweek, improved retirement benefits, and an immediate $10,000 per year raise. The media seized upon the seemingly exorbitant **salary** demands, though it was largely a bargaining chip to address what many workers felt was the central issue: reducing the stress of air traffic controllers who worked long hours with few breaks staring at radar screens. Lost in the drama of the strike was PATCO's appeal to public safety. The union claimed that the flying public was at risk due to conditions guaranteed to impair controllers' judgment. Also lost in subsequent events is the fact that PATCO had been negotiating with the FAA for months preceding the strike.

Striking air traffic controllers walk the picket line at the New York air route traffic control center in Ronkonkoma, N.Y., on August 5, 1981. With an 11:00 A.M. deadline passed, the traffic controllers continue their court-prohibited strike. © AP/Wide World Photos

Hours after the strike began, President Reagan issued an ultimatum, warning strikers that if they did not resume work within forty-eight hours, they would be terminated. The 11,350 controllers who ignored the president's ultimatum were fired on August 5. With a sweep of the pen, President Reagan replaced 70 percent of the nation's air traffic controllers. This action made him enormously popular with the business community and political conservatives, and it also played well with the public at large. Years of declining membership reduced organized labor's clout among the public and made it more receptive to corporate antiunion messages. Unions were blamed for a host of ills, including the stagnating economy. Reagan's actions also appeared decisive and bold, a welcome change to the political malaise of the 1970s.

The breaking of PATCO was one of the most dramatic labor events of the post–World War II era, and it had lasting negative consequences for organized labor in general. PATCO was formed in 1968 by air traffic controllers who expressed dissatisfaction with the long hours, low pay, and high stress that then characterized their jobs. After two stormy years, which saw PATCO stage a slowdown and two major **sick-outs**, PATCO finally established a stable organization and affiliated with the Maritime Employees Benevolent Association,

American Federation of Labor-Congress of Industrial Organizations (AFL-CIO), in 1970. It won its first **contract** with the FAA in 1973. Relations between PATCO and the FAA were generally troubled, with the union organizing sick-outs and slowdowns in 1974, 1975, and 1978. Relations deteriorated further after 1978, due to federal budget constraints, **pension** disputes, transfer policies, and several quality-of-work issues. Two separate studies indicated that morale among air traffic controllers was dangerously low, though the FAA ignored said findings. The FAA even ignored reports showing that controllers handled duties in excess of the FAA's own standards.

In response to this unrest, PATCO leaders initiated a strike plan for the expiration of the union's contract in 1981. The implementation of that plan accelerated when Robert Poli replaced longtime PATCO President John Leyden in 1980. The union's hopes that a strike could be averted rose briefly when Poli extracted vague promises to improve conditions from candidate Ronald Reagan. PATCO subsequently endorsed Reagan's 1980 presidential candidacy, only to become bitterly disappointed by the Reagan-staffed FAA during the contract negotiations of 1981. In July 1981, an angry union **rank and file** rejected an FAA offer that would have paved the way for significant wage increases, even though that offer broke new ground by including wage considerations in a federal contract. (Federal wage increases normally require congressional approval.) Insisting that the FAA's final offer did little to address most of their **grievances**, controllers staged the most significant strike of white-collar technical workers in U.S. history.

The Reagan administration was well prepared for the strike, using every legal means at hand to break it. Federal judges issued costly injunctions that assessed PATCO for damages resulting from the strike, quickly bankrupting the organization. Several strike leaders were arrested and jailed for defying the injunction, and a swift **decertification** vote among **scab** controllers removed PATCO as a bargaining unit. Meanwhile, military controllers, FAA supervisors, and hastily trained replacements were marshaled to break the strike. The AFL-CIO publicly supported PATCO and nationwide grassroots **solidarity** efforts sprang up as workers expressed their collective outrage at Reagan's antiunion tactics. International support for the strike came from several quarters as well, including the Canadian Air Traffic Controllers Association, which staged limited actions in support of PATCO. But unions in the U.S. airline industry did not honor PATCO picket lines, and the volume of air traffic steadily rose in the months following the walkout. As previously noted, PATCO also lost the battle for public opinion. About 90 percent of PATCO members were white males, who were perceived to be well-paid and privileged. PATCO credibility suffered further when long-delayed technological changes automated many of the more tedious air-traffic-controller tasks, thereby eliminating many of the quality-of-work issues that partly prompted the strike.

By the end of 1981, PATCO had been broken. This realization sent ripples throughout the United States, as Reagan's action was widely seen as encouraging private-sector companies to break unions as well. The PATCO strike touched off a new wave of **downsizing, decertification**, and **concessions** strikes. Within a few years, private employers had opted to replace permanently strikers at **Phelps Dodge**, International Paper, **Hormel**, and other major companies, contributing to a dramatic drop in strike rates in the United States that was not reversed by the end of the twentieth century.

Suggested Readings: Willis Nordlund, *Silent Skies: The Air Traffic Controllers' Strike*, 1998; Rebecca Pels, "The Pressures of PATCO: Strikes and Stress in the 1980s," in *Essays in History*, 1995; Michael Round, *Grounded: Reagan and the PATCO Crash*, 1999.

Joseph A. McCartin

Profit Sharing. Profit sharing is a plan that links a portion of a worker's yearly income to the company's profitability. Instead of an annual percent increase, the employee receives an added **bonus** when the company meets its expectations, but receives only his or her normal **salary** if the company fails to achieve expected goals. Profit sharing is designed to make workers feel that they have a stake in the continued success of the business. This has been a standard feature in American corporations since the Progressive Era and was a key component of **welfare capitalism**. By the late 1920s, over a million workers were enrolled in profit-sharing plans, though many of those systems collapsed during the Great Depression (1929–41).

Since employees are usually not given access to employer accounts, critics complain that profit-sharing plans are subject to abuse and can be dodges designed to avoid giving raises. Making pay raises contingent can also harm employees' long-term buying power. Deferred compensation can cause **wages** to lag behind the inflation rate. Because most profit-sharing plans pay their bonuses as a lump sum, it does not have the same cumulative effect as an annual raise, since the base wage remains stagnant. Moreover, these payments cannot be relied on for long-term financial planning.

Unions have long claimed that profit-sharing plans are also designed to deter unionization by creating the false impression that management will take care of workers without being pressured to do so. Despite problems associated with profit sharing, such plans began to reemerge in the 1970s as employers enlisted them as a way of being more competitive in an era of **globalization**. In theory, motivated employees with a vested interest are more productive. Many **contracts** contain profit-sharing language, despite union skepticism of its merits.

Suggested Readings: Everett Allen, *Pension Planning: Pensions, Profit Sharing, and other Defined Compensation Plans*, 7th Ed., 1992; Jay Conison, *Employment Benefit Plans in a Nutshell*, 1998; Douglas Krause, *Profit Sharing: Does it Make a Difference? The Productivity and Stability Effects of Employee Profit Sharing Plans*, 1993.

Joseph F. Rodgers

Protectionism. Protectionism is a term most commonly used in economics to describe regulations preventing free trade between countries. Although some economists do not believe that protectionist policies benefit a country's ability to distribute goods and services effectively, most find that these plans help developing "infant industries" that are new to the market of trade and exchange. Protectionism is usually created in the form of tariffs, import quotas, and trade regulations. Trade regulations are sometimes used when there is a concern regarding the quality of imports, such as automobiles.

Working people and their unions often favor some form of protectionism and argue that cheap imports endanger American jobs. Occasionally they find allies among manufacturers seeking alleviation from foreign competition to their products. Americans have hotly debated tariff issues related to protectionism since Colonial times. Past and present advocates of free trade argue that it benefits workers as both consumers and producers by providing low-cost goods for purchase while providing open markets for the goods and services workers create. A handful of labor activists, most notably **Henry George**, was dedicated to free trade, but most nineteenth-century workers favored protectionism; groups like the **Knights of Labor** employed paid lobbyists to pressure Congress to support protectionist legislation. In the twentieth century, protectionism's grip on workers relaxed somewhat, especially among urban consumers seeking cheaper products, but free trade remains a minority viewpoint. Farmers are split on the issue as they simultaneously fear competition from imported foodstuffs, yet want easy access to potential foreign markets. Most labor groups have been adamantly opposed to recent free-trade measures like the **North American Free Trade Agreement**, as well as the attempts of groups like the World Trade Organization to knock down international trade barriers.

The term protectionism is also used regarding **child-labor** issues. Used within this context, it refers to agencies, organizations, and institutions that advocate child-labor legislation to prevent children from being exploited in the workplace. Many contemporary critics of globalism cite child-labor abuses as another reason to oppose free-trade agreements.

In terms of labor law, protectionism refers to any legislation on the federal, state, or local level to increase the safety of employees at a workplace. These laws are also developed to promote the general welfare and interests of employees. This type of law is often called **protective labor legislation**.

Suggested Readings: Anne Krueger, ed., *The Political Economy of Trade Protection*, 1996; Charles Rowley, Willem Thorbecke, and Richard Wagner, eds., *Trade Protection in the United States*, 1995; Bureau of Labor Statistics Web site, http://www.bls.gov.export-import.

Amanda Busjit

Protective Labor Legislation. In its broadest terms, protective labor legislation refers simply to laws designed to protect human beings from the potentially damaging effects of work demands by their employers or inherent within work itself. It has proved problematic when designating special categories of workers as more deserving or needy of protection than others. It has been most often applied to children and women.

Protective labor legislation evolved out of Colonial debates between free labor and the reality of the changing nature of work. In theory, each Colonial worker was free to negotiate **wages**, hours, and working conditions according to the best bargain he or she could fashion. Custom generally dictated said terms, and a relatively closed economic system reinforced them. In an increasingly **capitalist** economy, however, competition rendered customary practices less viable. One of the first groups to push for work regulations was **journeymen**. After the American Revolution, journeymen carpenters led the move to

regulate the number of hours that constituted a legal day's work. Despite the fact that courts often declared journeymen associations illegal, the associations' efforts led to, first, the ten-hour movement and, later, the **eight-hour movement**. Female textile workers also played an important role in both movements. One of the earliest versions of protective labor legislation was an 1840 ten-hour bill for federal employees.

Child labor laws, one important type of protective labor legislation, sought to protect the rights and health of child workers, such as these coal mine breaker boys, who sorted the slag from the coal. © George Meany Memorial Archives/Library of Congress.

After the Civil War, however, protective labor legislation often broke down along gender lines, with state and federal courts playing a pivotal role. Courts routinely struck down laws regulating hours and conditions for male workers, but left them intact for women. Court decisions dovetailed with Victorian social and cultural systems that assumed women to be inferior in physical strength and intelligence. Victorians advocated separate spheres for men and women, with males suited for the public world of business, commerce, and work, while women's "natural" roles were those of homemaker and mother. Ideally, a male worker would earn a **family wage** sufficient to support his spouse and children. Few **working-class** males actually earned that amount, and women usually did not have the luxury of confining themselves to the private realm. However, Victorian customs excluded women from many jobs, especially those involving heavy toil or those that exposed women to moral dangers, like bartending or night work. Courts often opined that special protections for women were necessary to protect their presumably fragile reproductive systems and their delicate psychological health.

Ironically, nineteenth-century women were often protected better than children, as **child-labor** laws were notoriously lax throughout the century. This changed dramatically during the Progressive Era; by 1912, thirty-eight states adopted at least rudimentary child-labor laws. Progressive Era legislation and court decisions had far different implications for women, however. By 1900, many states regulated the number of hours women could work, and many male workers had won reduced hours. In 1905, the Supreme Court ruling in *Lochner v. New York* declared unconstitutional a New York state law regulating bakers' hours. Subsequent rulings stripped male workers of hard-fought reduced hours, but left shorter hours in place for women. Practice was cloaked in law in 1908 when the Supreme Court's **Muller v. Oregon** upheld shorter hours for women. Justice Louis Brandeis's majority opinion relied heavily on Victorian assumptions about women's health. By 1917, nineteen states fashioned laws based on the *Muller* decision.

Women's-rights activists faced a dilemma. On one hand, women were granted reduced hours, weightlifting restrictions, hazardous-waste-handling safeguards, and other protections that male workers still struggled to obtain through **collective bargaining**. To accept them without challenge, however, meant to accept an inferior status that many feminists found unacceptable. Groups like the **Women's Trade Union League** and the **International Ladies' Garment Workers' Union** were embroiled in hot debates over whether or not to acquiesce to gender-based protective legislation. Feminists correctly asserted that in lieu of an Equal Rights Amendment, women workers were vulnerable to unfavorable protective labor legislation.

New Deal legislation in the 1930s resolved some protective labor issues and engendered new ones. Job shortages during the Great Depression led numerous states to enact laws forbidding married women from holding most wage-earning jobs. New Deal job programs largely left said custom in place and excluded married women. However, programs like the **National Industrial Recovery Act** and the **Fair Labor Standards Act** instituted the eight-hour day, **minimum-wage** laws, **overtime** rules, and child-labor laws without regard to gender. Labor shortages during World War II negated bans on married-women's work. (World War II workplaces nonetheless continued to mandate rest periods for women, pay them lower wages, and restrict women from certain jobs.)

In the post–World War II period, protective labor legislation expanded. Greater awareness of workplace safety issues culminated in the 1970 **Occupational Safety and Health Act**, child-labor laws were tightened, and **workman's compensation**, minimum wage, and overtime laws were periodically updated. Customary gender biases remained, however, with entire categories of work being considered as gender-specific. Secretarial work, for example, was so heavily female (and so poorly compensated) that commentators spoke of it as a "pink-collar ghetto." Feminists in the 1960s began to challenge social customs, especially as they extended to the workplace. The 1963 **Equal Pay Act** outlawed differing wage scales for the same work, and Title VII of the 1964 Civil Rights Act referred sexual discrimination allegations to the Equal Employment

Opportunities Commission (EEOC). Other bills and executive orders took down more discriminatory barriers.

By the 1970s, women were found in numerous occupations once thought to be the preserve of men. Full equality was dealt a blow in 1982, however, when a proposed Equal Rights Amendment to the United States Constitution was not ratified. Many women complain that de facto protective legislation continues. Some jobs, most notably in the construction and parcel-post industries, continue to limit the amount of weight women can lift, and custom continues to dictate that certain jobs are inappropriate for women. Some critics also note that EEOC equal-pay provisions are circumvented by manipulating job titles instead of actual duties, a complaint that has spurred discussions of comparable worth. Women in many workplaces complain that their representation is more token than real, and that a **glass ceiling** prevents them from advancing.

Gender and race have also proved sticking points in protective labor legislation. **Affirmative Action** programs have led to complaints that women and people of color have been given unfair preference in hiring and promotion. Hiring quotas have been especially controversial, though rigid quotas were struck down by the Supreme Court's 1978 decision in *University of California Board of Regents v. Bakke*. Unions have steadfastly opposed any affirmative action interpretations of long-held **seniority** systems.

In recent years, workplace sexual-harassment complaints have skyrocketed. Ironically, the call for special rules to reduce sexual harassment have rekindled Progressive-Era dilemmas. The vast majority of complaints have been lodged by women, causing some males to raise questions of women's ability to cope in competitive and pressure-packed work environments. The same charges are leveled when women lobby for family leave, flexible hours, job sharing, or increased medical coverage for women's health issues. Once again the challenge is to adopt rules that protect workers in gender-neutral ways.

Overall, the track record of protective labor legislation is mixed. Obtaining it in some form or another is central to the mission of organized labor. Few would argue the wisdom of implementing child-labor laws, minimum-wage protection, and workplace-safety provisions, but laws that have applied only to certain categories of workers have proved controversial.

Suggested Readings: Rosalyn Baxandall and Linda Gordon, *America's Working Women: A Documentary History*, 1995; Alice Kessler-Harris, *Out to Work: A History of Wage-Earning Women in the United States*, 1982; Susan Lehrer, *Origins of Protective Labor Legislation for Women, 1905–1925*, 1987.

Robert E. Weir

Pullman Strike/Lockout. The Pullman Strike/Lockout of 1894 embodied many of the social ills and injustices of the late Gilded Age. Despite the crushing defeat dealt to the **American Railway Union (ARU)**, the strike catapulted **Eugene Debs** to national prominence, focused attention on the woes of the laboring classes, contributed to political realignment, and paved the way for needed reforms.

The events of 1894 took place against a backdrop of deep conflict and economic depression. The crushing of a nationwide railroad **strike** during the **Great Labor Uprising** of 1877 did little to bring quiescence to an industry that was marked by numerous subsequent strikes, especially during the **Great Upheaval** of the mid-1880s. Because rail workers were split into six brotherhoods, and the **Brotherhood of Locomotive Engineers (BLE)** was particularly loath to cooperate with other groups, rail workers' gains were modest during the 1880s. The **Knights of Labor (KOL)** proved more successful than any of the brotherhoods, but its decline after 1888 again left rail workers in a weak position. In 1893, Debs formed the ARU, an attempt at **industrial unionism** among railroad workers. His fledgling union won a victory against the Great Northern Railroad in 1893, but was ill-prepared to tackle the Pullman Palace Car Company in 1894. Debs, in fact, cautioned against the strike.

Industrialist George Pullman held a monopoly share of the lucrative sleeping-car industry. In 1880, Pullman purchased land twelve miles south of Chicago's central business district and constructed a new manufacturing facility. Pullman also responded to the growing urban social problems of the day and constructed what he hoped would be a model industrial town around his factory: Pullman, Illinois. The wide streets, sturdy homes, manicured lawns, and city services of

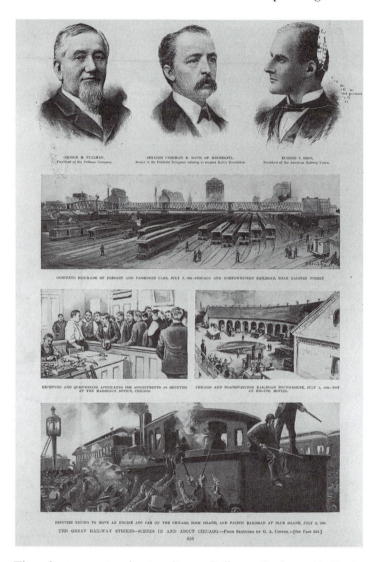

Three bust portraits showing George Pullman, Cushman K. Davis, and Eugene V. Debs; and four illustrations showing "blockade of railroad cars, applicants for appointments as deputies at the marshal's office, roundhouse, and deputies trying to move an engine and car at Blue Island." © Library of Congress.

Pullman stood in marked contrast to Chicago's slums, but Pullman was also a **company town** and workers' lives were much more controlled. Saloons and labor unions were banned from Pullman, and the town library did not even carry information on the latter. In addition, rents and utilities cost more in Pullman, and the company actually turned a profit on rent and services.

George Pullman's **utopian** vision was challenged by the collapse of financial markets in 1893. Tension between workers and employers was already high, and memories of the **Haymarket bombing** of 1886 remained vivid. The Panic of 1893 led to wide-scale business failures, bank closings, and massive layoffs. The Chicago area was hit even harder as the area had attracted numerous temporary laborers lured to construction jobs in preparation for the World Columbian Exposition that opened in 1893. Pullman exacerbated the region's unemployment by laying off nearly half of his 5,500 workers in 1893. His workforce rose to over 3,300 by April 1894, but Pullman slashed the **wages** between 25 and 40 percent. He did not, however, lower rents, utilities, or prices at company stores.

The immediate catalyst for the strike came in May, when Pullman rejected the pleas of a **grievance** committee that approached him for relief on rents. Despite his promise not to seek reprisals against the committee, he fired three members of it, possibly with the knowledge that all three belonged to the ARU. The ARU had a small presence at Pullman. Ironically, Pullman himself violated the no-union proviso by allowing a small **company union** to form; some of its members also joined the ARU. Pullman refused to submit the firings to **arbitration**, and on June 21, ARU locals in Pullman voted to issue a **boycott** of Pullman Palace cars unless he reconsidered. Rather than wait, Pullman preemptively closed his factory, thus officially making the events of 1894 a **lockout**. His actions were backed by a consortium of railroad executives, known as the General Managers Association (GMA), which was anxious to cripple the ARU.

The ARU officially issued its boycott on June 26, with union members staying on their jobs but refusing to handle Pullman cars. When companies attempted to fire those who refused to work with Pullman cars, entire crews walked off. Within days, the ARU tied up much of the freight traffic from Chicago to the West Coast, and the boycott threatened to expand to East Coast lines. At the height of the strike at the end of June, more than 25,000 workers were out. Public opinion was initially on the side of the workers, and Republican leaders like Mark Hanna called upon Pullman to arbitrate the dispute. The GMA, however, secretly schemed to create legal conflicts and incite violence to justify crushing the strikers and boycotters. This was accomplished largely through the importation of **scabs** from Canada and by attaching mail cars to Pullmans. The GMA also convinced Attorney General Richard Olney—a board member and stockholder in several railroads—to deputize more than 3,400 agents to make sure trains ran. Mainstream newspapers also fed the public a steady diet of antistrike propaganda.

Predictably, strikers clashed with scabs and deputies, and railroad property was destroyed. This prompted Olney to request that President Grover Cleveland send federal troops to protect the mails. Four divisions were dispatched over the protests of Illinois Governor John P. Altgeld. These actions initially energized strikers, but on July 2, Olney used several obscure Civil War–era laws and the recently passed **Sherman Antitrust Act** to obtain a court injunction from Judge Peter Grosscup expressly forbidding interference with mail delivery and interstate commerce. By early July, strikers faced more than 6,000 federal and state militia troops, in excess of 5,000 marshals, and some 3,100 police officers. Debs and the ARU contemplated a **general strike**, but those hopes were dashed when the **American Federation of Labor (AFL)** refused to sanction **sympathy strikes**. Despite support from the KOL and several unions that defied AFL leadership, the Pullman strike was doomed.

Several strike leaders, including Debs, were arrested for conspiracy to obstruct the mails, made bail, then were rearrested for contempt of court. The strike was officially raised on August 2, though troops were withdrawn several weeks earlier. Judge Grosscup sentenced Debs to six months imprisonment, an experience that Debs later claimed converted him to **socialism**.

Twenty-five workers died during the Pullman conflict, and 406 were seriously injured. Railroad losses totaled more than $5.3 million, and workers lost more than $1.7 million in wages. Many workers were blacklisted, and those who got their jobs back were forced to accept employers' terms as the ARU quickly collapsed. More damaging was the widespread use of injunctions during future strikes, Pullman supplying the model for their issuance.

Despite the rout, not all was lost. The Pullman strike, plus other traumatic events like the **Homestead Steel strike** and the march of **Coxey's Army**, convinced many Americans that reform was needed. The Panic of 1893 lasted until 1898, another indicator that industrial **capitalism** needed to be reined in, and even Olney was a reluctant convert to that conclusion. In 1898, some railway abuses were corrected by the **Erdman Act**. The Democratic Party was thoroughly repudiated by **working-class** voters and did not hold the White House again until 1912, after party officials reevaluated the party's overt probusiness biases. This paved the way for the election of a series of prolabor Democratic governors and legislators. Eugene Debs emerged from prison as a heroic figure and rallied tens of thousands to the socialist cause before his death in 1926.

Suggested Readings: Almont Linsey, *The Pullman Strike*, 1964; Richard Schneirov, Shelton Stromquist, and Nick Salvatore, eds., *The Pullman Strike and the Crisis of the 1890s*, 1999; Stanley Buder, *Pullman*, 1967.

Robert E. Weir

Pure and Simple Unionism. The term pure and simple unionism refers to the idea that a labor union's primary task is the pursuit of higher **wages**, shorter hours, and better conditions for its members. The concept derives from **Adolph**

Strasser and **Samuel Gompers**, officials in the Cigar Makers International Union (CMIU). Gompers made it a centerpiece of the ideology underpinning the **American Federation of Labor (AFL)**. The AFL was the first important labor federation to embrace pure and simple unionism.

Capitalism was still a contested concept in the nineteenth century, and most labor federations spoke of supplanting it with a more just economic system. By the 1880s, the nation's largest labor federation was the **Knights of Labor (KOL)**, and the CMIU was affiliated with it. Like most groups, the KOL embraced a broad reform agenda whose ultimate goal was nothing less than remaking the nation's cultural, economic, political, and social systems. Instead of capitalism, the KOL called for **cooperation**. **Socialist** and **anarchist** groups also called for the dismantling of capitalism and had equally broad reform agendas.

Socialist cigar makers in New York City quarreled with the CMIU in the early 1880s and eventually founded a rival organization. When the KOL backed the challengers, Strasser and Gompers led the CMIU out of the organization. Gompers, who claimed to have been a socialist in his youth, grew to have great disillusionment over what he thought their naïve and utopian views. He reached similar conclusions about the KOL and most other versions of reform unionism. To him and Strasser, too much energy was siphoned in pursuit of unobtainable goals, and both men felt the KOL's opposition to **strikes** was wrongheaded. They saw the strike as labor's weapon to force employers to grant what they did not wish to give. They further concluded that only individuals within the same trade unions would be able to maintain sufficient levels of **solidarity** to sustain strikes. Moreover, Gompers rejected popular sentiments to form a labor party, as he felt the two-party system was too entrenched and that politics only diverted energy from the workplace.

When the AFL was founded in 1886, Gompers and Strasser had effectively pared labor's agenda to that of wages, hours, and conditions. Many workers, reformers, and labor advocates of the time found the AFL's more modest goals too narrow, though its view ultimately prevailed. By stripping the AFL of partisan politics and social agitation, the organization gave implicit acceptance to the legitimacy of capitalism. That, plus its exclusionary membership policies, earned it the opprobrium of the **Industrial Workers of the World (IWW)**, which called the AFL the "American Separation of Labor." Ironically though, the IWW was the last important labor federation to call for the dismantling of capitalism.

Since the early twentieth century, most labor unions have accepted the permanence of the capitalist system. This has made the pure and simple approach the everyday operating philosophy of most unions, even if they adhere rhetorically to loftier future visions.

Suggested Readings: Bruce Laurie, *Artisans Into Workers*, 1989; Nick Salvatore, ed., *Seventy Years of Life and Labor: An Autobiography of Samuel Gompers*, 1984.

Robert E. Weir

Q

Quality Circles. Quality circles, in which small groups of managers and laborers work in tandem to plan and accomplish tasks, are an alternative to assembly-line production. Unlike the specialization of the assembly line (**Fordism**) or the relentless efficiency of scientific management (**Taylorism**), quality circles stress task diversity and cooperation between management and labor. Instead of individual workers performing a single task, each member of a quality-circle team performs multiple, changing tasks and sees the product through from planning to completion. The goal is to make workers feel less alienated toward the products they create, thereby ensuring high quality and a happier workforce.

Quality circles originated in Japan, though in many ways its central tenets hark back to 1930s human-relations theories developed by people like Elton Mayo. They began to catch on in the United States in the 1980s, especially in the auto industry, which had been hard hit in the 1970s by foreign imports and declining consumer confidence in domestic auto quality. Honda Motors was the world leader in using quality circles, with General Motors the first domestic auto manufacturer to adopt the method. By the 1990s, over 90 percent of all Fortune 500 corporations used quality circles to some degree. Some unions remain suspicious of quality circles, seeing them as a way for management to change work rules without negotiating such changes, though two National Labor Relations Board decisions in the early 1990s ruled that quality circles were subject to the **National Labor Relations Act**. An attempt by conservative Republicans to circumvent those decisions (the "TEAM Act") was vetoed by President Clinton in 1996.

Suggested Readings: Steve Babson, *The Unfinished Struggle: Turning Points in American Labor, 1877-Present,* 1999; Richard Florida and Martin Kennedy, "Transplanted Organizations: The Transfer of Japanese Industrial Organization to the US," in *American Sociological Review* 56 (1991): 381–98.

Robert E. Weir

Quickie. Quickie is another term for an unauthorized **wildcat strike**, a work stoppage that occurs without notice or approval by union officials or the national union. Such action usually violates **collective-bargaining** agreements and may, in some cases, be illegal. It can also refer to an authorized action of limited duration whose purpose is to demonstrate worker strength and serve warning to employers.

Quickies peaked during specific periods of labor history. During the 1930s and 1940s, quickies were frequent, despite management opposition. By the 1950s, one-third of all **strikes** were of this type, and **rank-and-file** members used them to force companies to renegotiate workplace-rights provisions. Even though these strikes seemed successful initially, they proved unsuccessful in the long run. The reason for the long-term failure is that companies agreed to increase **wage-** and benefit-packages demanded by workers but never shifted the balance of power of production and workplace issues to the employees. Such a loss of power forced employees to strike repeatedly over work conditions. Over time, wages and benefits weakened the impetus for such action.

Suggested Readings: Eugene C. Friedman, "Illegal and Unauthorized Strikes in Violation of Collective Bargaining Agreements: A Union View," in *NYU 36th Annual National Conference on Labor,* 1983; Martin Glaberman, *Wartime Strikes,* 1980; Florence Peterson, *American Labor Unions,* 1963.

Amanda Busjit

R

Racketeer Influenced and Corrupt Organizations Act (RICO). Passed by Congress in 1970, the Racketeer Influenced and Corrupt Organizations Act is designed to help the federal government prosecute organized crime. Although it does not pertain to labor as such, some unions have been involved in **racketeering** and other forms of union corruption. In fact, unions have been pursued as aggressively under RICO as groups like the Mafia and drug dealers. This has prompted some critics to charge that RICO has been applied against organized labor as much for political and ideological reasons as for actual corrupt practices.

The federal government has long found it difficult to break crime syndicates. Merely arresting corrupt individuals often does little to lessen crime; intact organizations simply replace them. The Federal Bureau of Investigation (FBI) was created in 1924 to replace a less-effective federal anticrime unit, and turned its attention to organized crime activities like bootlegging, gambling, extortion, and prostitution. Labor unions have also been investigated by the FBI and other federal agencies. A variety of pre-RICO federal legislation deals with possible union corruption. The 1935 **National Labor Relations Act** contains language to protect union members and employers from potential abuse by union officials. The rights of each were greatly enhanced by the 1946 **Taft-Hartley Act**. The Hobbs Act was also passed in 1946 to curtail union racketeering and protect employers during negotiations. Under the Hobbs Act, it became a federal crime to even attempt robbery or extortion in activities that involve interstate or foreign commerce. The latter provisions were directly incorporated into RICO. The 1959 **Labor-Management Reporting and Disclosure Act (Landrum-Griffin Act)** contained a union members' "bill of rights," as well as numerous provisions requiring union disclosure of internal procedures, use of union funds, and limits on an **international union's** rights to place locals in trusteeship.

Unfortunately, some unions have been guilty of racketeering. The **International Brotherhood of Teamsters** forged an alliance with organized crime that dates to the early 1950s, if not before. Some officials of the International Longshoremen's union were so infamous for their connections to the criminal underworld that their practices gave rise to the 1954 Hollywood film *On the Waterfront*. Smaller unions—like the bakers, laundry workers, and hotel and restaurant employees—have come under scrutiny. Beginning in 1957, the Senate Select Committee on Improper Activities in the Labor Management Field—better known as the McClellan Committee—investigated the Teamsters and others. Eventually, Teamster boss **James Hoffa** went to prison.

RICO was fashioned to aid the government's efforts to break crime syndicates. It makes it a federal crime punishable by up to twenty years in prison—or life, if the crime is one for which a life sentence can be imposed—to "conduct or conspire to conduct an enterprise whose activities affect interstate commerce by committing or agreeing to commit a pattern of racketeering activity." To be convicted under RICO, an individual must be proven to be a part of an organization whose history contains two or more racketeering episodes. RICO prosecutions take place for murder, extortion, jury tampering, gambling, mail fraud, counterfeiting, pornography distribution, drug trafficking, and a host of other activities. Usually, government agents are given wide leeway in investigating potential RICO violators.

One problem with RICO has been its ambiguity. Terms like "enterprise," "conspiracy," "pattern," and "racketeering" are subject to overly broad interpretation. Almost immediately, some employers saw RICO as a potential weapon to counter unions. A **strike**, for example, could be interpreted as affecting interstate commerce, and holding several could be seen as a pattern. A 1973 Supreme Court decision clarified this by exempting unions from prosecution if their activities were related to legitimate union objectives. One controversial section of that ruling also extended protection to illegal acts committed by members when the union itself was pursuing legitimate goals. RICO could not, for example, be used against an international union merely because some members of a local conspired to commit acts of vandalism.

RICO has been applied against unions on numerous occasions. The two best-publicized cases involved the Teamsters in 1988, and the Longshoremen two years later. Both were placed under federal trusteeship until **rank-and-file** reform groups could reorganize the unions along democratic lines. But there have also been many misapplications of RICO. In the late 1990s, for example, California building trades unions began setting up protect-labor agreements (PLAs) that required contractors to sign union contracts with at least one union on public-works projects. Contractor groups tried to sabotage PLAs by bringing RICO suits against the unions. (None was successful.) In 2000, AK

Steel brought suit against the **United Steelworkers of America (USWA)** and numerous officials, including USWA President **Richard Trumka**, charging them with RICO violations ranging from extortion and threats to attempted murder of AK Steel families. In 2002, those suits were dismissed as having no merit.

RICO remains a prosecutorial weapon with the potential to rid unions of corrupt practices, but also one that can be used unscrupulously.

Suggested Readings: Foster Dulles and Melvyn Dubofsky, *Labor in America,* 1984; U.S. Department of Labor, "Employment Law Guide," http://www.dol.gov/asp/programs/handbook/unions.htm.

Robert E. Weir

Raiding. Raiding is an inter-union squabble in which one union tries to represent organized employees already under another union's **jurisdiction**. Raiding does not exist when employees work within another union's jurisdiction but are not organized. A common motive for raiding occurs when a union seeks to increase its membership for purposes of bargaining power. Another reason a union may raid another union's membership is to retaliate against another for not cooperating on particular issues or with other organizations.

The American Federation of Labor-Congress of Industrial Organizations (AFL-CIO) created a no-raiding agreement as a precondition for merger in 1954. Affiliates pledged not to organize or represent employees where "an established bargaining relationship" already existed between the employer and another union. The agreement was effective for four years and, in 1958, its principles were incorporated in Article II, Section 8 and Article III, Section 4 of the AFL-CIO constitution, making the agreement mandatory for all affiliates. Raiding usually results in bitterness and it weakens the labor movement. In 1967, the **International Brotherhood of Teamsters** sought to raid Chicano workers allied with **Cesar Chavez** and the **United Farm Workers of America**. It took many years before the two unions cooperated with trust in one another. Raiding and jurisdictional issues have surfaced again recently in the wake of union mergers and the expansion of older industrial unions into workplaces outside their traditional constituencies.

Suggested Readings: Susan Ferriss, Ricardo Sandoval, and Diana Hembree, eds., *Fight in the Fields: Cesar Chavez and the Farmworkers Movement,* 1998; David Prosten, ed., *The Union Steward's Complete Guide,* 1998.

Amanda Busjit

Railroad Strikes of 1877. *See Great Labor Uprising.*

Railroad Strike of 1922. The Railroad Strike of 1922, also known as the Big Strike or the Great Railroad Strike of 1922, is often considered the largest strike in U.S. history. Between July and September 1922, some 400,000 skilled craft workers, known as shopmen, walked off their jobs to protest wage cuts and work-rule changes. It saw the most widespread use of injunctions in American labor history and resulted in a loss for the six unions involved.

The strike was a direct result of the breakdown of the **National Agreement**, a measure set up during World War I. The National Agreement created the Railroad Labor Board (RLB) to mediate wage and work disputes that might otherwise lead to stoppages that would jeopardize the movement of troops and war materiel. The RLB included representatives from the government as well as those from railroad carriers and unions. Vague promises of future cost-of-living increases were made, and the tripartite RLB resolved most wartime disputes peacefully. In 1920, however, the government's direct role in the RLB ended and power shifted to private carriers.

A postwar economic slump and a desire to break the power of **craft unions** led carriers to slash wages on July 1, 1921. Several lines, led by the Pennsylvania Railroad, also announced intentions to cease paying **overtime** rates for work on Sundays and holidays, and to change how **seniority** was calculated. The Pennsylvania Railroad added insult to injury by cutting more than 8,000 jobs during the winter of 1922, largely by **subcontracting** work once done by shopmen. Many of the Pennsylvania's actions were inspired by the **National Association of Manufacturers**, which had launched an **open-shop** drive to break the power of unions. In all, companies foisted about $60 million in wage cuts upon their employees, and most of their actions were in violation of the National Agreement. Craft unionists protested to the RLB, but the RLB acquiesced to carrier demands.

Newspaper coverage of the 1922 Railroad Strike. © George Meany Memorial Archives.

As conditions deteriorated in 1922, unions and carriers alike readied themselves for confrontation. Skilled shopmen had the potential to inflict severe economic damage to both railroads and the nation at large. Automobiles were not yet a fixture of American society, thus a sizable percentage of the nation's mail, commerce, and passengers was transported by rail. The carriers were dependent upon skilled carpenters, machinists, welders, repairmen, and others to keep the railroads running smoothly.

The first workers to leave their jobs were those employed in Pennsylvania Railroad shops, but it soon spread to other lines. A July 1 strike vote received the approval of 97 percent of the **rank and file** of the affected labor organizations, despite the fact that the RLB declared their strike illegal. Within days as many as 400,000 workers walked out. The strike was confined to skilled shopmen in six unions, including the **International Association of Machinists**, which negotiated through a joint Railway Employees' Department. Railroad brotherhoods like the carmen, firemen, and the **Brotherhood of Locomotive Engineers** were covered by separate agreements and continued to work after shopmen laid down their tools. This meant the railroads could continue to operate, and carriers recruited **scabs** from among management, the unemployed, college students, clerks, and those ideologically opposed to labor unions. The RLB authorized the hiring of scabs, and it turned a blind eye as machine guns and hired guards appeared in railyards across the East and Midwest.

The scabs were ill-prepared to take on such highly skilled work, leading railroad officials across the United States to seek injunctions to force workers back on the job; thousands faced arrest rather than yield. On July 28, President Warren G. Harding tried to broker an agreement that would have done little except protect seniority rights. The Railroad Employees' Department expressed reluctant acceptance, but railroad executives refused to discuss even Harding's modest proposal. Both the unions and President Harding were undermined by Harding's own attorney general, Harry Daugherty.

Daugherty played much the same role during the 1922 strike as Attorney General Richard Olney assumed during the **Pullman** boycott thirty years earlier. He sought broad injunctions against strikers, partly to protect his own investments, and partly because he had a pathological fear of communism. The Bolshevik Revolution took place in Russia five years earlier, and Daugherty claimed that railroad workers sought to emulate it. His interpretation was ludicrous, but red-baiting proved a successful strategy. Daugherty convinced Federal District Judge James Wilkerson to issue restraining orders on September 1, based on rather convoluted interpretations of the **Sherman Antitrust Act**. Again, like Pullman, alleged interference with the U.S. mail was used as one justification for injunctions.

Wilkerson's restraining order involved the widest use of injunction powers in U.S. labor history. He placed a total gag order on the unions, officials, and rank and file. Strikers were forbidden to **picket**, call strike meetings, issue press releases, or in any manner encourage the strike. His orders even forbade use of the mail or telegrams; in essence, Wilkerson outlawed free speech. Wilkerson's temporary restraining order also contained his defiant intent to defend **open shops**.

Hundreds of union members were jailed as a result of the injunction. In San Francisco, a $9 million judgment was ordered against striking unions; elsewhere even individuals filed lawsuits against the strikers. There was little unions could do in the face of such opposition except surrender. On August 25, 1922, less intransigent employers of the New York Central and Baltimore and Ohio Railroads settled with their workers. The so-called "B & O Plan" retained seniority systems and rehired most of the strikers at existing wage rates. This became the blueprint by which disputes on other lines were settled. Most strikes were over by mid-September, though some Pennsylvania Railroad workers remained on strike for more than two years.

In the short-term, the strike was a disaster for unions. Unions were weakened to the point where they couldn't muster opposition even when promises on seniority were broken. Tens of thousands of railroad workers were forced to quit their organizations and join **company unions**. It stands as the most dramatic example of the fate that befell most strikers in the 1920s. Union membership across the nation plummeted in the wake of a full-scale assault on the part of aggressive anti-union employers.

But rail carriers also paid the price. The Daugherty/Wilkerson injunctions were so outrageous than even some conservatives saw them as unreasonable. Daugherty's subsequent role in the Teapot Dome scandal crippled his credibility, and some awards against unions were either overturned or drastically reduced. Many workers responded to the political heavy-handedness of the strike by supporting the 1924 Progressive Party campaign of Robert La Follette, who garnered more than 4.8 million votes, more than half as many as Democratic challenger John Davis. In 1926, Congress passed the **Railway Labor Act of 1926 (RLA)** to correct some of the problems within the industry. In 1935, the **National Labor Relations Act** outlawed many of the abusive injunction methods used in 1922.

Suggested Readings: Irving Bernstein, *The Lean Years*, 1960; Foster Rhea Dulles and Melvyn Dubofsky, *Labor in America: A History*, 1984; Leonard Painter, *Through Fifty Years with the Brotherhood of Railway Carmen of America*, 1944.

Robert E. Weir

Railway Labor Act of 1926 (RLA). The Railway Labor Act of 1926 is the federal law that governs labor relations and **collective bargaining** in the U.S. railroad and airline industries. The act's objective is to avoid strikes and other forms of conflict which interrupt interstate commerce and weaken the economy. To do this, the act protects employee rights to form labor unions and mandates mediation of disputes by a federal agency.

The railroad industry receives special attention from lawmakers because of its critical importance in commerce and transportation. Stemming from disruptive and violent strikes during the **Great Labor Uprising** and the **Great Upheaval** from 1877 through 1888, a series of laws tried to achieve industrial peace in the railroad industry. The first of these laws was passed in 1888, and the 1926 Railway Labor Act was enacted to address the shortcomings of previous laws. It was a direct outgrowth of the **railroad strike of 1922**, which saw abusive use of injunction power against workers. Initially the RLA applied only to the railroad industry; airlines were added in 1934.

The act promotes collective bargaining and is administered by the National Mediation Board (NMB). When bargaining over pay and working conditions, strikes can only occur after the NMB releases the parties from mediation. The president of the United States can further delay a strike by creating a Presidential Emergency Board to investigate the dispute. Over 230 Presidential Emergency Boards have been formed since 1934. There are also provisions to prevent work stoppages over grievances.

To prevent strikes caused by employees trying to force an employer to recognize a union, the RLA authorizes secret-ballot elections conducted by the NMB. If a majority of workers vote for union representation, the union is certified and the employer must bargain with it. In addition to regulating railroad and airline labor relations, the RLA is significant because of its legal and operational influence on the drafting of the **National Labor Relations Act** of 1935, which governs labor relations in the rest of the private sector.

Suggested Readings: Douglas Leslie, ed., *The Railway Labor Act,* 1995; Charles Rehmus, ed., *The Railway Labor Act at Fifty: Collective Bargaining in the Railroad and Airline Industries,* 1977.

John W. Budd

Randolph, Asa Philip (April 14, 1889–May 16, 1979). Asa Philip Randolph was a trade unionist and civil-rights leader. He was the son of the Rev. James William and Elizabeth (Robinson) Randolph and completed high school in Jacksonville, Florida. In 1914, he married Lucille Greene. Shortly thereafter he moved to the Harlem section of New York City, and worked as an elevator operator while taking classes at City College of New York. Randolph's arrival in New York coincided with a flowering of political and cultural activity within the black community known as the Harlem Renaissance. He became a **socialist** and, in 1917, set up the United Brotherhood of Elevator and Switchboard Operators union. That same year, he and Chandler Owen began publication of

A. Philip Randolph in about 1930. © Bettmann/Corbis.

The Messenger, an independent socialist journal. That paper was sympathetic to the **Industrial Workers of the World** and critical of African American involvement in World War I. Randolph was arrested as a suspected **communist** in 1918, was briefly jailed, then drafted into military service, but the war ended and charges against him were dropped.

The Messenger advocated that African Americans join labor unions and was highly critical of both capitalism and the National Association for the Advancement of Colored People (NAACP), which Randolph felt was too conservative. In 1919, Randolph served on the executive board of the National Brotherhood Workers of America and, in 1920, he set up Friends of Negro Freedom, an organization to protect migrant and tenant rights. Randolph quit the Socialist Party when it moved too slowly on black issues. In 1925, he founded the **Brotherhood of Sleeping Car Porters (BSCP)** and commanded its twelve-year struggle to obtain a contract with the Pullman Corporation. In 1936, the BSCP affiliated with the **American Federation of Labor (AFL)**. He continued as president of the BSCP until his retirement in 1968.

Randolph was one of the most important civil-rights advocates of his era. He served on numerous commissions on race and, in 1936, co-founded the National Negro Congress to promote black job opportunities under the New Deal and protect black workers. His threat to organize a march of black workers on Washington, D.C. prompted President Franklin Roosevelt to establish the **Fair Employment Practices Committee** in 1941. During and after World War II, Randolph was an outspoken critic of military segregation. He was equally outspoken within the labor movement. As a delegate to the International Confederation of Free Trade Unions in 1951 and a member of the executive council of the American Federation of Labor-Congress of Industrial Organizations (AFL-CIO) after its 1955 merger, Randolph forcefully argued for full inclusion for people of color. In 1960 he founded the Negro American Labor Council to advance black union members. His militancy led to numerous clashes with cautious AFL-CIO leaders and, in 1961, the executive council censured Randolph. He was the national director of the 1963 March on Washington for Jobs and Freedom and addressed the rally just before the Rev. Martin Luther King, Jr. By the time of his death in 1979, the AFL-CIO had adopted many of the protections for black workers that Randolph advocated.

Suggested Readings: Jervis Anderson, A. *Philip Randolph: A Biographical Portrait*, 1972; Mari Jo Buhle, et al., *Encyclopedia of the American Left*, 1992; William Harris, A. Philip Randolph, "Black Workers, and the Labor Movement," in Dubofsky and Van Tine, *Labor Leaders in America*, 1987.

Robert E. Weir

Rank and File. Rank and file describes ordinary union members who do not hold office in the local union. Often, these workers are referred to as the union's grass roots. These are the participants whose interests the officers and other union officials represent during collective bargaining negotiations. In theory, these individuals belong to a democratic union whose procedures were formally stated in the **Labor-Management Reporting and Disclosure Act** of 1959. A union's bargaining power is established by the rank and file since, without the majority vote of workers, officers cannot be elected or undertake negotiations with an employer. Currently, there is insufficient worker-rights legislation to protect democracy within some unions. Unions like the **International Brotherhood of Teamsters** and the **United Mine Workers of America**

have witnessed rank-and-file insurgency movements to restore democratic union principles, but many unions continue to concentrate power in the upper echelons of their bureaucracies and employ complex rules and procedures that isolate officials from the rank and file.

Suggested Reading: Harry Kelber, "Why Drop Workers' Rights?" in *Weekly Labor Talk*, April 10, 1999.

Amanda Busjit

Rate Cutting. Rate cutting is a general term that applies to an employer's attempt to motivate workers to perform their jobs faster and more efficiently by reducing their pay or **piecework** rate. This type of reduction usually occurs in enterprises like textiles or the garment trade where the quantity of goods produced is essential to the firm's overall profit margin. Trade unionists usually oppose this type of system for two reasons. First, it is a de facto **speedup** in which increased efficiency and production far outstrip worker remuneration. Second, employers often abuse employees who have already mastered their skill and usually don't reward them financially for increased productivity. Sometimes, this term may refer to work situations where the pay rate to motivate employees has been higher than the salary of workers within the industry or in similar operations.

Rate cutting is primarily associated with jobs that pay either piece rates or a fixed sum for each article produced. It was also more common in the years before World War II than it is today. It was a key component in scientific management principles associated with **Taylorism** and often engendered fierce opposition from workers. For example, demand for production of wartime supplies in the early 1940s generated conflict and safety concerns at automotive plants such as Chrysler and Packard Motors. Workers challenged management consistently during this time over the right to maintain production standards and **incentive pay** rates. However, rate cutting still occurs wherever incentive pay is based on output, and in businesses intent on reducing costs and maximizing human resources.

Suggested Readings: Joyce Bagot, ed., *Source Book on Collective Bargaining*, 1998; Frederick Winslow Taylor, *The Principles of Scientific Management*, 1998.

Amanda Busjit

Ravenswood Lockout. The Ravenswood Lockout was a protracted struggle between the **United Steelworkers of America (USWA)** and the Ravenswood Aluminum Company (RAC). To some observers, the USWA's partial victory in 1992 signaled an important reversal of union fortunes in the 1980s and is a portent for organized labor's potential for renewal.

Problems at Ravenswood were part and parcel of the merger mania that marked American corporate culture in the 1980s. The aluminum reduction and fabrication plant in this small West Virginia Ohio River town opened in

1954, as part of the Kaiser Aluminum Company (later known as ALCOA). In 1958, the USWA organized plant workers in local 5668. For many years, capital/labor relations were marked by **paternalism**, union/management cooperation, and civic benevolence on the part of the corporation. By the 1970s, however, ALCOA's market share declined in the face of competition from imports and its own outmoded manufacturing processes. Jobs were eliminated in Ravenswood and other facilities. ALCOA management forced local 5668 to accept deep **concessions** in 1984. By 1986, however, ALCOA was still deeply in debt. Two years later, Ravenswood was part of an ALCOA sell-off that placed the RAC under the control of an international holding company clandestinely financed by corporate raider and tax-evader Marc Rich.

Safety conditions and morale were already in decline at the RAC and the plant's new management was openly hostile to the USWA. The deaths of several Ravenswood workers brought matters to a head in 1990. On November 1, RAC management issued a **lockout** of the plant's 1,700 workers, declared it a non-union facility, and began hiring **scabs** to replace USWA members. For the next eighteen months the USWA battled the company on the picket line, in domestic and international courts, before the National Labor Relations Board, in the political arena, and on the public-relations front. The USWA launched an especially effective **corporate campaign** that exposed Ravenswood's ties to Marc Rich, by then an international fugitive from justice living in Switzerland. It also showed how cost-cutting measures took place in violation of the **Occupational Safety and Health Act (1970)**, and how the firm routinely violated provisions of the Clean Air and Clean Water Acts.

RAC workers also maintained inspiring levels of solidarity throughout the struggle. Even more impressively, local 5668 was able to build bridges with overseas union movements that collectively placed pressure on Rich, banks doing business with Ravenswood, and politicians who coddled questionable corporate practices. The union also convinced important RAC clients—like Coca Cola and Anheuser-Busch—to stop purchasing scab-made cans. The union's anti-Rich campaign took them to Australia, England, Finland, France, The Netherlands, Romania, Russia, Spain, Switzerland, and five other nations. It successfully linked Rich's consortium to labor struggles around the globe and pressured Rich holdings worldwide. Faced with international pressure, mounting legal bills, and overwhelmingly negative public opinion, the RAC settled its dispute with USWA local 5668. On June 12, 1992, members ratified a new contract and, on June 29, jubilant workers marched into the plant singing "Solidarity Forever."

For many observers, Ravenswood—like 1990s victories by United Parcel Service workers, NYNEX workers, Fieldcrest employees, and others—shows that organized labor is on the cusp of a renewal. Ravenswood workers received high praise for their creativity, their international organizing efforts, and their steadfast refusal to cave in. Some observers see the Ravenswood lockout as proof that modern labor conflicts must go beyond traditional trade union reliance on strikes. The final settlement was not a complete victory for the USWA. Ravenswood nearly went bankrupt during the lockout and its uncertain financial future threatens to delay promised safety improvements, job guarantees, and pension schemes. The $2,000 in back pay given to each worker hardly compensated their loss, and several hundred workers did not get their jobs back. Moreover, the USWA had to welcome into the union over 300 scabs who took vacant positions. In 2001, President William Clinton pardoned Marc Rich, an act seen by many USWA members as an insult. It remains to be seen if Ravenswood truly was a turning point for labor.

Suggested Readings: Tom Juravich and Kate Bronfenbrenner, *Ravenswood,* 1999; Joshua Green, "Union Square Off," www.thenewrepublic.com/express/green.020801.html; Russell Mokhibu and Robert Weissman, "A Rich Pardon," www.sfbg.com/focus/120.html.

Robert E. Weir

Reece, Florence (April 12, 1900–August 3, 1986). Florence Reece was a social activist, poet, and songwriter. Born in Sharps Chapel, Tennessee, she grew up in a coal camp at Fort Ridge, Tennessee. Florence Reece was the daughter of a coal miner who loaded a ton and a half of coal for thirty cents. At age of fifteen, the year after her father was killed in a slate fall, she married Sam Reece. Reece was also a coal miner, who had gone to work in the mines at the age of eleven to earn sixty cents a day. Her mother opposed the marriage and the two crossed the state line to Kentucky where her mother's permission was not needed. Reece had ten children, some of whom went into the mines as boys to help support the family.

Florence Reece lived in Harlan County, Kentucky in the 1930s when the **United Mine Workers of America** attempted to unionize coal miners. She saw miners and their families—hard-working people—going hungry. She saw thugs prowling her county to keep coal miners from affiliating with the union. Her husband Sam would come home wearing frozen clothes after lying in water all day to mine coal. Sam Reece was one of the labor organizers for the United Mine Workers of America in "bloody" Harlan County. During the Harlan County strike, which is called the Battle of Evarts, Sheriff J. H. Blair led his deputies on a violent rampage of beating and murdering union leaders. One night in May 1931, while Reece was alone with her children, Sheriff Blair and a band of deputies broke into her home. She demanded of the sheriff, "What are you here for? You know there's nothing but a lot of little hungry children here." The men ransacked the house in search of Sam, but could not find him. While the sheriff and his thugs waited for Sam, she managed to get word to her husband not to come home. Days later, while waiting for her husband to return, she wrote "Which Side Are You On?" on an old wall calendar, written to the tune of an old Baptist hymn called "Lay the Lily Low." The Battle of Evarts, immortalized in this Appalachian woman's coal-miner protest song, is one of the most famous labor songs in history and communicates hope and inspiration.

Come all you poor workers,
Good news to you I'll tell,
How the good old union
Has come here to dwell.
Which side are you on?
Which side are you on?
We're starting our good battle,
We know we're sure to win,
Because we've got the gun thugs
A lookin' very thin.
Which side are you on?
Which side are you on?
If you go to Harlan County,
There is no neutral there,
You'll either be a union man
Or a thug for J. H. Blair.
Which side are you on?
Which side are you on?

In 1941, a version recorded by the Almanac Singers—comprised of Woody Guthrie, Lee Hays, Millard Lapell, and Pete Seeger—made the song famous. The song is still sung at labor worker gatherings and other social causes, worldwide. (See **Music and Labor**.)

A lifelong activist, Reece wrote *Against the Current,* a collection of short stories and poems. Reece also criticized President Reagan for his cuts in programs for the poor and needy in her song "You Can't Live On Jellybeans," which is a reference to one of the president's favorite foods.

Florence and Sam lived happily together for sixty-four years, until he died in 1978 of pneumoconiosis, or Black Lung Disease. Florence died from a heart attack in Knoxville, Tennessee.

Suggested Readings: William Serrin, "Labor Song's Writer, Frail at 83, Shows She Is Still a Fighter," in *The New York Times* no. 160 Late City Final Edition (March 18, 1984, Sunday); Hilda Wenner, *Here's to Women,* 1987; Deana Martin, "Appalachian Protest Songwriters," http://athena.English.vt.edu/~appalach/writersM/protestsongs.htm.

Patricia Shackleton

Reeves v. Sanderson Plumbing Products, Inc. *Reeves v. Sanderson Plumbing Products, Inc.* is a Supreme Court decision rendered in June 2000 that makes it easier for employees to file bias lawsuits against their employers. The plaintiff, Roger Reeves, was a supervisor in the Sanderson Plumbing Products firm of Columbia, Mississippi. In 1995, he was fired after working for the firm for forty years. The company alleged that Reeves was dismissed for poor record keeping and lax supervisory skills, but Reeves maintained that he was fired because of his age. A company manager told the fifty-seven-year-old Reeves that he was "too damn old," several months before his dismissal. This followed a similar slight several months before.

Reeves's job reviews were exemplary and he thus filed suit alleging that he was a victim of age discrimination. Reeves won, but the original verdict was overturned by a federal appeals judge who ruled that Reeves failed to demonstrate discrimination, even though the company's stated reasons for firing him were untrue. In June 2000 the Supreme Court unanimously sided with Reeves and reinstated the original verdict. The court also ruled that employees need only demonstrate that an employer's explanation for a hiring or promotion decision was false, and that it was the task of juries to determine whether or not discrimination occurred. Unions and worker advocates hailed the decision, which no longer requires employees to provide concrete evidence of discrimination. Legal scholars predict it will dramatically increase discrimination suits against employers.

Suggested Readings: Marcia McCormick, "Reeves v. Sanderson Plumbing: Turning Back the Tide on Summary Judgment in Federal Employment," in *Washington Post*, June 13, 2000. "DCBA Brief Online," http://www.dcba.org/brief/octissue/2001/art31001.htm; *Reeves v. Sanderson*, http://supct.law.cornell.edu/supct/html/99–536.ZS.html.

Robert E. Weir

Replacement Worker. Replacement worker is the term used to describe a person who takes the place of another during a **strike** or **lockout**. It has only gained currency since the late 1970s and has been part of concerted, professional attempts to defeat and discredit unions. The term has been actively promoted in an attempt to escape the opprobrium associated with the older term "**scab**."

Although businesses have long attempted to operate as non-union concerns and many have succeeded in routing organized labor from their businesses, the usual practice was to rehire most strikers once a union was broken. In strikes like the **Professional Air Traffic Controllers Organization (PATCO) strike** in 1981, the **Phelps-Dodge strike** in 1983 (miners), and the **Hormel strike** in 1985 (meatpackers), however, management replaced their entire workforce. A 1993 attempt by the 103rd Congress to amend the **National Labor Relations Act** and prohibit the hiring of permanent replacement workers was killed by Republican filibuster. Under current law, permanent replacement workers remain legal hires if the strike is deemed purely an economic action on the part of the union. Unions have countered by filing **unfair labor practices** in order to refute the right to hire replacement workers. (An unfair labor practice would mean the strike was not entirely economic.)

Suggested Readings: Stanley Aronowitz, *From the Ashes of the Old*, 1998; Charles Baird, "Strikers and Scabs," http://www.libertyhaven.com/theoreticorphilosophicalissues/economics/employmentandunemployment/strikersandscabs.html; Thomas Geoghean, *Which Side Are You On?*, 1991.

Robert E. Weir

Republicanism. Republicanism was the political ideology that formed Americans' core political beliefs and institutions. In the antebellum years, republicanism helped shape the views of workers and their unions as well. Throughout the eighteenth and nineteenth centuries, many denounced the inequalities of colonialism, slavery, and industrialization by employing the tenets of republicanism: virtue, citizenship, community, liberty, and equality. British labor agitator Thomas Paine, for example, emigrated to America, where he wrote *Common Sense* (1776). Seeking farmers' and artisans' participation in the American Revolution, Paine proclaimed "the floor of Freedom is as level as water." Many workers were attracted to Paine's challenges to constituted authority and his insistence that true liberty was radically democratic. Among artisans, Thomas Paine's birthday was a de facto workers' holiday. Thomas Jefferson was also much honored for his perceived radicalism and support for farmers and other commoners.

Vague republican precepts also resonated among slaves. In 1800, Gabriel Prosser rallied more than 1,000 slaves under the slogan "Death or Liberty." Prosser invoked the same principles as Patrick Henry's famous revolutionary proclamation, thereby demonstrating that the promises of republicanism were being denied to slaves.

Despite most Americans' use of republicanism to stress economic individualism, workers employed republicanism to critique industrialization and commercialization that they believed amassed wealth and power and threatened their independence. The **Workingmen's Movement** of the 1820s and 1830s helped shape labor republicanism. An Albany paper proclaimed that "the farmers, mechanics, and workingmen are assembling [with] those principles of liberty and equality unfolded in the Declaration of Independence." By the 1830s, labor republicanism was a loose nexus of ideas that critiqued existing social and economic elites and called for equal rights, essentially demanding American society honor the democratic ideals embedded within the Declaration of Independence and the Bill of Rights. To that end, advocates called for banking regulations, land reform, mechanics' **lien laws**, shorter work hours, reform of inheritance-tax laws, and universal public education. They also called for the abolition of debtor prisons, laws requiring males to drill in local militias,

WHITE SLAVES.

It is of the greatest importance to the workingmen of the United States to understand the true sentiments and objects of the leading traitors of the South. Their opinions of workingmen---who earn their support by their daily labor--- are clearly set forth in the following extract from the speech of Mr. Hammond, of South Carolina, in the Senate of the United States, on the 4th of March, 1858.

" In all social systems there must be a class to do the mean duties, to perform the drudgery of life---that is, a class requiring but a low order of intellect, and but little skill. Its requisites are vigor, docility, fidelity. . . . . It constitutes the very mud-sills of society and of political government; and you might as well attempt to build a house in the air, as to build either one or the other except on the mud-sills. Fortunately for the South, she found a race adapted to that purpose to her hand. . . . We use them for the purpose, and call them slaves.

The man who lives by daily labor, and scarcely lives at that, and who has to put out his labor in the market, and take the best he can get for it---in short, your whole class of manual laborers and operatives, as you call them, are SLAVES. The difference between us is, that our slaves are hired for life, and well compensated; there is no starvation, no begging, no want of employment among our people, and not too much employment either, Yours are hired by the day. . . . YOUR SLAVES ARE WHITE, OF YOUR OWN RACE---you are brothers, of one blood. Our slaves do not vote. We give them no political power. Yours do vote; and, being the majority, they are the depositories of all your political power. If they knew the tremendous secret, that the ballot-box is stronger than an army with bayonets, where would you be!---Your society would be reconstructed. . . . Not by meetings in parks, with arms in their hands, but by the peaceful process of the ballot-box."

The law-abiding and union-loving workingmen of the Union---whom the Senator denounces as " White Slaves," went to the ballot-box, according to the Constitution, and effected "a peaceful revolution." But the "gentlemen" traitors of the South, less loyal and less honest, went " with arms in their hands," and treason in their hearts, and have compelled the workingmen of the South to rise against their brothers of the North, in order to make "white slaves" of them all.

There are many other advocates of the doctrine of Senator Hammond who can be produced.

These things being true, I charge,

1st. That the rebellion of the South Carolina traitors is an attempt to destroy the interests of the democratic working classes of the Union.

2d. That it is an effort to build up forever a system by which "*Capital shall own Labor.*"

3d. That it is an attempt to make slavery---and property in slaves---the controlling interest of the Union.

4th. That Slavery is, and from its nature must be, the deadly enemy of Free Labor.

5th. That the success of the traitors will be a death-blow to the interests of Free Workingmen, North and South.

6th. That self-interest and patriotism both call upon Workingmen to stand by the government firm as a rock till the rebellion is put down, and peace restored by the constitutional authorities.

I challenge Hon. Fernando Wood, Hon. Benjamin Wood, C. Godfrey Gunther, Esq., and Prof. Mason, of New York; F. W. Hughes, Esq. and Hon. Geo. B. Woodward, of Pennsylvania; and Hon. C. L. Vallandigham and Hon. G. E. Pugh, of Ohio, to disprove my quotations or the correctness of my conclusions.

A Democratic Workingman.

NEW YORK, Sept. 28th, 1863. ☞ *PLEASE POST THIS UP.*

This Civil War declaration of a workingman contains a description of the concept of "wage slavery," which many southerners, and some northerners, viewed as the North's version of slavery. © George Meany Memorial Archives.

and the formation of monopolies. A key idea was expansion of suffrage; some even supported women's right to vote.

Women working in New England textile mills employed the term "wage slavery" to denounce class structures and workplace injustices. Over time, this became a key link for those who associated labor's cause with abolition. After the Civil War, workers joined the **eight-hour movement** to bring about the "republicanization of labor, as well as a republicanization of government." In the 1880s, the **Knights of Labor**'s motto, "an injury to one is the concern of all," tapped workers' republican idealism. From Virginia to California, Knights participated in labor parties and took control of local politics, causing a San Francisco newspaper to proclaim that the Knights were "regenerators of the Republic."

The post–Civil War period also saw the penetration of imported ideologies, like **anarchism**, **Lassalleanism**, Marxism, and other varieties of **socialism**. In addition, American-style liberalism began to cast off its associations with laissez-faire **capitalism** and merge with republican precepts. By the 1890s, the term republicanism began to fall out of favor, though its ideals continue to resonate in working-class movements. In recent years, labor historians have found republicanism a useful idea in helping explain why socialist movements in the United States have been weaker than those in other western industrialized nations. According to this line of reasoning, American workers were less susceptible to imported socialism because they were grounded in an older and better-entrenched radical tradition that drew on Paine's democratic idealism and Jefferson's rural (and rhetorical) radicalism.

Suggested Readings: Leon Fink, *Workingmen's Democracy: The Knights of Labor and American Politics*, 1983; Eric Foner, *Tom Paine and Revolutionary America*, 1976; Sean Wilentz, *Chants Democratic: New York City and the Rise of the American Working Class, 1788–1850*, 1984.

John Whitmer

Rerum Novarum. *Rerum Novarum* was an encyclical issued by Pope Leo XIII in 1891 that, among other things, removed the Roman Catholic Church's blanket condemnation of secret societies and recognized the legitimacy of labor unions. It offered critiques of both **socialism** and **capitalism**, arguing that capital and labor must recognize that their interests are inextricably linked.

Prior to *Rerum Novarum*, Catholic workers faced a dilemma. In the wake of the anti-Masonic agitations in the early nineteenth century and violence associated with the clandestine **Molly Maguires** in the 1870s, the Catholic Church reaffirmed views against secret societies that dated to medieval times. The Church similarly took a dim view of burgeoning socialist movements, both in Europe and in the United States. Catholics joining any sort of secret order faced the threat of excommunication.

In the United States, however, the church's position ran afoul of other social trends. First, the post–Civil War period saw a proliferation of fraternal orders, most of which practiced some degree of ritual secrecy. Second, many labor unions also maintained levels of secrecy. In the absence of labor laws protecting **collective-bargaining** rights, workers faced severe sanctions merely for associating with a labor union. To protect membership, many chose to operate clandestinely. For Irish, German, and French-Canadian Catholic immigrants the church's condemnation imposed a special burden: obeying the church's prohibition meant avoiding fraternal groups and labor unions important to helping immigrants assimilate into American society. It also fueled already deep nativist suspicions of foreign-born workers. Moreover, many workers were attracted to socialism, and many immigrants had been involved in movements prior to arriving in America.

The Catholic Church's position became untenable with the growth of the **Knights of Labor (KOL)** in 1880s. Because the KOL practiced a concealed ritual and operated in complete secrecy until 1882, it was roundly condemned by Catholic clerics. In Canada, Catholic workers were forbidden to join the KOL, and those in America faced church discipline. The KOL's leadership, however, was heavily Roman Catholic and, at least until 1886, so too was the bulk of its membership. Forced to choose between their church or their union, many choose the latter.

The KOL took the lead in attempting to ameliorate disputes with Rome. In 1879, Knights changed wording in their ritual to allow communicants to reveal parts of it to their priests, and KOL head **Terence Powderly**, a practicing Catholic, led the move to make the KOL a public organization in all but its ritual. He also cultivated an alliance with the powerful James Cardinal Gibbons of Baltimore, who admired the KOL and saw no threat to the faith in its precepts. Gibbons lobbied Rome to make policy changes. At first he was rebuffed, but after 1885, so many workers were joining the KOL that Gibbons argued that the Church would be irreparably harmed by continuing a blanket ban against secret orders and labor unions.

The Catholic Church was still officially a mission church in the United States for much of the nineteenth century. Catholics were suspect, and outbreaks of anti-Catholic discrimination were common, especially against Irish and Irish-Americans. Powderly himself came in for intense criticism for attempting to placate the Church. Gibbons parlayed all of this into a successful plea in Rome. Canadian parishes were ordered to cease excommunicating Knights and, in 1891, Pope Leo XIII issued *Rerum Novarum*.

Rerum Novarum pales when compared with the pronouncements of Protestants involved in the Social Gospel movement. The document offers only tepid acceptance of labor organizations, though it did recognize their struggle for social justice. It did, however, place the blame for industrial strife upon the shoulders of capital rather than labor. It also valorized manual labor, echoing views of the dignity of toil found in popular labor manifestos. Officially, it endorsed neither capitalism nor socialism. Instead, the encyclical upheld a vague mutualism rooted in principles of Christian fraternity and charity.

Nonetheless, it had a profound impact on the American labor movement. Ironically, the KOL was in deep decline by 1891 and *Rerum Novarum* did little to revive its sagging fortunes. But many future labor leaders were Roman Catholic, and the encyclical allowed Catholic workers to join unions with a clear conscience. Rome's periodic reaffirmations of *Rerum Novarum* also insulated it somewhat from charges of complicity with oppression. The most significant of these was *Quadragesimo Anno* issued by Pope Pius XI in 1931, which contained blistering condemnations of unemployment. As an ironic footnote, *Rerum Novarum* also led to the founding of a large Catholic fraternal order that uses secret rituals: the Knights of Columbus.

Suggested Readings: Sidney Ahlstrom, *A Religious History of the American People*, 1975; Henry Browne, *The Catholic Church and the Knights of Labor*, 1949; Ken Fones-Wolf, *Trade Union Gospel: Christianity and Labor in Industrial Philadelphia 1865–1915*, 1989.

Robert E. Weir

Reuther, Walter (September 1, 1907–May 9, 1970). Walter Reuther was born in Wheeling, West Virginia, the son of German immigrant parents.

Reuther's father, Valentine, worked as a brewery-wagon driver and insurance agent and was active in the trade union and **socialist** movements. Walter Reuther and his two younger brothers, Roy (1909–1968) and Victor (1912–), were inculcated with their father's working-class idealism and commitment to social justice. In 1923, Walter dropped out of high school to become an apprentice die maker and, in 1927, moved to Detroit where he worked as a die maker for Ford Motor Company. While working full-time at Ford, Reuther finished high school and enrolled at Detroit City College (later Wayne State University). Reuther was involved

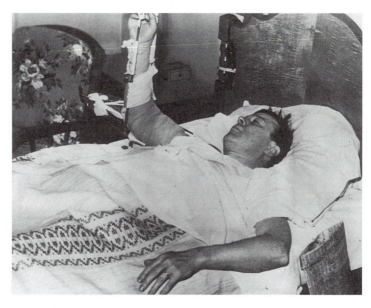

Walter Reuther recovering after an assassination attempt. © George Meany Memorial Archives.

in campus politics and worked actively for the election of Norman Thomas, socialist candidate for the presidency in 1932. Reuther joined the Auto Workers Union, affiliated with the communist Trade Union Unity League, but found himself laid off, a victim of the Great Depression. In 1933, Walter and his brother Victor traveled abroad where they witnessed the Nazi seizure of power and briefly worked with the underground resistance. Traveling to the Soviet Union, the Reuther brothers were employed at the Gorki automotive factory where their experience at Ford proved valuable. The Stalinist regime proved too oppressive for the Reuthers and they remained in the Soviet Union for only two years. Upon return to the United States, Walter Reuther became involved in the labor movement. He attended the 1935 **American Federation of Labor (AFL)** convention, where **John L. Lewis** led the movement for industrial unionism, arguing that mass organization on an industry-wide basis rather

Walter Reuther (speaking) and his younger brother Victor Reuther (seated). © George Meany Memorial Archives/Nate Fine Photo.

than organization by skilled craft was the future of organized labor. Reuther, without a job, obtained a union card in a small **United Auto Workers (UAW)** local of GM workers. Reuther was a delegate at the UAW's South Bend, Indiana, convention in 1936, where his ambition, self-confidence, ability, left-leaning reputation, and oratorical skills propelled him to a position of leadership. Reuther became president of the tiny Local 174. Reuther and his brothers led a **strike**, in December 1936, against Kelsey-Hayes Corporation, a brake and wheel supplier for Ford. This strike spurred tremendous growth for Local 174. Immediately following the Kelsey-Hayes settlement, the Flint, Michigan, General Motors (GM) **sit-down strike** began. Walter's brothers Victor and Roy were deeply involved in the Flint strike. On May 26, 1937, Reuther and other UAW organizers were viciously attacked by Ford Service Division goons at the Battle of the Overpass, outside the River Rouge plant. Newspapers throughout the nation published vivid photographs of Reuther, Richard Frankensteen, and other bloodied UAW organizers, thus establishing Reuther as one of labor's heroes.

Between 1936 and 1939, the UAW was fraught with internecine warfare between numerous factions, not only communists and conservatives, but also those who feuded with the leadership over tactics, strategy, and organization. By 1939, Reuther had emerged as head of the potentially important GM Department, which Reuther transformed from a paper organization into a critical part of the UAW by organizing the tool and die makers. Reuther saw that, without the labor of the tool and die makers, GM would be unprepared to roll out its 1940 models, thus the company was compelled to recognize and bargain with the UAW.

As the United States entered World War II, Reuther proposed the conversion of auto plants to military production, with the goal of 500 aircraft per day. Reuther saw the war as an opportunity for labor to achieve a more nearly equal voice with the companies in workplace management. Reuther proposed a series of new ideas that gained him national attention. Once reconversion to peacetime production began, Reuther challenged GM's argument that it could not afford wage increases without increases in the cost of automobiles. Reuther challenged GM to "open the books" to prove the company's contention. No other labor group joined Reuther in his challenge, though, and labor obtained wage increases while companies passed along significant price increases to consumers.

In 1946, Walter Reuther defeated the ineffective R. J. Thomas for UAW president. Thomas and George Addes, UAW secretary-treasurer, had been among Reuther's staunchest opponents. Reuther purged the UAW leadership of all remnants of the Thomas-Addes caucus and, in 1948, was the subject of a shotgun assassination attempt. In 1949, his brother Victor was the subject of a similar attempt; Walter suffered a paralyzed arm, Victor lost an eye. Neither crime ever resulted in an arrest, but Reuther beefed up personal security for the remainder of his life. Following 1948, Reuther led the purge of communists from the **Congress of Industrial Organizations (CIO)**. In 1949, eleven communist-dominated unions were expelled and Reuther, once seen as a leftist himself, was the most prominent leader in the movement to purge the left-wing unions. Politically, Reuther had slowly become more centrist. He abandoned the Socialist Party and became a stolid supporter of Franklin D. Roosevelt's New Deal, coming to believe that the Democratic Party was the only practical way for labor to achieve national political influence. He dreamed of a realignment of American politics whereby the Democrats would take on the role of Europe's labor and social democrats. He became a force within the Democratic Party, solidly backing John F. Kennedy and Lyndon B. Johnson and enthusiastically supporting Johnsons's civil rights and Great Society programs.

Reuther's labor strategy evolved to the identification of one target firm among auto's big three. That firm would bear the brunt of strike actions. Then, once a settlement was reached with the target firm, the gains made there would be used as a model for settlement with the other two giant auto firms. Under Reuther's bargaining strategy, tremendous gains were made for auto workers in the postwar era. Productivity increases were linked to **cost-of-living** increases at GM in 1948; employer-funded pensions were introduced at Chrysler in 1950; medical insurance for workers began at GM in 1950; unemployment benefits that supplemented those available through the government were introduced by Ford in 1955. Reuther's strategy in a prosperous postwar world was to offer shop-floor stability and discipline in exchange for gains in wages, benefits, and job security. Reuther's critics charged that this transformed the union from a vital, radical force for social change into a disciplinary arm of the auto companies' personnel departments.

Reuther's practical successes made the UAW the largest union in the CIO, however, when President Philip Murray died in 1952, Reuther succeeded him. As CIO president, Reuther started the negotiations that would lead to the merger of the AFL and CIO in 1955 under the presidency of **George Meany**. Reuther eventually clashed with Meaney, largely over Meaney's support of the Vietnam War, but also over issues such as minority rights and environmental abuses. By 1968, the UAW left the AFL-CIO. Following this, Reuther devoted his efforts to the UAW's Black Lake Recreation and Education Center. He and his wife were killed in an airplane crash in Pellston, Michigan, on May 9, 1970, while traveling to inspect the construction of the center. Roy Reuther worked as an organizer for voter-registration drives as well as for progressive political causes, continuing his formal association with the UAW until his death in 1968. Victor Reuther remained active with the UAW until 1971, but grew disaffected with the union's leadership and direction and became a harsh critic of UAW leaders and policies.

Suggested Readings: John Barnard, *Walter Reuther and the Rise of the Auto Workers*, 1983; Nelson Lichtenstein, *The Most Dangerous Man in Detroit: Walter Reuther and the Fate of American Labor*, 1995; William Serrin, *The Company and the Union: The "Civilized Relationship" of the General Motors Corporation and the United Automobile Workers Union*, 1973.

James P. Hanlan

Rice, Monsignor Charles Owen (November 12, 1908–). Charles Owen Rice was born in New York City on November 12, 1908. After his mother (Anna O'Donnell) died in 1912 while giving birth to her third child (Ellen), Charles and his older brother Patrick were sent to Ireland to live with his father's family. (The sister, Ellen, died a month after birth.) The two brothers moved from Ireland to Pittsburgh in 1920 and lived with their Uncle Joe and their father, Michael, who was an A & P food store warehouse foreman. Michael Rice had remarried his dead wife's eldest sister, Jennie. Charles's Uncle Joe eventually became an organizer in the **Congress of Industrial Organizations (CIO)** and had a significant influence on the political development of his nephews.

The family was strongly Irish Catholic. Charles and his brother both attended parochial schools in Pittsburgh. Charles graduated from St. Mary's Elementary School (1922) and St. Mary of the Mount High School (1926). Charles followed his older brother when he entered Duquesne University in 1926, Patrick's senior year at the college. After graduating from Duquesne in 1930, Charles entered St. Vincent's Seminary and was ordained as a priest in 1934.

Coming of age as a priest during the Depression impacted Rice. He became socially active soon after being assigned assistant pastor of St. Agnes Parish in Pittsburgh in 1935. Between 25 percent and 50 percent of his parishioners were on public assistance. Rice's own father lost his job at the market in the 1930s and had great difficulty finding work. In 1931, while Rice was a student in the seminary, Pope Pious XI issued *Quadregisimo Anno*, a papal decree that reaffirmed Pope Leo XIII's **Rerum Novarum** (1891). These papal pronouncements encouraged Catholic social activism in organized labor and guided a generation of socially active priests who supported trade unions and a more organized form of capitalism.

Rice and two other Pittsburgh priests, Father Carl Hensler and Monsignor George Barry O'Toole, formed the Catholic Radical Alliance (CRA) in 1937. The CRA initially followed the philosophy of, and was allied with, Dorothy Day's Catholic Worker (CW) Movement. The CRA established a CW-type hospitality house to help clothe, shelter, feed, and comfort Pittsburgh's poor. But the CRA also focused on supporting organized labor causes in Pittsburgh. Rice and the others formed a Pittsburgh chapter of the **Association of Catholic Trade Unionists (ACTU)** in 1938. A number of fissures developed between the CW movement and Pittsburgh's CRA. Rice did not agree with the CW movement's uncompromising pacifism and opposition to U.S. entrance into WWII. The CW movement was also less critical of individual Communist Party members' activities in reform and labor organizations than Rice and the Pittsburgh ACTU.

Rice and many of the other Pittsburgh ACTU activists (often called actists) were vigorous anticommunists who redbaited their foes in the labor movement. Indeed, a strong strain of the motivation for ACTU was for Catholics to counter Communist Party influ-

Monsignor Charles Rice. © George Meany Memorial Archives.

ence in the working class, as well as a sincere support of unionism. By the time that Rice and the Pittsburgh ACTU hosted the first national ACTU convention in 1940, the connections with the CW movement had been severed, and Rice was well on his way to becoming one of the best-known and most influential labor priests in the country.

Through the Pittsburgh ACTU, Rice became increasingly enmeshed in the political battles in the labor movement throughout the 1940s. He was very close to important Catholic national labor leaders, like CIO President **Philip Murray**. Rice sought to rid the CIO unions of communist influence. He was perhaps the most visible, forceful, and active anticommunist cleric involved in the labor movement. He wrote, spoke, and actively red-baited the left in the CIO, particularly in the years immediately following World War II. He was especially active, for example, in the bitter internal battle for control in the **United Electrical Workers (UE)** union. ACTU, Rice, and the other anticommunists supported the CIO's purge of eleven CIO international unions, including the UE, for being communist dominated in 1949 and 1950. They supported the CIO's creation of the **International Union of Electrical Workers (IUE)**, which was formed to replace the UE in the CIO. Rice also provided information to the FBI and collaborated with the House Un-American Activities Committee (HUAC) when it held hearings in Pittsburgh in August 1949. After the death of Rice's friend, Philip Murray, in 1952, he receded from the limelight and, in 1958, he was made pastor of a large parish in Washington, Pennsylvania.

Although he was never again as active or nationally important as in the 1940s, Rice continued to champion social causes. In the 1960s he opposed the U.S. military role in Vietnam. Rice also became critical of the complacency and inactivity of the labor movement in the 1960s. He supported progressive **rank-and-file** reform movements in a number of national unions, including the **United Steel Workers** and the **United Mine Workers** in the 1960s and 1970s. In the 1980s, he also supported activists and steelworkers who attempted to keep their plants from closing in the Monongahela Valley, Pennsylvania.

Rice has openly questioned the stridency of his anticommunism of the 1940s. He regrets some of the red-baiting tactics he used in the internecine labor battles then and how they may have contributed to the general conservatism of organized labor.

Suggested Readings: Neil Betten, "Charles Owen Rice: Pittsburgh Labor Priest, 1936–1940." *The Pennsylvania Magazine of History and Biography* XCIV no. 4 (1970): 518–32; Charles J. Mc-Collester, ed., *Fighter With a Heart: Writings of Charles Owen Rice, Pittsburgh Labor Priest*, 1996; Patrick McGeever, *Reverend Charles Owen Rice: Apostle of Contradiction*, 1989.

Joseph Turrini

Right-to-Work. Right-to-work is the belief that workers should not be forced to join a labor union or pay union **dues** to work. If a union contract contains a **union shop** or agency shop clause, all employees must pay union dues to continue their employment. Opponents argue that this is compulsory unionism which violates individual freedoms: individuals have a right-to-work, that is, the right to choose whether or not to join a union and/or pay union dues.

Since unions must represent all employees, members and nonmembers, unions argue everyone should have to join or pay dues because it is unfair to allow free riders to benefit from union representation without sharing the costs. Also, in democratic institutions, everyone is bound by what the majority decides and a union or agency shop clause is only present when a majority approves it. Many unions also charge that right-to-work campaigns are little more than thinly disguised attacks on **collective bargaining** rights and are part and parcel of an overall campaign of union-busting on the part of unscrupulous employers and ideological conservatives.

U.S. labor law does not prohibit union and agency shop clauses, but Section 14 (b) of the 1947 **Taft-Hartley Act** allows states to pass right-to-work laws, thus making agency and union shops illegal. States with these laws are called right-to-work states. As of 2001, there were twenty-two right-to-work states, primarily in the South and Midwest. The National Right to Work Committee lobbies for right-to-work legislation and the National Right to Work Legal Defense Foundation provides legal representation for workers trying to challenge union membership requirements. Right-to-work laws have made union organizing drives quite difficult in some areas, especially in the South and Southwest. Most unions call for the overturn of right-to-work laws, but have made little headway in accomplishing said goal.

Suggested Readings: Thomas Haggard, *Compulsory Unionism, the NLRB, and the Courts: A Legal Analysis of Union Security Agreements*, 1977; Fred Witney, Fred Taylor, and Benjamin J. Taylor, *Labor Relations Law*, 1995; "National Right-to-Work Committee," http://www.right-to-work.org.

John W. Budd

Robinson, Cleveland Lowellyn (1915–August 23, 1995). Cleveland Robinson was the authoritative voice of the Coalition of Black Trade Unionists (CBTU), a civil rights advocate, and labor official. He and his long-time associate, **A. Philip Randolph**, were considered the leading voices for greater participation by African Americans inside the American Federation of Labor-Congress of Industrial Organizations (AFL-CIO). The two frequently clashed with AFL-CIO President **George Meany** in efforts to get the organization to take a stronger stance on **minority labor**.

Robinson was born in Swabys Hope, Jamaica, in 1915 and emigrated to the United States in 1944, settling in New York City. He took employment with a Manhattan dry goods store and quickly took up the task of unionizing workers. In 1947, Robinson became an organizer for District 65 of the Distributive Workers of America, a union of about 30,000 retail and wholesale employees affiliated with the Retail, Wholesale, and Department Stores Employees Union. Both were absorbed by the **United Auto Workers (UAW)** in 1969. District 65 was one of the nation's more liberal labor organizations in matters of civil rights, and Robinson became one of its vice presidents in 1950. He held that post only two years and, in 1952, became the secretary-treasurer for District 65, a post he held until his retirement in 1992.

Robinson himself was active in the civil-rights movement. He served as a labor advisor to the Reverend Martin Luther King, Jr. and was the administrative chair of the 1963 march on Washington. He was also served mayors Robert Wagner and John Lindsay on New York City's Human Rights Commission. Robinson felt that the causes of labor and civil rights were inextricably linked and challenged the AFL-CIO to make said connection. He served as vice president, then president of the Negro American Labor Council, the forerunner of the CBTU. By the late 1960s, black workers inside the AFL-CIO were restive, and militant **rank-and-file** groups like the **Dodge Revolutionary Union Movement** were on the rise. Robinson grew convinced that the AFL-CIO's **voluntarism** was untenable. When Meany pledged the federation to neutrality in the 1972 presidential election, Robinson admonished that the re-election of Richard Nixon would result in "four more years of favored treatment for the rich and powerful . . . and [insensitivity] to the rights of workers, minorities, and the poor." He and four other black leaders announced the formation of the CBTU to pressure the AFL-CIO to pay more attention to the concerns of African American trade unionists. The CBTU greatly increased the number of African Americans in union leadership positions. He played an active role in the CBTU even when his personal life was marked by tragedy. In 1976, his wife, Susan Jenkins Robinson, passed away. In 1977, he married the former Doreen McPherson.

Robinson continued to merge interests in labor and civil rights. In 1985, he became the vice chairman of New York state's Martin Luther King, Jr. Commission, a group lobbying to make the Reverend King's birthday an official holiday and, later, in charge of commemorative events, educational programs, and social justice programs to honor King. Robinson became chair when Harry Belafonte stepped down in 1987, and he continued to serve on the commission until his death. He was also an outspoken opponent of the apartheid system in South Africa and pressured the AFL-CIO to call for boycotts of the nation and its products. In 1990, he co-chaired the committee that sponsored Nelson Mandela's visit to New York City.

Robinson retired from District 65 and the labor movement in 1992. When he died in 1995, the mourners and speakers at his funeral included such political and civil-rights luminaries as Mayor David Dinkins of New York, former United Nations ambassador Andrew Young, singer Harry Belafonte, the Reverend Jesse Jackson, and Coretta Scott King, the widow of Martin Luther King, Jr. Both President Mandela of South Africa and President William Clinton also sent condolences. The CBTU remains an active force in advancing the cause of African American union members.

Suggested Readings: "Coalition of Black Trade Unionists," http://www.cbtu.org/2003 website/aboutcbtu/robinson.html; Wolfgang Saxon, "Cleveland Robinson, 80, Civil-Rights Advocate," obituary in *New York Times*, August 26, 1995; Philip Foner, *Organized Labor and the Black Worker, 1619–1981*, 1982.

James P. Hanlan
Robert E. Weir

Runaway Capital/Shops. The term runaway capital/shops refers to the business practice of moving operations in whole or in part to another state, area, or country to escape the effects of a unionized workforce or government regulations. Historically the Northeast and northern Midwest regions of the United States contained the greatest density of industrialization. For this reason, unions and protective labor laws were more prominent. Beginning in the early nineteenth century, some employers sought to circumvent the countervailing power of strong employee representation. Early captains of industry like Samuel Slater did not hesitate to close textile mills and build entirely new **company towns** to avoid challenges to his authority. After the Civil War, however, the customary practice was to move (or threaten to move) operations to regions—often the South—where unions were weak and wages were lower.

Ironically, the 1935 **National Labor Relations Act** exacerbated this trend by further encouraging union membership in those areas where it was already strongest. The 1947 **Taft-Hartley Act** allowed state legislatures to pass **right-to-work** laws that prohibited compulsory union membership. Since 1947, twenty-two states in the South and the Midwest have passed right-to-work laws, the most recent of which was Oklahoma in 2001. These states have been favored by labor-intensive industries as a way to lower production costs through reduced wages. The Northeast, for example, saw most of its textile, shoes, and machine-tool industries leave the region and relocate in the South.

The debate over runaway shops has become ideological and is seen by opponents of unions as a way to curb their political influence and power. It has taken on new urgency now that the practice of runaway industries has become global. By the 1970s, even right-to-work states began to experience job losses as businesses left to secure even cheaper labor outside the United States' border. Moreover, new investments frequently take place in low-wage nations. The controversial **North American Free Trade Agreement (NAFTA)** removed many tariff barriers between the United States, Canada, and Mexico. Many free-trade advocates wish to extend NAFTA throughout Central and South America. To opponents, this move toward **globalization** threatens the very future of American jobs and wages.

Suggested Readings: Thomas A. Kochan, Harry C. Katz, and Robert B. McKersie, *The Transformation of American Industrial Relations,* 1994; John Mehring, "Labor Loses 'Right-to-Work' Fight in Oklahoma," *Labor Notes,* vol. 272, (November 2001); Robert B. Reich, *The Work of Nations: Preparing Ourselves for 21st Century Capitalism,* 1992.

Pete Gingras

S

Sabotage. Sabotage is a commonly (or deliberately) misunderstood word when applied to labor relations. In common parlance it refers to wanton destruction of property resulting from a dispute between two parties. It is often used to refer to damages inflicted by workers on the property of recalcitrant employers, especially during a **strike** or **boycott**. Most labor unions, however, adhere to a definition developed by the **Industrial Workers of the World (IWW),** in which sabotage meant a systematic withdrawal of worker efficiency. For example, assembly line workers might deliberately slow the pace of their work so they meet only exact production quotas, or fail to meet them altogether. Many labor supporters advocate sabotage as a form of what the IWW called "striking on the job." Workers can disrupt work processed by withholding specialized knowledge they possess that management does not. A group of workers might, for instance, feign ignorance of how to repair a broken machine, thereby slowing production.

Unions have, however, engaged in direct destruction of property. Destructive sabotage was quite common during the **Great Labor Uprising** of 1877, and some IWW members used it as part of a larger program of **direct action** aimed at disrupting **capitalism**. Many observers claim the term comes from the French word *sabot*, or wooden shoe. One school of thought credits the term to a 1910 French rail strike in which workers damaged the shoes (*sabots*) holding rails together. Still others claim it comes from the practice of disgruntled machine tenders hurling their *sabots* into machines in the early days of the French industrial revolution. The latter claim seems more probable, as the practice of both wanton and passive forms of sabotage assuredly predates 1910. As numerous IWW supporters were fond of pointing out, the act of ancient Hebrew slaves spoiling Egyptian bricks was a form of sabotage, as were acts of antebellum slaves filling the bottoms of cotton bags with stones.

Destructive sabotage has often provided the pretext for employers to request government assistance in defeating strikes. When several hotheaded strikers derailed a train during an 1890 strike against the New York Central Railroad, for example, the railroad used the incident to justify the hiring of **Pinkerton** detectives (which was actually done before the incident) and to convince reluctant state governments to send National Guard troops into numerous locales. Likewise, striking miners who dynamite pits or commit other acts of destructive sabotage have often found themselves subject to state repression in the wake of their violence.

For the most part, however, destructive sabotage has been less common than striking on the job. Management often exaggerates or invents sabotage threats to justify heavy-handed crackdowns. In some cases, management employs **agent provocateurs** to either incite strikers to commit property damage or make it appear that unions did damage that was done by company thugs. The 1936 **La Follette Committee** revealed that this was a widespread tactic. The use of agent provocateurs, like destructive sabotage itself, is illegal, but both continue to occur occasionally. For the most part, however, destructive worker sabotage has been an act of frustration, not a tactic authorized, endorsed, or condoned by their unions.

The modern form of sabotage as a way of withdrawing efficiency is the **work-to-rule** tactic. In such a case, workers follow the letter of the law in their contracts and refuse to take on any task not specifically enumerated in the contract. Truckers in the **International Brotherhood of Teamsters** have several times won employer concessions simply by driving the speed limit at all times, taking breaks exactly as mandated in the contract, and by refusing to do any loading or unloading of cargo not specifically mandated. Teachers have found work-to-rule an especially effective tool when contract talks stall. Since most teachers perform myriad tasks not required under their contracts—like staying after hours to work with students, supervising bus loadings, advising clubs, meeting with parents, making photocopies, correcting homework at night, informally handling discipline problems, and taking on extra duties during unexpected emergencies—a well-run work-to-rule campaign can severely disrupt how schools operate. Work-to-rule and striking on the job campaigns of all sorts have gotten more attention in recent years as strikes have become harder to win and **replacement workers** easier to obtain.

Suggested Readings: Frank Bohn, "Some Definitions: Direct Action—Sabotage," and Ben William, "Sabotage," in Joyce Kornbluh, ed., *Rebel Voices: An I.W.W. Anthology*, 1968; Martin Sprouse, ed., *Sabotage in the American WorkPlace: Anecdotes of Dissatisfaction, Mischief and Revenge*, 1992.

Robert E. Weir

Sacco and Vanzetti. Nicola Sacco and Bartolomeo Vanzetti were Italian immigrants convicted of murdering two people during a 1920 payroll robbery in suburban Boston. They were executed in 1927, despite the lack of credible evidence against them. In the annals of American jurisprudence, their executions rank among the **Molly Maguire** executions, the convictions following the **Haymarket bombing**, and later cases like the Scottsboro Boys and the Rosenberg electrocutions as severe miscarriages of justice that violate the rules of evidence.

Both Nicola Sacco, a shoemaker, and Bartolomeo Vanzetti, a fish peddler, were anarchists attracted to the views of Italian theorist and revolutionary Luigi Galleani, and members of the East Boston anarchist debate society Gruppo Autonomo. This combination proved fatal in the aftermath of World War I when a red scare broke out. Attorney General A. Mitchell Palmer's near pathological fear of radicalism led to authorized crackdowns against **anarchists, communists**, members of the **Industrial Workers of the World**, and even moderate **socialists** who advocated ballot-box politics. Such famed radicals as **Eugene Debs, Bill Haywood**, and **Emma Goldman** were arrested; Goldman and various other resident aliens were deported. A bad situation was exacerbated when some anarchist groups responded with the very violence the public feared. In June 1919, anarchist bombs rocked seven U.S. cities.

On April 15, 1920, a payroll heist occurred outside a shoe factory in East Braintree, Massachusetts, a Boston suburb. Robbers made off with $16,000 and killed two guards in the process. Sacco and Vanzetti were arrested on May 4, when they went to pick up a car police had connected with the robbery. The trial that ensued was marked by many unethical procedures, including the prosecution's coaching of witnesses and Judge Webster Thayer's overt prejudice against the defendants. More seriously, the prosecution quashed evidence that exonerated Sacco and Vanzetti. Both were convicted in a case that, in essence, put their anarchism on trial. Shortly after both were indicted in September 1920, an anarchist bomb planted on Wall Street in New York City killed forty people. In such a tense atmosphere, neither defendant stood much of a chance. Both were convicted on July 14, 1921 and sentenced to death. Lengthy appeals and worldwide protests served only to delay their electrocution until August 23, 1927. Their deaths took place even though another man confessed to the crime in 1925.

Organized labor had little connection to Sacco and Vanzetti; their anarchist beliefs made them unwelcome in most unions. Although several unions held strikes to protest their impending execution and many union workers endorsed clemency, organized labor was largely silent on the matter. Only unionists associated with the political left dared to speak vociferously in defense of Sacco and Vanzetti. This was partly because all unions were under attack in the 1920s. Post–World War I red-baiting proved a disaster for labor unions, irrespective of their ideological leanings. The **open-shop** movement was in full swing, and workers across the country found themselves subject to indignities like **company unions** and **yellow-dog contracts**. The dramatic Sacco and Vanzetti case was another tool used by employers to tar labor unions and other progressives with murderous intent and to justify crackdowns.

Neither man was the martyred saint that romantics made them out to be. It is possible, even probable, that both were involved in some aspect of the June 1919 bombings. That said, however, few legal scholars believe either should have been convicted for the East Braintree murders. In the end, theirs appears to be a state-sanctioned murder. Sacco and Vanzetti have never been exonerated, though in 1977, Massachusetts Governor Michael Dukakis declared that they had not received a fair trial and proclaimed Sacco and Vanzetti Day on the fiftieth anniversary of their execution.

Suggested Readings: Paul Avrich, *Sacco and Vanzetti: The Anarchist Background*, 1991; Irving Bernstein, *The Lean Years*, 1960; Katharine Porter, *The Never-Ending Wrong*, 1977.

Robert E. Weir

Salary. Salary is the compensation for the time during which an employee is required to be on the employer's premises or on duty at a prescribed work place. Salary is the total remuneration paid by an employer to an employee for labor or services in accordance to a previously agreed upon rate, secured either via collective bargaining or individually. Unlike **wages**, salaries are usually not pegged to an hourly rate.

The 1938 **Fair Labor Standards Act (FLSA)** governs most employment relationships, though six major categories of employees are exempted: executive, administrative, professional, elected officials, recreational (i.e. entertainers), and agricultural employees. Under the exemptions these employees are to be considered salary-based and thus receive a fixed payment for any pay period without regard to the number of days or hours worked. Unless contracts specifically stipulate otherwise, salary deductions can be made for all such work absences as personal reasons, illness, or disability. The FSLA forbids deductions for jury duty, court service, or temporary military leave. Many salaried employees complain of long work hours, burdensome job duties, and abusive supervisors. Some labor observers believe that professional and white-collar workers are ripe for union-organizing drives. Many professions, including teachers, nurses, and journalists, have already organized in some areas.

Suggested Readings: Maurice B. Better, *Contract Bargaining Handbook for Local Leaders*, 1993; David B. Lipsky and Clifford B. Donn, *Collective Bargaining in American Industry*, 1987; Juliet B. Schor, *The Overworked American: The Unexpected Decline of Leisure*, 1991.

Pete Gingras

San Francisco General Strike (1934). *See Depression-Era Strikes.*

Scab. Scab is the term used to refer to workers who refuse to participate when their colleagues strike, or to workers who are hired by management to replace strikers. To loyal union supporters, there is no greater insult than to be dubbed a scab.

The exact origin of the term is disputed. Its first known use in English occurred in 1529 as a synonym for moral decay. By 1590 it was used generally to refer to persons of low character. Its first recorded use to refer to strike breakers occurred during a 1777 cordwainers' strike in Bristol, England, though it's likely the term was in currency long before then. The term appeared in the United States as early as 1806 during a boot and shoemakers' strike. For much of the nineteenth century it vied with blackleg as the favored term of abuse, though the latter has fallen from popular use. Printers also commonly used the terms fink, rat, and/or ratfink.

Imported scabs have long been a staple of capital/labor disputes, with management attempting to maintain production and thus break strikes. Until recently, most scabs have been recruited from among the ranks of immigrants, itinerant laborers, and the unemployed. In some cases, workers were unaware that they were strike breakers until they arrived at their jobs. Some of the tension between African American and Caucasian labor can be traced to the deliberate importation of blacks into strike-torn situations. Since the late 1970s, employers have turned increasingly to professional strike-breaking firms and the hiring of permanent **replacement workers**. This supplants an older practice in which scabs were terminated once a dispute was settled and all or most strikers were rehired. Labor advocates have taken some solace in the fact that the term scab has withstood several legal challenges from those claiming they were libeled or injured by its use. Most recently, a 1999 11th Circuit ruling in *Dunn v. ALPA* stated that the use of scab to describe pilots who crossed picket lines was accurate and non-libelous.

During the 1877 railroad strike, strikers in Chicago attack scab switchmen and brakemen. © George Meany Memorial Archives/Public Affairs Press.

Suggested Readings: Stanley Aronowitz, *From the Ashes of the Old,* 1998; Archie Green, *Wobblies, Pile Butts, and Other Heroes,* 1993.

Robert E. Weir

Schneiderman, Rose (April 6, 1884?–August 11, 1972) Rose Schneiderman was an important leader of the **Women's Trade Union League (WTUL)**, the **International Ladies' Garment Workers' Union (ILGWU)**, and numerous other organizations. She was born in either 1882 or 1884 in Saven, a Polish town then controlled by Russia, the daughter of Samuel and Deborah (Rothman) Schneiderman. Her Jewish parents emigrated to the United States in 1890, and settled in New York City's Lower East Side. Soon after their arrival, Schneiderman's father, a tailor, died of influenza. Economic pressure dispersed the Schneiderman children to orphanages and the homes of relatives. Rose's public-school education ended when she was thirteen, and she went to work in a department store. She left for a factory job stitching cap linings.

The brutal conditions of factory work led Schneiderman to **socialism** and trade unionism. She was instrumental in the formation of New York Local 23 of the United Cloth Hat and Cap Makers of North America (UCHCM), and was elected its secretary. At the time, the UCHCM did not even officially admit women, a policy Schneiderman helped reverse. She also helped direct a successful 1905 strike that increased wages for city hat makers. Schneiderman's efforts attracted notice and, in 1907, she was elected as vice president of the New York Branch of the WTUL. She also received a scholarship to attend classes at a preparatory school while working as an East Side organizer. She and Leonora O'Reilly were key figures in organizing a 1908 strike against the Cohen Company for better wages and an end to the **piecework** system. The strike was successful and the dressmakers' union affiliated itself with the ILGWU.

Schneiderman came to national attention following a rousing speech she gave after the **Triangle Factory Fire of 1911**. Schneiderman spoke at a funeral held by the city for the unclaimed dead and marched in the procession to represent the WTUL. After the fire, Schneiderman organized workers with increased vigor. She was an ILGWU organizer from 1914 to 1916. Her ILGWU duties took Schneiderman across the country to unionize workers in Boston, Philadelphia, Cleveland, and Chicago. In Chicago, Schneiderman was a valuable contributor in the successful Herzog glovemaker strike of 1915. She also served as WTUL vice president from 1919 to 1926, and as its president in 1918 and from 1926 to 1947. She spent much of her career organizing Jewish and Italian working women in the garment industry of the Lower East Side. Schneiderman claimed that Eastern European Jewish women were the most loyal unionists. In addition, she was an ardent believer in women's suffrage and campaigned heavily for the right to vote.

Schneiderman attended the 1920 International Congress of Working Women, and served as a trustee of **Brookwood Labor College** from 1924 to 1929. She was an early supporter of Franklin Roosevelt and, in 1933, became the sole female labor unionist on the board of the National Industrial Recovery Administration. She also served as secretary to the New York Department of Labor from 1937 to 1944. Her friendship with Eleanor Roosevelt provided White House access and some consider Schneiderman to have been among the brain trust that helped Roosevelt formulate New Deal policy. By the 1940s, however, the WTUL was in severe decline, and some critics fault Schneiderman for distancing the WTUL from the **Congress of Industrial Organizations**. Others blamed her for holding onto the WTUL reins for too long. She finally dismantled the national WTUL in 1949 and retired. Schneiderman died in 1972.

Suggested Readings: Alice Kessler-Harris, "Rose Schneiderman and the Limits of Women's Trade Unionism," in Melvyn Dubofsky and Warren Van Tine, *Labor Leaders in America,* 1967; Rose Schneiderman and Lucy Goldthwaite, *All for One,* 1967; Leon Stein, *Out of the Sweatshop: The Struggle for Industrial Democracy,* 1977.

Cristina Prochilo

Scientific Management. *See Taylorism.*

Scissorbill. Scissorbill is an out-of-fashion term for a worker who lacks class consciousness, has bourgeois pretensions, and refuses to join a union. The term was sometimes spelled scissorsbill. It was a favored slang insult among members of the **Industrial Workers of the World (IWW)**. Scissorbill was first applied to refer to late-nineteenth-century law-and-order vigilantes in Western states and probably came to the IWW through Western miners who changed its meaning. IWW members were especially scornful of scissorbills and songwriter **Joe Hill** parodied them in verses set to the popular "Steamboat Bill." In the song, Hill called them "the missing link Darwin tried to trace." The term faded from use when the IWW declined.

Suggested Reading: Joyce Kornbluh, *Rebel Voices,* 1968.

Robert E. Weir

Secondary Labor Force. Secondary labor force is a pool of reserve and/or less skilled laborers whose labor is deemed less valuable than that of workers in the top echelon of a particular job or trade. Historically, **child labor** and **minority labor** (including women) made up the bulk of the secondary labor force. Workers in smaller firms in industries dominated by large-scale, high-wage companies were also included in the secondary labor market. Craft workers and labor unions argued that these workers were used by unscrupulous employers to depress across-the-board wages within an industry. Employers frequently drew upon secondary labor during labor disputes when seeking replacement workers.

In more recent times, unions and some economists maintain that the American capitalist system continues to exploit the secondary labor market through two-tier wage systems, the use of temporary workers, the recruitment of foreign and immigrant labor, and the maintenance of a vast low-wage underclass. As these critics view it, workers find it difficult to press for better wages and benefits when management can draw upon large labor reserves that will work more cheaply. Debate rages as to whether such conditions are natural within **capitalism** or if they are part of a deliberate management strategy to hold down costs, increase stockholder profits, and discipline the work force.

Suggested Reading: David Gordon, Richard Edwards, and Michael Reich, *Segmented Work, Divided Workers*, 1985.

Robert E. Weir

Senate Civil Liberties Committee. *See La Follette Committee.*

Seniority. Seniority is customarily defined as the length of full-time service or work by an employee without a break in service. Less than full-time employment can be credited on a prorated basis. Seniority determines a worker's standing relative to fellow employees. Those with greater service or work time usually receive more privileges with regard to appointments, promotions, consideration for vacant positions, work-location preferences, scheduling of vacations, and overtime opportunities. Seniority also frequently determines who gets laid off during economic downturns, with employees lacking seniority being the first to lose their jobs and the last to be recalled when conditions improve.

Seniority has concerned the labor movement since the nineteenth century. Many unions sought seniority considerations to curb the practice of dismissing older workers in favor of younger ones who employers felt would be more productive. Many craft unions struck bargains that recognized seniority, though not always for the protection of all workers. While the length of service rewarded employees for service time, some unions barred African Americans from bargaining units. Other programs made it impossible for black workers to move out of unskilled job classifications. As women entered the labor market in greater numbers during World Wars I and II, they experienced unequal treatment due to a union's rigid seniority provisions. Even the **United Auto Workers**, prior to World War II, maintained a privileged seniority list for the all-white skilled and semi-skilled job categories, and separate lists for women, and yet another for all-black unskilled classifications.

During World War II, the War Labor Board established principles of nondiscriminatory seniority known as industrial jurisprudence. In 1961, President Kennedy created the President's Committee on Equal Employment Opportunity (PCEEO), to administer a fair seniority system for federal employment. Such legislation helped ease past discrimination, but problems remain in some industries and unions where the seniority principle of last hired, first fired prevails.

Suggested Readings: Richard Freeman and James Medoff, *What Do Unions Do?*, 1984; Clark Kerr and Paul Staudohar, *Labor Economics and Industrial Relations: Markets and Institutions*, 1994.

Pete Gingras

Service Employees International Union (SEIU). The Service Employees International Union (SEIU) represents more than 1.6 million workers, most of whom are employed in the service sector of the economy. Its members range in occupation from custodians and nurses to taxi drivers and window washers. At a time in which many unions have struggled to maintain their strength, SEIU has more than doubled its ranks since 1980. It is also one of the most diverse unions in the United States. More than thirty percent of its **rank-and-file** are racial minorities, and fifty-three percent is female.

SEIU was founded by a group of Chicago janitors in 1921 and was chartered by the **American Federation of Labor (AFL)**. It was known as the Building Service Employees International Union (BSEIU) until 1968, when it changed its name to SEIU. Although the BSEIU has not received the attention from scholars that the **industrial unions** of the 1930s have, it organized hospital workers and public employees during the 1930s at a time in which no other major union was attempting to do so. It was most active in large cities, including New York, where local 32B won several strikes that resulted in wage increases for members.

The BSEIU began to grow in the 1960s, due in no small part to shifts in the American economy that led to an expanding service sector. Its growth coincided with the resurgence of feminism and the union found itself inexorably drawn into the organization of women, especially in the health care industry. In 1974, the newly renamed SEIU was one of the major supporters of the **Coalition of Labor Union Women (CLUW)**, a group that seeks to address women's issues and place more women in union leadership roles. In 1975, the SEIU chartered **9 to 5**, a union of women clerical workers. Although 9 to 5 has since spun off into a separate organization, the SEIU maintains a powerful clerical **district** number 925. The SEIU was also deeply affected by the civil rights movement, as many custodians and office support staff have been (and are) African American and Latino. In 1985, SEIU members in Denver created Justice for Janitors, a campaign to organize office cleaners and custodians. Since its inception, it has spread to other cities, including Los Angeles and Boston, where heavily non-English-speaking immigrant workforces won wage and benefit concessions in the 1990s.

The SEIU has also enjoyed a reputation for being among the more democratic unions in the modern American Federation of Labor-Congress of Industrial Organizations (AFL-CIO). Its individual locals maintain a high level of autonomy within the **international union**. The SEIU suffered a minor setback in 2000, when its Canadian affiliates representing 30,000 workers disaffiliated. Publicly, Canadian leaders claimed a desire for a more uniquely Canadian perspective, but most observers cite dissatisfaction with lower wage rates in negotiated settlements in the United States. Nonetheless, the SEIU's aggressive organizing successes coupled with its reputation for diversity sensitivity ,have led many observers to see it as a model for future union organizing. The AFL-CIO itself recognized this when, in 1995, it tapped SEIU President **John Sweeney** to head the AFL-CIO. The current president of the SEIU is Andrew Stern.

Suggested Readings: Thomas Beadling et. al., *A Need for Valor: The Roots of Service Employees International Union, 1902–1992,* 1992; John Jentz, "Citizenship, Self-Respect, and Political Power: Chicago's Flat Janitors Trailblaze the Service Employees International Union," *Labor's*

Heritage 9, no. 1 (Summer, 1997), pp. 4–23; Anne Kornhauser, "Reader's Companion to U.S. Women's History—Service Employees International Union," http://college.hmco.com/history/readerscomp/women/html/wm_019611_serviceemplo.htm.

Robert E. Weir

Shanker, Albert (September 14, 1928–February 22, 1997). Albert Shanker was an advocate for teacher unions and president of the **American Federation of Teachers (AFT)** from 1974 until his death in 1997. He was born in New York City to Jewish immigrant parents. His father, Morris, delivered newspapers and his mother, Mamie, was a garment worker. After he graduated from high school in 1946, Shanker attended the University of Illinois and earned a B.A. in philosophy. He earned an M.A. in mathematics and philosophy from Columbia, but never finished the Ph.D. program in which he enrolled. In the early 1950s he became a mathematics teacher in the New York City public schools.

Shanker soon became active in the local teachers' union, the Teachers' Guild. He helped to organize the school in which he taught and, in 1959, became a full-time organizer for the union. In 1960, the guild merged with the High School Teachers' Association to form the United Federation of Teachers (UFT). Even though New York state laws prohibited teachers' **strikes**, on November 7, 1960, over 5,000 UFT members struck to demand **collective bargaining** rights. In 1961 New York teachers chose the UFT as their sole bargaining agent, and it negotiated the first comprehensive collective bargaining agreement in a major city. The 1960 **New York City Teachers' Strike** inspired public schoolteachers across the country to demand collective bargaining rights.

Shanker's New York activities thrust him into the national limelight. In 1962, Shanker was elected UFT secretary and in 1964, he succeeded Charles Cogen as the second UFT president, a position he held until 1986. In the 1960s he was twice jailed for breaking the state law that barred public-employee strikes. The first time was in 1967 during a strike over smaller classes and more funding for public education, and the second came after the 1968 Ocean Hill-Brownsville strike, which centered on an African American community's attempt to replace white schoolteachers.

During the 1970s, Shanker was one of the most widely known labor leaders in the United States. In 1972, he helped to bring about the merger between the New York State AFT affiliate and the state chapter of the rival **National Education Association (NEA)** to form the New York State United Teachers (NYSUT). NYSUT became the largest and most influential statewide union in the country, and Shanker served as its executive vice president from 1973 to 1978. He wrote a regular "Where We Stand" column in *The New York Times*, and made such regular appearances on radio and television that comedian Woody Allen satirized him in the 1973 futuristic film, *Sleeper*. In 1974, Shanker was elected AFT president and became a member of **American Federation of Labor-Congress of Industrial Organization (AFL-CIO)** executive council. During New York City's fiscal crisis in 1975, he was widely credited with helping save New York from bankruptcy by using the UFT's pension money to buy the city's financial bonds.

Shanker used his position with the AFL-CIO executive council as a platform for supporting government Cold War policies. As head of the AFL-CIO's International Affairs Committee, he financially backed pro-American labor unions around the world. In 1993, Shanker became the founding president of Education International, the pro-Western worldwide teacher-union federation. Education International had been formed by the merger of the International Federation of Free Teachers' Unions (IFFTU), to which the AFT belonged, and the World Confederation of Organizations of the Teaching Profession, with which the NEA affiliated.

Shanker also increasingly supported the call of conservative commentators for national educational standards. He espoused greater classroom discipline and teacher testing and blamed parents for student failure. From 1976 to 1996, he was a regular delegate to the Democratic National Convention, and was an education advisor to U.S. presidents from Jimmy Carter through Bill Clinton. Shanker died of cancer in 1997 at the age of 68, leaving behind four children from two marriages.

Suggested Readings: Dickson A. Mungazi, *Where He Stands, Albert Shanker of the American Federation of Teachers*, 1995; Philip Taft, *United They Teach: The Story of the UFT*, 1974; United Federation of Teachers web site: http://www.uft.org.

John F. Lyons

Shape-Up. The term shape-up refers to a method of hiring for short-term work. Usually this system applies to unskilled day laborers. A shape-up occurs at a gathering spot for unskilled workers looking for short-term job assignments. The gathering could take place at a work site—such as on the docks—in a union hall, or a streetscape known by both workers and employers as a place where men and women in search of work tend to gather. Economists refer to this as the "casual labor market."

Workers were typically selected by hiring foremen from a milling crowd seeking jobs at the morning shape-up, or call. This system was particularly infamous on the docks well into the 1950s. The decasualization of longshore labor was a struggle that took decades. Under the shape-up system, the hiring foreman controlled access to work. The system encouraged kickbacks to the foreman, favoritism, and an arbitrary method of selecting workers in which a wide variety of discrimination was possible. The inequities of the shape-up system gave rise to repeated **strikes**, job actions, and corruption. Union officials, employers, and politicians attempted to work within the shape-up system. Union officials tried to use the shape-up to favor the selection of union members. Politicians often sought preferential hiring for particular ethnic groups. Employers saw the system as a way to prevent casual workers from gaining strength in the workplace. The shape-up allowed union officials, employers, and politicians alike to exploit workers and keep them in line. One of the more famous films about labor, *On the Waterfront*, is based on shape-up abuses among dock workers. (See **Films and Labor**.)

While the evils of the system were widely recognized, the solution to the arbitrariness of the shape-up was different in various labor markets. San Francisco and New York, for example, found different solutions to the problem of longshore workers. On the West coast, a 1939 arbitrator's decision, written by Wayne Morse, opened the door for a new era of industrial relations when it replaced the shape-up system with the union hiring hall. Under the hiring hall system, workers still shaped-up, but work opportunities were assigned on a fair rotational basis among all union members who sought work. The **rank-and-file** elected dispatchers who assigned work, via a set of posted rules, and employers were forbidden from bypassing the hiring hall. The International Longshore and Warehouse Union (ILWU) used union hiring halls on the West coast docks, while in New York, arbitrary work assignments on the docks persisted into the 1950s.

The shape-up continues to be practiced in agricultural labor and in day labor, where labor contractors use the system as a means to avoid regulations governing workplace health and safety. It also thrives among immigrant laborers, illegal aliens, and homeless individuals anxious to secure employment under any condition. In 2003, the General Accounting Office estimated the **contingent workers** comprised thirty percent of the workforce. On July 24, 2003, Rep. Luis Gutierrez (D-IL) introduced legislation (H.R. 2870) aimed at protecting day laborers from the abuses of the contemporary shape-up system.

Suggested Readings: Charles P. Larrowe, *Shape-up and Hiring Hall: a Comparison of Hiring Methods and Labor Relations on the New York and Seattle Waterfronts*, 1955; Wayne Morse Center for Law and Politics, University of Oregon, http://libweb.uoregon.edu/speccoll/exhibits/morse/; Howard Kimledorf, *Reds or Rackets?*, 1988.

James P. Hanlan

Albert V. Lannon

Sherman Antitrust Act. The Sherman Antitrust Act was passed by Congress in 1890, ostensibly to curtail monopolistic business methods. In practice, the Sherman Act was applied more vigorously against labor unions than monopolists. The bill was drafted by Senator John Sherman of Ohio in response to the rise of trusts and monopolies in the two and one-half decades after the Civil War. The Sherman Act outlawed combinations deemed a restraint of trade or commerce, including cartels, price-fixing schemes, and other impediments to competition. Moreover, the act allowed the federal government, as well as private parties, to initiate restraint-of-trade lawsuits. The act was enforced by the Department of Justice, and violators could be fined and/or imprisoned. If the courts so desired, triple damages could be levied against violators.

From its inception, organizations like the **National Association of Manufacturers** opposed applying the Sherman Act to regulate business practices, but sought to use it against labor unions. The Sherman Act was invoked during the 1894 **Pullman lockout** and the courts obliged by issuing injunctions against the **American Railway Union (ARU)**. ARU President **Eugene Debs** spent six months in prison for violating court injunctions. In 1895, the Supreme Court ruled in *United States v. E. C. Knight* that manufacturing was not covered by the commerce clause of the Constitution. This effectively eviscerated much of the act's original intent and opened the door for broader use of the act against labor. President Theodore Roosevelt used the Sherman Act against the Standard Oil Corporation and several other trusts, but government pursuit of business monopolies remained rare.

The **American Federation of Labor (AFL)** made reform of the Sherman Act a high priority for its legislative lobbyists. This stand later caused tension within the **National Civic Federation**, a labor/management board upon which AFL President **Samuel Gompers** sat, but the importance of reform was obvious to most working people. By 1901, eighteen suits had been brought, but half of them were against labor. The following year saw the D. E. Loewe Company of Danbury, Connecticut, bring suit against the striking **United Hatters, Cap, and Millinery Workers International Union**. The courts awarded Loewe $240,000 in damages and declared most secondary **boycotts** illegal. Liens were placed on both union bank accounts and the homes of individual hatters. The AFL was stunned when the Supreme Court upheld the awards. In 1903, the Kellog Switchboard and Supply Company and the American Anti-Boycott Association brought a successful suit against the **International Brotherhood of Teamsters**, who urged a boycott to support Kellog strikers.

The AFL included the use of the Sherman Antitrust Act against labor among the list of wrongs it presented to Congress in its 1906 Bill of Grievances. In that same year, however, an AFL boycott of the **Buck's Stove and Range Company** of St. Louis led to injunctions against the AFL. Gompers was sentenced to a year in jail for contempt, though the conviction was later overturned and Gompers never served the sentence. The Sherman Act remained a thorn in labor's side until most labor activity was placed beyond "restraint of trade" interpretations by the 1914 **Clayton Antitrust Act**.

Suggested Readings: Ronald Filippelli, *Labor in the USA: A History*, 1984; Philip Foner, *History of the Labor Movement in the United States*, Vol. 3, 1964; Walter Licht, *Industrializing America: The Nineteenth Century*, 1995.

Robert E. Weir

Shoemakers Strike of 1860. The Shoemakers Strike of 1860 took place in New England and was the largest strike to take place before the Civil War. As many as 20,000 workers left their jobs in Massachusetts, New Hampshire, and Maine. The strike is notable also for the role women played and for the manner in which sexism undercut the strike's potential.

Although shoemaking was a highly skilled craft during the Colonial era, it was not a lucrative one and even **master craftsmen** were often quite poor. It remained a poorly paid profession into the nineteenth century, even as it was transformed by centralization and mechanization. The introduction of machines, especially sewing machines, deskilled shoemaking. Paralleling changes in textile production, by the 1830s, shoes were being produced in urban centers like Lynn, Massachusetts. Like textile workers, increasing numbers of shoemakers were women, especially those involved in pattern-making, stitching, and binding. Although firms centralized, a substantial amount of shoemaking still took place in private homes. As in cigar making and the needle trades, married women took on a lot of shoemaking **homework**. Technological advances gradually reduced the number of homeworkers and, by extension, the number of women working in the shoe trade; but by 1860, women still made up about 40 percent of Lynn's shoeworkers.

Union organization was weak in the shoe industry. In 1831, Lynn women formed the short-lived Society of Shoebinders, which demanded that women be treated as equals as well as receive higher wages. Two years later they created the Female Society of Lynn and Vicinity for the Promotion of Industry. Men formed the Society of Cordwainers, best known for its labor paper, the *Awl*. The Society also admitted women in a special auxiliary. However, neither men nor women had an organization strong enough to challenge manufacturers.

Industry downturns led to discontent in the 1850s. The roots of the 1860 strike lay in a **journeymen**'s dispute in 1859 related to wage cuts the previous year. What came to be called the Great Strike began on February 22, 1860, Washington's Birthday. It began in Lynn and quickly spread to other shoe towns like Danvers, Haverhill, Natick, Newburyport, and Marblehead in Massachusetts; and Dover, Farmington, and Rochester in New Hampshire. The early morning of February 23 saw the strike's only violence, when some Lynn strikers attempted to prevent a shipment of bottoms and uppers from leaving town. Boston police and militia were called in and strike leaders denounced both their presence and all acts of violence. Initially, women were called upon to support the strike in the hope that their involvement would lend moral force to the strikers' demands.

The role of women proved more complicated than mere appeals to morality, however. Male workers touted the ideal of a **family wage** to demand higher compensation. Basic to the family wage is the principle that a man's wage ought to be sufficient to support his dependents. The concept of the family wage resonated with married female homeworkers, but Lynn also contained hundreds of young, single women employed as factory stitchers who had their own issues. Led by Clara Brown, more than 300 Lynn factory women voted their own strike and issued separate wage demands. Several meetings were held that affirmed Brown's actions and, by the end of February, as many as 2,000 women supported the strike. Ruptures soon occurred in their ranks, however.

The men's efforts were being coordinated by Willard Oliver and Alonzo Draper, head of the Lynn Mechanics' Association and editor of the *New England Mechanic*. They planned a massive parade for March 7. On March 2, Clara Brown learned that the demands of women strikers had been softened without her knowledge. She protested this action and was told by Oliver and Mary Damon that existing demands were unreasonable. Damon represented female homemakers who supported a family wage; both she and Oliver argued that high wages on the part of women factory workers threatened to destroy homework jobs and undermine the male-wage structure.

Heated meetings and discussions took place, bifurcating women's ranks. In the end, about 800 women joined the March 7 protest parade in Lynn. Many carried banners bearing defiant slogans like "American Ladies Will Not Be Slaves." Some estimates put the total number of marchers at around 4,000, making it one of the largest antebellum protests in American history. The march marked the highwater mark of the strike, and solidarity and resolve weakened in the ensuing weeks. Brown's refusal to endorse the actions of Draper, Oliver, and Damon isolated her and her followers, as did Brown's outspoken remarks about the folly of the others' decision. Manufacturers also sought to undermine unity by offering wage increases that affected only homeworkers. Those offers bred resentment, but the strike began to fizzle after most male workers obtained wage increases. On March 31, Oliver advised all women remaining on strike to return to work under existing low-wage scales and without signed agreements.

Some have interpreted the shoemakers strike of 1860 as a partial victory, though the historical record suggests that is an overly optimistic reading of the events. The strike was dramatic because of its size but strikers accomplished very few of their goals and manufacturers refused to recognize any unions. One could easily conclude that male strikers undermined chances for success by remaining committed to the concept of the family wage and by refusing to meet Brown and her charges as equals.

Suggested Readings: Mary Blewett, *Men, Women, and Work: Class, Gender, and Protest in the New England Shoe Industry, 1780–1910*, 1988; Alan Dawley, *Class and Community: The Industrial Revolution in Lynn*, 1976; Walter Licht, *Industrializing America: The Nineteenth Century*, 1995.

Robert E. Weir

Shop Steward. The shop steward is the frontline union representative who carries out the business of the union in the workplace. Shop stewards handle grievances, collect dues, and recruit new members. Generally the shop steward is elected by union members in the workplace or appointed by higher elected union officials. Most shop stewards continue to work a regular job and handle union duties on a part-time or release-time basis. Often the term is now interchangeable with union steward.

The evolution of the shop steward over the history of the labor movement symbolizes the dynamic nature of employee representation. Initially, the position of steward embodied strength; typically it was a male able to intimidate employer and co-worker alike. Before labor laws assured unions a legal right to exist, the steward had to fight the employer as well as wrangle dues from colleagues. Now that laws like the **National Labor Relations Act** legitimate the existence of unions, agents are able to enforce mutually-agreed-to work policies. This has transformed the shop steward from a physical enforcer to a legal enforcer, as well as a generalist who combines many roles in servicing the representational needs of fellow workers. The major obligations of this duty are to serve the interests of all union members without discrimination, and to exercise discretion with good faith and honesty.

Suggested Readings: Bruce S. Feldacker, *Labor Guide to Labor Law*, 2000; Terry L. Leap, *Collective Bargaining and Labor Relations*, 1991.

Pete Gingras

Sick-Out. A sick-out is a concerted job action, sometimes sanctioned, in which a large number of workers do not report to work on a predetermined day. Uniformed workers like police and fire fighters sometimes refer to this as the blue-flu. The purpose of this type of job action is to force concessions from an employer without resorting to a formal strike or other job action that would negatively impact workers' wages or threaten their jobs.

Sick-outs have been a form of labor protest since Colonial times and have been an occasionally effective tactic since. Unions like the **United Mine Workers** have used it to demonstrate workers' collective might and hasten stalled contract negotiations. Sick-outs have also been used as a form of protest when a **no-strike pledge** or **contract** language precludes the possibility of a formal work stoppage. Diverging from strikes has taken on renewed urgency since the 1980s, given the relative ease with which employers now utilize temporary and **replacement workers** to replace strikers. Although some sick-outs violate existing labor laws, they often prove safer than formal actions, and they frequently generate publicity for worker grievances.

Suggested Readings: Bruce S. Feldacker, *Labor Guide to Labor Law*, 2000; William Gould, *Agenda for Reform: The Future of Employment Relationships and the Law*, 1993; David B. Lipsky and Clifford B. Donn, *Collective Bargaining in American Industry*, 1987.

Pete Gingras

Sit-Down Strikes. Sit-down strikes occur when workers refuse to leave their place of employment or continue production until a grievance or contract is settled. This form of job action has its roots within the **Industrial Workers of the World (IWW)** at the beginning of the twentieth century, although IWW tactics did not catch on until a generation later during the Great Depression of the 1930s. The **Congress of Industrial Organization (CIO)** split from the **American Federation of Labor** in this period to organize mass production workers. The CIO employed a number of IWW methods, especially the sit-down strike. While the **General Motors Sit-Down Strike** in Flint, Michigan in 1936–37 was not the initial use of a sit-down strike by the CIO, it garnered national publicity for the fledgling organization as it took on the world's largest corporation. The sit-down in Flint featured a disciplined group of auto workers who stayed warm and dry in the confines of their factory, while supporters surrounded the perimeters. Because of insurance regulations, General Motors was unwilling to shut off utilities and was unable to introduce **scabs**. Instead the National Guard was mobilized. However, public and political support for the strikers eventually carried the day and General Motors finally agreed to recognize the union in February 1937.

Subsequently, workers around the globe engaged in a series of sit-down strikes that brought the labor movement great success and influence. Culturally, the seizing of private property by a group of workers claiming "sweat equity" in a facility clashed head-on with an endearing tenet of free enterprise mentality. Although the United States Supreme Court outlawed the practice in 1939, the use of the tactic continues sporadically.

A striking autoworker reclines on an automobile bench-seat during the 1930s sit-down strikes against General Motors. © George Meany Memorial Archives/Library of Congress.

Suggested Readings: Richard O. Boyer and Herbert M. Morais, *Labor's Untold Story*, 1955; Jeremy Brecher, *Strike!*, 1972; Sidney Lens, *The Labor Wars*, 1973.

Scott Molloy

Skidmore, Thomas (August 13, 1790–August 7, 1832). Thomas Skidmore was an important early labor radical and a member of New York's Workingmen's party. He was born in Newton, Connecticut, the eldest of ten children, to John and Mary Skidmore. He was a precocious and brilliant child who, at the age of thirteen, became a teacher in the Newton school district. He taught there for five years before moving on to teach in Connecticut, New Jersey, Virginia, and North Carolina. He left teaching in 1815 to pursue an interest in the chemical properties of gun powder. He moved to New York in 1819 and married Abigail Ball two years later.

Skidmore held exceedingly progressive views for his day. He advocated free, universal education; the ten-hour workday; racial equality; property redistribution; and equal rights for women. He worked for the presidential campaign of John Quincy Adams in 1828, and was a cofounder of the New York Workingmen's party in 1829. He was largely responsible for writing the party platform. His 1829 book, *The Rights of Man to Property*, stands as a radical testament to his views on land reform. In it, Skidmore advocated the abolition of inheritance rights, a nationalization of property, and land redistribution by lottery. Skidmore's views gained immediate currency and he narrowly lost an 1829 bid for the New York legislature. He published a short-lived labor paper, *The Friend of Equal Rights*.

Skidmore was a temperamental man who quarreled with other leaders. As the Workingmen began to splinter and falter, he tried to salvage a radical wing that he called the Original Workingmen, or the Poor Men's Party. In 1832, he was ousted from the very party he founded, and he died that summer of cholera. His work stands as a radical example of the emphasis that nineteenth-century labor activists placed on land reform.

Suggested Readings: Edward Pessen, *Uncommon Jacksonians*, 1967; Ronald Walters, *American Reformers 1815–1860*, 1978; Alden Whitman, ed., *American Reformers*, 1985.

Michele Bernier
Robert E. Weir

Smith-Connally Act. *See War Labor Disputes Act.*

Social Darwinism. Social Darwinism was a philosophy embraced by the business community and many members of the middle and upper class in the middle- and late-nineteenth century. It sought to apply Charles Darwin's evolutionary models to society, particularly his assertion that within nature a struggle for existence rages, and that survival of the fittest dictates which species gets access to limited resources. Proponents of Social Darwinism perverted Darwin's biological findings to argue that wealth and poverty were natural products of social struggle, therefore, those who made great fortunes were more "fit" than those who lived in poverty. Quite conveniently, Social Darwinists ignored factors like inherited wealth, corrupt financial and political practices, and exploitation. In their eyes, entrepreneurs of the emerging business class, investors, and the rich were a more completely evolved species than the toiling masses. Eugenicists, nativists, and racists also cast these principles in ethnic and racial terms.

Social Darwinism was, in some respects, a logical outgrowth of the underlying principles of **capitalism**. In Adam Smith's classic treatise, *The Wealth of Nations*, he argued that economic activity ought to be free of external regulations and controls and subject only to the natural laws of supply and demand. Those views found few adherents among Colonial-American artisans, and were roundly challenged by workers after the American Revolution. Many advocates of the **Workingmen's Movement** in the 1830s offered devastating critiques of an unregulated economy and lambasted any attempts to institute special privileges or class legislation.

Capitalism expanded during the antebellum period, but did not reach its take-off phase until after the Civil War. The rise of mass industry, the birth of modern corporate structures, and the advent of new managerial techniques gave rise to manufacturers, investors, and business owners who had fewer ties to local communities and/or the customary social arrangements of the past. With sheer profit as the driving motive for many such individuals—who were dubbed "robber barons" by their critics—business competition was often cutthroat and the exploitation of workers brutal. Yet these same ruthless forces helped the national economy expand exponentially, pushing the United States to first-tier status among the world's economic and military powers. Enormous fortunes were made in the last third of the nineteenth century, and they were used to buy political influence. Economic expansion also led to more complete articulation of the middle class, which was small by contemporary standards, but more stratified. Its upper echelon consisted largely of the nouveau riche who were wealthy, but who lacked the social pedigrees of long-standing elites. New industrialists, managers, and professionals tended to identify with the social and cultural practices of the elites but, like the working classes, had to work for their compensation. Social Darwinism thus served to both justify amoral business practices and confer social status on the upwardly mobile.

The primary theorists of Social Darwinism were English philosophers Herbert Spencer and Walter Bagehot, and American sociologist/economist William Graham Sumner. Industrialists like John Rockefeller and Andrew Carnegie also added to Social Darwinian thought through their many speeches and essays. By the 1870s, Social Darwinism was the hegemonic social philosophy within the United States. Ministers, mainstream newspapers, orators, and writers praised its virtues and lampooned its critics. In practice, Social Darwinism was a marriage between laissez-faire economics and conservative politics, and the courts routinely turned aside legal challenges. Social Darwinists justified their great wealth and power by arguing that their alleged virtues—like sobriety, thrift, investment acumen, and hard work—were hallmarks of being more highly evolved than those who failed to attain their levels of success. Such thinking was in accord with late-Victorian beliefs. The concept of social problems had not yet been articulated; rather, misfortune was associated with sin and personal moral failings.

Not surprisingly, the American working class begged to differ. Trade unions and the **Knights of Labor** mounted powerful rhetorical challenges, with the labor press churning out stories of exploitation, graft, and illegalities on the part of allegedly moral and upright Social Darwinists. Among workers, the writings of **Henry George**, Victor Drury, David Ricardo, Karl Marx, and other social critics were widely discussed, as were various forms of **anarchism**, **communism**, **socialism**, **Bellamyite nationalism**, cooperation, and other ideas that challenged capitalism and Social Darwinism.

More than rhetoric, however, it was workers' direct challenges to Social Darwinism that loosened its grip. So many workers boycotted Social Darwinian churches that conferences were held to discuss ways to win them back to the pews. The Vatican summoned American cardinals and priests to Rome because many Catholics were giving up the church for their unions. In 1891, Pope Leo XIII issued the encyclical **Rerum Novarum**, which removed the Vatican's objections to organized labor and contained strong condemnations of unbridled capitalism (as well as most forms of socialism). By the 1890s, many Protestant churches were abandoning Social Darwinism in favor of the Social Gospel movement, with its messages of alleviating poverty and its warnings against materialism.

Even more powerful were the challenges offered at the workplace and the voting booths. **Strikes** were frequent and violent after the Civil War, including the 1877 railroad strikes of the **Great Labor Uprising** and the voluminous work stoppages during the **Great Upheaval** of 1885 through 1890. Labor- and agrarian-based third parties dislodged numerous Republicans and Democrats on the local and state level, and threatened to do so nationally. The social Darwinian cause was hurt further by the numerous panics and recessions that threw the nation into economic turmoil. In all, the late-nineteenth century was so chaotic that even members of the middle class—especially those of moderate wealth or less—concluded that reform was necessary. The Gilded Age gave way after 1901 to the Progressive Era, the first significant reform movement that also involved local, state, and federal governments. Many of that period's leading reformers were members of the middle class, while unions and labor advocates continued to press for economic and social changes.

The American labor movement deserves credit for exposing the inequities, fallacies, and ruthlessness of Social Darwinism. The development of modern sociology also helped reveal the naiveté of attributing social problems to individual weakness. By the early-twentieth century, Social Darwinism had lost its moral force and was widely viewed as indefensible. The business community contained numerous individuals who were as heartless as their Gilded Age predecessors, but Social Darwinism was no longer the dominant social or cultural philosophy within the United States. Those who openly practiced its precepts were roundly criticized by many of the same forces that once defended its practices: the church, the media, and liberal politicians. Most people in the business community gave at least rhetorical support to philanthropy and moderate reform; some even experimented with **welfare capitalism**. It would be a mistake, however, to assume that Social Darwinism passed from the American scene. Its major assumptions continue to be held by many conservatives and some modern business practices are as cruel as those of an earlier age. Though social Darwinism is no longer the prevailing philosophy, it retains vigor.

Suggested Readings: Richard Hofstadter, *Social Darwinism in American Thought*, 1955; Robert McCloskey, *American Conservatism in the Age of Enterprise 1865–1910*, 1951; Norman Pollack, *The Populist Response to Industrial America*, 1962.

Robert E. Weir

Socialism. Socialism refers to an ideology whereby the means of production are in collective hands and are used for the benefit of the larger society rather than for a restricted group of individuals. For the most part, socialists envision a greater role for the state than communists or anarchists support. Socialists distrust many forms of private property and seek to make all wealth serve the broader community rather than single individuals. It rejects capitalist logic that links wages, prices, and the supply of goods and services to market forces.

It is a broad term encompassing many forms of collectivism, ranging from faith-based idealism to state-planned economies.

Socialist groups have suffered repression, though usually not as much as companion leftist ideologies. Because its ideals run counter to the logic of American **capitalism**, its overall impact on U.S. society has been less than that of most other industrial societies. At various moments, however, socialism has resonated with sizable segments of the population. Numerous religious groups, like the Shakers and various German Pietist groups, practiced rudimentary forms of socialist collectivism. Many labor activists and organizations have supported at least limited forms of socialism.

Like Marxism and **anarchism**, to which many forms of socialism are related, socialism was largely conceived in Europe and imported to the United States through literature and the influx of class-conscious immigrant laborers and social activists. The wide popularity of the *Manifesto of the Communist Party* (1848) by Karl Marx and Frederic Engels stimulated discussions about socialism in the United States. Many nineteenth-century European immigrants contributed to the discourse. In the antebellum period, German immigrants like laborer Herman Kriege and political activist Wilhelm Weitling sought to organize their comrades under socialist ideas. In New York City, Joseph Wedemeyer organized the Proletarian League that lasted until 1854. After the Civil War, doctrinal reinvigoration brought by Karl Marx and Ferdinand Lasalle inspired American socialists to organize socialist associations. The 1876 Union Congress tried to unite the disparate groups. That attempt largely failed; diversity is a hallmark of American socialism. The Socialist Labor Party, founded in 1877, and the Socialist Party (SP)—formed in 1901 when the Social Democratic Party absorbed several smaller groups—have been the foremost organized political expressions of American socialism.

Throughout the late-nineteenth and early-twentieth centuries, socialists wrestled with internal and external challenges. Internally, the socialist movement was both invigorated by the participation of new immigrants and hampered by the cultural contradictions brought by ethnic diversity. American-born socialists like **Eugene V. Debs** did not always agree with immigrant radicals like **Daniel DeLeon**. In addition, ideological disputes arose. **Lassallean** socialists placed more hope in the ballot box than did many Marxists, but socialists frequently clashed over whether or not socialism could be achieved peacefully. Despite disagreements, ongoing economic decline in the 1890s and the repression of labor activism helped socialism gain supporters. Debs became the leading SP politician of the day. In 1912, he gathered nearly a million votes for president, and there were over 300 socialist newspapers in circulation. The 1917 Russian Revolution also reinvigorated socialism, as well as the debate over how to achieve it. Socialists won a variety of state and local offices between 1910 and 1918, and the independent socialist Victor Berger was elected to Congress in 1910. The SP reached its highwater mark in 1918, when it had over 100,000 dues-paying members and many more supporters.

Externally, socialism faced three challenges: electoral politics, bourgeois reformers, and political repression. Groups that embraced electoral politics saw Republicans and Democrats co-opt many of their more moderate ideas. Moreover, ballot-box politics did not appeal to potential allies like the **Industrial Workers of the World**, which advocated anarcho-socialism. Reformers outside the major parties also borrowed from socialism: **Henry George**, Edward Bellamy, Jacob **Coxey**, and others borrowed socialist language and concepts, though their exact ideology was more hazy. Periodic repression has been an even bigger obstacle. Federal, state, and local governments frequently used repressive devices to muzzle socialist leaders. Many, like Debs, were persecuted for opposition to World War I. Postwar repression of better-established socialist groups and disappointment over Robert La Follette's failed 1924 presidential bid partly explain why communists held a higher profile during the Great Depression than did the SP. The SP did revive under the leadership of Norman Thomas, who garnered 800,000 votes for president in 1932. Upton Sinclair polled well in his bid to become governor of California in 1934, but the SP proved unable to avoid renewed doctrinal debates or compete with Franklin Roosevelt's popularity among working-class voters. Roosevelt's New Deal incorporated moderate socialist ideals in programs like Social Security and unemployment compensation.

Few radical groups weathered post-World War II political repression well, and most socialist groups declined precipitously even though most socialists became ardent anticommunists during the Cold War. In the 1950s, labor unions increasingly embraced **business unionism** and distanced themselves from leftist ideology of all sorts. A few advocates like Michael Harrington and the League for Industrial Democracy served left-labor interests well into the 1960s, and socialism as a whole enjoyed a brief revival during the 1960s. Nonetheless, socialism as a movement is small and its impact on American society remains marginal. A few unions continue to espouse socialist collectivist principles, but their current profile is low.

Nonetheless, socialism continues to provide an ideological critique of capitalism, potential connections to the international workers' movement, and language for conceptualizing leftist political activism in the United States. It also provides intellectual critiquing tools popular in American universities. Most recently, socialist criticism of **deregulation** and **globalization** has energized protest groups. Ideals of personal politics, open processes, democratic participation, social capital, community enterprise, human rights, and other progressive sentiments spring from age-old socialist doctrines.

Suggested Readings: Paul Buhle, *The Immigrant Left in the United States*, 1996; John Diggins, *The American Left in the Twentieth Century*, 1973; James Weinstein, *Ambiguous Legacy: The Left in American Politics*, 1975.

Timothy Draper

Social Reform Unionism. Social reform unionism refers to an activist philosophy that sees the labor movement as a force for larger change in society. Social unionism runs the gamut from socially sanctioned reform efforts to revolutionary ideology. Government authorities and business leaders have historically viewed organized workers with suspicion and treated them with antagonism—except during wartime when labor peace is deemed necessary to maintain uninterrupted production. Labor's programs over the decades thus reflected not only the **pure and simple unionism** principles of wages, hours, and working conditions, but also a need to tackle larger social problems to ensure the acceptance of unions. The liberal and, at times, radical outlook on society required a freer social structure and involved working-class movements in broad-based reform efforts. This often made labor a target for corporate and political opponents whose wealth and influence gave them greater access to those channels influencing public opinion.

The first real flowering of unions in the 1830s combined demands for shorter hours and higher wages with a political program that attacked child labor, municipal corruption, and property requirements for voting that disqualified working men in some states. Child labor usually went hand in hand with illiteracy, thereby subjugating factory hands to a de facto manufacturing caste system, and the ineligibility to vote often translated into a prohibition against workers serving on juries. These shackles severely undermined unions' ability to fight for smaller pure-and-simple objectives. This led early worker movements like the **Workingmen's Movement** and the **National Labor Union** to call for wholesale revamping of political and economic conditions.

During the Gilded Age, the **Knights of Labor (KOL)**, with its broad constituency, advocated changes as sweeping as mandatory **arbitration** of strikes, the abolition of the wage system, racial and gender equality, temperance, and land reform. A determined employer counteroffensive eliminated the Knights, but paved the way for the more exclusive **American Federation of Labor (AFL)** and its conservative craft mentality, which tried to match a skilled worker monopoly against corporate trusts. The AFL largely rejected the KOL's social unionism in favor of a pure-and-simple agenda. In the early 1900s, however, an insurrectionary version of social unionism found expression in the **Industrial Workers of the World**, which called for the overthrow of the free-enterprise system.

The AFL outlasted its union and corporate foes by maintaining a hard-nosed fixation on everyday working conditions and by using tactics that did not threaten the larger political framework. This evolutionary approach brought the AFL through the depression of 1893 and helped it gain acceptance as an alternative to the IWW during World War I. Even the AFL declined in the 1920s when businesses returned to prewar hostility and eviscerated all of organized labor by the time of the stock market crash and the onset of the Great Depression.

Ironically, the economic disaster of the 1930s rekindled social reform unionism, especially in the unskilled and semi-skilled ranks of the new **Congress of Industrial Organizations (CIO)**. The upsurge in labor militancy dovetailed with the radical policies of President Franklin Roosevelt's New Deal. The CIO embraced Roosevelt programs that liberalized the nation's archaic and restrictive labor laws, precipitating a large scale organizing drive, especially in mass-production industries. Labor's new **rank and file**—swelled by previously ignored immigrants, women, and people of color—became an army for social change. Leftists were instrumental in fashioning this alliance, though their socialist and communist ties later haunted the labor movement.

After World War II, the United States abandoned its alliance with the Soviet Union and the Cold War ensued. Opponents of the labor movement, as well as conservative forces within the AFL, found it easy to discredit progressive labor forces through red-baiting. By extension, other forms of social activism—like African American civil rights—were deemed suspicious, if not disloyal. The red scare in the 1950s provided the rationale to expel radicals from the labor movement. By the time the AFL and CIO merged in 1955, most unions had banned radicals from membership. The purge included small numbers of actual communists, but the climate of fear also sacrificed larger numbers of progressives espousing less extreme versions of social reform unionism. This sanitized version of the labor movement temporarily enjoyed the fruits of economic expansion and the emergence of a consumer society.

By the 1970s, however, the energy crisis, **runaway shops**, and the pressures of **globalism** caught the AFL-CIO unprepared for the new world order. Labor's first line of defense, its left-wing militants had been muzzled or expelled. The conservative forces of **business unionism**, confronted by economic change and a hostile political environment, discovered that their roles as junior partners in a corporate-dominated society served only to make them an easy target for those managers seeking to discredit the labor movement. This downward spiral for the labor movement also included massive job losses in former union strongholds like steel making, automobile production, and machine shops. Sophisticated personnel relations also undercut the union appeal, as management practiced enlightened workplace policies during flush economic times. Many unions began to lament lost militancy and question their blithe acceptance of prevailing economic and political arrangements. In 1995, **John Sweeney** was elected president of the AFL-CIO, largely on the strength of promises to reinvigorate the federation with social reform unionism principles. To date, the AFL-CIO's versions of social unionism and activism seem tepid when compared with that of the KOL, IWW, or early CIO, but they mark a promising revision of business unionism. How well it will play out in the new global economy remains to be seen.

Suggested Readings: Simeon Larson and Bruce Nissen, eds., *Theories of the Labor Movement*, 1987; Kim Moody, *An Injury to All*, 1989; Philip Taft, *The Structure and Government of Labor Unions*, 1962.

Scott Molloy

Solidarity. Solidarity is a term that encapsulates the central organizing principle of most labor unions. It denotes the collective ideal that only in unity can working people attain their objectives and goals. It implies mutualism and community and entails both rights and responsibilities for individuals. Solidarity unionism, ideally practiced, educates and supports individuals and their families, but individuals are expected to forgo private goals if doing so would better serve the union. Solidarity can express itself in classic Marxist perspectives on social class, or in less precise notions of interdependence, fellowship, or comradeship. The goal of most unions is to foster solidarity among the **rank and file** though, in practice, solidarity is usually strongest in moments of struggle and challenge, like **strikes, contract** negotiations, or external oppression.

The term derives from the French *solidarité* and was used by those intellectuals and workers who formed the short-lived Paris Commune in 1871. It probably came to the United States via immigrant anarchists and communists shortly after 1871. The term was used in the late-nineteenth century, but greater popularity came after 1915, when **Industrial Workers of the World** songwriter Ralph Chaplin penned "Solidarity Forever." That song became the unofficial anthem of the American labor movement for workers of all ideological dispositions. (See **Music and Labor**.)

Since 1915, solidarity has passed into general usage and has become a shorthand phrase for organizers and unionists expressing the need for unity. Appeals to solidarity are used to mute internal union bickering, justify coalitions with other groups, and substantiate calls for greater rank-and-file involvement in their unions. It has also come to imply a near-mythic ideal of unity, harmony, and strength. In 1980, unionized Polish workers opposed to the ruling Soviet-style government dubbed themselves *Solidarność*. Their struggles revitalized use of the term solidarity within the United States. In 1981, the American Federation of Labor-Congress of Industrial Organizations called a Solidarity Day to oppose the economic policies of President Ronald Reagan. An estimated half million people rallied in Washington, D.C., perhaps the largest labor protest in American history. That same year, Pope John Paul II defended the concept of solidarity in the papal encyclical *Laborem Exercens*.

Despite the imprecision of the term and the abstractions for which it sometimes stands, solidarity remains the highest ideal of the labor union movement.

Suggested Readings: Jeremy Brecher, *Strike!*, 1972; Bang Jee Chun, *The Impact of Solidarity or Conflict on Participation in a Labor Union*, 1997; Simeon Larson and Bruce Nissen, eds., *Theories of the Labor Movement*, 1987.

Robert E. Weir

Speedups. Speedups are any form of increased work and productivity requirement without a parallel increase in pay or benefits. In a manufacturing facility, a company might accelerate the movement of the assembly line or require workers to produce a greater number of goods. In a service-sector scenario, delivery routes might be increased or office personnel assigned a larger number of tasks. The speedup was once a standard feature in industries like textiles and automobiles, with companies often employing it to build up excess inventory prior to contract negotiations as a hedge against possible **strikes**. Such unilateral work changes occur most frequently in non-union settings, however, because many **collective bargaining** agreements have provisions blocking such management practices without prior negotiations.

Today, many multinational corporations with labor-intensive operations avoid speedup prohibitions by relocating North-American and European production plants to developing nations where unions are weak. The new era of labor-management relations, beginning with the energy crisis and the dawn of **globalism** in the 1970s, introduced a host of new work practices which circumvented earlier restraints against speedups. For example, computers measuring in nanoseconds can also be used to monitor and time employee tasks. Although such acceleration predominates in union-free environments, the competitive pace has affected labor contracts as well. Telephone operators, postal workers, and keypunch operators are among those groups of workers who have complained of modern-day speedups.

Suggested Readings: Carroll R. Daugherty and John B. Parrish, *The Labor Problems of American Society*, 1952; Mike Parker and Jane Slaughter, *Working Smart: A Union Guide to Participation Programs and Reengineering*, 1994.

Scott Molloy

Staley Lockout. The Staley Lockout took place between June 1993 and November 1995. It was one of three labor disturbances in Decatur, Illinois during the early- to mid-1990s, making the city of about 85,000, in the words of workers, a "war zone." In addition to the A.E. Staley Manufacturing Company, a corn processor, local facilities of **Caterpillar** Tractor and **Bridgestone-Firestone** were involved in clashes that pitted multinational corporations against workers' rights. The fundamental importance of the lockout to U.S. workers and unions was captured in occasional references to Decatur as the **Homestead** of the 1990s, a comparison to the infamous 1892 labor-management confrontation in Homestead, Pennsylvania. Like Homestead, the Decatur actions ended badly for affected workers and their unions. Some pessimists cite these three incidents as proof of organized labor's inexorable decline toward irrelevance.

The battle began in the fall of 1991, when members of the **United Auto Workers** (UAW) struck two Caterpillar factories in Decatur and Peoria, and the company responded by locking out union workers at two other Illinois plants. Caterpillar management sought a six-year **contract** that would break UAW **pattern bargaining** in the tractor industry and create a two-tier wage system that would establish a lower wage scale for new hires. The issues remained unresolved when, in the spring of 1992, Caterpillar threatened to hire **replacement workers**. In response, the UAW ended the **strike**, but without a new contract. Nearly two years of tense relations on the shop floor followed, marked by frequent disputes between union members and managers, and firings of union activists.

Also in 1992, officials of Tate & Lyle, PLC, a London-based multinational corporation that purchased the nearly century-old Staley company in 1988, sought to lower labor costs and increase management flexibility by insisting on a new contract featuring twelve-hour, rotating shifts. Workers affiliated with the Allied Industrial Workers Union (AIW) refused to discuss the contract proposal. Although the plant employed as many as 2,300 workers in the late 1960s, the 1992 workforce was about 740 and the company indicated its intent to make further reductions. A brief walkout by AIW workers in early June 1993 was followed a few weeks later by the company's **lockout**. Staley workers retained labor consultant Ray Rogers and launched a **corporate campaign** against Tate & Lyle, hoping to marshal public and financial pressure to end the lockout and soften the company's contract demands.

Confrontation also brewed at the Bridgestone/Firestone plant, located midway between Staley and Caterpillar on Decatur's east side. Bridgestone, a Japanese firm, purchased Firestone in 1988. Six years later, claiming it was responding to increasing competition in the industry, Bridgestone/Firestone sought a new contract with the **United Rubber Workers (URW)** that also included twelve-hour, rotating shifts; productivity-linked wage hikes; cuts in vacation time, and a two-tiered wage system. In July 1994, the URW struck and the company responded by hiring **scabs** at 30 percent lower wages. Efforts by the Clinton administration to withdraw government contracts from the tire maker in response to its hiring of replacement workers failed. Massive demonstrations, civil disobedience—including the arrest in June 1994 of a priest and several nuns and police use of pepper gas against peaceful demonstrators at Staley—Rogers's corporate campaign, and the efforts of Staley "road warriors," who traveled about the United States rallying support from other unions, focused national attention on Decatur. It did little, however, to cushion the crippling losses that ensued.

Following a late 1995 change in the local's leadership, Staley workers—reorganized as members of the **United Paperworkers International Union**—accepted the company's contract. Of the 740 workers employed at the time of the lockout, just 146 returned to work. As the decade ended, the plant employed only 270 laborers with that figure projected to drop to 200. In June 1994, UAW leadership called a new strike against Caterpillar that continued until December 1995 when, despite rejection of a contract offer by the membership, workers were ordered by the union to return to their jobs. Within three years, UAW members ratified a new contract similar to Caterpillar's original offer. Firestone workers, now affiliated with the **United Steel Workers of America**, ratified a new contract in late 1996, an agreement that included twelve-hour, rotating shifts.

To workers and students of labor history, the Decatur disputes placed in doubt the future of working-class gains in hours, wages, and conditions won over the previous sixty years. Organized labor has not yet fashioned an adequate response to the aggressive demands of multinational corporations in labor relations. Two of the unions involved—the AIW and the URW—disappeared into mergers that were, in part, brought on by the disputes. Relations between unionized Firestone union workers, picket-line crossers, and replacements were improving when, in December 2001, the plant closed following negative publicity involving tire problems in certain Ford vehicles that used their tires. About 1,500 men and women were left unemployed.

Suggested Readings: Stephen Franklin, *Three Strikes: Labor's Heartland Losses and What They Mean for Working Americans*, 2001; Tom Juravich and Kate Bronfenbrenner, *Ravenswood*, 1999.

Robert D. Sampson

Standard Time. Standard time was a creation of **Taylorism**. Scientific management experts calculated the exact time necessary for a worker to complete a particular task. Frederick Winslow Taylor, who founded this school of thought, employed stopwatches to standardize every movement that went into assembling a product. In a quest for total efficiency, management dissected jobs into steps and taught employees how to repeat processes in a more time-efficient way. The savings in time, multiplied by each worker over the course of the year, created a gargantuan leap in productivity, at least on paper. The robotic nature of the system was not lost on workers, who faced deskilling of their jobs and dehumanizing conditions. Taylor and his followers tried to entice factory hands by offering **incentive pay** to those who could beat the clock. Time, rather than the making of so many items, became the benchmark of this accelerated work life.

Labor unions bitterly contested this **speedup** and many workers imposed an informal **stint** that applied pressure to workers who bought into standard time. Assembly-line workers sometimes even resorted to sabotage to resist the dehumanizing effects of standard time. Ultimately, most firms determined that strict adherence to standard time was impractical. Despite eventual widespread societal disillusionment with the system, however, it lingers into the present and permeates the up-tempo life of contemporary America. Computerization modernized the old concepts of time-and-motion studies by fracturing time into humanly unfathomable bits, such as nanoseconds. Some vestiges of the old assembly line speedup can still be witnessed in fast food restaurants, where even the shaking of salt on french fries is carefully timed. For the most part, high-end production facilities have abandoned standard time in favor of team management.

Suggested Readings: American Social History Project, *Who Built America?*, Vol. 2, 2000; Eric Schlosser, *Fast Food Nation*, 2001.

Scott Molloy

Steel Strike of 1919. Like other strikes that occurred this same year, the Steel Strike of 1919 had its origins in World War I. The National Committee for Organizing Iron and Steel Workers, led by John Fitzpatrick of the Chicago Federation of Labor and former **Industrial Workers of the World (IWW)** organizer

William Z. Foster, began a campaign to unionize steelworkers nationwide in 1918. At first, steel producers were reluctant to fight organization because the administration of President Woodrow Wilson would not have tolerated labor disruptions that put government war contracts at risk. For this reason, the committee signed up thousands in the waning days of the war. This was the first sustained effort to organize steelworkers since the **Homestead lockout** of 1892 had largely driven unions from the industry.

When the war ended, union leaders requested negotiations with industry executives in the hope of receiving a contract. Steel producers refused to recognize or even meet with them. Even though the National Committee wanted more time to organize before striking, **rank-and-file** pressure forced it to call a nationwide steel strike on September 22. The two main issues were union recognition and a reduction in working hours from the ten- to twelve-hour days that remained a steel-industry standard.

Strike leader at Gary, Ind., advising steel strikers, 1919. © Library of Congress.

The strike affected firms differently. On the first day of the strike the majority of workers did not show up at most of the facilities owned by industry-giant U.S. Steel. By contrast, Bethlehem Steel, U.S. Steel's largest competitor, experienced only scattered disruptions. Best estimates put the total number of strikers at 250,000 nationwide, approximately half the workers in the industry.

Steel producers fought the strike by using three successful strategies. First, they immediately hired **scabs** to replace as many strikers as possible. Since the committee tended to attract unskilled workers, it proved relatively easy to replace them. Second, steel producers deliberately inflamed racial and ethnic tensions in the workforce. For example, U.S. Steel paid African Americans in Gary, Indiana, to march through the streets rather than to make steel, anticipating that this would engender fear among white strikers that blacks would take their jobs. Finally, the industry encouraged the media to attack the politics of the strike and its organizers. Most of these attacks centered on Foster, whose previous career with the IWW gave the committee's enemies an easy way to make the campaign seem dangerously radical.

The committee's best hope for winning concessions of any sort came during an industrial conference called by President Wilson in October. But when U.S.

Steel Chairman Elbert Gary refused to accept voluntary government **arbitration**, all hopes for compromise disappeared. Striking workers gradually returned to their jobs—without union contracts—all across the country. The committee formally ended the strike on January 8, 1920, although production had returned to normal levels weeks before. Steel remained largely nonunion until the Steel Workers Organizing Committee won major victories in the late-1930s.

Suggested Readings: David Brody, *Labor in Crisis: The Steel Strike of 1919*, 1987; Interchurch World Movement, *Public Opinion and the Steel Strike*, 1921; Interchurch World Movement, *Report on the Steel Strike of 1919*, 1920.

Jonathan Rees

Steel Strike of 1959–60. The Steel Strike of 1959–60 was the last nationwide and industry-wide strike of steelworkers. One of the largest and most successful strikes in United States' history, it was the culmination of many decades of labor's efforts to establish and consolidate its power in basic industries. For steelworkers, it evoked memories of historical struggles like the **Homestead steel strike**, the **steel strike of 1919**, and the **Depression-era strikes**. On July 15, 1959, more than 500,000 steelworkers, all members of the **United Steel Workers of America (USWA)**, struck the twelve major steel companies, including U.S. Steel. The strike closed over 90 percent of the American steel industry and idled close to one percent of the United States' entire labor force. In terms of idled hours, the strike was the largest in U.S. history. The workers were out for 116 days, returning to the mills November 7 by mandate of the **Taft-Hartley Act**. In early January 1960, the steel companies gave up. The settlement was a sweeping victory for the steelworkers and a humiliating defeat for management.

The steel companies sought a strike to roll back much of what the steelworkers had gained in previous contracts. Management precipitated the walkout in hope that a long strike would cause the **rank-and-file** to abandon USWA leaders. Ultimately, the companies wanted to severely reduce the union's and workers' power on the shop floor. Section 2-F of the steelworkers' contract forced company management to negotiate with the union over work processes. The companies' goal was to force the union to abandon section 2-F, thus returning all shop-floor power to management. The USWA saw section 2-F as vital to protecting jobs and workers and refused to negotiate changes to it.

The strike became a battle of attrition, and a settlement was reached only due to the intervention of the federal government. In October, the strike began to affect the national economy and President Dwight Eisenhower declared it a threat to national security. On October 9, Eisenhower invoked the eighty-day cooling-off provision of the Taft-Hartley Act to force the steelworkers back into the mills. USWA President David McDonald accused Eisenhower of strike-breaking, but once Taft-Hartley was in effect, negotiations began in earnest for the first time. In mid-October, Kaiser Steel agreed to the USWA's terms. Under order by the U.S. Supreme Court, the workers returned to work on November 7. The cooling-off period expired in January 1960. Recognizing the rank-and-file's willingness to renew their strike, the Eisenhower administration convinced the companies to settle on the USWA's terms. A settlement was announced on January 5. The steelworkers earned a wage increase and no reduction in their various benefits. Section 2-F remained intact.

The USWA maintained **solidarity** among steelworkers. Despite a four-month strike and two more months of intense management lobbying to convince workers to drop their support of the union, the rank-and-file remained committed to their union. This was all the more remarkable given that few younger steelworkers favored the original strike. Veterans of previous strikes argued that a show of force was necessary to defend the union and preserve wages, various benefits, and shop-floor power. Management intransigence served only to focus rank-and-file anger, determination, and solidarity. Left with little choice, the federal government allied with the workers and convinced the steel companies to capitulate. The USWA hailed the contract as its best ever. Ironically, it may remain so. By the 1970s, the steel industry was in deep decline, with foreign imports undercutting domestic prices, hastening the closing of aging plants, and leading to overall retrenchment. Giants like U.S. Steel began to shift assets out of production and diversify their investments. USWA membership declined among a shrinking steelworker pool until it expanded organizing efforts to workers in other fields.

Suggested Readings: Anthony F. Libertella, "The Steel Strike of 1959: Labor, Management, and Government Relations," Ph.D. dissertation, Ohio State University, 1972; Jack Metzgar, *Striking Steel: Solidarity Remembered*, 2000.

Mark Marianek

Steel Workers Organizing Committee. *See United Steel Workers of America.*

Steward, Ira (March 10, 1831–March 13, 1883). Ira Steward was a machinist who was one of the influential early advocates for the **eight-hour movement**. He was born in New London, Connecticut. His father was a laborer, and Steward was largely self-educated. By 1850, Steward was an apprentice machinist whose grueling twelve-hour workdays kindled his interest in reducing the strain of long hours on workers. He joined the International Machinists' and Blacksmiths' Union (IMBU)—a forerunner of the International Association of Machinists—which, in 1863, passed resolutions demanding an eight-hour workday. Steward quickly became a leader, and the IMBU provided him with seed money to build a workers' movement in support of the eight-hour goal.

Steward set up several organizations in the greater Boston area, including the Labor Reform Association and the Grand Eight-Hour League (which later was known as the Boston Eight-Hour League). In 1868, federal employees won an eight-hour day. He ran afoul of progressive Massachusetts labor advocates like Wendell Phillips for his anti-Chinese views, but Steward did help pressure the Massachusetts legislature to grant a ten-hour day for women and children in 1874. In 1878, he and J. P. McDonnell founded the International Labor Union (ILU). Although the ILU was short-lived, many of its views on **cooperation**, shorter workdays, and redistributing wealth inspired future labor leaders, especially **George McNeill**, who idolized Steward.

Steward is credited with being among the first to make cogent arguments about how shorter hours would improve workers' lives and society. His numerous articles and pamphlets were often mined by others seeking to defend shorter hours. Among Steward's claims was the argument that shorter hours would lead workers to improve themselves morally. He even argued that the overall economy would benefit because reduced hours would give workers more time to become consumers. That said, there can be no doubt that Steward saw the eight-hour day as part of a larger program to undermine capitalism through redistributing wealth.

Steward married twice. His first wife, Mary, died in 1878, and, in 1880, he married Jane Henning. He died in Plano, Illinois, in 1883. Steward remained an important symbol for the eight-hour movement for most of the nineteenth century, but he was largely forgotten by the time the 1938 **Fair Labor Standards Act** put the force of federal law behind the eight-hour day.

Suggested Readings: David Montgomery, *Beyond Equality: Labor and the Radical Republicans, 1962–1872,* 1967; Timothy Messer-Kruse, "Eight Hours, Greenbacks, and Chinamen: Wendell Phillips, Ira Steward, and the Fate of Labor Reform in Massachusetts," *Labor History* 42, no. 2 (2001); Paul R. Taylor, *The ABC-CLIO Companion to the American Labor Movement,* 1993.

Bruce Cohen

Stint. Stint refers to an informal agreement among workers as to what constitutes a reasonable pace and amount of work. Often expressed under the rubric a fair day's work for a fair day's pay, the stint was an important part of the nineteenth-century work mentality that persists to the present. Employers routinely attempt to break worker stints through methods ranging from **piecework** rates to **speedups**, but frequently encounter resistance when they do so. Unlike organized protests, the stint requires little more to maintain than tacit agreement among workers. It is considered an important aspect of shop-floor culture that illustrates how laborers exert some degree of control over production, even in nonunionized companies. Overly zealous workers who do not respect the stint are usually ostracized by others. Employers face resistance ranging from deliberate slowdowns and **grievance** filings to sabotage.

Suggested Reading: David Montgomery, *Workers' Control in America,* 1984.

Robert E. Weir

Stool Pigeon. A stool pigeon is an informer used as a decoy to entice individuals into a trap. In the workplace the term stool pigeon is used to describe a company or government spy in the ranks of workers. A stool pigeon is comparable to an **agent provocateur**, though the latter also incites illegal actions as well as spying. Other terms with similar connotations include: company spy, company spotter, fin, rat, and labor spy. Stool pigeon derives from a fowling practice in which a pigeon was tied to a stool to attract birds of prey. Stool is a variant of the archaic stale, meaning decoy or, more specifically, of the French *estale*, a pigeon that entices hawks or other pigeons into a net. The modern sense of the term dates from the fifteenth-century alternative spelling *stall*, which was jargon for a pickpocket's accomplice who distracted a victim while the co-conspirator fleeced a victim. By the end of the sixteenth century, a person who worked to entrap another was generally referred to as a stool pigeon.

In the United States, one of the earliest known uses of the phrase was in an 1830 *Workingman's Gazette*, which used it to illustrate how political parties used human decoys to attract voters, much as a huckster might use a fake testimonial to peddle his goods. Its first use in the context of industrial espionage is difficult to pinpoint. The rise of factory spies and the use of **Pinkerton** detectives in the labor struggles of the Gilded Age certainly provided the opportunity for the use of the term. In one famed incident, Pinkerton detective James McParlan allegedly infiltrated the **Molly Maguires**. His evidence sent ten Pennsylvania miners to the gallows in 1875, and fourteen more to jail. During the West Virginia-Kentucky bituminous coal strikes of the 1920s, stool pigeons acted as agent provocateurs and committed illegal acts that justified harsh crackdowns. The use of police informants to break organized crime rings during the Prohibition era brought the term to greater prominence, but stool pigeons continued to be used against labor unions as well. The practice was condemned by the 1937 **La Follette Committee**, but the report did little to stop the practice. Many 1960s social reform movements, including unions, were troubled by internal spies. Stool pigeons also kept management apprised of union activities during the 1997 Detroit newspaper strike.

Suggested Readings: Edward Levinson, *I Break Strikes!*, 1969; Jean Spielman, *The Stool Pigeon and the Open Shop Movement*, 1923.

Mark Noon

Strasser, Adolph (1844–January 1, 1939). Adolph Strasser was a major figure in the early Socialist Labor Party, Cigar-Maker's International Union (CMIU), the **Knights of Labor (KOL)**, and was a cofounder of the **American Federation of Labor (AFL)**. Strasser is credited with being the ideological father of **pure and simple unionism**.

Strasser was a German-speaking Hungarian who emigrated to America around 1872. Not much is known of his early life. His knowledge of British trade unionism indicated that he probably spent some time in England, and some people—including AFL leader **Samuel Gompers**—surmised that Strasser had upper-class origins. Upon his arrival New York City, the twenty-eight-year-old Strasser became an active participant in the socialist movement, joining the American Section of the International Workingmen's Association of the Marxist First International. He also took an active role in the CMIU, where he worked with Samuel Gompers.

Strasser was disappointed in the faction-ridden, German immigrant character of the International, and joined a group of American-born activists in organizing the **Tompkins Square** unemployment demonstration on January 13, 1874, which ended in violence. His participation violated the rules of the American Section, and Strasser, **Peter J. McGuire**, and several others were expelled. Strasser and McGuire then organized the Social Democratic Workingmen's Party (SDWP), Strasser becoming its executive secretary. He contributed extensively to its paper, *The Socialist*, which was later renamed *The Labor Standard*.

Though Strasser was an active, visionary force in the SDWP, he was never able to stem the arguments raging in the German-American community on the tactical merits of trade union organization versus political action. This issue was hotly debated in the pages of the SDWP's journal, and it caused serious disruption at an April 1876 Unity Convention in Philadelphia of various socialist groups. Strasser's statements on the need to focus on immediate achievements—provision of jobs, high wages, short working hours, unemployment insurance, and sick benefits—as opposed to participation in political campaigns, was the major point of contention in the meetings. After much debate, the Workingmen's Party of the United States—soon to be re-christened the Socialist Labor Party (SLP)—was formed. Most of the other participants insisted upon the primacy of political campaigning, and Strasser was removed from his leadership position.

In 1877, Strasser was promoted from organizer to president of the CMIU, a position he occupied for the next fifteen years. When he took over the CMIU, membership had sunk to just over 1,000 members. Within three years, the CMIU membership climbed to over 4,000. Both Strasser and Gompers soon shed their socialism and developed pure and simple unionism. Strasser insisted unions should focus on **collective bargaining** and short-range political action. Although this strategy was the antithesis of the utopianism of the Socialist Labor Party, pure and simple unionism became the bedrock model for American trade unionism by about 1890.

The first major action of the Strasser/Gompers-led CMIU was the campaign against tenement cigarmaking. The CMIU organized a campaign that emphasized the unsanitary conditions of tenement labor, and introduced a **union label** on cigars to distinguish them from the tenement-made brands. In 1878, the union appealed to the federal and state legislatures to ban commercial production in residential dwellings. The several bills introduced all failed, and further alienated socialists within and without the CMIU. In consequence, CMIU members of the SLP bolted from the union to form the SLP-affiliated Progressive Cigar-Maker's Union (PCMU). In New York City, the PCMU was chartered as a Knights of Labor local assembly, a move that angered Strasser and Gompers, who were nominal members of the KOL. The fight between the

CMIU and the PCMU weaned Strasser from any remaining vestiges of socialism and touched off bitter jurisdiction battles between the CMIU and the KOL. Strasser actively worked to subvert the PCMU. He also became a harsh critic of the KOL and, in 1886, demanded that the Knights stop organizing workers in skilled trades.

Though Strasser was a central figure in the formation of the AFL in 1886, he preferred thereafter to focus his energies on the CMIU. He did serve the AFL's legislative committee and on its executive council. In the latter position Strasser is credited with pushing through the expulsion of the **Brewery Workers** Union in 1907, when it embraced an **industrial unionism** philosophy. Strasser vacated the CMIU presidency in 1892, but continued to serve the cigar makers in a variety of lower-level capacities. Later in life he moved a great deal, first from New York City to Buffalo, then to Chicago from 1905 to 1911, and then back to Buffalo in 1914 when he retired from the labor movement and spent four years as a real-estate agent.

Little is known of Strasser's personal life. A CMIU newspaper article published at the end of his presidency said "personally, or rather socially, he makes few friends. . . . " In 1930, Strasser moved to Florida, and his apparently deliberate low profile left him an almost-forgotten figure in the AFL. He had no further contact with the CMIU, and spent his last years living in the home of a dressmaker, dying there on January 1, 1939. Strasser's considerable stock portfolio and savings were depleted during the Depression. He died nearly penniless, his burial expenses being paid by the state of Florida. Several years later the CMIU paid to have his remains exhumed and shipped to Chicago for reburial. Only three people attended Strasser's interment in the Forest Home Cemetery.

Suggested Readings: Patricia Cooper, *Once a Cigarmaker: Men, Women, and Work Culture in American Cigar Factories, 1900–1919*, 1987; H. M. Gitelman, "Adolph Strasser and the Origins of Pure and Simple Unionism," *Labor History* 6, no. 1 (Winter 1965): 71–83; Julie Greene, *Pure and Simple Politics: The American Federation of Labor and Political Activism, 1881–1917*, 1988.

Jeff McFadden

Strike. A strike is the cessation of work initiated by employees in protest against perceived injustices on the part of an employer. It is also commonly referred to as a work stoppage, suspension, or walkout. Issues like low pay, poor working conditions, long hours, or fringe benefits are among those that precipitate strikes. The strike is the primary weapon of organized labor and is one of the most significant forms of social protest in the United States. Strikes can take a variety of forms including the **sit-down strike**, the **sympathy strike**, or the **wildcat strike**. However, the most common form involves a decision among workers to withhold their labor by walking off their jobs and staying away until their demands are negotiated. A dominant feature of the strike is the use of a **picket** line in which workers voice their demands, alert the public of their plight, and attempt to prevent strikebreakers from entering the business or factory.

The first recorded use of the term in the context of a concerted refusal to work dates from 1768, and likely originated in the sailors' practice of striking, or lowering, a ship's sails to symbolize their refusal to go to sea. The first documented strike in the United States occurred in Philadelphia in 1786, when printers sought a minimum wage of $6 per week. With the development of labor organizations in the late-nineteenth century, strikes became more frequent, with the first nationwide strike occurring in 1877, when railroad workers protested a series of wage cuts. The opening decades of the twentieth century witnessed several important industry-wide strikes by miners, steelworkers, and autoworkers. Significantly, until New Deal legislation in the 1930s gave unions the right to organize, courts routinely ruled that strikes were illegal and forced employees back to work. Since World War II, the number of strikes has been on the decline with some of the most significant strikes occurring among public employees such as teachers and municipal workers.

In 1948, during a strike at the Univis Lens Company in Dayton, Ohio, replacement workers enter the plant under the protection of Ohio National Guardsmen. © George Meany Memorial Archives.

Suggested Readings: Jeremy Brecher, *Strike!*, 1997; E. T. Hiller, *The Strike: A Study in Collective Action*, 1969.

Mark Noon

Subcontracting. Subcontracting is the practice whereby production and/or services purchased from one firm are assigned to another by the firm under contract. It is especially commonplace in the building trades. A consumer—which could be an individual, a municipality, or even the federal government—signs an agreement with a contractor. The contract usually specifies the amount the consumer will pay for the project and the time in which the contractor will complete it, or reasonable estimates in the case of larger undertakings. Contracts are often quite detailed regarding the nature and quality of the work to be completed. In addition, building codes and consumer laws may apply.

It is the contractor's responsibility to complete the project, but that individual or firm may have great flexibility in how to do so. Few general contractors complete all the work themselves. They may choose, for example, to subcontract the plumbing to one firm, landscaping to another, and electrical work to still a different company. It is usually the original contractor's responsibility to make certain all work is completed properly.

Subcontracting has long been a feature of American industry, and not just in the building trades. Auto manufacturers, for example, often subcontract parts fashioned in one place, but assembled at another. The same is true in the apparel industry, where cloth or even basic garments might be woven or cut in one location and tailored somewhere else.

Organized labor concerns itself with subcontracting when it undermines the jobs and wages of union workers. In recent years, subcontracting has emerged as another way for less scrupulous firms to subvert wages under the guise of frugality. Hospitals, for example, have replaced staff nurses with subcontracted care from firms that generally pay lower wages. Many airlines now subcontract plane maintenance, a practice that has cost jobs among union workers in the **International Association of Machinists and Aerospace Workers**. Abuses are widespread in the building trades, where large construction firms may actually set up nonunion subsidiaries toward which they channel projects. Apparel-industry workers complain that subcontracted **homework** is little more than **sweatshop** production in a new guise. Malls and office complexes routinely subcontract services like security, maintenance, rubbish removal, and cleaning to outside firms. In larger cities, badly paid subcontracted work often goes to immigrants and the poor, though campaigns by groups like Jobs with Justice and Justice for Janitors have helped in some cities. For the foreseeable future, subcontracting is likely to remain a point of contention between unions and management.

Suggested Reading: Barbara Ehrenreich, *Nickel and Dimed*, 2001.

Robert E. Weir

Sugar, Maurice (August 12, 1891–February 15, 1974). Maurice Sugar was born on August 12, 1891, in Northern Michigan. His parents were Lithuanian Jews who immigrated to the United States in the early 1880s. His father was a salesman who eventually opened his own small shop in the lumber boom town of Brimley, Michigan. The family moved to Detroit in 1900, but returned to live in Brimley in 1906. When Maurice entered University of Michigan law school, there was no indication of the radicalism that would motivate much of his legal career. At University of Michigan, Maurice met and fell in love with Jane Meyer, a committed **socialist**. By the time Sugar graduated in 1913, he firmly embraced the Socialist Party of **Eugene Debs**. Meyer and Sugar eloped in 1914 and moved to Detroit.

The politically active and motivated Sugar quickly gained the trust of the local labor movement and the Socialist Party of America (SP) in Detroit. In the few years after he moved to Detroit, and prior to World War I, Sugar worked for the International Typographical Union Local #18 (Detroit) during a strike, and assisted the Detroit Federation of Labor in its attempts to stop the use of injunctions in labor disputes in Michigan. Sugar and his wife also became leaders in the Detroit and Michigan chapters of the SP. Sugar supported the SP's antiwar and anticonscription positions as the United States entered World War I.

Like other SP members, Sugar was convicted and jailed for his opposition to United States entrance into World War I and for failing to register for conscription. On November 25, 1918, two weeks after WW I ended, the Supreme Court refused to hear his appeal and Sugar entered the Detroit House of Corrections. He spent the next ten months in jail. Perhaps more alarming to the young attorney, the Detroit Bar Association argued successfully for Sugar's disbarment soon after he was sentenced in early 1918.

Frank Murphy, in 1923 a young, ambitious Detroit judge, thought Sugar's disbarment unjust. Murphy had been an opposing attorney at some of Sugar's earlier labor cases and respected Sugar as an attorney and as a person. Murphy, who later became mayor of Detroit (1930–33), governor of Michigan (1937–38), and then a Supreme Court justice (1940–49), prepared and argued successfully Sugar's case for reinstatement to the Michigan Bar. The paths of Murphy and Sugar continued to intersect, sometimes as allies and sometimes as adversaries, throughout their careers.

Now able to practice law again, Sugar returned to the labor movement and worked on civil-liberties cases as well. He was a local advisor to Clarence Darrow in the Ossian Sweet defense case, a landmark Detroit civil-rights trial. Although he did not return to membership in the SP in the 1920s, he remained close to the left in Detroit and provided legal assistance to both the International Labor Defense (ILD) and the Unemployed Councils (UC). Both the UC and the ILD were close to the Communist Party (CP). Although he does not appear to have been a member of the CP, he was also active in other CP-allied organizations like the John Reed Club. He and his wife visited the Soviet Union in 1932.

By the mid-1930s Sugar became more formally connected with the local labor movement. In 1933 he was hired as the legal counsel for the **Mechanics Educational Society of America** (MESA), an independent union of skilled craftsmen located primarily in the Detroit area. While working for MESA he became an expert on the legal workings of the New Deal agencies that had increased the federal government's involvement in labor relations. He represented MESA, for example, at the Automobile Labor Board hearings of the National Recovery Administration (NRA). Perhaps more important, he was called upon as an advisor for the fledging **United Auto Workers** union (UAW) at the historic Flint **sit-down strike**. Sugar penned "Sit-Down," one of the better known labor songs of the twentieth-century in 1938, as Detroit exploded in sit-down strikes in the wake of the Flint workers' success. More than a few of Detroit's sit-down strikers called Sugar for advice and legal representation.

His association with the UAW grew quickly and, in 1939, he was hired as the UAW general counsel. Sugar established a modern and quite skilled legal department in the UAW. Although Sugar became increasingly skeptical of the labor movement's reliance on the federal government, he and his UAW staff utilized federal-government-established labor relations machinery, like the National Labor Relations Board and the **National War Labor Board**, as successfully as any other union in the country. But Sugar was much more than the UAW's general counsel. From the beginning he was deeply involved in the overall functioning, decision-making, and politics of the union. He helped develop strategies in the drive to organize the Ford Motor Company, particularly between 1939 and 1941, for example. Although not an elected official, he regularly attended executive board meetings. Sugar also participated in the factional political struggles that wracked the union after World War II. He opposed the rise of **Walter Reuther** to the presidency in 1946 and Reuther's successful campaign to gain control of the executive board eighteen months later in 1947. Soon after gaining control of the UAW, Reuther moved to fire many of his factional enemies' supporters, including Sugar. Many unsubstantiated charges were filed against Sugar as the executive board debated his disposition for eight hours before deciding to terminate his relationship with the union. Sugar was clearly a casualty of the left-wing faction's loss to Reuther.

Sugar was politically and personally committed to the UAW and his ouster was unpleasant. Especially difficult for Sugar was that the UAW did not allow him to respond to unfair accusations made by his political opponents. After being released from the UAW, Sugar receded from politics and moved north to Black Lake. His private practice was the first integrated law firm in Detroit. It included African American George Crocket, who was also fired by Reuther from a UAW post in the late 1940s, and Ernest Goodman. Sugar died on February 15, 1974.

Suggested Reading: Christopher Johnson, *Maurice Sugar: Law, Labor, and the Left in Detroit, 1912–1950*, 1988.

Joseph Turrini

Supplemental Unemployment Benefits. *See Guaranteed Annual Wage.*

Sweatshop. Sweatshops are generally defined as small manufacturing concerns, often within a residential setting, in which men and especially women and children labor under substandard conditions, for long hours and low pay. Beginning in the nineteenth century, American workers, many of them recent immigrants, toiled in urban tenements making clothes, shoes, and cigars, paid by the piece. During the 1880s, the Cigarmakers International Union was among the first trade unions to demand regulation of sweatshops. Progressive Era social reformers also expressed concern for sweatshop workers, as well as the possibility that disease could be spread to unwary consumers through goods produced in unhealthy settings. The garment industry was especially dependent on "sweated" labor, which trade unionists argued kept all garment makers' wages low. The **International Ladies' Garment Workers' Union** in particular lobbied against the proliferation of sweatshops. The horrible **Triangle Factory Fire of 1911** focused public attention on sweatshop and factory conditions and stimulated ordinances to control them. Federal laws, passed during the New Deal in the 1930s, further restricted the use of sweatshop labor. Nonetheless, inhuman labor conditions, especially in the production of clothing, continue in the twenty-first century. In addition, many unions charge that **subcontracted homework** replicates sweatshop conditions in private homes. Moreover, many American-based firms have moved their manufacturing operations to low-wage nations where sweatshop conditions are the norm. In response, activist groups like Sweatshop Watch and labor organizations like UNITE seek to publicize both American and global sweatshop labor by mounting **boycotts** and sponsoring organizing campaigns.

Suggested Readings: Eileen Boris, *Home to Work: Motherhood and the Politics of Industrial Homework in the United States,* 1994; Miriam Ching Yoon Louie, *Sweatshop Warriors: Immigrant Women Workers Take on the Global Factory,* 2001.

Kathleen Banks Nutter

An 1888 illustration depicting the evils of New York sweatshops. © George Meany Memorial Archives/Library of Congress.

Sweeney, John Joseph (May 5, 1934–). John J. Sweeney is the current president of the American Federation of Labor-Congress of Industrial Organizations (AFL-CIO). He was elected in 1995, and has pledged to reverse decades of declining union membership in the United States. He is the son of working-class Irish immigrants and was raised in the Bronx borough of New York City. His father, a bus driver, was an active member in the Transport Workers Union and his mother was a domestic worker. Sweeney attended Roman Catholic schools and obtained a B.A. in economics from Iona College in 1956. He is married and has two children.

He worked briefly for IBM, before leaving to earn substantially lower pay as a researcher for the **International Ladies' Garment Workers' Union**. By 1960, he was working for the Building Service Employees International Union (BSEIU) as a contract director. His affiliation with the BSEIU grew as he steadily took on tasks more central to the union's operations. Four years after the BSEIU changed its name to the **Service Employees International Union (SIEU)** in 1968, Sweeney became a part of the union's executive board. Soon after, he became a vice president. In 1976, Sweeney assumed the presidency of SEIU Local 32B in New York City and confronted two problems hampering union efforts: corporate disregard of workers and union passivity. In the first four years of his presidency of Local 32B he addressed both concerns. Two fierce and swift **strikes** won important wage and job security **concessions** for 70,000 workers.

Sweeney was elected SEIU international president in 1980 and was also elected as a vice president of the AFL-CIO. During the 1980s, Sweeney led a number of successful campaigns including Justice for Janitors in 1985, and the Work and Family Campaign begun in 1986. Sweeney also agitated for legislative changes, including the federal Family and Medical Leave Act. Under his watch SEIU also made a concerted effort to bring gender and racial diversity to the union. In addition, gays and lesbians found expression in the union's Lavender Caucus.

In response to what Sweeney saw as AFL-CIO apathy and its inability to confront conservative politicians and deteriorating working conditions, he challenged Lane Kirkland's hand-picked candidate for the presidency of the AFL-CIO in 1995. Sweeney won the election and vowed to expand SEIU policies and militancy throughout the federation. He also announced intentions to concentrate on recruitment drives. As SEIU president, Sweeney spent one-third of its budget on organizing campaigns, and SEIU was one of the few AFL-CIO unions to experience growth during the antiunion administrations of Presidents Ronald Reagan and George H. Bush. Similarly, when Sweeney assumed the presidency of the AFL-CIO, he immediately launched an aggressive organizing drive backed by $20 million of newly allocated funds. This campaign also sought to diversify AFL-CIO membership and leadership through active recruitment of women and minorities. Sweeney also vowed to promote union democracy, a call that ruffled several notoriously autocratic affiliate heads.

Another constant in Sweeney's leadership has been his dedication to consider the plight of all working Americans, not just union members. He is an outspoken critic of modern corporate management strategies used to maximize profit: **deregulation, downsizing**, capital flight, reducing employee benefits and **pensions**, and ignoring worker security. He also maintains that corporate managers have persuaded the government to enact laws that protect property but not people. Current and recent AFL-CIO campaigns include making workplaces conform to principles of ergonomics, enforcing workplace safety laws, safeguarding the right of workers to organize, recognizing new categories of occupational injury, preserving the current Social Security program, and equalizing incomes as a means to achieve greater social stability worldwide.

The **Teamsters'** 1997 victory in the **United Parcel Service strike** heartened many union supporters, and AFL-CIO unions reversed a 1980s trend by winning more strikes than they lost. Sweeney, however, has not been successful in stopping the AFL-CIO's membership slide; in fact, it has decreased at a faster rate than it did under Kirkland. Very few unions have honored Sweeney's call to devote 30 percent of their budgets to organizing. Attempts to assist the **United Farm Workers** in organizing strawberry pickers flopped, as did an expensive campaign to unionize Las Vegas construction workers. The federation has also been plagued by defections, most notably the United Transportation Union, which quit over conflicts with the **Brotherhood of Locomotive Engineers**, and the 500,000-strong **United Brotherhood of Carpenters and Joiners**. Some critics charge that methods used by SEIU will not work in businesses subject to movable capital, though most analysts feel it is too early to evaluate Sweeney's effectiveness.

Suggested Readings: *Current Bibliography Yearbook,* 1996; Jo-Ann Mort, *Not Your Father's Union Movement: Inside the AFL-CIO,* 1998; "Leadership: AFL-CIO Top National Officers," www.aflcio.org/aboutaflcio/leaders/.

Simon Holzapfel

Sweetheart Contract. Sweetheart contract is a sarcastic term for bargaining agreements worked out secretly between a few union officers and management without the input or even knowledge of **rank-and-file** unionists. Historically such arrangements have been associated with corrupt practices by either party and usually involve a kickback to a labor official. The **American Federation of Labor-Congress of Industrial Organizations** condemned this method as a violation of trade union ethics. Although the practice was never widespread, except in a handful of local and national unions with ties to organized crime, most corrupt vestiges had been eliminated by the start of the twenty-first century. The term itself, however, lingers on in the lexicon of the rank and file as a simile for an unpopular **contract**, even if it was negotiated legally. Some union leaders simply find it easier to work out an agreement in private and then sell the contract to a skeptical membership, or purposefully avoid grassroots involvement fearing that the rank and file will not understand the larger issues and problems facing the industry. The negotiator tries to address these concerns privately in good faith to avoid temporarily the wrath of the union constituents. Such procedures invariably lead to cynicism among union members' ranks and are now a hallmark of **business unionism** rather than criminal intent.

Suggested Reading: Florence Peterson, *American Labor Unions: What They Are and How They Work,* 1963.

Scott Molloy

Swinton, John (December 12, 1829–December 15, 1901). John Swinton was one of the leading **labor journalists** and reform activists of the late-nineteenth century. He was born in Salton, Scotland, the son of William and Jane Swinton. He received little formal education before emigrating to Montreal, Canada, with his parents at the age of fourteen. He worked briefly as a **journeyman** printer at the Montreal *Witness*, before his family moved to New York City, and then to Illinois, where Swinton worked on small-town newspapers. Swinton studied theology for a short time at the Williston Seminary in Massachusetts, however, his interests in writing and social reform led him toward a career in labor journalism.

As a journeyman printer, Swinton traveled extensively through the South and the West, trips that sharpened his sympathies for the oppressed. In South Carolina, he confronted the horrors of chattel slavery, an experience that converted him to abolitionism. As a compositor in the state printing office, he taught African Americans to read and write at considerable personal risk. His antislavery sentiments drew him to Kansas in 1856, where he edited the *Lawrence Republican*, aided Kansas free-soil forces, and took part in a raid led by John Brown. In 1857, he briefly studied medicine at the New York Medical College, but did not complete his courses.

On the strength of some articles on medicine, he joined the staff of the *New York Times*. By 1860, he was its chief editorial writer. He left the

John Swinton. © George Meany Memorial Archives.

Times in 1870 and worked at the rival *New York Sun* until 1883. Swinton's special interest was union news, and he gained a reputation as an inspirational speaker on behalf of labor groups. On January 13, 1874, he was the principal speaker at a demonstration at **Tompkins Square** to protest injustices to workers. Swinton's speech was interrupted when police and militia moved in to disperse the crowd, resulting in a riot. His popularity inside the labor movement prompted the Industrial Political Party, an affiliate of the Socialist Labor Party, to nominate him for mayor of New York City in 1874. Although he did not win, Swinton worked to abolish tenement house cigar making—a notoriously exploitative practice—and helped lead an 1875 mill **strike**. Swinton also spoke out against **child labor** and deplorable conditions in the **sweatshops**. In 1886, he provided testimony at a U.S. Senate Committee on Labor and Education hearing and offered ideas on legislation to benefit working people.

Swinton is best remembered for his effort to create a newspaper whose content was free from the influence of big business. The first issue of *John Swinton's Paper* debuted on October 14, 1883. The six-column, four-page weekly sought to improve the economic welfare of the laboring classes by organizing protests, promoting reform legislation, and encouraging organized labor. Many readers relied on Swinton for news of the **Knights of Labor** and the **American Federation of Labor**. *John Swinton's Paper* also reported on living and factory conditions, strikes, wage-and-hour statistics in individual trades, and the abuse of power by Gilded Age robber barons like Jay Gould and William H. Vanderbilt. The paper's 1885 exposés on contract immigration labor led to legislation prohibiting the practice.

Swinton's insistence on the paper's independence eventually brought about its downfall, as he refused to accept financial backers or gifts. In addition, Swinton turned down opportunities to affiliate the paper with specific unions. Subscriptions and advertising were not enough to keep up with expenses, and the paper was forced to fold in August 1887. Swinton lost his life savings—approximately $40,000—on the venture.

After the collapse of the paper, Swinton made an unsuccessful bid for the New York State Senate on the Progressive Labor Party ticket. He then continued his campaign for social justice as a freelance writer and a public speaker. Swinton eventually returned to the New York *Sun,* and he wrote for European journals. Failing eyesight plagued Swinton and he depended on his wife to assist him. Despite being totally blind by 1889, he continued his crusade for social reform by completing two books, *Striking for Life: Labor's Side of the Labor Question* (1894) and *A Momentous Question: The Respective Attitudes of Labor and Capital* (1895). He died in Brooklyn Heights in 1901. Swinton's career embodied many of the virtues and frustrations of the independent labor crusader. Autonomy and outspokenness won Swinton scores of admirers and provided labor with a truly independent advocacy voice. In the end, however, Swinton's lack of affiliation and firm alliances provided little cushion against insolvency, nor did he possess the means to widen his audience beyond its small devoted core.

Suggested Readings: Sender Garlin, *John Swinton, American Radical, 1829–1901,* 1976; Frank Reuter, "John Swinton's Paper." *Labor History* 1, no. 3 (Fall 1960): 298–307.

Mark Noon

Sylvis, William H. (November 26, 1828–July 27, 1869). William H. Sylvis was a Philadelphia iron molder and the founder of the **National Labor Union (NLU)**. He was born in Armagh, Pennsylvania, the son of Nicholas and Maria (Mott) Sylvis. His father was a failed wagon maker who moved his family frequently as he searched for work. When he was eleven, William boarded with a Whig politician, and his several years there provided his only formal education. At eighteen, Sylvis was apprenticed as an iron molder. He married fifteen-year-old Amelia Thomas in 1852, and moved to Philadelphia two years later.

Molders, who made stoves and other iron products, were highly skilled craftsmen whose wages exceeded that of most other trades. Until the 1850s, they retained great control over their craft and often operated their own foundries. Sylvis himself was briefly part owner of a foundry, though he usually worked as a **journeyman** molder. By the mid-1850s, however, a separate proprietary class was emerging in the molding trade, with owners seeking to wrest workplace control from mechanics. Sylvis participated in a **strike** in 1857, and was soon chosen as secretary for his local union. In 1859, he organized a Philadelphia convention to explore forming a national molders union. In 1860, the National Union of Iron Molders came into being, with Sylvis serving as treasurer. He also authored a fiery constitution that accused organized wealth of degrading common labor.

The Civil War threw the union into disarray. Sylvis, a Democrat, was an ardent supporter of the Union cause and served in a workers' militia during the war. He left active duty in 1863, returned to union activism, reorganized his trade as the Iron Moulders' International Union (IMIU),

William H. Sylvis. © George Meany Memorial Archives.

and served as its president. Sylvis was a tireless organizer and by 1865, two-thirds of all molders belonged to the IMIU. Employers responded by increasing the number of unskilled hands in the foundries, thereby driving down journeymen's wages. Several also banded together to combat the IMIU, hoping to rid the trade of union activity. Sylvis, however, built a strong strike fund and brought union locals under the control of the parent organization. A 1866 strike forced owners to capitulate.

Despite success, Sylvis recognized that the coming struggle between capital and labor required greater coordination between unions. Like many others of his time, he was also a booster of worker-controlled **cooperatives**. Although several appeared in the iron molding trade, they did not supplant **capitalism** as Sylvis and other advocates hoped. Sylvis felt that labor needed a national umbrella organization that would represent all trades in order to press for legislation beneficial to workers. He was the moving force behind the 1866 Baltimore labor congress that created the NLU, though he did not attend. Sylvis became the co-editor of the NLU's journal, the *Working Man's Advocate*. At an 1868 convention, Sylvis was elected NLU president.

The NLU proved to have more rhetorical than political clout, but Sylvis did what he could to put teeth into the organization's demands. He was among the many voices that urged President Ulysses S. Grant to enforce a recently enacted eight-hour-day law for federal employees. He was also an ardent supporter of the **greenback** movement seeking to reform the nation's monetary policy. Sylvis grew convinced that a working-class/middle-class alliance was necessary to advance favorable labor legislation and thus urged the seating of non-workers as NLU convention delegates. Already an advocate of limited suffrage for women, he also welcomed Susan B. Anthony, **Kate Mullaney**, and two other women to the 1868 convention, despite some organization resistance. When Sylvis ascended to the NLU presidency, he promptly appointed Mullaney as an assistant secretary in charge of organizing female workers.

Sylvis also pressed the NLU to work closely with the International Workingmen's Association (IWA), a European socialist organization, and he attended an 1869 IWA congress in Switzerland. He also urged African Americans to join the NLU, and several attended its 1870 congress, a mere two years after the NLU had rejected a proposal to admit black members. For a time, the NLU worked closely with the **Colored National Labor Union**.

Alas, much of the NLU's promise evaporated after Sylvis's death. Never a robust man, Sylvis died in July 1869, shortly after returning to his Philadelphia home from an organizing tour of the South. Without his guidance, NLU ties to women, African Americans, and the IWA weakened and the organization disappeared shortly after the 1872 election. Sylvis is considered by many scholars to have been the prototype of a more modern labor leader. Many of his ideas and tactics were well in advance of the times.

Suggested Readings: John R. Commons, *History of Labour in the United States*, Vol. 2, 1946; Jonathan Grossman, *William Sylvis: Pioneer of Labor*, 1945; David Montgomery, "William Sylvis and the Search for Working-Class Citizenship," in Melvin Dubofsky and Warren Van Tine, eds., *Labor Leaders in America*, 1987.

Ralph Shaffer

Sympathy Strike. A sympathy strike is a work stoppage in support of another group of workers who have walked out or been locked out, rather than a grievance against one's own employer. It is rooted in ideals of class **solidarity** and in the hope that capitalists will exert pressure on each other to resolve labor disputes. For example, during the 1934 San Francisco dock **strike**, Atlantic dock workers considered using the tactic to express their solidarity with the struggle of their west coast comrades. The 1947 **Taft-Hartley Act** outlawed use of sympathy strikes, though many workers ignore the law. Between 1980 and 2000, a variety of workers have engaged in sympathy strikes. In 1996, members of the **United Auto Workers** walked off jobs in Michigan in support of striking Dayton, Ohio, brake workers. Pilots and flight attendants have ignored the ban, as have teachers striking in support of support workers. The sympathy strike remains a potent, if risky, tactic.

Suggested Readings: Helen Marot, *American Labor Unions*, 2001; United Transportation Union, http://www.utu.org/worksite/history/LaborHistory.htm.

Evan Daniel

T

Taft-Hartley Act. Taft-Hartley Act is the popular name for the Labor-Management Relations Act, a bill sponsored by Senator Robert Taft (Ohio) and Representative Fred Hartley (New Jersey). It became law in June 1947, when the Republican-dominated Congress overrode President Harry Truman's veto, and is regarded by unions as one of the worst pieces of antilabor legislation in U.S. history. It was consciously designed to weaken the **National Labor Relations Act (NLRA)**, which the business community and its Republican allies felt gave unions too much power.

By the end of World War II, nearly 25 percent of the workforce was unionized, and half of the existing union **contracts** contained closed-shop, or **preferential-shop**, hiring provisions. Conservative attempts to scuttle the NLRA faltered in 1937, when the Supreme Court affirmed its constitutionality. Tactics then switched to securing legislative remedy. The Taft-Hartley Act represents the culmination of over a decade of opposition to the NLRA, although it was often touted as merely correctives and amendments to the NLRA.

The law has nine major clauses. Among its most important provisions, it outlaws closed shops, allowing a union-controlled shop to exist only if a union represents the majority of eligible voters and accords new members equal rights with existing members. The act mandated a sixty-day cooling-off period before a union could resort to a **strike**, and another provision gave the federal government the authority to seek injunctions for an eighty-day cooling-off period in essential industries. Both employers and unions were empowered to sue each other for breach of contract. Republicans also exploited the emerging red scare to secure a clause that required union officers to file affidavits stating that they were not members of the Communist Party, a proviso that had the effect of silencing some of labor's more radical voices. Moreover, unions were required to file their constitutions and yearly financial statements with the **Department of Labor (DOL)**. This section rankled many union leaders, as private corporations were not required to make their finances public. Reacting to the union-Democratic Party alliance forged by the New Deal, another clause forbids unions from

making direct or indirect campaign contributions, a proviso largely sidestepped when unions set up political action committees. The act also allowed employers to discontinue the **dues checkoff** system, if they so choose.

Congressman Hartley hated unions and hoped his bill would destroy them. That did not happen, but Taft-Hartley's impact has been devastating. The right to strike was severely curtailed and the wave of postwar militancy that emerged in 1945 quickly petered out. Anticommunist provisos and the need for leaders to quash **wildcat strikes**

A labor rally against the Taft-Hartley bill. © George Meany Memorial Archives.

further depleted militant ranks. Under the Taft-Hartley Act, employers gained the right to initiate **decertification** hearings, a power that unions charge has led to intimidation and unfair labor practices. There is no question that labor-management relations grew more litigious after the passage of Taft-Hartley, with disputes often moving from the shop floor to the courtroom.

In the late 1940s and early 1950s labor lost a golden moment to overturn Taft-Hartley, which did not enjoy popular support initially. Unions, however, failed to mobilize uniform working-class opposition. Some unions, like the **United Mine Workers of America (UMWA)**, openly defied the law. The **Congress of Industrial Organizations (CIO)** threatened to conduct **general strikes** until the bill was repealed, but it failed to follow through on its bluster. Most unions placed their hopes in a political solution, backing liberal politicians and lobbying for prolabor appointments to the National Labor Relations Board. The Taft-Hartley Act moved unions even more solidly into alliance with the Democratic Party, which has consistently supported—though never implemented—changes to the law. Nearly every union in the nation has called for repeal of the Taft-Hartley, but it remains law. It is not solely responsible for the demise of organized labor in recent decades, but it has hurt labor's ability to defend itself, and current labor law remains tilted in favor of employers.

Suggested Readings: James Alteson, *Values and Assumptions in American Labor Law*, 1983; Melvin Dubofsky, *The State and Labor in Modern America*, 1994; Christopher Tomlins, *The State and the Unions*, 1986.

Andrew E. Kersten

Taylorism. Taylorism is a production system based on principles outlined by Frederick Winslow Taylor in 1911 and somtimes known as scientific management. Efficiency, defined as maximizing worker output, is the key to Taylorism. Taylor sought to break down all labor into a series of easy-to-learn tasks. He then used time-and-motion studies pioneered by Frank and Lillian Gilbreth to reorganize work tasks efficiently by eliminating needless motion. All work was designed by a planning department, which delegated the overseeing of worker efficiency to line supervisors. Taylor recommended separate supervisors for setup, line speed, quality, and repairs. Taylor recommended using motivational tools such as **incentive pay** and **piecework** to get workers to increase their output, but a major component of the system was the constant surveillance of the workforce.

Taylor's methods were so harsh and dehumanizing that most business leaders adopted modified versions. In 1933, sociologist Elton Mayo challenged Taylor's assumptions and redefined efficiency as a worker's social capacity. He developed methods today known as human relations, which focuses on benefit packages, group work, respect, and workplace culture. In some form or other, though, Taylorist central planning, time-and-motion studies, incentive pay, piecework, and worker surveillance became common features in American business firms. Most workers deeply resented Taylorism, especially when combined with assembly-line production **(Fordism)**. As Mayo predicted, workers found informal and formal ways to resist Taylorism, ranging from **stint** or **sabotage** to union organizing and **strikes**.

Suggested Readings: Frank Gilbreth and Lillian Gilbreth, *Cheaper by the Dozen*, 1949; Frank Gilbreth and Lillian Gilbreth, *Motion Study*, 1911; Elton Mayo, *The Human Problems of Industrial Civilization*, 1933; Frederick Winslow Taylor, *Scientific Management*, 1911.

Robert E. Weir

Team Act. *See Company Union.*

Textile Strikes (1934). *See Depression-Era Strikes.*

Textile Workers Union of America. *See Amalgamated Clothing Workers of America.*

Time and Motion. *See Taylorism.*

Tompkins Square Riot. The Tompkins Square Riot was an 1874 clash in New York City that signaled worsening relations between capital and labor. Some see it as a harbinger of the **Haymarket** Square riot that convulsed Chicago in 1886.

General insecurity and unemployment resulting from the depression of 1873 led to calls for direct governmental intervention and public-works programs to assist unemployed workers. Though this movement was widespread, efforts were largely uncoordinated. By late 1873, only New York City workers had managed to unite many of their various factions. On January 1, 1874, several thousand workers, including **socialists**, trade unionists, and antimonopolists, founded the Committee of Safety to pressure the city government to provide unemployment relief. All efforts to meet with authorities were rebuffed, and the city press furiously denounced the committee.

After the failure to schedule a meeting with officials, the Committee of Safety distributed a circular demanding that $100,000 be allotted to a Labor Relief Bureau comprised of committee members and city aldermen, and announced a January 13 meeting in Tompkins Square to show the strength of the movement. Meanwhile, a rival organization headed by bricklayer Patrick Dunn denounced the committee and its leaders as **communists** and tried to organize a march to City Hall on January 5. Dunn was almost universally discredited, but some workers did turn up on January 5. They were greeted by two committee leaders, **Peter James McGuire** and Theodore Banks, who led the march to City Hall. Mayor William Havemeyer was absent, and the committee had an unfruitful meeting with the Board of Aldermen.

Meanwhile, impatience on the part of the workers for action caused Banks to reschedule the next meeting for January 8. On that date, approximately 1,000 workers met in Union Square, but another proposed march to City Hall was cancelled, and participants marched instead to Tompkins Square, where McGuire and about 200 others were waiting. McGuire asked the assembled to join together in ward organizations set up by the committee and to meet again on January 13. McGuire also called upon the city government to halt the evictions of unemployed tenants and to deliver public aid to them. He also affirmed the willingness of the ward organizations to distribute food to the needy.

But while the participants were satisfied, the city government was alarmed. At the January 5 meeting, more than 150 police officers stood outside City Hall, and several hundred others entered Union Square after the crowd's departure for Tompkins Square. On January 8, the press reported that several thousand cases of ammunition had arrived at the armory on 35th Street, and the mayor and police commissioner held a meeting to decide on tactics for the upcoming demonstration. The committee was granted a permit to meet in Tompkins Square, but the police refused its request to march to City Hall. Police officers were instructed to arrest anyone who encouraged workers to leave their posts to take part in the demonstration. McGuire protested these restrictions and pled the case of suffering immigrant workers, only to be chided by Police Commissioner Oliver Gardner that he should confine his concerns to American citizens. When told that the police would arrest anyone nearing

City Hall, McGuire pointed out that no city statute gave the police such power. Gardner told him pointedly that it didn't matter; protestors would be arrested anyway. Appeals to Mayor Havemeyer were ignored.

While having difficulties with city officials, the committee's tenuous hold over its factions began to unravel. The committee president George Blair resigned; the New York City local of the Iron Molder's International Union denounced the committee as communists, internationalists, and **anarchists**; and Patrick Dunn and a group of his supporters appeared before the police board and warned of the committee's communistic character. The latter charge was based on the involvement of the American Section of the International Workingmen's Association (IWA).

On the morning of January 13, plans for the demonstration were unclear. At first, the mayor was scheduled to speak, then rumors circulated that the parade permit had been revoked. The permit had, in fact, been revoked, but word did not reach most of those who turned out. Though the temperature was well below freezing, between four and six thousand people gathered in Tompkins Square that morning; most were immigrants, and many were women and children. Among the crowd were about 1,200 members of the German Tenth Ward Workingmen's Association, and among the participants were future **American Federation of Labor (AFL)** dignitaries **Samuel Gompers** and **Adolph Strasser**, as well as Lucian Sanial, later prominent in the Socialist Labor Party.

At the office of the police board, meanwhile, the First Mounted Squad of the city police department awaited instructions, along with the rest of the 1,600 members of the police force who had been mobilized en masse that morning. Because of IWA's involvement and the intent of radicals to speak, superiors were given orders to suppress all meetings held during the day. Several dozen officers were stationed at public buildings throughout the city; others were posted outside of Tompkins Square, prepared to arrest anyone who showed seditious intent. Later that morning the *New York Graphic* published its daily issue with the headline "A Riot Is Now in Progress in Tompkins Square."

Around 11 A.M., the First Mounted Squad was ordered to fall in behind a group of the committee members who were marching toward Tompkins Square. By then, about 7,000 people were crowded into the square. Police Commissioner Abram Duryee and several policemen with nightsticks walked into the center of the crowd and ordered them to go home. The police officers immediately began clubbing bystanders, and the crowd began to scatter. In the corner of the square, however, the German Tenth Ward Workingmen's Organization refused to move. One German, Joseph Hoefflicher, hit an officer with a cane. An officer who then attacked Hoefflicher was hit with a hammer by another German, Christian Mayer. Just then, a group of mounted police entered the square and chased away the remaining protesters.

After Tompkins Square was sealed, more mounted policemen chased the fleeing crowds down the city streets, clubbing and beating them in what Samuel Gompers later called "an orgy of brutality." According to Gompers, for the next several hours squads of policemen attacked any group of poorly dressed persons standing or moving together. Those who gathered outside of the Fifth Street Police Station and protested the forty-six arrests made that day were also beaten. In other parts of the city, wild rumors circulated about immigrant plots to steal diamonds to trade for weapons, or of Hungarian workers planning to burn a schoolhouse. Most of the protesters arrested that day were foreign-born; most were charged with disorderly conduct, and a young German socialist named Justus Schwab was charged with inciting a riot and waving a red flag. None of those arrested could afford bail, and all remained in jail pending their arraignments.

City officials and most local newspapers defended the actions of the police, as did Mayor Havemeyer and Police Commissioner Duryea. *Harper's Weekly* evoked the specter of the Paris Commune and reminded its readers that such ways were "alien to American thought and methods." *The Philadelphia Inquirer* advised police to deal similarly with future demonstrations, even advocating lethal force to suppress such activities. Only a handful of newspapers were even mildly critical of the police; they included the *New York Sun*, the *New York Graphic*, and the *Cincinnati Enquirer*.

The protest coalition fell apart after the riot. The Committee of Public Safety reorganized as the Industrial Political Party, and several other parties were formed, but all were short-lived. Some in the labor movement saw Tompkins Square as an indication that democratic political institutions could no longer contain their demands. Many were radicalized by the experience, among them *New York Sun* editor **John Swinton**, who ran for public office on a labor ticket in 1874, and later started his own labor newspaper; and P. J. McGuire, who with Adolph Strasser, organized the Social Democratic Workingmen's Party later in 1874. Samuel Gompers, however, came to the conclusion that organized labor's association with radicalism was injurious to the movement and began to repudiate the socialism of his youth. Eventually, Strasser also adopted that position.

The police board created a special detective bureau to spy on socialist and trade-union meetings. The two German workers charged with assault on police, Joseph Hoefflicher and Christian Mayer, were both sentenced to several months in prison. On January 30, 1874, a large meeting in support of free speech and against police brutality was held at the Cooper Institute. A large and diverse coalition of groups and individuals, especially Germans, supported the right of workers to petition for public aid. Their call came to naught, as did efforts to punish or dismiss the police board. Another meeting was held in Tompkins Square on August 31: it secured the pardon of Christian Mayer. The meeting was peaceful, though it attracted little attention. One exception was in Chicago, where newspapers began warning authorities of the possibility of similar incidents in their city. The *Chicago Tribune* encouraged the wealthy in the city to fund and support a local militia to deal with agitators. In October, Cyrus McCormick became an honorary member of the First Regiment of the

Illinois National Guard. Chicago was therefore on its way toward mobilizing its police forces well before the 1886 **Haymarket** incident.

Tompkins Square heralded a more confrontational phase in capital/labor relations. Violence erupted in the coalfields of northeast Pennsylvania, where the **Molly Maguires** were rumored to be responsible and, in 1877, the traumatic railroad strikes associated with the **Great Labor Uprising** led to the loss of many lives and millions of dollars in property damage. An unfortunate legacy of Tompkins Square and ensuing clashes is that U.S. labor history has been stained by violence.

Suggested Readings: Iver Bernstein, *The New York City Draft Riots: Their Significance for American Society and Politics in the Age of the Civil War,* 1990; Samuel Gompers, *Seventy Years of Life and Labor: An Autobiography,* 1925; Herbert Gutman, "The Tompkins Square Riot in New York City on January 13, 1874: A Re-examination of Its Causes and Its Aftermath," *Labor History* 6, no. 1 (Winter 1965): 44–70.

Jeff McFadden

Trade Union Unity League. The Trade Union Unity League (TUUL) was the labor federation of the **Communist** Party-USA (CP); it was initiated in 1929 and officially dissolved in 1935. The Trade Union Unity League was an outgrowth of the Trade Union Educational League (TUEL), which had been started by **William Zebulon Foster** in 1920 and supported by the CP since 1922.

The TUEL's objectives were to work within the existing **American Federation of Labor (AFL) craft unions**, advocating for **industrial unionism** and organizing the most militant workers into the TUEL. However, the TUEL was largely unsuccessful. By 1928 a campaign to expel communists from the AFL and a string of TUEL failures coincided with a change in the perspective of the Communist International (Comintern): the capitalist economies were held to be entering a third period in which stability was threatened and revolution was on the agenda. CP-affiliated labor groups such as the TUEL were instructed to organize workers into revolutionary unions. This policy of **dual unionism**—setting up organizations in competition with existing unions—directly contradicted the official TUEL strategy of "boring from within," but actually reflected its more recent practice. (For example, the TUEL set up the National Miners Union [NMU] and the National Textile Workers Union [NTWU] in 1928 after being expelled from AFL unions.)

After its formal creation in 1929, the TUUL organized dozens of dual unions along with new unions in industries untouched by the AFL. Together, these industries included mining, textiles, steel and metal, auto, the needle trades, shoe and leather, tobacco, lumber, cannery and agricultural, packinghouse, machine tool and foundry, food, marine transport, furniture, and lumber. In addition, the TUUL organized in specific locales, such as pharmacies and dried goods in New York City.

Industrial unionism, **direct action, rank-and-file** independence, and the centrality of interracial solidarity characterized the TUUL unions. The slogan of the organization was "Class against Class," and it was overtly and unapologetically a part of the Communist Party. However, class-war rhetoric and pro-Soviet propaganda for the most part took a back seat to the demands for union recognition, better wages, and better conditions, which dominated most TUUL organizing work. The organizers were admirably audacious or disastrously foolhardy, depending on whom you ask; hardworking or fanatical, their ideological commitment certainly helped to provide the courage and perseverance necessary for organizing when and where they did. Sometimes, TUUL unions would plan **strikes**, but more often, the TUUL provided leadership during spontaneous workplace actions.

Nearly all of the TUUL battles followed identical trajectories: committed political and organizational work, direct action, violence from various authorities, and defeat. The first TUUL union to gain substantial recognition was the NTWU, in a tragic and bloody battle at the Loray Mill in **Gastonia**, North Carolina, in 1929. The NMU led a series of similarly failed strikes in Pennsylvania, Ohio, West Virginia, and, most famously, in Harlan County, Kentucky, where the struggles were immortalized in the **Florence Reece** song "Which Side are You On?" From 1930 through 1934, TUUL activities in the south and west among farmworkers resulted in multiracial unions like the Share Croppers Union and the Cannery and Agricultural Workers Industrial Union. They fought against evictions and for government relief. TUUL also led strikes, some of which eventually met with some success. The Marine Workers Industrial Union was one of the strongest in the TUUL, and its waterfront actions helped transform hiring practices in the industry on the East Coast.

Alongside trade-union work, the TUUL participated in much of the CP organizing among the unemployed. By early 1930, under TUUL auspices, the Communist Party began to create a network of unemployed councils, which fought for public work, government relief, unemployment insurance, and mortgage moratoriums, and against evictions in communities around the country. In 1930, the TUUL helped mobilize the March 6 Hunger March, simultaneous nationwide demonstrations that brought out close to one million jobless into the streets of most major cities. In 1932, the local TUUL led the Ford Hunger March from Detroit to the Ford River Rouge plant in Dearborn, Michigan. Autoworkers and their families presented Ford with a series of demands at the gate and, as fights with security and local police broke out, police began to fire into the crowd. The march became known as the Ford Massacre after four marchers were killed and twenty-three others shot.

By 1933, in spite of extraordinary levels of activity, the TUUL had little concrete to show for its efforts, and its membership consisted, in the main, of unemployed and blacklisted workers. The staggering number of unemployed, the despair and fear felt by many, and the extreme reaction against unions by employers accounted for most of this failure. The propagandizing of the red unionists during the third period surely contributed as well: Their revolutionary ideology isolated them from many workers, and gave employers and local authorities greater impetus and leverage for retaliation. Additionally, the TUUL's principled insistence on racial equality in its campaigns and organizations generated intense hostility in the South in particular, and was used as a divisive tactic by employers to break **solidarity**. However, the radicalism of the TUUL also stood it in good stead with those workers who were drawing radical conclusions in light of the country's depression, while, for many others, the TUUL's willingness to fight overrode political questions they might have about the organization. In the end, accurately assessing the extent to which the TUUL's politics stood in its way is difficult: Organizing attempts by the AFL in textiles, mining, and other industries proved just as unsuccessful during the early depression era.

The events of 1933–34 tested the TUUL's dual unionism even further. With a partial economic recovery and the passage of the National Recovery Act, thousands of workers were now streaming into unions, and the AFL and other traditional unions gained the vast number of new recruits. Although its membership stood at an impressive 100,000, the traditional unions dwarfed the TUUL; in response, it began disbanding its unions to join with AFL or other independents in their industries. The end of the TUUL corresponded with another change in the CP line toward a united, or Popular Front, with reformists against fascism. In this sense, the TUUL could be interpreted as a mistaken revolutionary experiment that was ultimately rejected by its own initiators.

Viewed in another light, however, the TUUL's legacy of militant, industrial, antiracist organizing laid important groundwork for the industrial unionism of the mid-1930s. Thousands of organizers and workers who cut their teeth in the TUUL played crucial roles in building the **Congress of Industrial Organizations (CIO)** and its member unions. Beyond the skills of its organizers, much of the organizing in the mid-1930s owed a great deal, tactically and at times politically, to the TUUL. Finally, unions from the TUUL were themselves, alone or in combination with others, the nuclei of later CIO affiliates: The **United Auto Workers (UAW)**, New York City's Transport Workers Union, the **United Electrical, Radio, and Machine Workers of America (UE)**, and the International Longshoremen's and Warehousemen's Union were among the more important unions formed with TUUL influence. Finally, the influx of communists and communist supporters from the TUUL into the traditional unions set the stage for the reaction to their presence, which itself had profound effects on the overall shape of the U.S. labor movement.

Suggested Readings: Michael E. Brown, et al., eds., *New Studies in the Politics and Culture of U.S. Communism,* 1993 (cf., Roger Keeran, "The Communist Influence on American Labor"); Irving Howe and Lewis Coser, *The American Communist Party, a Critical History,* 1957; Fraser M. Ottanelli, *The Communist Party of the United States: From the Depression to World War II,* 1991.

Penny Lewis

Trautmann, William Ernest (1869–?). William Ernest Trautmann was a radical unionist and cofounder of the **Industrial Workers of the World (IWW)**. He was born in New Zealand to German American parents and was raised in Germany and Poland, where he served an **apprenticeship** in the brewing industry. Trautmann moved to Germany after he became a master brewer, but was eventually expelled for agitation on behalf of child bottling-shop workers and exploited brewery workers. He immigrated to the United States in the 1890s, settled in Ohio, and became an organizer for the United **Brewery Workers** Union (UBW), an early **industrial union**. In 1900, he became editor of the UBW newspaper, *Brauer-Zeitung*, and used its pages to criticize the exclusionary policies of the **American Federation of Labor (AFL)**, whose **craft union** perspective sacrificed the welfare of workers who were female, African American, and unskilled.

When the UBW moved closer to the AFL, Trautmann gravitated toward the militant Western Federation of Miners (WFM). In 1905, Trautmann quit the UBW and joined forces with WFM and Socialist Labor Party leader **Daniel DeLeon** to form the Industrial Workers of the World (IWW). At a 1908 convention, IWW members were split over their tactics. Trautmann supported the **direct action** tactics espoused by former WFM colleague Vincent St. John over the electoral strategy advanced by DeLeon. DeLeon's faction quit the organization and formed a rival IWW based in Detroit.

Between 1909 and 1912, Trautmann was an IWW organizer, and he participated in several **strikes**. The 1909 Pressed Steel Car strike at **McKee's Rock**, Pennsylvania, led to a gun battle in which a dozen workers died, but it resulted in a partial victory for workers, one of the few in the steel industry until the 1930s. Trautmann was also an organizer and bookkeeper in the famed 1912 Bread and Roses strike in **Lawrence**, Massachusetts. When $20,000 turned up missing, Trautmann blamed St. John and other IWW leaders for misusing funds.

Trautmann resigned because of the fund debacle and, in 1913, joined DeLeon's Detroit IWW. He was an outspoken critic of U.S. involvement in World War I and penned the pamphlet *War Against War*. In 1915 and 1916, he worked as a carpenter in Universal City, California, where he constructed sets. He also appeared as an American Indian extra in a film, and he claimed to have written several scripts that were used by studio executives. He also worked on the Los Angeles-Owens Valley aqueduct, but was fired for trying to unionize workers.

In 1919, Trautmann moved to Chicago and became a factory worker. He became disillusioned with unions, but helped workers organize informal workshop councils. In the 1920s, he participated in a strike by sugar-beet workers in Colorado. He wrote two books, *Riot*, a novel based on the Pressed Steel Car strike, and *America's Dilemma*, a book critical of labor unions. In the 1930s he moved back to California where he worked on a New Deal highway project and finished his autobiography, *Fifty Years: The Rise and Fall of the Industrial Workers of the World*. He was known to have lived until 1939, but the date and place of his death are unknown.

Suggested Readings: Melvyn Dubofsky, *We Shall Be All*, 1969; Patrick Renshaw, *The Wobblies*, 1968.

Jay Miller

Travel Card. *See Permit Cards.*

Tresca, Carlo (March 9, 1879–January 11, 1943). Carlo Tresca was a radical, an organizer for the **Industrial Workers of the World (IWW)**, and a crusader against fascism. He was born in Sulmona, Italy, the sixth child of Filippo and Filomena Tresca. He finished secondary school and harbored ambitions of becoming a lawyer, though his mother wanted him to become a priest. His family fell into debt in the 1890s, lost their land, and Tresca embraced free thought and **socialism**. He joined the Italian Railroad Workers Federation, and in 1900, he became a branch secretary and editor of their newspaper. Tresca organized peasant workers, was arrested several times, and faced a libel charge that spurred him to immigrate to the United States in 1904 where he settled in Philadelphia. He married Helga Guerra shortly before fleeing Italy. She joined Tresca in 1905 and the couple had a daughter, but their marriage quickly failed. In 1908, Carlo was indicted for assault, rape, and adultery for a liaison with a fifteen-year-old girl; he served nine months in jail for adultery.

From 1904 to 1906, Tresca edited *Il Proletario,* the official journal of the Italian Socialist Federation of North America, then began his own paper. He edited three short-lived Italian-language radical papers between 1906 and 1917. Tresca immersed himself in the struggles of Italian immigrant workers, especially miners and mill workers in Pennsylvania. His editorials in *La Plebe* engendered opposition from the Catholic Church, as well as capitalists, government officials, and the Italian consulate. His exposés of the "Black Hand" Mafiosi figures he alleged had ties to the church and right-wing political movements also gained him enemies.

Nonetheless, Tresca embodied a strong radical tradition among Italian immigrant workers, many of whom joined socialist and anarchist movements. Over time, Tresca converted to **anarchism**, though socialism was so strong among Italian workers that Tresca easily deflected charges of anarchism by claiming to be a socialist. Tresca was not an ideologue, though opposition to **capitalism** and authoritarianism of any sort remained constants in his speeches and writing. His popularity was such that the IWW invited him to speak during the 1912 **Lawrence textile strike**, and his powerful oratory helped maintain solidarity among Italian workers that was threatened when officials arrested Joseph Ettor and Arturo Giovanniti. He met **Elizabeth Gurley Flynn** at Lawrence, and the two became lovers shortly thereafter.

Tresca took part in several IWW job actions, including the **Paterson silk strike** in 1913, and a miners' strike in the Mesabi Range in Minnesota in 1916. During the latter strike, Tresca was charged with murder and was almost lynched. Tresca was freed from the trumped-up charge in a complicated plea bargain in which some IWW members agreed to plead guilty to other charges. IWW secretary **William Dudley Haywood** lashed out against the agreement, and Tresca soon quit the IWW. He, like many IWW members, was arrested in 1917, but he moved to have his case tried separately and charges were dropped, although he was under surveillance for much of the rest of his life.

For most of the 1920s and 1930s, Tresca was an independent voice in defense of freedom and worker rights. He raised money and public support on behalf of **Nicola Sacco and Bartolomeo Vanzetti**, two Italian anarchists accused of bank robbery and murder in 1920. He also worked hard on their appeal efforts, although the two were executed in 1927. Tresca was embroiled in numerous free-speech fights, several of which elicited support from the American Civil Liberties Union. In 1922, fascists under Benito Mussolini took control in Italy. Mussolini's government pressured the United States to silence Tresca and his latest publishing venture, *Il Martello*. In 1925, Tresca was arrested and jailed for obscenity, because *Il Martello* ran an advertisement for birth control. He was sentenced to a year in jail, but served only four months before President Calvin Coolidge yielded to public outrage and commuted his sentence. Tresca redoubled his editorial attacks on fascism and many observers claim his efforts did much to sour Italian Americans on Mussolini. He was active in the antifascist Mazzini Society. Tresca originally supported the Bolshevik Revolution in Russia, but he reluctantly attacked Josef Stalin when he concluded that Stalin was as authoritarian as Mussolini. The expulsion of Leon Trotsky from the Communist Party in 1927 and the Spanish Civil War in the 1930s deepened Tresca's anarchism and his hatred for all forms of fascism. Tresca took part in the Italian American Victory Council in the early 1940s and zealously weeded out those he felt were fascists, mafiosi, or communists.

Tresca was gunned down in New York City on January 11, 1943, and his murder has never been solved. Assassination theories range from the possible to the fanciful, with the motives of everyone from communists to the Catholic Church being suspect. Most historians point the finger at future Mafia boss Vito Genovese who, in 1943, was a lieutenant in the Luciano crime syndicate and was perhaps acting on behalf of pro-Mussoloni forces. Recent evidence bolsters this theory, but the controversial Tresca never lacked enemies.

Tresca holds significance for the labor movement on several levels. He was an important radical voice in the immigrant community, a group often spurned by more conservative union leaders as unorganizable. Tresca's efforts at Lawrence and elsewhere proved the unsoundness of that assertion. He is also an important example of an independent drive for workers' rights that takes place outside the formal structure of unions. Finally, he illustrates the way in which labor rights are linked to broader questions of freedom and social justice.

Suggested Readings: Dorothy Gallagher, *All the Right Enemies*, 1988; Nunzio Pernicone, "Tresca, Carlo," in *Encyclopedia of the American Left*, eds., Paul Buhle, et al., 1992.

Robert E. Weir

Triangle Factory Fire of 1911. The Triangle Factory Fire of 1911 was one of America's most infamous industrial accidents. For many, it symbolized rapacious unbridled **capitalism** at its worst, and the tragedy became a rallying cry for reformers and labor activists. The official cause of the fire remains unknown. It began on the eighth floor of New York City's Asch Building near the close of business on Saturday, March 25, 1911. (The exact time of the fire is in dispute as factory owners commonly set back the clocks to extract a longer workday from employees.) The fire started as workers collected their paychecks and belongings to go home for the weekend.

Initially, the fire was small but it quickly raged out of control as flames engulfed the shirtwaist fabric. As the workers, largely young women, fled the fire, panic ensued when they found doors locked, an elevator out of order, and the windows blocked. When the fire department arrived, its ladders only reached to the seventh floor. By then, floors eight through ten were engulfed in flame. As the fire spread and the workers grew increasingly desperate, some chose to jump from the windows. Firefighters tried to save the workers by holding nets to brace their falls, but the plummeting bodies tore through their nets. The result was macabre, with corpses piling as women jumped to imminent death. At the end, 146 workers had died in the blaze. Many of those who remained inside were burned beyond recognition and remained in the city morgue for days before family members could retrieve their loved ones.

The New York Times reported that the Asch Building was fireproof, but the building did not meet safety codes. Doors opened inward instead of outward, and the doors were bolted during working hours to ensure workers would be unable to take breaks. Additionally, there were only two narrow staircases in the building. Manslaughter charges were brought against Triangle Factory owners Max Blanck and Issac Harris, both of whom escaped the building unharmed. They were acquitted on December 27, 1911. On March 11, 1913, Harris and Blanck settled, agreeing to pay seventy-five dollars for each life lost.

The 1911 fire culminated a series of labor disasters associated with the Triangle Factory. A spontaneous walkout in 1909 failed to address worker concerns and both the **Women's Trade**

Firefighters try to put out the catastrophic 1911 fire at the Triangle Shirtwaist Factory Building which killed 146 workers as a result of locked doors and missing fire escapes. © Underwood & Underwood/Corbis.

Union League (WTUL) and the **International Ladies' Garment Workers' Union (ILGWU)** failed in their numerous attempts to organize Triangle Factory workers. The company also remained relatively unaffected by the 1910

Uprising of the 20,000 (1909) in which New York City's immigrant female shirtwaist workers successfully struck for better working conditions, shorter hours, and wage increases.

After the blaze, ILGWU Local 25 organized relief services and proposed a day of mourning. Thousands of people poured into the streets for the memorial and public funerals. The ILGWU also organized a rally against unsafe working conditions at which **Rose Schneiderman** made a scathing speech about the inequities of working conditions.

The fire's graphic horror and senseless deaths attracted nationwide attention and outrage. Unions and reformers used the tragedy to advance their causes, and the fire became a symbol of the horrendous working conditions under which factory workers toiled. The WTUL fought for sweeping code regulations and building inspections. Although reforms were not as sweeping as advocates desired, the fire did lead to a spate of state and local factory safety laws.

Suggested Readings: *New York Times*, (March 26, 1911); Leon Stein, *The Triangle Fire*, 1962; "The Triangle Five" http://ilr.cornell.edu/trianglefire/.

Cristina Prochilo

Trolley Wars. The Trolley Wars were a series of understudied **strikes** that bridged the Gilded Age and the Progressive Era and that illuminate late-nineteenth- and early-twentieth-century labor-management relations. Conflicts regularly erupted between horsecar and trolley companies and the drivers, motormen, and conductors who operated their vehicles in small cities and urban metropolises in this period. For almost forty years, streetcar workers and legions of their riders waged a relentless war to reform and politically control traction companies.

The earliest battles involved horsecar employees who, spontaneously or under the leadership of the **Knights of Labor (KOL)**, rocked the urban landscape beginning in the 1880s. Drivers and conductors usually triggered walkouts with demands for shorter workdays, higher **wages**, and union recognition. Surprisingly, the public joined in street demonstrations that often ended in mayhem, transportation paralysis, and mobilization of the local militia. Citizen hostility targeted the corporate influence of transit companies who did everything in their considerable power to obtain inexpensive, long-term charters to monopolize the streets of any given city. Owners resisted lower fares, refused to implement transfer tickets, and packed their vehicles like freight cars. Although the concerns of the public, especially the emerging middle class, differed from the demands of the car men, they made common cause to curtail the power of urban transportation firms whose machinations undermined the democratic process, especially in city councils and state legislatures.

As the urban, mass-transit industry switched from horsepower to electricity during the 1890s, the changeover to an accelerated system only aggravated earlier worker and patron complaints. Streetcars the size of steam locomotives could reach blistering speeds on suburban, private rights of way, which led to accidents and carnage rivaling that of the railroad system. Gone, too, were the amenities that a slower-paced world provided through horsepower and accommodating drivers and conductors. Employees chafed under the ruthless dictates of systemized routes, which eliminated time for layovers or passenger courtesy. The protests packaged together a host of these complaints, sometimes spawning clean-government campaigns in their wake. Several hundred strikes punctuated the quarter century before World War I.

In 1892, a new militant national union, the Amalgamated Association of Street Railway Employees, organized the industry's discontented workers. Combining the ugly threat of class warfare on the streets with a civilized offer to arbitrate any differences with hostile companies, the Amalgamated provided the organizational muscle to bring parity and progress to the workforce. The union displayed tremendous resiliency despite many dramatic losses. In some cities, the **strikes**—like those in St. Louis in 1900 and Philadelphia in 1909—resembled insurrections rather than industrial conflict. Eventually, efforts during the Progressive Era ushered in a system of nationally standardized wages and conditions. One of the nation's most unusual alliances between service workers and passengers held firm, especially when traction companies turned to **scabs** to replace admired motormen and conductors. The establishment of a **National War Labor Board** during World War I mediated disputes and solidified the union, which is now over a century old.

Suggested Reading: Scott Molloy, *Trolley Wars: Streetcar Workers on the Line*, 1996.

Scott Molloy

Trumka, Richard Louis (July 24, 1949–). Richard Louis Trumka is a union organizer and secretary-treasurer of the American Federation of Labor-Congress of Industrial Organizations (AFL-CIO). Trumka was born to Italian- and Polish-American parents in the coal-mining town of Nemacolin, Pennsylvania. He received an excellent education and obtained several degrees from Pennsylvania State University and Villanova University Law School. Upon graduation from Villanova, Trumka joined the legal staff of the **United Mine Workers of America (UMWA)**.

At the time, the UMWA was moribund, and Trumka quit his post and worked as a miner for five years. In 1981, he was elected as the southwest Pennsylvania representative on the international executive board of the UMWA. A year later, Trumka rode a tide of **rank-and-file** insurgency to the presidency of the UMWA. At age thirty-two, he became the youngest-ever president of a major union. Trumka set out to reestablish militant unionism at a time in which many other labor organizations were moving sharply rightward. He helped reverse a downward spiral in UMWA membership. By 1998, the union's 240,000 members represented about 42 percent of the nation's miners.

Trumka left the presidency of the UMWA when he became the youngest secretary-treasurer in the history of the AFL-CIO in 1995. He, along with president **John Joseph Sweeney** and Linda Chavez-Thompson, promised to reinvigorate the labor movement by focusing on organizing, independent politics, and coalition-building. Trumka is an unabashed liberal who rejects the **business unionism** of the post–World War II labor movement and calls upon labor to commit acts of civil disobedience when necessary. He served on President Clinton's Bipartisan Commission on the Deficit, where he argued vociferously against changes in the Social Security system. Trumka is also an outspoken opponent of the **North American Free Trade Agreement (NAFTA)** and of the World Trade Organization.

Suggested Readings: *The Columbia Encyclopedia*, 2000, s.v. "Trumka, Richard"; *Current Biography*, 1986 s.v. "Trumka, Richard."

Don Binkowski

Two-Tier Wage Structure. *See Concessions.*

U

Unfair Labor Practices. The term unfair labor practice stems from Section 8 of the **National Labor Relations Act (NLRA)**. The NLRA creates rights and obligations for unions, management, and employees in a workplace represented by a labor union. If either labor or management fails to perform its obligations, an unfair labor practice charge may be filed with the National Labor Relations Board. Such a charge may also be filed if either side interferes with the rights of the other party. Employees are empowered to file charges against either employers or representative unions.

The NLRA makes it illegal for management to threaten or retaliate against employees for seeking union representation or refuse to provide information necessary for the union to fulfill its representational responsibilities. At the same time, unions are not allowed to intimidate management, retaliate against other employees who do not join the union, or refuse to represent nonunion workers during contract talks. Each group is required to bargain with the other in good faith. If any party fails to do so, the NLRA is empowered to compel good-faith bargaining.

Historically, unions have filed the most unfair labor practice suits, often during organizing drives during which management oversteps its legal authority in seeking to dissuade workers from joining a union. Suits are also common during **contract** talks in which negotiations stall. More recently, some employers have used unfair labor practice charges as a prelude to **decertification** votes, or to sap union strength by bottlenecking them in the cumbersome and slow bureaucracies associated with legal challenges.

Suggested Readings: American Bar Association, *The Developing Labor Law,* 2001; Frank and Edna Elkouri, *How Arbitration Works,* 1997.

Cornelia McAndrew

Union Label.

The union label, or *bug* as it is known in printing trades, is a tag, imprint, or design attached to an article as evidence that it was produced by union labor. The invention of the union label is credited to the Carpenters' Eight-Hour League in San Francisco, which adopted a stamp in 1869 for labeling products produced by mills employing men working an eight-hour day (as opposed to ten). Six years later, in 1874, the cigar makers of San Francisco created a white labor label as part of an ongoing campaign against a cheaper (and greatly exploited) nonunionized Chinese labor force, which had come to dominate that industry in California. The Cigar Makers International Union quickly recognized the potential support that working-class consumers could provide in encouraging the production and sale of union products, especially as new technologies in cigar manufacturing began pushing out skilled (unionized) labor. The union adopted the first national union label in 1880. Other unions quickly followed suit in the next decade, including those representing typographers, garment workers, coopers, bakers, and iron molders.

The labels of unions affiliated with the American Federation of Labor in 1903. © George Meany Memorial Archives.

A Union Label Department, created by the **American Federation of Labor (AFL)** in 1909, worked vigorously to spread the label's use. **William Green**, president of the AFL in 1939, noted that the label's appearance on a product was "emblematic of a high standard of living, of tolerable conditions of employment, of those conditions surrounding working men and women, which makes for a higher and better standard of living." A modern "look for the union label" campaign was launched by the **International Ladies' Garment Workers' Union (ILGWU)** in 1975 to build consumer awareness about the products that Americans buy. The campaign is an effort that the Union Label and Services Department of the American Federation of Labor-Congress of Industrial Organizations (AFL-CIO) carries on today.

Suggested Readings: Ira B. Cross, *A History of the Labor Movement in California,* 1935; Tony Hyman, "'Look for the Union Label': A Guide to Union Labels for Collectors," *The Antique Trader Weekly* (11 March 1987): 68–72; Union Label Section of San Francisco, *1939 Union Label Catalogue-Directory,* 1939; Union Label and Service Trades Department, AFL-CIO.

Susan Sherwood

Union Local. In simplest terms, a union local is the smallest **bargaining unit** in the union process. It refers to those members of a particular union who are defined as a bargaining unit. The union local takes care of the day-to-day operations that concern workers the most. It negotiates **contracts**, oversees the **grievance** procedure, galvanizes members for political activity, collects and distributes **dues**, supervises **business agents**, and leads **strikes** and **boycotts**, should they become necessary.

A union's locals usually comprise workers within a single locale, although that's not always the case. Often, not even all members of a certain profession working in a single place belong to the same local. Procedures for defining a local are determined by each parent union. Union locals usually have their own bylaws, officers, and procedures. Locals then cooperate with one another in larger alliances, like district councils and national (or international) unions. Many of the latter send representatives to larger federations with which they are affiliated.

The **United Auto Workers (UAW)** typifies the above structure. Its 750,000 members are spread across more than a 1,000 union locals. Each elects a nine-member executive board to coordinate important member services. For example, Local 160 represents 1,600 General Motors (GM) employees in Warren, Michigan. The same city also sports Local 909, which represents GM workers at its Powertrain facility. Local 400 is an example of a union local that spans several locations, as it represents 5,500 Visteon and Ford workers in Chesterfield, Highland Park, and Utica, Michigan. All three locals belong to UAW District 1, which has its own executive board and officers; altogether, there are twelve UAW regions and subregions. These regions report to the international UAW, which is affiliated with the American Federation of Labor-Congress of Industrial Organizations (AFL-CIO).

Depending on the union, locals often operate with great autonomy. The term union local came into widespread use only after the founding of the AFL in 1886. Since earlier organizations such as the **Knights of Labor (KOL)** and the **Brotherhood of Locomotive Engineers (BLE)** were modeled, in part, on fraternal orders, the terms lodge and assembly were often preferred.

Suggested Reading: "Welcome to the UAW," http://www.uaw.org.

Robert E. Weir

Union of Needletrades, Industrial, and Textile Employees (UNITE). The Union of Needletrades, Industrial, and Textile Employees was founded in 1995, when the **International Ladies' Garment Workers' Union (ILGWU)** and the **Amalgamated Clothing and Textile Workers Union** voted to join forces as one union. It is the latest attempt to organize workers in the historically union-resistant textile and garment industries, though UNITE's reach extends beyond such firms. At its formation, UNITE represented more than 250,000 workers in the United States, Puerto Rico, and Canada. Since then, UNITE has led drives against **sweatshop** labor, expanded its representation to thousands of other workers, and has been a part of the growing student protest movement against exploitative labor conditions around the globe.

In 1996, in response to news reports of widespread sweatshop labor in the United States, Central America, and Asia, UNITE began a Stop Sweatshops campaign that seeks to bring together trade unions, students, consumers, civil-rights activists, and women's groups to publicly ban sweatshop labor within the United States and abroad. Innovative summer internships with UNITE increased student activism on campuses across the United States and led to the formation of a nationwide organization, the United Students Against Sweatshops, in 1998. A year later, in 1999, UNITE took part in the demonstrations against the World Trade Organization in Seattle and in several other U.S. cities. At the same time, UNITE has continued to organize workers, including 5,000 workers at the **Fieldcrest** Cannon textile mills in North Carolina who, in 2000, ratified a contract that included precedent-setting guarantees such as paid sick days, improved working conditions, and expanded retirement benefits. UNITE has also sought to expand its membership to industries other than the needle trades. Beginning in 1998, UNITE increased its representation among industrial laundry workers when it organized almost 3,000 National Linen workers in twenty-nine plants in southern United States. In 2001, the Laundry and Dry Cleaning International Union joined UNITE, bringing with it almost 40,000 union laundry workers, totaling 90 percent of all union laundry workers in the United States.

UNITE lobbied for a 2001 effort that saw passage of an antisweatshop law in New York City that makes illegal the use of tax dollars to purchase city employee uniforms made under sweatshop conditions. Additionally, UNITE continues its commitment to improved labor conditions around the world with its most recent campaign, Global Justice for Garment Workers. By 2001, UNITE claimed 300,000 active members from a variety of industries including textiles, laundries, auto parts, and in Xerox manufacturing plants across the United States, Canada, and Puerto Rico.

Suggested Reading: "UNITE," http://www.uniteunion.org.

Kathleen Banks Nutter

Union Shop. A union shop, also called a closed shop, is a situation in which a worker is required to join a union as a condition of employment. Unions involved in successful organizing drives have sought such provisions since the nineteenth century, and they proved especially attractive in extractive industries such as mining and timber. Under current law, several sections of the **National Labor Relations Act** allow such arrangements, though the act sets limits. Employees subject to union-shop clauses have at least thirty days to join the union. Furthermore, the union-shop clause can be invoked to secure a discharge only if the employee refuses to pay **dues**, or initiation fees, and only if the requirement is enforced on a uniform, nondiscriminatory basis. Finally, the union's authority to enter into a union-shop agreement can be discontinued by majority vote of employees in an election held pursuant to section 9(e) of the act.

Many critics see union-shop agreements as a violation of an individual's right to free association. Unions often counter that it is unfair to allow single individuals to reap the same benefits as dues-paying members in a union **collective bargaining** unit. Some union advocates also oppose closed shops on the grounds that they breed resentment and that coerced membership is counterproductive. In recent times, union shops are less popular than so-called agency shops in which those employees who opt not to join a union are compelled to pay a fee to the union that negotiates their **contract**.

Suggested Reading: American Bar Association, *The Developing Labor Law*, 2001.

Cornelia McAndrew

Union Steward. *See Shop Steward.*

United Auto Workers (UAW) Strike of 1945–46 (General Motors). After Victory in Japan Day (V-J Day), conversion from wartime to peacetime production went slowly, and more than 300,000 Michigan workers were unemployed. Within the UAW, there was a struggle for the future direction of the union and who would lead it. The most likely leader was **Walter Reuther**, but prominent UAW figures George Addes, R.J. Thomas, Richard Frankensteen, and Richard Leonard allied against Reuther, who warned against a reenactment of the post–World War I **open-shop** drive. *The New York Times* columnist James Reston observed that both labor and management seemed eager for a fight. From the summer of 1945 through the end of 1946, **strikes** were rife in the auto, steel, electrical equipment, meat-packing, longshore, and trucking industries. The most bitterly contested of the battles was the General Motors strike, which began in November 1945, and lasted for 113 days. Walter Reuther's controversial strategy was to demand both a 30 percent **wage** increase and a stipulation that GM hold the line on car price increases. Reuther argued that, in the past, carmakers had simultaneously conducted two sets of negotiations: one with workers for wages and working conditions, and the other in the marketplace with consumers who were seeking price increases to cover more than whatever **concessions** had been made to workers. Reuther argued that labor unions should use their clout to prevent manufacturers' price increases from paying their workers' wage increases with "the wooden nickels of inflation." To the complaint of GM that the UAW demands would prevent the corporation from making a fair profit, Reuther offered to accept less than 30 percent if GM would open its books to the union and show their entire cost and earnings record. GM charged that Reuther's demands would lead to a **socialistic** nation. A fact-finding board appointed by President Harry Truman recommended a 17.5 percent increase, which the board believed the company could easily afford. GM ignored the recommendations, and Truman declined to pursue the matter further. As it turned out, Reuther badly miscalculated the willingness and ability of GM to take a long strike. Under the wartime excess-profits tax, GM had earned what it was allowed for the year. In effect, the federal government would be making strike payments to the corporation. Industry settlements were reached with Ford and Chrysler, which offered approximately eighteen cents per hour. By the end of January, a single cent separated GM and the UAW, and workers' savings were exhausted. On March 13, 1946, GM agreed to eighteen and one-half cents, with additional provisions for plant-pay differentials, vacations, and **overtime**. Although Reuther failed to get the auto companies to open their books, the strike propelled Reuther to national attention with the assurance that he would be elected union president. Later critics viewed Reuther's settlement with GM as a missed opportunity for labor to co-manage the economy.

Suggested Readings: John Barnard, *Walter Reuther and the Rise of the Auto Workers,* 1983; Nelson Lichtenstein, *The Most Dangerous Man in Detroit: Walter Reuther and the Fate of American Labor,* 1995.

James P. Hanlan

United Brotherhood of Carpenters and Joiners (UBC). The United Brotherhood of Carpenters and Joiners (UBC) represents about 520,000 carpenters, millwrights, cabinetmakers, and assorted woodworkers in the United States and Canada. Like many modern unions, the UBC has also absorbed other groups not involved in woodcrafts, including the former **granite cutters** union.

The UBC was founded in 1881 in response to changes in the post–Civil War building trades industry. In Colonial and antebellum America, skilled carpenters and joiners enjoyed tremendous bargaining power. Woodworking trades replicated the medieval guild system with its hierarchy of **apprentice, journeymen**, and **master**. They established a book of prices that regulated the trade across North America. Most projects were small and the functions of contractor, master, and capitalist were often identical. Face-to-face negotiations made it easier for skilled artisans to resolve disputes. After the Civil War, however, technological changes, changes in building techniques, and the expansion of the American economy unraveled the already frayed customary arrangements between contractors and carpenters. Masters reappeared as independent contractors, whose incentive was to hold down labor costs, which was also the goal of the venture capitalists, stockholders, developers, and government officials that authorized and funded large-scale projects.

The UBC was largely the brainchild of **Peter J. McGuire**, a New York City carpenter who had witnessed such Gilded Age capital/labor clashes as the 1874 **Tomkins Square riot**, and railroad strikes associated with the **Great Labor Up-**

rising of 1877. McGuire was also a member of the **Knights of Labor (KOL)**. The UBC was founded in August 1881, with just over 2,000 members; McGuire served as union secretary, and Gabriel Edmonston was its first president. McGuire, though a **socialist**, became increasingly committed to **pure and simple unionism**. He and the UBC were instrumental in creating the **American Federation of Labor (AFL)** in 1886.

The UBC supported the **eight-hour movement**, and it took a key part in planning a **general strike** in support of eight hours on May 1, 1886. Although some UBC members won reduced hours, the 1886 strike was not a success, and it culminated in the **Haymarket bombing** in Chicago. In 1890, the UBC led another AFL-sanctioned general strike for the eight-hour day, and it bore better fruit; more than 23,000 carpenters won an eight-hour workday and another 32,000 were reduced to nine. By the early twentieth century, the eight-hour day was the norm for most carpenters.

UBC-AFL **craft unionism** conflicted with the principles of many within the KOL, and the UBC often found itself in **jurisdiction** disputes with the KOL. Relations between the two groups were tense after 1886, but many UBC members held dual membership in the KOL and AFL until the early 1890s. By 1903, the UBC contained 167,200 members, far more than the moribund KOL.

The first two decades of the twentieth century saw the UBC battle against the **open shop movement**. Employers in numerous major cities engaged in **lock-outs** against the UBC in attempts to reduce wages and hire non-union carpenters. For the most part, such efforts served only to increase UBC strength; in 1910, the union contained more than 200,000 members. In 1915, **William Hutcheson** took over as UBC president, and was successful in thwart-

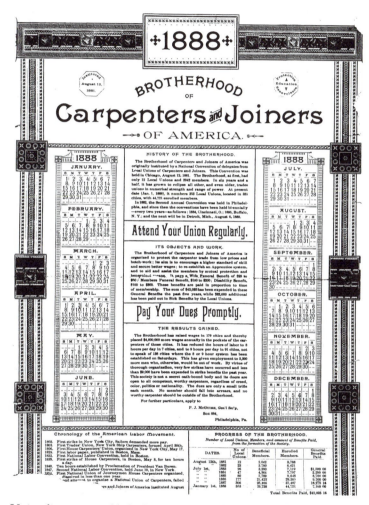

Union literature published by the United Brotherhood of Carpenters and Joiners (UBC) in 1888. © George Meany Memorial Archives.

ing the Wilson administration's back-door attempts at open shops during World War I. The 1920s were more difficult, however. Employers advocating the open shop, now under the guise of the **American Plan, locked out** UBC members in many cities. The UBC defeated open-shop plans in Chicago and San Francisco, which crippled the American Plan, but UBC membership fell in the 1920s. The union also faced internal challenges from **communists** attempting to assert control over UBC locals.

The Great Depression also proved difficult, with only about 30 percent of UBC members gainfully employed at any moment. Hutcheson grew increasingly conservative and launched bitter attacks against radicals and advocates of **industrial unionism**. At the 1935 AFL convention, Hutcheson called **John L. Lewis** a "bastard" for supporting industrial unionism, and Lewis bloodied him with a haymaker. Many historians credit the intransigence of conservative craft unionists like Hutcheson as hastening the formation of the **Congress of Industrial Organizations**. Even some UBC members complained that leaders were out of touch with **rank-and-file** concerns. UBC leaders historically embraced the AFL **voluntarism** principle with its built-in distrust of government intervention in capital/labor relations, but they reluctantly supported key New Deal programs and lobbied for unemployment compensation and **minimum-wage** programs.

The UBC enjoyed a resurgence during World War II, and Hutcheson's son, Maurice, served on the Wage Stabilization Board. Membership surged from 320,000 in 1940 to over 700,000 by 1945. The UBC lost a key battle in 1946, however, when the **Taft-Hartley Act** was passed over President Truman's veto. Section 14 (b) of that bill gave legal status to hated **right-to-work** provisos against which the UBC had long battled. Nonetheless, the UBC benefited from the building boom of the 1950s, and grew to 850,000 members by 1958. Critics continued to complain that the UBC was a **business union**, and cited its purchase of properties in New Jersey and Florida and its new Washington headquarters (opened in 1961) as examples of its inattention to the rank-and-file. In 1952, Maurice Hutcheson succeeded his father as UBC president, and some complained his style was autocratic.

Whether or not the critics were correct, the UBC took a big hit in the 1970s. Although the UBC was over 800,000 strong in 1973, the end of the construction boom during the recession that began in 1973 and lingered for a decade greatly reduced its ranks. Developers—spearheaded by groups like the Chamber of Commerce and the Business Roundtable—renewed efforts to hire nonunion carpenters. Business efforts were buoyed by conservative politicians, especially the antiunion administrations of Ronald Reagan (1981–89) and George H. Bush (1989–93). In 1969, approximately 80 percent of all carpenters were unionized; by 2000, the figured slipped to about 30 percent.

In the 1990s, the UBC renewed efforts to organize workers, and UBC President Doug McCarron (elected in 1995) reversed some of the policies the rank and file found distasteful. Recently, the UBC has fought campaigns to preserve

prevailing wage structures as established by the 1931 **Davis-Bacon Act**, a law conservatives seek to repeal.

Suggested Readings: Walter Galenson, *The United Brotherhood of Carpenters*, 1983; Richard Schneirov and Thomas Suhrbur, *United Brotherhood, Union Town: The History of the Carpenters' Union of Chicago, 1863–1987*, 1988; "UBC Union History," http://www.carpenters.org/history.

Robert E. Weir

United Electrical, Radio, and Machine Workers of America (UE). The United Electrical, Radio, and Machine Workers of America was founded in 1936 during the wave of **depression-era strikes**. It was once the third largest affiliate of the **Congress of Industrial Organizations (CIO)**, but was badly hurt by the anticommunist red scare that emerged after World War II. In a much reduced state, the UE still exists and is headquartered in Pittsburgh, Pennsylvania.

After a successful strike in 1933, Philadelphia Radio (Philco) locals were recognized by the **American Federation of Labor (AFL)** and granted a union charter. Jurisdictional disputes arose between established **craft unions** within the AFL and the newly federated **industrial unions** like that at Philco. When AFL leadership assigned Philco locals to the International Brotherhood of Electrical Workers (IBEW), they quit the AFL and joined forces with the newly formed electrical manufacturing locals from Lynn, Massachusetts, and Schenectady, New York, and created the United Electrical and Radio Workers of America (UERW). These unions affiliated with the CIO. In 1937, James Matles led the 15,000-member **International Association of Machinists** out of the AFL and into the UERW, with a resultant name change.

As early as 1933, union activists saw New Deal labor legislation as a golden opportunity to build industrial unions. Originating from individual local unions in Westinghouse, General Electric, Philco Radio, and other locations, union activists like **James Barron Carey**, Julius Emspak, Al Coulthard, and William Turnbull joined forces to fight union-recognition battles within the electrical and radio industries. The UE became known for its militant and democratic unionism. It began with about 30,000 members and ballooned to 720,000 by 1944.

The UE did not shy from using talented left-wing organizers, and from its inception, the UE battled charges that it was dominated by **communists**. It faced a constant barrage of attacks from anticommunist crusaders in federal and state government, business, and other labor unions. UE leadership split over the issue of communist influence. At the 1941 UE convention, Carey proposed banning fascists and communists from holding union office. Matles, Emspak, and Albert Fitzgerald, a popular member from Lynn, Massachusetts, united to defeat Carey's motion. The same coalition ousted Carey and installed Fitzgerald as the new UE president.

World War II (1941–45) brought boom years, and the UE's largest membership gains took place during the war. Challenges emerged after the war when the 1947 **Taft-Hartley Act** focused renewed attention on communist influences in organized labor and required leaders to sign anticommunist affidavits. When the UE refused to do so, it became vulnerable to raids from other unions. At the 1949 CIO convention, the UE pressed for a resolution forbidding further union **raiding** of the UE. When the convention refused the UE's request, it stopped paying CIO **dues** and was expelled. The 1949 convention also chartered a rival union, the **International Union of Electrical, Radio, and Machine Workers of America (IUE)**.

Raiding of UE locals continued through the 1950s and into the 1960s. In addition, the IUE operated in the same shops and factories as the UE, thus forcing repeated run-off elections. By the mid-1960s, the once dominant UE was reduced to a shadow of its former self. This proved disastrous for electrical workers. Where the UE had been the main institution representing electrical manufacturing workers, operatives were now represented by sixteen different unions. This made unified **collective bargaining** with conglomerates like General Electric and Westinghouse nearly impossible.

Battered and wounded by the internecine union battles, the UE began to rebuild in the late 1960s, only to suffer greater losses during the 1970s and 1980s due to **downsizing** and plant closings. The UE remains proud and defiant, however, and boasts a core of loyal members that has allowed it to survive into the twenty-first century. It touts its independence from the AFL-CIO and is viewed by some as a model of independent **rank-and-file** democratic unionism. The UE publishes its own monthly newspaper, maintains a vibrant Web site, and represents about 35,000 members. It has expanded its organizing focus to embrace workers as diverse as plastic injection molders, warehouse workers, custodians, and graduate teaching assistants.

Suggested Readings: Ronald Filippelli and M. D. McColloch, *Cold War in the Working Class: The Rise and Decline of the United Electrical Workers*, 1995; James Matles and J. Higgins, *Them and Us: Struggles of a Rank-and-File Union*, 1974; Ed Rosswurm, ed., *The CIO's Left-Led Unions*, 1992.

Mike Bonislawski

United Farm Workers of America (UFW). The United Farm Workers of America is the union that represents about 27,000 agricultural workers in the United States. It has locals across the United States and Canada, though the bulk of its membership is located in California and the Southwest. Members come from many ethnic backgrounds, but historically the UFW has been an important voice for Chicano workers. The UFW is affiliated with the American Federation of Labor-Congress of Industrial Organizations (AFL-CIO).

Despite the political rhetoric of modern-day xenophobes, the border between the United States and Mexico has long been a fluid boundary, and Chicanos a fixture of American society. In the 1820s, Americans moved into what was then Mexican territory in search of new farmlands to replace those worn out by cotton cultivation. Many settlers came despite prohibitions by the newly independent nation of Mexico. The desire of southern agriculturalists to bring slaves into sections of Mexico was among the issues that led to the Texan war for independence in 1836. The United States annexed Mexico in 1845, and border disputes precipitated the Mexican War in 1848. Under terms of the Treaty of Guadalupe Hidalgo, the United States seized about one-third of Mexico, including parts of the present-day states of Arizona, California, Colorado, Nevada, New Mexico, and Utah. Thousands of Mexicans found themselves American citizens overnight. The border proved equally porous during the 1870s and 1880s, with Mexican *vaqueros* providing much of the manpower for cattle drives.

United Farm Workers President Cesar Chavez talks to striking Salinas Valley farm workers during a large rally in Salinas, Calif., on March 7, 1979. © AP/Wide World Photos.

Chicanos, Central Americans, Caribs, and South Americans often sought employment opportunities in the United States. Cubans, for example, played an important role in the south Florida cigar trade by the early twentieth century, Filipino farm laborers entered after the 1898 Spanish-American War, Puerto Ricans began coming to the mainland in the 1920s, and large numbers of Mexicans sought employment in mining, railroading, and the auto industry between 1910 and 1930. The **Industrial Workers of the World (IWW)** had some success in organizing agricultural workers of various ethnic backgrounds in the 1910s.

Fewer Latinos came to the United States during the Great Depression (1929–41) and, in some cases, those who were not U.S. citizens were forcibly repatriated. The U.S. government encouraged new waves of Latino immigration during World War II. Growers complained of manpower shortages, and the government set up the *bracero* program to recruit Mexican agricultural workers, many of whom stayed in the United States irrespective of their temporary guest-worker status. In 1951, the tacit agreement between the United States and Mexico was formalized as Public Law 78, with a stipulation that guest workers could not replace domestic workers, a proviso seldom enforced. Contrary to popular belief, however, the majority of Latino farmworkers are American citizens, with many UFW members having deeper American roots than nativist critics.

Both *braceros* workers and American farmworkers faced appalling conditions. Agricultural labor was exempt from the 1935 **National Labor Relations Act (NLRA)**, leaving farmworkers to negotiate whatever deals they could. Only those in the *braceros* program were regulated to any degree, and even their wages hovered around $1.40 per hour in 1964, the year the program ended; others averaged about $.90 per hour. Moreover, sanitary conditions, health standards, educational opportunities, and housing were inferior to those of America's worst ghettos. Life expectancy for farmworkers was only forty-nine years.

The UFW came about after a series of small steps taken by other organizations. In 1958, **Dolores Huerta** sought AFL-CIO support for a group called the Agricultural Workers Association (AWA); one year later the AFL-CIO absorbed the AWA as part of the **Agricultural Workers Organizing Committee (AWOC)**. AWOC contained some Anglo and African American workers, but the bulk of its membership was Filipino and Chicano, with Huerta and Larry Itliong, a Filipino, providing much of AWOC's leadership. In 1962, **Cesar Chavez** and Huerta created the National Farm Workers Association (NFWA) to organize Chicano farm laborers in and around Delano, California. In 1965, the NWFA struck a California rose farm at the same time the AWOC struck California grape growers who were not complying with the end of the *braceros* program. Both **strikes** enjoyed some success, but neither resulted in a union **contract**.

The UFW was born out of a joint NWFA/AWOC strike against grape growers in the Delano/Bakersfield area of California's southern San Joaquin Valley. AWOC called the strike on September 8, 1965, and growers began to import Chicano **scabs**. On September 16, Chavez convinced the NWFA to join the largely Filipino strike. Within weeks, more than thirty farms found themselves unable to field a workforce. By most accounts, the event that made the strike and led to the founding of the UFW was Chavez's decision to launch a nationwide **grape boycott** of California table grapes. Inspired by the nonviolent tactics of Gandhi in India and civil rights leaders like Martin Luther King, Jr., in the United States, Chavez proved a capable and charismatic organizer. Grassroots mobilization spread awareness of the **boycott** across the nation, roving **pickets** tied up a 400-square-mile region, and organizers convinced numerous scabs to leave the fields. Chavez also led a 340-mile protest march from Delano to Sacramento in March, 1966, that gathered intense media attention for the farmworkers' cause.

The giant Schenley conglomerate buckled under the pressure and signed an agreement with the NFWA, the nation's first **collective bargaining** agreement between farmworkers and growers. Several weeks later, the DiGrigorio corporation agreed to hold union elections. That move, however, temporarily hurt the farmworkers' cause when the **International Brotherhood of Teamsters (IBT)** tried to organize farmworkers, touching off bouts of **raiding** and wholesale boycotting of the first election by NWFA members. A second election ordered by California governor Pat Brown resulted in NWFA victory.

Despite victory over Schenley and DiGrigorio, however, other growers remained intransigent. On August 22, 1966, the NWFA and the AWOC merged to form the Farm Workers Organizing Committee (FWOC), under the aegis and with the support of the AFL-CIO. The name was subsequently changed to the United Farm Workers of America (UFW); by 1970, most growers had settled with the UFW. Public opinion largely pressured the settlements, shaped in no small measure by Chavez's twenty-five-day water-only fast to publicize the cause. Contracts covered issues ranging from housing and access to clean drinking water to the handling of pesticides. The UFW also set up a credit union, a health clinic, Radio Campesina, and a union hiring hall. The UFW's stylized eagle became an instantly recognizable icon, and posters emblazoned with *Huelga! (Strike!)* and *Viva La Causa (Long Live Our Cause)* proved so popular that they became UFW slogans.

The UFW grew rapidly in the late 1960s, peaking at about 80,000 by 1970. Each campaign it undertook proved a bruising battle, however. Three picketers were killed in 1972; the UFW renewed its grape boycott; Chavez underwent a second fast; and the Teamsters continued to sign side agreements with growers that undermined UFW efforts. Particularly nasty was the fight to eliminate the short hoe, which took its toll on the backs and posture of workers; growers insisted long hoes damaged plant roots. One of the UFW's biggest victories came in 1975, when California passed the **Agricultural Labor Relations Act (ALRA)**, which extended legal collective bargaining rights to farmworkers and set up structures that parallel those under the NLRA.

UFW fortunes waned in the latter half of the 1970s and into the 1980s. The UFW called a lettuce boycott in 1979, but it failed to capture the same support as had the grape boycott, and many California growers simply refused to comply with the ALRA. Several more farmworkers died during strikes between 1979 and 1983. Studies revealed that farmworkers suffered higher cancer rates and miscarriages than the general public, problems linked to the handling of and exposure to toxic pesticides. The UFW achieved very little in negotiations with growers over pesticide use. In 1984, Chavez and the UFW called for a third worldwide boycott of all sprayed grapes. The boycott lingered until 2001, when the UFW called it off.

By the late-1980s, the UFW was in serious trouble. It lost more union elections than it won, and its official membership plunged to around 10,000; in truth, it was probably about half that. Chavez underwent a thirty-six-day "Wrath of Grapes" fast in 1988 to call attention to pesticide poisoning and the renewed grape boycott. Publicity, however, was perhaps as much due to the support of celebrities like Whoopi Goldberg, Martin Sheen, and Emilio Estevez as to the public's sympathy for the UFW. Some UFW supporters complained that Chavez was autocratic and that too many of the union's strategies revolved around appeals to charisma and public opinion.

But even critics were stunned by Chavez's premature death on April 23, 1993. He was succeeded by Arturo Rodriquez, his son-in-law through marriage to Linda Chavez. Rodriquez has, thus far, attempted to balance dramatic public actions with grassroots organizing. To mark the one-year anniversary of Chavez's death, Rodriquez and the UFW recreated the 1965 Delano to Sacramento march, an event in which 20,000 participated. The UFW has slowly rebuilt its membership base and, since 1994, has won nearly all representation elections. Contracts with Gallo Vineyards, strawberry workers at Coastal Berry, and several mushroom growers represent significant strides forward.

The UFW's future contains numerous challenges. Ending the grape boycott was due as much to public indifference as to tangible gains. To date, two of the five pesticides that sparked the 1984 grape boycott remain in use, and overall pesticide use is up. In 2002, the UFW launched a boycott against Pictsweet mushrooms and encouraged the public to pressure Pizza Hut, a major buyer, to cease its use of Pictsweet products. Taking on United Foods, which owns Pictsweet, has not been an easy struggle. Moreover, studies reveal that nearly half of all growers still flunk field sanitation standards.

Despite its waxing and waning fortunes, UFW achievements for an organization built on large numbers of **part-time** and **contingency** workers is impressive. In addition to winning union contracts, UFW farmworkers have a union pension plan, health benefits, **profit sharing**, and parental leave policies. Its biggest challenge will be to raise wages; in 1999, farmworkers still averaged less than $7,500 per year.

Suggested Readings: Susan Ferriss, Ricardo Sandoval, and Diana Hembree, *The Fight in the Fields: Cesar Chavez and the Farmworkers Movement*, 1998; Patrick Moore and Theo Majka, *Farmers' and Farm Worker Movements: Social Protest in American Agriculture*, 1994; "UFW History," http://www.ufw.org/ufw.htm.

Robert E. Weir

United Food and Commercial Workers Union (UFCW). The United Food and Commercial Workers Union is an international union that represents about 1.4 million workers, mostly in the United States and Canada. Its members are currently concentrated mostly in food retail, food processing, and meatpacking industries, though it also represents workers in a variety of professions including distillery and wine workers, health care workers, garment workers, and those employed in chemical and fertilizer processing plants. The UFCW bears watching, as it hopes to be a major force in organizing the fast food and retail industries, two varieties of service industry work that have grown rapidly since the 1960s, but which are largely nonunion. The UFCW was formed in 1979, when the Retail Clerks International Association and the **Amalgamated Meat Cutters and Butcher Workmen of North America (AMCBW)** merged.

The struggles of butchers and meatpackers are among the most dramatic and difficult ones in American labor history. The invention of refrigerated railcars led to a national meat industry that was dominated by corporate giants like Armour, Cudahy, Morrell, Swift, and Wilson. Both stockyards and meatpacking plants proved hard to organize. A traumatic strike loss in 1886 led by the **Knights of Labor (KOL)** in the Chicago stockyards retarded union efforts for a time, but the AMCBW formed in 1897 and obtained a charter from the

American Federation of Labor (AFL). It made modest gains, but more significant progress was made in the 1930s by the **United Packinghouse Workers of America (UPWA)**, which was affiliated with the **Congress of Industrial Organizations (CIO)**. The two unions ceased **raiding** each other's membership prior to the AFL-CIO merger in 1955, but maintained separate identities until 1968, when the UPWA joined the AMCBW. Many supermarket meat cutters and butchers are union members, though the packinghouses remain a challenge for unions, and membership has declined in recent years.

Retail clerks have been affiliated with the AFL since 1890. Retail has proved a union-resistant industry due to its historically high employee turnover rate, intransigent employers, seasonal employment cycles, and sexism. (Women often dominate the ranks of retail clerks and many unions have, in the past, not given their concerns attention equal to the concerns of male industrial workers.) From the outset, however, the UFCW has had a good record in matters of gender equality. More than half of its members are women, and many hold positions of authority within the UFCW. In 1987, UFCW President Lenore Miller became the first female union president to be elected to the AFL-CIO's executive council.

Much of the UFCW's success has been in organizing grocery and supermarket employees. In 1998, Wal-Mart—the world's largest corporation—entered the supermarket business. Its entry hastened a merger process already underway and placed cost pressures on Wal-Mart competitors. The UFCW has faced pressure to grant **concessions** to unionized supermarket chains. In 1999, it began a campaign to organize Wal-Mart, a virulently antiunion corporation. It has also launched campaigns against so-called big box stores like Home Depot, as well as McDonald's and other fast-food chains.

If the UFCW is successful in its efforts, it could emerge as one of the most important labor unions of the twenty-first century. Its opposition is formidable and commands enormous financial resources, but most UFCW targets are not likely to become **runaway shops**, a factor in its favor.

Suggested Readings: Barbara Ehrenreich, *Nickel and Dimed*, 2001; Eric Sclosser, *Fast Food Nation*, 2001; "UFCW: A Voice for Working America," http://www.ufcw.org.

Robert E. Weir

United Hatters, Cap, and Millinery Workers International Union. In 1934, the United Hatters of North America merged with the Cloth Hat, Cap, and Millinery Workers Union to form the United Hatters, Cap, and Millinery Workers International Union (UHCMWIU). From earliest times, men and women wore functional head coverings to protect themselves from sun, rain, cold, and the hazards of the environment. Early nomadic Asian tribes are believed to have discovered the use of felted sheep's wool for making tents and clothing. By the late fourteenth century, the hat began to be important as a source of fashion as well as practicality, and fancy materials such as silk, velvet, taffeta, leather, and felted beaver were used by hat makers, whose trade would always be subject to the notoriously fickle whims of fashion.

The hat-making trade was long known as a sick trade, largely due to the illnesses to which hatters were prone and the environmental hazards to which they were subjected. Mercury nitrate salt was used to prepare and soften fur and wool fibers in the felt-making process. This was regarded as a trade secret by the hat makers, who would inevitably suffer the effects of mercury poisoning, hence the phrase, mad as a hatter. For hundreds of years, hatters suffered from hatters' shakes, uncontrollable shaking of the hands of hat-industry workers. Hatters struggled to conceal the shakes from employers since the first sign of the shakes endangered continued employment in the trade. It was not until December 1, 1941, that the United States Public Health Service brought an end to the use of mercury by hat manufacturers as a result of individual negotiations with manufacturers in twenty-six states. Union president Max Zaritsky had convinced Surgeon General Thomas Parran to investigate mercury poisoning. The Health Service found that one in five workers in the hat industry suffered from the shakes. The Public Health Service, as well as the union, claimed credit for the elimination of the use of mercury. The efforts on both sides were doubtless boosted by the war-time shortage of mercury.

In addition to the battle to eliminate the workplace environmental health hazards of mercury, the UHCMWIU and its predecessors fought to eliminate prison labor, **sweatshops**, and crippling **jurisdictional** battles. Similarly, the hatters struggled to drive **racketeers** out of the industry and to fight charges of **communist** domination during years of red-baiting following both world wars. Among the most famous of the hat industry struggles was the fight over the use of the secondary boycott during the so-called Danbury Hatters Case (**Loewe v. Lawler**, 1908). The decision in that case was a major setback for all of organized labor but was particularly devastating for the hatters.

In the period immediately after World War II, the hatters were led by Zaritsky, who had been involved in hat unions since 1907. The UHCMWIU advocated labor-management cooperation to promote the hat, cap, and millinery industry in the face of a decline in the fashion of wearing hats by both men and women. In an effort to seek greater strength and form alliances with other unions in the garment and needletrades, UHCMWIU became part of the Amalgamated Clothing and Textile Workers Union (ACTWU) in 1983. In 1995, ACTWU merged with the **International Ladies' Garment Workers' Union (ILGWU)** to form **Union of Needletrades, Industrial and Textile Employees (UNITE)**.

Suggested Readings: Donald B. Robinson, *Spotlight on a Union: the Story of the United Hatters, Cap, and Millinery Workers International*, 1948; David Bensman, *The Practice of Solidarity: American Hat Finishers in the Nineteenth Century*, 1985.

Patricia Shackleton

James P. Hanlan

United Mine Workers of America (UMWA). The United Mine Workers of America has engaged in numerous bitter disputes with coal mine operators over wages, working conditions, and benefits for miners. It represents miners of various kinds, though its historic strength has been in anthracite and bituminous coal fields.

The miners' struggle is among the bloodiest and most bitter in American labor history. Mines were often located in remote areas and mine owners ran their operations as if they were personal fiefdoms. Workers often toiled in **company towns** and were subject to rigid rules that regulated both work and life off the job. Some workers were paid in scrip, and many mining camps were marked by squalor, backbreaking labor, and crushing poverty. The first effort to organize coal miners came in 1860. It and other efforts yielded only modest success. The first miner unions to have more than a regional presence were those affiliated with **Knights of Labor (KOL)** National Trade District 135 and the 1885 National Federation of Miners and Mine Workers, which affiliated with the newly formed **American Federation of Labor (AFL)** in 1886.

The UMWA was formed when the National Progressive Union of Miners and Mine Laborers merged with KOL District 135 in 1890. It affiliated with the AFL. The UMWA constitution forbade discrimination based on race, religion, or ethnicity. In 1898, the UMWA won an **eight-hour** day for most of its members. Dynamic leadership aided UMWA growth. **John Mitchell** was the UMWA president from 1898 to 1908. Although he was a conservative man, Mitchell was a good tactician. He was a member of the **National Civic Federation** and parlayed his contacts into bargaining advantage. In 1902, more than 150,000 miners struck in protest of low pay and

A 1902 certificate of membership in the United Mine Workers of America (UMWA). © George Meany Memorial Archives.

appalling safety records in the mines. Mitchell offered to submit **grievances** to binding **arbitration**, and when operators refused, President Theodore Roosevelt intervened on behalf of the miners. This event is widely heralded as the beginning of a change in government attitudes toward organized labor.

Many UMWA campaigns were contentious. Hard-rock miners in the west faced especially difficult conditions, with nearly constant **strikes** involving the UMWA and the Western Federation of Miners from the 1890s through 1914. Many lives were lost in pitched battles that led to such notorious episodes as the 1897 **Lattimer massacre** and the **Ludlow massacre** of 1914. The UMWA agreed to a **no-strike pledge** during World War I and grew to over 500,000 members during this period of industrial peace. Strikes broke out anew after the war, spurring the government to create the Bituminous Coal Commission in 1920 that gave miners large raises and recognized the UMWA as the miners' **bargaining unit**. This did little to prevent horrendous violence in Kentucky and West Virginia, including the infamous 1920 shootout between miners and Baldwin-Felts agents in **Matewan**, West Virginia. Its aftermath led to the **Battle of Blair Mountain** in which more than two dozen lives were lost. In all, some 10,000 miners battled police, company forces, and the government for over a year, until miners were forced to capitulate. The same sort of conflict lived on in Kentucky, where violence was so pronounced that one county was dubbed "bloody Harlan" in 1932.

In 1920, **John Llewellyn Lewis** became UMWA president. Under his tutelage, UMWA members secured retirement **pensions** and higher pay. Lewis grew increasingly restless with the AFL's slowness to recognize the need for **industrial unions** and its parsimony in funding organizing efforts. He was the leading spirit behind the establishment of the Committee for Industrial Organization, that later became the **Congress of Industrial Organizations (CIO)**. Although a formal break did not come until 1937, the UMWA was effectively out of the AFL in 1935. Lewis rose in national prominence becoming the first CIO president and riding a tide of worker militancy to win wage and benefit **concessions** for UMWA members. Lewis supported Franklin Roosevelt in 1932 and 1936, but opposed him in 1940 and resigned as CIO president when Roosevelt was reelected. In 1941, Lewis demanded and won a closed-shop agreement in captive mines owned by steel firms. In 1942, Lewis abruptly pulled the UMWA out of the CIO and, unlike most other unions, the UMWA refused to take a no-strike pledge during World War II. Lewis was twice cited for contempt of court during the **coal miners' strike of 1943**. Some historians believe that UMWA actions during the war fueled postwar antilabor legislation.

The UMWA rejoined the AFL in 1946, then quit in 1947 when Lewis refused to commit the UMWA to noncommunist affidavits required under the **Taft-Hartley Act**. The UMWA also defied the act through a series of short strikes, **memorial strikes**, and other tactics designed to test its limitations. From 1947 through 1950, the UMWA interrupted national coal supplies on numerous occasions, with President Harry Truman issuing an injunction against new strikes in 1950, whilst Congress debated seizing coal mines.

Lewis resigned as UMWA president in 1959. Although his leadership had been dynamic, it was also autocratic. **Automation** began to displace workers by the 1960s, and the UMWA progress stalled on key campaigns like worker safety and occupational diseases like **black lung**. In 1963, William Boyle succeeded to UMWA presidency and almost immediately charges of corruption swirled. A miners-for-democracy movement grew within the UMWA, and it supported **Joseph A. Yablonski**'s bid to unseat Boyle in 1969. Boyle was reelected and Yablonski was murdered several weeks later. A federal judge invalidated Boyle's reelection as fraudulent, and Boyle was later convicted of Yablonski's murder. Reformer Arnold Miller became UMWA president and was in charge during a brutal 1973–74 battle against Duke Power Company in Brookside, Kentucky. In 1982, **Richard Trumka** became UMWA president, and he is credited with completing the restoration of **rank-and-file** democracy. Under Trumka, the UMWA also made headway on black lung disease, though it remains a touchstone issue for the union. Trumka led the UMWA back into the AFL-CIO and became secretary-treasurer of the latter organization in 1995. In that year, Cecil Roberts, Jr., became UMWA president. The UMWA currently has about 240,000 members and represents over 40 percent of all American coal miners.

Suggested Readings: Melvyn Dubofsky, *John L. Lewis,* 1986; J. M. H. Lasslett, *The United Mine Workers of America,* 1996; Paul Taylor, *Bloody Harlan,* 1990.

Shalynn Hunt
Robert E. Weir

United Mine Workers Strike of 1943. *See Coal Miners Strike of 1943.*

United Packinghouse Workers of America (UPWA). The United Packinghouse Workers of America was created in 1943 as the **industrial union** that succeeded the Packinghouse Workers' Organizing Committee (PWOC, 1937–43). Both the PWOC and the UPWA were affiliated with the **Congress of Industrial Organizations (CIO)**, and were the culmination of many decades of struggle to secure **collective-bargaining** rights for workers in the meat industry. In the 1880s, the **Knights of Labor (KOL)** organized packinghouse workers in small firms, but industry giants like Swift and Armour proved intransigent, and the KOL's efforts faltered during a disastrous 1887 strike in Chicago.

The **American Federation of Labor's (AFL) Amalgamated Meat Cutters and Butcher Workmen of North America** formed in 1897 and enjoyed its greatest success during World War I. After the war, however, most firms broke agreements with the Amalgamated Meat Cutters and Butcher Workmen of North America, and other AFL workers **scabbed** on it during struggles against Armour. Moreover, the AFL largely ignored the immigrant workforce that made up the bulk of slaughterhouse workers. The harsh conditions and long hours under which they toiled was the subject of Upton Sinclair's famed novel, *The Jungle,* the title derived from a term used to describe work in the stockyards. If anything, those conditions worsened once the Great Depression began.

Many PWOC leaders were left-wing radicals, and some held associations with the Communist Party. The Autoworkers Organizing Committee also supplied logistical support for the PWOC. Ideology was put into practice, with the PWOC maintaining strict codes of racial and gender solidarity. It also broke down barriers that separated pork butchers from those working in beef, who viewed themselves as more skilled. Although the UPWA probably never contained more than 125,000 members, its activist traditions allowed it to succeed where prior efforts had faltered. Its "night riders" tactic transported workers and leaders from one packing town to another to facilitate quick organizing drives and maintain **solidarity** between cities, thereby lessening the likelihood of scabbing during labor disputes. Kansas City workers defeated Armour in 1937, and the firm soon settled in other cities. Two years later, the PWOC forced firms to pay men and women equal wages for equal work.

The progressive PWOC swamped the Amalgamated Meat Cutters and Butcher Workmen of North America in most elections held under the **National Labor Relations Act** and, by 1943, was the largest union in the stockyards. In 1946, the UPWA elected Ralph Helstein as its president. He was dedicated to maintaining the union's activism. Helstein and the union attacked the segregation policies of southern plants and the glaring **wage differentials** vis-a-vis northern workers. Although the UPWA managed to raise wage rates in the South, it was less successful dealing with Jim Crow policies that relegated African American workers to the worst jobs available.

The UPWA maintained its commitment to racial equality even when it cost them white members. In the 1950s, the union moved its headquarters to the heavily African American "Black Belt" in Chicago's South Side, and when whites dropped out, promoted African Americans to positions of leadership. The UPWA also conducted a militant fourteen-month strike and boycott against Boston's Colonial Provision Company between 1954 and 1956, which saw remarkable levels of racial cooperation despite red-baiting and other brutal company tactics.

The UPWA declined in the 1960s, as mechanization replaced line workers and firms relocated to nonunion areas. In addition, industry consolidation eliminated jobs and new corporate ownership groups instituted antiunion policies. In 1968, the UPWA merged with the Amalgamated Meat Cutters and Butcher Workmen of North America. Further union streamlining resulted in the creation of the **United Food and Commercial Workers Union (UFCW)** in 1979. Its 1.4 million members represent stockyard workers, butchers, grocery workers, and other food-industry employees.

Suggested Readings: Rick Halpern, *Down on the Killing Floor*, 1997; Roger Horowitz, *Negro and White, Unite and Fight*, 1997; Shelton Stromquist and Marvin Bergman, eds., *Unionizing the Jungle*, 1997.

Sara Pleva
Robert E. Weir

United Paperworkers International Union (UPIU). The United Paperworkers International Union (UPIU) was one of two large unions attempting to organize paper industry workers in the twentieth century, the other being the International Brotherhood of Pulp, Sulphite, and Paper Mill Workers (IBPSPW). The UPIU tended to represent skilled workers, whereas the IBP-SPW was more of an **industrial union**. The UPIU—under the name of the International Brotherhood of Paperworkers (IBP)—was formed by Holyoke, Massachusetts, paperworkers in 1884 and ceased as an independent entity on January 4, 1999, when it merged with three other **international unions** to form PACE, the Paper, Allied-Industrial, Chemical, and Energy Workers International Union, an organization that represents about 320,000 workers in the United States and Canada.

During its 155-year history, the UPIU changed its name numerous times. The IBP, a forerunner of the UPIU, was chartered by the **American Federation of Labor (AFL)**. Through time, AFL **craft unionism** made increasingly less sense as the paper industry underwent mechanization changes that eroded the centrality of skilled craft workers. Many locals of both the IBP and the IBP-SPW cast their lot with the **Congress of Industrial Organizations (CIO)** in the late 1930s, while others remained inside the AFL. CIO locals were reorganized under the banner of the United Papermakers and Papermakers (UPP). In 1957, two years after the AFL and CIO merged, the UPP and remaining AFL locals merged to form the UPIU.

Skilled and semiskilled paperworkers in both the AFL and CIO often battled a common enemy: the International Paper Company, a company that formed in 1898, when it consolidated more than 1.7 million acres of forests in eastern Canada with milling operations in New England and New York. International soon became the world's largest paper, pulp, and forest products industry in the world, a status it retains to the present. The UPIU began its struggle for an **eight-hour** day beginning in 1912, one of many contentious issues that led to a five-year-long strike against International Paper in the 1920s. After that, strikes against International Paper become a relatively constant part of the UPIU's history, although relations took a turn for the better in the 1970s. In 1985, however, a new company management team headed by John Georges demanded wage cuts from employees and announced plans to close several operations. The UPIU found itself embroiled in a well-publicized sixteen-month **downsizing, decertification and concessions strike** against International Paper during 1987 and 1988. At the center of the controversy was **local union** number 14, which represented about 900 workers in the Androscoggin Mill in Jay, Maine. Local 14 attracted world attention and brought luminaries like the Reverend Jesse Jackson, consumer advocate Ralph Nader, and Amy Carter, daughter of the former president, to this remote part of Maine. It also waged a **corporate campaign** against International Paper that exposed the company's deplorable environmental record. The strike was lost when the UPIU struck a deal with International Paper that was unfavorable to Maine workers, many of whom lost their jobs to **replacement workers**. Many union advocates expressed anger against the UPIU and accused it of **business unionism** strategies not in keeping with **rank-and-file** interests.

The UPIU has also struggled to become more racially diverse. From 1975 to 1981, African American workers brought a series of lawsuits against Gilman Paper Company operations in Georgia, charging that it, often in collusion with the union, confined black workers to bottom-rung positions in the company. The UPIU was a codefendant in many of these suits, most of which were won by plaintiffs. The UPIU did improve its civil rights record but negative publicity coupled with losses in the 1980s served to sap its strength.

The UPIU was not alone in its plight. During the late 1980s and into the 1990s, many weakened unions merged to create larger and presumably more powerful entities. PACE was born from this impulse. It brought together the UPIU, the **Oil, Chemical, and Atomic Workers Union (OCAW)**, cement workers in the former Allied Industrial Workers of America, and the Allied Industrial Workers of America, the remnant of autoworkers who did not bolt the AFL for the **United Auto Workers** in 1937.

Suggested Readings: Peter Kellman, *Divided We Fall: The Story of the Paperworkers' Union and the Future of Labor*, 2003; Julus Getman, *The Betrayal of Local 14: Paperworkers, Politics, and Permanent Replacements*, 1998; "One Great Union PACE History," http://paceunion.org/one_great_union.htm.

Robert E. Weir

United Parcel Service (UPS) Strike. The United Parcel Service Strike occurred in 1997 when 185,000 workers walked out on the United Parcel Service. It resulted in a thorough victory for the **International Brotherhood of Teamsters** (IBT). Some analysts hailed the union's victory as a sign that organized labor was poised to reverse its two-decade decline. The **strike** also focused attention on the plight of **part-time** and **contingency labor**.

At the time of the strike, UPS was the nation's largest private handler of packages. Like many companies, it used the rubric of competitiveness to increase its use of part-time and contingency workers. UPS had added 46,300 new jobs in the four years preceding the strike, but 38,500 of them were part-time. In all, nearly 60 percent of the UPS workforce consisted of part-time workers. Also akin to other companies, UPS maintained a two-tier **wage** structure under which new hires and part-timers were paid a lower rate than full-time workers; most part-timers made about $11 per hour, whereas full-time workers averaged more than $23.

The IBT wisely chose to make the plight of part-time workers the centerpiece of its fight against UPS, and it called upon the company to create more full-time positions. This struck a responsive chord as millions of Americans were working part-time, often not by choice. This was certainly the case at UPS, where three-quarters of those leaving the company claimed to have done so because they could not secure full-time work with the firm. In 1996, UPS trained more than 182,000 part-time workers, of whom just over 40,000 remained after a year. (The IBT strategically ignored the fact that a sizable number of these were seasonal employees working on a predetermined limited term.) The issue of part-time work resonated in urban areas—where many UPS terminals were located—because higher costs of living made it more difficult to make ends meet without full-time work. UPS offered to promote 10,000 part-timers, but only to fund 1,000 new full-time jobs; others would have to wait for openings created by retirements, resignations, and firings.

The IBT also opposed UPS's plan to administer the employee **pension** plan. The IBT managed UPS pensions as part of a multiemployer group. Under the UPS proposal, the company would have removed funds from the IBT-managed group and established its own fund. Although it promised higher rates of return than the IBT currently offered, the union feared that future contributions would not exceed the tax breaks UPS received, a level that might not keep pace with rising prices. More importantly, the IBT feared the risks involved in a corporate-run fund in which management would be free to shift money from the pension fund to other accounts.

The IBT and UPS also quarreled over safety issues, weight limits, and **subcontracting**. The company's safety record—though not bad overall—was marred by its seeming indifference to accidents. To many, the company's requirement that line workers be able to lift 150 pounds also appeared excessive. For the IBT, however, a more substantive issue was the company's plan to subcontract feeder driver jobs. Feeder drivers transport parcels between UPS terminals; if subcontracted, such a plan would reduce the number of drivers.

The strike began on August 4, 1997, and ended fifteen days later. From the outset, the IBT won the public-relations battle. IBT president Ron Carey was articulate throughout the strike and came across as more reasonable than UPS officials. It was also apparent that the union was far more prepared for the strike than UPS. UPS tried to move managers onto the line, but it did not have an in-place reserve of **scabs** to make good its threat to layoff or fire strikers. As a result, the IBT was able to reduce the volume of packages from twelve million per day to under one million through a combination of manpower shortages, **picketing**, and encouraging the public to use other shippers.

The IBT maintained remarkable solidarity throughout the fight, even though the union strike fund was low. It received solid support from the American Federation of Labor-Congress of Industrial Organizations (AFL-CIO), whose financial assistance helped strikers draw $55 per week strike pay. AFL-CIO President **John Sweeney** was also instrumental in helping the IBT on the political front, where the IBT's biggest danger lay. Under the **Taft-Hartley Act**, the president of the United States has the authority to order an eighty-day cooling off period if a strike creates a national emergency. President William Clinton had used that power earlier in 1997 to avert a pilots' strike at American Airlines. UPS officials argued that the strike threatened five to seven percent of the national output, as firms were dependent on UPS to deliver parts, contracts, and goods. President Clinton chose not to evoke Taft-Hartley, a decision that conservatives claimed was driven by AFL-CIO and IBT contributions to his reelection campaign. (Politics may have been involved, but the presence of numerous parcel post carriers—the United States Postal Service, Federal Express, Guaranteed Overnight Delivery, Emery, and others—tends to vindicate Clinton's decision that no national emergency existed.)

On August 19, 1997, UPS capitulated. Under the terms of a five-year contract, UPS agreed to create 10,000 new full-time jobs, and that five of every six new full-time openings would be filled by promoted part-time workers. Part-timers also won annual increases of 7 percent, while full-timers won 3 percent raises. The IBT also maintained control over pension funds and got UPS to agree to discuss weight and safety issues. UPS also agreed to abandon plans to subcontract feeder routes.

The IBT victory was marred by one sour note. IBT President Ron Carey was forced to resign when a federal mediator ruled that his 1996 election over James Hoffa, Jr., was tainted by fraud and misappropriation of union funds. New elections were ordered, and Carey was barred from seeking reelection. (Hoffa was elected IBT president in April 1998.) Carey, the IBT, and the AFL-CIO were also alleged to have made illegal contributions to the Democratic National Committee, but investigations did not sustain those charges.

The significance of the UPS strike divides along ideological grounds. Conservatives chastised the ineffectiveness of the Clinton administration and argued that UPS was permanently damaged by a capricious strike. They further claimed that members lost wages that would take years to recover, that UPS lost so much business that it would not be able to create new jobs, that the company pension plan was superior, and that the strike did not change the ratio of full- to part-time workers. As of 2002, only the last charge appears to have merit. The strike's short duration and generous wage increases quickly led to recouped wages, and Wall Street scandals have called into question the long-term viability of employer-administered pension plans.

Liberals hailed the UPS victory as the harbinger of a new labor movement that would reverse losses suffered from the 1970s on. The AFL-CIO drew upon the UPS victory in its campaign to organize new workers and hailed it as an example of workers' hunger to join unions. More than five years after the strike, the liberals' hopes appeared no more prescient than the conservative critique. Organizing gains have barely offset losses, and organized labor struggles to maintain its rate of representing about 14 percent of the American workforce.

There are, nonetheless, concrete lessons to be drawn from the UPS strike. First, the IBT was very well prepared for its action, indicating that offensive strikes are more likely to succeed than defensive ones. Second—as the contingency issue indicated—favorable public opinion is an important issue in helping win strikes. In that regard, actions like the UPS strike and the **Ravenswood lockout** of 1990–92 stand in marked contrast to public relations nightmares like the 1981 **PATCO strike**. Third, organized labor's remarkable **solidarity** during the UPS action was vital in helping achieve victory.

The UPS strike probably also validates those who claim that short, decisive actions have more chance of success than drawn-out clashes. It also shows that politics plays an important role. The neutrality of the Clinton administration contrasts sharply with the antiunion stance of presidents Reagan and Bush in the 1980s. Finally, the strike highlights the problems of contingency workers. This is likely to form the basis of future clashes between capital and labor.

Suggested Readings: Kathleen Barker and Kathleen Christensen, *Contingent Work: American Employment Relations in Transition*, 1998; David Bacon, "The UPS Strike—Unions Win When They Take the Offensive," http://www.igc.org/dbacon/Strikes/07ups.htm; Leo Troy, "The UPS Strike: Labor Tilts at Windmills," http://www.heritage.org/library/backgrounder/bg1165.html.

Robert E. Weir

United Rubber Workers of America (URWA). The United Rubber Workers of America had its roots in the late-nineteenth-century Eastern boot and shoe business, especially in New England. Operatives in the field first organized under the banner of the **Knights of Labor (KOL)** and tried to unite the industry on a national basis before the companies formed a trust in 1892. Internal strife within the KOL and the eventual demise of the organization allowed the cartel—the United States Rubber Company—to dictate labor-management relations without the intervention of labor unions during the 1890s. Production soon outgrew the narrow confines of rubber footwear and expanded into the manufacture of tires for bicycles, then automobiles. Innovations in the creation of rubber, the industry's continual search for **automation**, and periodic **speedups** transformed the workforce from **artisan** bootmakers to semi-skilled and unskilled tire makers.

In the 1890s, the **American Federation of Labor (AFL)**, under **Samuel Gompers**, tried to pick up the organizational pieces left by the KOL by chartering **federal labor unions**. Numerous federal locals banded together to create the short-lived Amalgamated Rubber Workers Union. Both the **Industrial Workers of the World (IWW)** and the machinists' union attempted to organize the field workers at the rubber tire citadel of Akron, Ohio, but were not successful. With the stimulus of New Deal labor legislation in the 1930s, the AFL once again led the field with the establishment of a Rubber Workers Council in 1934. However, the AFL's penchant for splitting mass-production workers into **craft union** affiliates weakened its appeal, but the AFL formed the United Rubber Workers of America in 1935. Almost immediately, URWA leaders rebelled against the AFL's skill mentality and pushed for **industrial unionism**.

The infant union shocked the labor world with a massive **sit-down strike** at the Goodyear Rubber Company in Akron in 1936, as well as subsequent **wildcat strikes**. Such actions moved the rubber workers into the more hospitable orbit of the **Congress of Industrial Organizations (CIO)** that same year and led to a signal triumph against the Firestone Rubber Company. Under government supervision, the URWA won victories over other major tire enterprises, including the United States Rubber Company, the industry pacesetter. The URWA continued its momentum during World War II and expanded its jurisdiction and title to the United Rubber, Cork, Linoleum and Plastic Workers of America (URCLPWA) at the end of the conflict to reflect new categories of workers under the union's jurisdiction.

Like other CIO unions in the postwar era, the rubber workers union split into left-wing and conservative factions that destabilized the organization for several years. As in similarly divided unions, the postwar red scare encouraged the URCLPWA to adopt a middle-of-the-road stance. With a politically acceptable ideology, the union achieved an organizational durability that gained master contracts in the field of rubber and increased membership, especially in the burgeoning field of plastics. By the 1970s, the union had almost a quarter of a million members.

Globalism and **concessionary** bargaining emerged at about the same time the union reached its organizing zenith. Rubber companies continually sought synthetic rubber, instituted automation, and eventually moved many jobs to underdeveloped countries with lower labor costs. As **runaway** plants eroded union membership rolls, the rubber workers merged with the **United Steel Workers of America (USWA)** in 1995.

Suggested Readings: Daniel Nelson, *American Rubber Workers and Organized Labor*, 1988; Bryan D. Palmer, *Goodyear Invades the Backcountry: The Corporate Takeover of a Rural Town*, 1994.

Scott Molloy

United Steel Workers of America (USWA). The United Steel Workers of America grew out of the Steel Workers Organizing Committee (SWOC). The **Congress of Industrial Organizations (CIO)** created SWOC and similar organizing bodies in 1936 to organize nonunion industries that the **American Federation of Labor (AFL)** had previously ignored. The CIO paid particular importance to steel because many steel companies controlled coal mines that the **United Mine Workers of America (UMWA)**, the CIO's largest **industrial union**, wished to organize fully. The UMWA lent the SWOC experienced organizers, including union executive **Philip Murray**, who served as SWOC's chairman. The USWA ultimately organized the notoriously antiunion steel industry, the culmination of decades of struggle that produced upheavals like the 1892 Homestead lockout and the **steel strike of 1919**.

SWOC focused its organization efforts on **company unions** at U.S. Steel, the industry's largest firm. By convincing independent employees that an outside union could offer them more than a company-dominated organization, the SWOC managed to rally workers to their cause. In March 1937, secret negotiations between CIO President **John L. Lewis** and U.S. Steel Chairman Myron Taylor resulted in a SWOC contract. For the first time since the **Homestead** lockout of 1892, an independent trade union represented a significant portion of America's steelworkers. The SWOC hoped that the $5 per day, forty-hour workweek **contract** with U.S. Steel would become an industry standard.

Other large firms, dubbed "Little Steel" simply because they were smaller than U.S. Steel, did not succumb to union pressure until after World War II began.

The SWOC began the Little Steel Strike in mid-1937, but its efforts stalled because the leaders of these firms had a near pathological hatred for organized labor. The Memorial Day Massacre of 1937, during which police killed ten defenseless strikers outside a steel plant in Chicago, demonstrated the resolve of Little Steel to resist unionization. However, once the war began, the administration of Franklin Roosevelt forced most of the industry to recognize unions to ensure uninterrupted war mobilization-efforts. The SWOC's June 1942 decision to change its name to the United Steelworkers of America signified its newly acquired permanence.

With more than 700,000 steelworkers enrolled, the USWA called a nationwide strike in January 1946 in an effort to make its recent contract gains permanent. The **walkout** lasted less than a month. President Harry Truman partially lifted wartime price controls, and steel producers gave workers an eighteen-and-a-half-cent hourly wage increase. Four other industry-wide strikes between 1945 and 1959 resulted in new wage increases for USWA members. It also obtained important **concessions** on job classification and supplemental unemployment benefits during this period. David McDonald became USWA president upon Murray's death in 1952 and served until 1963. He helped ease the USWA into the newly merged American Federation of Labor-Congress of Industrial Organizations (AFL-CIO) in 1955.

Steel workers constructing the Chase Manhattan Bank building in New York in the late 1950s. The steel industry was an important sector of industrial employment and industrial unionism. © George Meany Memorial Archives.

In retrospect, the USWA's highwater mark came during the **steel strike of 1959–60**, which lasted 116 days and idled 519,000 steelworkers in addition to 250,000 workers in related industries. Its ripple effect on the national economy was practically unparalleled.

Saddled with aging equipment, high labor costs, and a flood of cheaper steel imports, the American steel industry waned in the mid-1960s. The USWA did what it could to help employers cope, effectively abandoning strikes as a weapon from 1960 through 1983. From 1973 through 1983, the USWA and the steel industry formally agreed to submit their differences to **arbitration** under an arrangement known as the Experimental Negotiating Agreement (ENA). **Wages** continued to increase under the ENA, even as the industry contracted. In the 1980s, though, remaining steel firms demanded concessions and give-backs from the USWA.

Layoffs accompanying the steel industry's decline profoundly influenced the direction of the USWA. Plant closings and production cutbacks created massive unemployment in the union's ranks during the 1980s and 1990s. To compensate for these losses, the USWA began organizing workers in other industries. The merger of the USWA and the United Rubber, Cork, Linoleum, and Plastic Workers union in 1995 is the clearest symbol of this effort.

Hardship also radicalized many of the union's members. Once an organization consisting mostly of conservative, highly-paid white males, the USWA led some of the longest, bitterest strikes of the 1990s, including campaigns like the **Ravenswood lockout** of 1990 to 1992, and the **Bridgestone-Firestone strike** of 1994 to 1996. The USWA has also become more ethnically and racially diverse. Today, it represents about 675,000 members. USWA membership fluctuates monthly, as under its rules members only pay **dues** when they're employed. It also represents about 600,000 retired workers in the United States and Canada. Its broad-based membership includes steel, aluminum, copper, container, brick, glass, and technical workers.

Suggested Readings: Paul Clark, Petter Gottleib, and Donald Kennedy, eds., *Forging A Union of Steel: Philip Murray, SWOC, and the United Steelworkers*, 1987; John Hoerr, *And the Wolf Finally Came*, 1988; "United Steelworkers of America," http://www.uswa.org/uswa/program/content/index.php.

Jonathan Rees

Uprising of the 20,000 (1909). Approximately 20,000 workers, 80 percent of them women, mostly between the ages of sixteen and twenty-four, and almost entirely Jewish, were involved in the manufacture of ladies' garments in New York City in 1909. The strikers were mostly women but the leadership of the **International Ladies' Garment Workers' Union (ILGWU)** was mostly male. The **strike** was called in reaction to the brutality of the police against **picketers** at the Triangle Shirtwaist Factory, where workers were on strike. Employers retaliated by hiring thugs to beat workers and by hiring prostitutes to harass the young women on the picket lines and suggest, lasciviously, that the young women turn to prostitution if they were dissatisfied with garment-industry **wages**. The strike called attention to the ease with which employers could fire troublesome employees, the sixteen-hour workdays during the garment season, and the periods of compulsory unemployment in the off-season. High-paying jobs, such as tailoring and cutting, were reserved for men, while women were confined to labor-intensive sewing, basting, and finishing. Prior to the uprising of the 20,000, women in New York City's garment trade were widely regarded as unorganizable. Although the strike was not a success, it caused the **American Federation of Labor (AFL)** to reconsider its stance on organizing women, and it strengthened the ILGWU.

Suggested Readings: Charlotte Baum, Paula Hyman, and Sonya Michel, *The Jewish Woman in America,* 1976; Elizabeth Ewan, *Immigrant Women in the Land of Dollars,* 1985.

James P. Hanlan

Utopianism. Utopianism is a belief in an ideal society free from social and economic imperfections. The term dates to the early-sixteenth-century writing of Sir Thomas More, though ideological uses of the term utopian are of more recent vintage. During the nineteenth century, numerous workers, thinkers, and social activists sought to reorganize society and ameliorate the ills brought by inequality and industrialization. American labor and social activists imported much of their utopian bent from Europe. During the French Revolution, François-Noël Babeuf led a secret movement that laid the groundwork for early-nineteenth-century schemes in European utopianism. Others followed. Charles Fourier, in his 1820 *Theory of Social Organization,* called for a new social order featuring the phalanx, which would organize labor on a more rational basis and allow greater flexibility in a worker's life. Numerous short-lived Fourier-inspired phalanxes appeared in the antebellum United States.

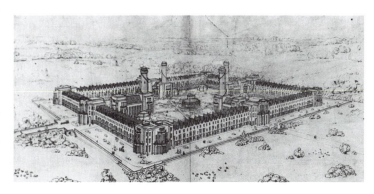

A depiction of Robert Owen's utopian community at Harmony, Indiana. © George Meany Memorial Archives/Library of Congress.

The **Workingmen's Movement** of the 1830s drew inspiration from Robert Owen's experiments in New Lanarck, Scotland. Both Owen and his son, **Robert Dale Owen**, immigrated to the United States in 1824 to establish a New Lanarck spin-off at New Harmony, Indiana, one of the best-known models of American utopianism. While promoting a **cooperative** ethos, New Harmony could not sustain its viability as an independent, cohesive community and soon folded.

In antebellum New York, the Oneida community offered a particularly American version of utopianism by combining radical versions of economic, religious, and sexual life. Under the leadership of John Humphrey Noyes, Oneida lasted for several decades, emphasizing the notions of Biblical communism, Christian perfectionism, and gender equality. Like New Harmony, ideological and cultural differences surfaced and doomed the community. The very nature of these experiments, however, suggested that the revolutionary nature of industrializing **capitalism** forced many Americans to reappraise their relation to the evolving social order and seek new alternative lifestyles.

Radicals often admired utopian experiments, even while criticizing them. In the *Communist Manifesto*, Karl Marx and Frederick Engels viewed the utopian impulse as a significant working-class movement, though one that failed because its adherents lacked an understanding of class struggle. As they saw it, inattention to class dynamics caused utopians to rely on bourgeois interests and place too much hope in nonrevolutionary palliatives. For most of the nineteenth century, however, belief in human perfection remained a powerful ideal. After the Civil War, the Grange, Farmers' Alliances, and the **Knights of Labor (KOL)** engaged in numerous **cooperative** experiments. Utopian novels enjoyed wide popularity, especially Edward Bellamy's *Looking Backward*. That book inspired a movement known as **Bellamyite Nationalism** that involved thousands of Americans in the effort to make the writer's fictive utopia a social reality.

Utopian movements weakened in the twentieth century, though New York City's Greenwich Village fostered a communal movement prior to World War I, and counterculture activists revived those ideals in the 1960s and 1970s. During the 1930s, New Deal programs experimented with collective farms and village settlements. Within the labor movement, however, the utopian impulse largely gave way to concentrating more intently on issues of **wages**, hours, and working conditions.

Suggested Readings: Spencer Klaw, *Without Sin: The Life and Death of the Oneida Community*, 1994; "The Robert Owen Museum," http://robert-owen.midwales.com/index.html.

Timothy Draper

V

Voluntarism. Voluntarism is the reliance on uncoerced action to maintain an institution, carry out a policy, or achieve an end. It is used particularly in reference to joining a union and was one of the foundational principles of the early **American Federation of Labor (AFL)** under **Samuel Gompers**. Voluntarism also involves distrust of governmental authority. It values the liberty of workers to determine their own forms of union organization and methods without outside interference.

According to Gompers, voluntarism advances labor unionism in a number of ways. First, it binds workers to a union that delivers health, unemployment, and retirement benefits. Second, voluntarism isolates workers from hostile state power by limiting government interference in the labor movement and making workers immune from antilabor courts. Finally, voluntarism's values of individual ingenuity and initiative allegedly give workers more power to put pressure on employers to recognize the right of self-organization.

Voluntarism is a vague self-help construct that was more likely clear to Gompers than to most **rank and file** AFL members. In practice, its political nonpartisanship and suspicion of all governmental action often led to decisions that members questioned. The AFL's refusal to endorse political candidates or embrace popular third-party movements engendered tension. Likewise, many AFL members questioned Gompers's logic in 1919, when he opposed unemployment compensation on the grounds that workers and their unions, not the state, needed to solve the problem of joblessness. Although never officially repudiated, the concept of voluntarism was dealt a mortal blow in the 1930s, when New Deal policies altered the relationship of workers to the state.

Suggested Readings: Ronald Filippelli, *Labor in the USA: A History*, 1984; Bruce Laurie, *Artisans Into Workers*, 1989.

Cornelia McAndrew

Vorse, Mary Heaton (October 9, 1874–June 14, 1966). Mary Heaton Vorse was a **labor journalist**, reformer, and feminist. Born in New York City, Vorse was the only child of Hiram and Ellen (Blackman) Heaton. She was raised in Amherst, Massachusetts, in a well-to-do home. Her father owned a prosperous inn in the Berkshires, and Mary regularly traveled to Europe, where she received much of her education. In 1898, she married writer Albert Vorse, and the couple maintained homes in New York and Provincetown, Massachusetts, where she organized a Montessori school and was involved with the Provincetown Players, an experimental theater group. Vorse also began her career as a writer, submitting articles on Italian education to the *Woman's Home Companion*.

In 1910, her husband died, and Vorse turned to her writing for financial and emotional support. Much of Vorse's early writing included sketches and short stories that appeared in various periodicals. Her labor activism dates from the 1912 **Lawrence textile strike**, which she covered for *Harper's Weekly*. Some credit her colorful dispatches as a reason why the **Industrial Workers of the World (IWW)** were able to win said strike. The Lawrence strike led her to befriend IWW leader **Elizabeth Gurley Flynn** and radical journalist Joseph O'Brien. She married O'Brien in 1912, and their son was born two years later.

The Lawrence strike radicalized Vorse, and she began devoting her life and writing to progressive and labor causes. Among the **strikes** Vorse covered were those involving Minnesota iron-ore miners in 1916, the national **steel strike of 1919**, and the 1920 **Amalgamated Clothing Workers of America** strike. Vorse also attended the Women's International Peace Conference at The Hague in 1915, and she covered several international conferences devoted to women's suffrage. During World War I, Vorse worked as a war correspondent for the Hearst newspaper chain, and she reported on the famine gripping the Soviet Union in 1921–22. She also covered the **Sacco and Vanzetti** case and was convinced of their innocence.

Joseph O'Brien died of cancer in 1915; to ease her grief, she was prescribed morphine, to which she became addicted. In 1920, she cohabited with Robert Minor, a cartoonist for *The Masses* and later the secretary of the Communist Party USA. After a miscarriage and separation from Minor, Vorse's morphine addiction worsened, and she did not free herself of its grip until late 1925. Vorse then resumed her career as a labor journalist and reported on numerous upheavals, including textile strikes in Passaic, New Jersey, in 1926, and in Gastonia, North Carolina, in 1929. From those experiences came two novels.

During the 1930s, Vorse chronicled the rise of fascism in Europe, events inside the Soviet Union, and the emergence of the **Congress of Industrial Organizations (CIO)** at home. The latter inspired her 1938 book *Labor's New*

Millions, her best-known book. She also served briefly with the Bureau of Indian Affairs. Vorse was a target of post–World War II red-baiting. Her last major work of investigative journalism was a 1952 analysis of internal corruption in waterfront unions controlled by organized crime. She remained an unrepentant radical throughout the 1950s, a situation that led to de facto retirement. Vorse's commitment to labor, feminism, global peace, and democratic **socialism** helped rehabilitate her image in the 1960s. The **United Auto Workers** awarded her its Social Justice Award in 1962. She died at her Provincetown home on June 14, 1966.

Suggested Readings: *AFL-CIO News* June 25, 1966; Dee Garrison, *Mary Heaton Vorse,* 1989; Barbara Sicherman, *Notable American Women: The Modern Period,* 1980.

Leslie Juntunen

Robert E. Weir

W

Wage Differential. The term wage differential refers to the difference in **wages** earned by workers in the same job. It occurs most often on shift-work jobs, wherein a worker on a late-night shift might get a higher wage than someone on the more desirable day shift. Wage differentials also occur on jobs that require more skill. For example, a worker with knowledge of maintaining a machine might get a higher wage than a line worker. Wage differentials are usually negotiated between unions and management through **collective bargaining**.

Wage differentials also exist regionally, and these regional differentials are of more concern to unions. For many decades, textile workers in the South received lower pay than those in the North. This had the effect of deflating wages across the industry, and made constant the threat to close factories in the North and relocate them in South. In recent years, the same threat looms from low-wage developing nations.

Suggested Reading: American Bar Association, *The Developing Labor Law*, 2001.

Cornelia McAndrew

Wages. Wages are the set amount of monies paid to workers. The term wage does not apply to all remuneration for labor, but more specifically to that paid to the hourly employee. The wage is payment for labor hired on a short-term basis or workers employed in actual production, as distinct from the payment made to hired professional and white-collar employees, which is called **salary**.

Unions generally see wage negotiation as one of their primary tasks during **contract** bargaining, although this has not historically been the case. In the nineteenth and early twentieth centuries, unions like the **Knights of Labor** and the **Industrial Workers of the World** called for an end to the wage system. **Capitalism** was still contested, with many workers seeing wages as a form of social and economic dependency. They were also troubled by the fact that under the wage system, investors, speculators, and management generally made more money than ordinary workers yet did no productive labor. Those opposed to the wage system advocated replacing it with economic arrangements that linked productive labor to remuneration. Those included **cooperatives**, communal labor, and syndicalism.

The **American Federation of Labor** was the first important labor organization to endorse the wage system unequivocally, and today, wage labor is considered the norm. In unionized environments, unions usually negotiate hourly wages. In nonunion businesses, employers unilaterally set monetary scales, but must often take into account the compensation in the industry or a local region. Some businesses will pay a union scale to dampen labor organizing.

Suggested Readings: American Bar Association, *The Developing Labor Law*, 2001; Frank Elkouri and Edna Elkouri, *How Arbitration Works*, 1997.

Cornelia McAndrew

Wage Stabilization. Wage stabilization is a government policy usually instituted during wartime or under extreme economic conditions to control **wages** and prices through legislative action. Beginning in World War I, federal agencies intervened in industrial conflicts as mediators to try to strike a balance between the demands of labor and management to maintain peace in the workplace and ensure uninterrupted production of war material. During the Great Depression, President Franklin Roosevelt's New Deal programs promoted wage increases, but only as a way of taming political and economic unrest until the economy improved. World War II took the economy out of the depression, but that same conflict also ushered in a whole new series of government initiatives like the **National War Labor Board**, which, for the most part, froze wages. However, organized labor managed to gain **concessions** in other areas making it easier to recruit new members on jobs with federal **contracts**. Similar, but less draconian, stabilization efforts reappeared during the Korean and Vietnam Wars. Although labor unions usually chafed under such policies, they routinely bargained for legislative tradeoffs that bore future dividends.

Suggested Readings: Jack Barbash, *The Practice of Unionism*, 1956; Melvyn Dubofsky, *The State and Labor in Modern America*, 1994.

Scott Molloy

Walsh-Healey Public Contracts Act (1936). The Walsh-Healey Public Contracts Act of 1936 provided general employment regulations for employers who received contracts from any department, agency, or instrumentality of the federal government in any amount exceeding $10,000. Federal contractors were required to pay the federal **minimum wage** plus an established **overtime** rate (time and a half) for hours in excess of eight hours per day, or forty hours per week. Males under sixteen years of age and females under eighteen years of age were barred from employment by contractors as was convict labor (except under carefully defined circumstances). Contractors were required to maintain safe and sanitary working conditions. Enforcement of the act was the responsibility of the secretary of labor. Contractors accused of violating the law's provisions were entitled to a hearing, but failure to comply could result in fines, penalties for actual and liquidated damages, and the cost of recontracting the work. Equally as important, violators could be placed on a list of debarred bidders, effectively eliminating a company's ability to obtain work under any federal contract. Contractors were required to keep certain information about their employees, including logs of hours worked, wages paid, and dates of birth for a period of three years and to make a public posting of the law's requirements at the place of employment.

The Walsh-Healey Act has been amended since its enactment but remains in effect to the present time. Its provisions remain a staple of human resouces departments throughout the country.

Suggested Readings: U.S. Department of Labor, http://library.dol.gov/oasam/regs/statutes/41-35.htm; Arnold Thieblot. Jr., *Prevailing Wage Legislation: The Davis-Bacon Act, State "Little Davis-Bacon" Acts, the Walsh-Healey Act, and the Service Contract Act, 1986.*

James P. Hanlan

War Labor Disputes Act (Smith-Connally Act). The War Labor Disputes Act was an attempt by conservative Democrats and Republicans to curtail strikes and rising union might during World War II. It passed in June 1943 and is also known as the Smith-Connally Act for its congressional sponsors, Virginia Democrat Howard Smith and Texas Democrat John Connally. It was precipitated by a series of labor shortages, predominately in the coal industry, that idled some 1.3 million workers in the first half of 1943. Public-opinion polls revealed widespread support for shackling the **United Mine Workers of America (UMWA)** and its president, **John L. Lewis.**

The bill gave the government the right to take over any production facility involved in the war effort if the workforce went on **strike,** and it allowed for the prosecution of those who instigated strikes. The bill further required union leaders to notify management of its intention to walk out, mandated a thirty-day cooling-off period before a strike could proceed, and required the National Labor Relations Board (NLRB) to hold a strike vote after thirty days to determine if workers still wished to strike. The bill also prohibited union contributions to political campaigns.

Both the **American Federation of Labor (AFL)** and the **Congress of Industrial Organizations (CIO)** opposed the bill, while Lewis denounced it as a "slave act." President Roosevelt vetoed the bill, arguing that government-imposed cooling-off periods and strike votes would only encourage **walkouts.** Congress overrode Roosevelt's veto, but his reservations proved prophetic. In the first three months the bill was in effect, the NLRB held fifty-three strike votes resulting in forty-seven work stoppages. Moreover, workers engaged in over 1,900 walkouts in the last half of 1943 without paying any attention to the act.

Ironically, the bill also increased labor's participation in politics. In July 1943, the CIO established its Political Action Committee (PAC) to funnel money to prounion candidates. Following the advice of Lee Pressman, the CIO's general counsel, the CIO advised its affiliates that the Smith-Connally Act did not prohibit contributions for primary candidates, nor did it prevent unions from spending money on candidates through intermediary groups. The PAC ultimately increased interest in politics and led the CIO to push voter education and registration. The act's many loopholes rendered it ineffective, but it nonetheless signaled congressional intent to limit union power. Key parts of the bill resurfaced in antiunion bills like the **Taft-Hartley Act** and the Labor Management Reporting and Disclosure Act.

Suggested Readings: James Foster, *The Union Politic*, 1975; Joel Siedman, *American Labor from Defense to Reconversion*, 1953; Robert Zieger, *The CIO, 1935–1955*, 1995.

James Wolfinger

Watsonville Strike. The Watsonville strike was a **strike** from 1985 to 1987 of some 1,000 women against the Watsonville Canning Company. The strike ultimately pitted the mostly Latina, Mexicana, and Chicana workforce against their own **International Brotherhood of Teamsters (IBT)** union. Although it ended in wage **concessions**, the strike inspired the labor movement because of its **solidarity**, as well as its role in helping reform the Teamsters. It also demonstrated that a supposedly hard-to-galvanize group, Spanish-speaking women, were in fact capable labor unionists.

The Watsonville Canning Company in California's Salinas Valley was among the many firms that demanded concessions during the 1980s. Although its largely female workforce made only $6.66 per hour, Watsonville demanded cuts to $4.25 and an end to health-care benefits. Watsonville officials were also intent on breaking IBT **pattern bargaining** in the region. They were joined by Richard Shaw, Inc., which also demanded wage concessions.

The workers faced seemingly insurmountable odds. First, the strike came during the antilabor administration of President Ronald Reagan, which saw numerous **downsizing, decertification, and concessions strikes** end in routs of the affected unions. Second, the strikers were largely Latina, whereas the local town council and agribusiness management were Anglo. Third, the IBT was a troubled union around which swirled charges of union corruption that were soon verified. By most accounts, Teamster officials were ready to grant concessions to both Watsonville and Shaw.

Teamsters Local 912 managed to unify workers at both plants, and on September 9, 1985, more than a thousand women walked out. Local 912 received logistical support from Teamsters for a Democratic Union (TDU), a reform movement of dissident IBT members. Although TDU could not offer much, it did help strikers organize their own strike committee and set up needed support systems. The women of Watsonville maintained unparalleled levels of solidarity; not a single member crossed **picket** lines. They also proved adroit at soliciting support from other sources, especially Spanish-speaking members of the **Hotel Employees and Restaurant Employees International Union** and the **United Farm Workers of America (UFW)**. UFW President **Cesar Chavez** attended a Watsonville rally, as did the Reverend Jesse Jackson. San Francisco–area women also raised money for the strikers during a 1985 International Women's Day rally.

The most remarkable achievement of the strikers was their ability to cultivate family and transnational networks. Watsonville attempted the popular tactic of importing **scabs**, declaring them **replacement workers**, and encouraging them to **decertify** the union. Since most of the scabs were also Latina, strikers called upon a vast kinship network that applied pressure to families of replacement workers as distant as Mexico and Texas. Watsonville officials were stunned when in August 1986, replacement workers voted to retain Local 912 as its **bargaining unit**.

That action did not bring the strike to a close, however. Wells Fargo Bank loaned Watsonville $23 million in 1985. At the suggestion of Cesar Chavez, a modified **corporate campaign** targeted the bank. In May 1986, Local 912 began encouraging local unions to withdraw funds from Wells Fargo. Within weeks, Wells Fargo drove Watsonville into bankruptcy. It was purchased by Gill Davis, a grower owed millions by Watsonville. The Teamsters immediately accepted his offer to end the strike.

By then, however, the IBT no longer had the respect of the Local 912 **rank and file**. Membership rejected the new **contract**, as some workers lost medical benefits under it. The IBT cut off strike funds to Local 912 and tried to place it under trusteeship. Instead, Local 912 ousted its president, Richard King, and replaced him with Sergio Lopez, who was sympathetic to the strike's continuation. Finally, on March 11, 1987, Davis offered a contract that extended health care to all workers.

The Watsonville strike was not a complete success. In the end, workers saw their **wages** cut to $5.85 an hour, the amount Shaw workers accepted in early 1986. Given their already-low wages, it took years to recoup lost wages. Nonetheless, the willingness of Latina women to hold out for eighteen months inspired union workers across the country. The strikers also brought more light to the internal corruption of the Teamsters, paving the way for long-needed reforms.

Suggested Readings: Jeremy Brecher, "Resisting Concessions," http://www.zmag.org/ZMag/articles/brechermay98.htm; James Green, *Taking History to Heart: The Power of Building Social Movements*, 2000; Kim Moody, *An Injury to All: The Decline of American Unionism*, 1989.

Robert E. Weir

Welfare Capitalism. Welfare capitalism is a practice whereby employers provide a variety of benefits for their workers in the hope or expectation of ensuring a loyal workforce. It has been a popular business practice, especially in good economic times, since the nineteenth century. In the nineteenth century, factory owners sometimes saw themselves in a **paternal** role, taking care of the workers in exchange for their loyalty and hard work. Such employers tended to see worker unions and **collective bargaining** as betrayals of this reciprocal relationship. In the twentieth century, employers utilized welfare capitalist measures often specifically to counteract the appeal of union membership by providing services and benefits as good as, if not better than, those the union could provide. Typical welfare capitalist benefits of the twentieth century included **pensions**, paid vacation, sick leave, and **profit sharing**. Services at the workplace might be provided, such as cafeterias, well-appointed restrooms, libraries, and lounges. Loyalty and a feeling of stake holding might also be obtained through worker-advisory councils and recreational activities such as company picnics or athletic contests. Large companies used welfare capitalism extensively in the prosperous 1920s, but the practice declined quickly during the Great Depression of the 1930s as companies cut costs. As laws became friendly to organized labor in the 1930s, and collective bargaining became the norm in labor management relations, companies increasingly negotiated with unions over providing benefits as part of their labor **contracts**. No longer were pensions and vacations due to the "benevolence" of the company, they were demands to be fought for. By the 1950s and 1960s, they had become expectations.

In the last decades of the twentieth century, many nonunion firms, especially those in technological industries, looked again to welfare capitalism to attract and retain quality workers. Some employers revived earlier practices such as athletic teams and company picnics. Others took into account the modern realities of two-income families or single parenthood by allowing for flexible start times or providing on-site child-care centers. Employee concerns with physical fitness were sometimes met with company-provided exercise facilities, keeping the workers physically and psychologically connected to the workplace. Welfare capitalism has the potential for virtually infinite variations and has been a highly adaptable practice.

Suggested Readings: Stuart D. Brandes, *American Welfare Capitalism, 1880–1940*, 1970; Sanford M. Jacoby, *Modern Manors: Welfare Capitalism Since the New Deal*, 1997.

Elizabeth Jozwiak

West Virginia Mine War, 1919–22. The series of violent confrontations collectively known as the West Virginia Mine War began in late 1919 with the start of the **United Mine Workers of America (UMWA)** organizing campaign in the largely nonunion southern West Virginia coalfields. Mine operators had kept the region nonunion through a combination of **contracts** that prohibited miners from joining unions (commonly called **yellow-dog contracts**) and operatives of the Baldwin-Felts Detective Agency, who enforced the contracts. When the UMWA's organizing campaign began, those miners who joined the union or supported it were fired and evicted from their company homes. As the conflict dragged on into the spring, tent colonies of striking miners and their families began to appear throughout southern West Virginia. The first major confrontation between miners and operators came in May 1920 at the village of **Matewan** in Mingo County. Eleven Baldwin-Felts detectives, including Albert and Lee Felts, brothers of one of the agency's partners, arrived at Matewan by train to evict striking miners in the area. The evictions themselves were carried out without difficulty. However, when the detectives returned to the train station at Matewan, they were confronted by the town sheriff Sid Hatfield, the town's mayor, and a large group of angry miners. Hatfield apparently ordered the detectives to surrender their weapons. When the detectives refused, an argument ensued. At some point, a shot was fired, and the street in front of the station erupted in a gun battle that left seven detectives, including Albert and Lee Felts, dead. The Matewan mayor and two miners were also killed.

The battle at Matewan made headlines all over the nation and inaugurated months of violent conflict. Armed miners throughout the region began closing down the mines. Operators responded by importing strikebreakers and more detectives. Shootouts between prounion miners and mine guards and **scabs** became commonplace. Company property, including shaft houses and coal cars, was also destroyed. Finally, the governor declared a state of martial law and brought in federal troops to maintain order. With the introduction of troops, the fighting stopped. However, when the troops were withdrawn in September 1920, the violence began again. In May 1921, a three-day battle erupted around the town Merrimac on the Tug River between striking miners and a combination of mine guards, state police, and deputy sheriffs. The battle spread up the river and across into Kentucky. When it was finally over, nearly twenty people had been killed.

Tension levels remained high, and President Warren Harding was hesitant to send federal troops into the area again, possibly out of fear that the West Virginia governor saw federal troops as his private police force. Instead, the governor of West Virginia took matters into his own hands. The state police force was enlarged, and the National Guard was reconstituted. Both of these institutions began enlisting and training anyone who would join. Local communities also began deputizing local businessmen for service in the conflict. These new forces quickly moved to suppress the miners. Under martial law, all meetings were prohibited, and any conversation between two or more miners was forbidden. Union miners were also arrested for carrying any prounion literature and were not released until they promised to leave the state. National Guard troops, state police, and local sheriffs invaded and destroyed the tent colonies where the evicted miners lived.

In January 1921, Sid Hatfield and several others who had taken part in the shootout at Matewan were tried for the murder of the seven detectives at Matewan. All the defendants were acquitted. However, Hatfield and his friend, Ed Chambers, were called before a grand jury in McDowell County for questioning in another shooting. When Hatfield and Chambers arrived at Walsh, the county seat, in August, they were gunned down in front of their wives on the courthouse steps by Baldwin-Felts detectives. The murder of Sid Hatfield, who had become a local hero after Matewan, enraged the miners. Throughout the region, miners began to assemble at Lens Creek, south of Charleston, with the intention of marching through Logan and Mingo Counties, breaking martial law and liberating union miners from jail. As the small army of miners began to move toward Logan County, their organization became apparent. Although there was no "general" leading the army, it had its own medical and commissary facilities as well as passwords and patrols. As they marched, they confiscated whatever supplies they needed from local communities, or brought them from Charleston. They also hijacked trains and cars to increase their progress.

In response to the miners army, the sheriff of Logan County, Don Chafin, began to assemble his own army. A combination of National Guard, state police, deputized businessmen, and conscripted strikebreakers, armed with rifles, machine guns, and even a few airplanes, Chafin's army met the miners at **Blair Mountain**. The fighting at Blair Mountain lasted for over a week, but in spite of fierce fighting on both sides, little was accomplished, and neither side could dislodge the other. With the reports of fighting in Logan County, the federal government acted by declaring southern West Virginia in a state of insurrection. Federal troops under the command of General Henry Bandholtz descended on the region from several directions. The presence of federal troops effectively ended the fighting. Although the miners bitterly hated the mine operators and their supporters, they were unwilling to confront the federal government. Miners began turning over their weapons to federal troops, or simply hid them, and returned to their homes. Don Chafin's army returned to a hero's welcome.

In the aftermath of the West Virginia Mine War, some 550 individuals were brought up on charges ranging from treason to murder. However, as the miners' army had no significant leader to blame, it proved very hard to establish treason. Also, the heavy involvement of the mine operators in support of the prosecution cast doubt on the purpose of the trials. As a result, most of the miners were acquitted.

Suggested Readings: David Alan Corbin, *Life, Work, and Rebellion in the Coal Fields: The Southern West Virginia Miners 1880–1922*, 1981; *Matewan* [video] Los Angeles: Evergreen Entertainment, 1996; Lon Savage, *Thunder in the Mountains: The West Virginia Mine War, 1920–21*, 1990.

Jim Riordan

White-Collar Workers. *See Blue-Collar Workers.*

Wildcat Strike. A wildcat **strike** is an unplanned, spontaneous, and short-lived work stoppage. Most occur in response to local conditions and are not authorized by the union. Relatively few of them involve **wages**. Instead they often involve issues to which labor leadership does not attribute much importance or feels lie outside its purview. While radical unions such as the **Industrial Workers of the World** advocate the tactic, most contemporary unions view wildcat strikes as anathema. The 1947 **Taft-Hartley Act** prohibited the use of wildcat strikes, and unions are subject to heavy fines if members engage in them and the union does not do its utmost to end them. Safety issues often trigger wildcats, especially in mining where local stoppages often occur after a worker is injured. During the 1960s and 1970s, some **rank-and-file** workers engaged in wildcat strikes to express their displeasure with union leadership. Wildcat strikes are rare, however, as workers engaging in them abrogate most legal protection. A 1970 Supreme Court decision, *Boys Market Inc. v. Retail Clerks Union Local 770*, dealt a further blow to wildcat strikes when the court ruled that no-strike clauses were implied in union **contracts**, even if they were not specifically stated.

Suggested Readings: Leigh Benin, *The New Labor Radicalism and New York City's Garment Industry: Progressive Labor During the 1960s*, 1999; Jeremy Brecher, *Strike!*, 1997; Martin Glaberman, "Wildcat Strikes" in Mari Jo Buhle, Paul Buhle, and Dan Georgakas, *Encyclopedia of the American Left*, 1992.

Evan Daniel

Winpisinger, William W(ayne) (December 10, 1924–December 11, 1997). William Winpisinger served as president of the **International Association of Machinists and Aerospace Workers (IAM)** from 1977 through 1989 and as a vice president of the American Federation of Labor-Congress of Industrial Organizations (AFL-CIO). Known to his friends as "Wimp" or "Wimpy," he was once described by A. H. Raskin as "the Stanley Kowalski of American Labor," due to his gruff manner and beefy appearance. Winpisinger described himself as a self-conscious seat-of-the-pants **socialist**. He was born in Cleveland, Ohio, the son of a **journeyman** printer at the Cleveland *Plain Dealer*. Winpisinger dropped out of high school to join the navy during World War II, serving in the Mediterranean and the English Channel, where he learned and practiced the trade of a diesel mechanic from 1942 to 1945. Upon discharge, Winpisinger returned to Cleveland and, opposing his father's wishes that he become a newspaper stereotyper, worked as a mechanic. An active member of Lodge 1363 of the IAM, by 1949 Winpisinger was elected president of the 1,300-member local. Winpisinger's skills at **contract** negotiation, **grievance,** and **arbitration** cases, and organizing led to his appointment with the IAM's Midwestern field staff and by 1958 his transfer to IAM headquarters in Washington, D.C. At headquarters, Winpisinger organized truck and auto mechanics, served in the aerospace unit, and performed masterfully as a special troubleshooter for the union's president. He became national automobile coordinator with responsibility for 120,000 members. Eventually his responsibilities included railroad and airline workers as well. By 1977, Winpisinger was administrative chief of staff for the IAM.

The IAM was chiefly for skilled workers, and its members and leaders alike took an elitist viewpoint of restricting membership to the skilled. Winpisinger was an advocate for **industrial unionism** within the IAM and favored mass organizing based on the model of his heroes **John L. Lewis** and **Walter Reuther**. Realizing that his views were in the minority, Winpisinger did not raise the hackles of his fellow union leaders, who tolerated his views because of his superb skills at **collective bargaining** and his tendency to get the best possible deal for his members. When president Floyd E. (Red) Smith retired in 1977, Winpisinger was the natural choice to succeed him.

The union that Winpisinger took over had grown from its 1888 roots as a union of railroad mechanics to encompass the transportation, electronics, and aerospace industries. It was the third largest affiliate of the AFL-CIO and the fifth largest union in North America. Only the **International Brotherhood of Teamsters** had a more diverse industrial base. Nevertheless, membership had dropped from a high of 1 million to about 750,000. Winpisinger insisted that both the IAM and the AFL-CIO needed a dose of old-fashioned activism to restore membership. Within two years, Winpisinger had the membership rolls back to about 900,000. He began quietly by forming alliances with other AFL-CIO leaders known as the "progressive bloc," a group critical of the lethargic and conservative leadership provided by **George Meany**. Winpisinger took to the road to present the case both for the IAM and for unionism in general. His goal was to restore the tarnished image of unions and make a case for stabilizing and improving the economic position of America's union workers. His task, he argued, was formidable, for the reputation of labor unions was "just ahead of Richard Nixon and just behind the used car dealers." Winpisinger began youth programs, sponsored prizes for auto-race mechanics, and insisted that broadcasters present an unbiased view of labor unions or face opposition to license renewal in front of the Federal Communications Commission. Winpisinger did not shrink from political activism and insisted on backing only those politicians whose labor records were solid. In this context, he once referred to President Jimmy Carter as "the best Republican president since Herbert Hoover." Similarly, he referred to Energy Secretary James R. Schlesinger as "a nazi." Winpisinger took public stances on energy policy and limiting defense spending (in spite of his union's large presence in the defense industry). The IAM's Machinists Non-Partisan Political League became the nation's eighth largest nonpartisan political donor and was fifth largest among union political contributors. Winpisinger served as a vice president of the Americans for Democratic Action and was a prominent member of Michael Harrington's Democratic Socialist Organizing Committee.

In spite of his radical views, Winpisinger remained enormously popular within the IAM. He was seen as a man who rose through the ranks, who fought for, and advanced, the interests of his members, who never lost touch with his **working-class** roots, and who bargained pragmatically and creatively with employers. He was even admired by Eastern Airlines President Frank Borman for his willingness to consider innovative **salary** agreements. Thus members of a conservative union could embrace Winpisinger in spite of what Sidney Lens called "the sharpest [recent] indictment of American **capitalism** uttered by a prominent union official." Winpisinger viewed the American worker and the government alike as potential victims of the corporate state, where the rhetoric of a free-market economy and free-enterprise propaganda endangered both economic and political freedoms. His down-to-earth manner, devotion to working for progressive and pragmatic change, as well as the power of his intellect, endeared him to his union. William Winpisinger and his wife, Pearl, had five children, two of whom followed their father into the mechanic's trade. William Winpisinger died in Howard County, Maryland, on December 11, 1997.

Suggested Reading: William Winpisinger, *Reclaiming Our Future: An Agenda for American Labor*, 1989.

James P. Hanlan

Wobbly. Wobbly is a term used to refer to members of the **Industrial Workers of the World (IWW)** and sometimes shortened to "Wob." The exact origins of the term are unknown, and it does not appear in usage until 1913. The term may be related to the verb wobble. Many members of the IWW toiled in unskilled positions on docks and railroads. One theory holds that the term may have originated from either longshoremen wobbling under their loads or from railroad men prying long tamping irons under rails and lifting themselves into the air to gain leverage. The latter created a midair wobble. Still another theory links the term to Chinese members' attempts to pronounce the difficult *w* consonant. Those with little English proficiency might pronounce IWW as "eye-wobble-u-wobble-u." Still others postulate Australian or exotic-dance connections. There is no conclusive proof for any theory. After 1913, however, union members freely and proudly appropriated the term.

Suggested Reading: Archie Green, *Wobblies, Pile Butts, and Other Heroes: Laborlore Explorations*, 1993.

Robert E. Weir

Women and Labor. *See Minority Labor. See also Protective Labor Legislation, as well as specific organizations and individuals.*

Women's Trade Union League (WTUL). The Women's Trade Union League (WTUL) was founded in Boston in 1903 to campaign for shorter hours, higher **wages,** and better working conditions for working women. The WTUL partially filled the void in women's trade unionism left by the decline of the **Knights of Labor,** as most unions affiliated with the **American Federation of Labor (AFL)** either excluded women or showed little interest in organizing them. The American WTUL was patterned after an eponymous group founded in England in 1874. A 1902 **boycott** by housewives of kosher butchers inspired William English Walling, a New York City settlement-house worker, to go to England and learn how the WTUL operated there. Walling and **Mary Kenney**

O'Sullivan drew up plans for an American WTUL with the aid of **Samuel Gompers**, though future AFL support for the WTUL was minimal.

Many of the early WTUL leaders were drawn from the settlement-house movement and included figures like Lillian Wald, Agnes Nestor, Vida Scudder, **Leonora O'Reilly**, and Jane Addams. The WTUL hoped to promote the cause of women trade unionists and convince women workers to join unions, but its membership also included sympathetic middle-class women who were not wage-earners, a structural arrangement for which some criticized it. The WTUL grew under the dynamic leadership of Margaret Dreier Robins, who served as president from 1906 until 1922. The organization played an important role in the 1909 **Uprising of the 20,000**, raising money to support strikers, urging **boycotts** of firms being struck, and organizing mass protests. The strike was said to be the largest strike of women in labor history to that point. The WTUL also investigated the **Triangle Factory Fire of 1911** and used the tragedy to promote its causes. It also supported the **Industrial Workers of the World** during the 1912 Bread and Roses strike in **Lawrence**, Massachusetts.

The all-female staff working in the headquarters of the Women's Trade Union League of New York during the Shirtwaist Strike, January 1910. © Hulton/Archive.

Robins's leadership was marked by controversy. The WTUL supported **protective labor legislation** for women on the grounds that a **minimum wage** and **eight-hour day** were true labor reforms. As these applied only to women, however, feminists decried the essentialist implications of such legislation, and the AFL felt that the WTUL undermined its own **collective bargaining** efforts. Moreover, the WTUL's willingness to work with both the middle class and radicals led some in both camps to distrust it. Thus the WTUL had good relations with some unions—notably the **Amalgamated Clothing Workers of America**—but strained contacts with most AFL trades.

The WTUL also immersed itself in the suffrage movement and provided important **working-class** support for the National American Woman Suffrage Association. By the 1920s, much of its work was more political in nature, with the WTUL continuing to lobby for protective labor legislation for women. The election of Franklin Roosevelt in 1932 gave the WTUL a boost, as First Lady Eleanor Roosevelt was a long-time WTUL member. The WTUL's **Rose**

Schneiderman gained access to the White House and was said to have influenced several pieces of New Deal legislation, including the Social Security Act. The WTUL was less successful in its campaign to remove laws and customs barring married women from working during the Great Depression.

The WTUL's influence waned on the eve of World War II, though it continued to offer classes for working women in everything from history to vocational training. It officially dissolved in 1950, but should be considered the forerunner of such groups as the **Coalition of Labor Union Women** and various women's caucuses within the organized labor movement.

Suggested Readings: Philip Foner, *Women and the American Labor Movement*, 2 vols., 1980; Alice Kessler-Harris, *Out to Work: A History of Wage-Earning Women in the United States*, 1982; Jone [sic] Johnson Lewis, "Women's History," http://womenshistory.about.com/.

Robert E. Weir

Working Class. Historian E. P. Thompson argues that the only way to understand class is to see it as a "social and cultural formation" that develops over a long period of time. Any study of class must take place within this context and must consider not only the people, but also their relationships and their environment. Thompson's comments concerned the English working class, but can be applied to the American working class as well.

Classes are groups of people connected to one another, and made different from one another, by the ways they interact when producing goods and services. The working class is an economic and social class, involving both men and women, with a particular income, status, and lifestyle. The people who make up this class do not own their own businesses, but rather are hired, paid labor. It is with the help of these people that businesses, and those who own them, are able to accomplish their work and make money.

The working class only started to appear in the United States in the early nineteenth century. Before that, the majority of the population in the United States was either self-employed or slave labor. An increase in industrial activity, as well as population growth, led to hired labor becoming the majority of the population and the subsequent development of a working class. In the beginning of its development, the United States had an active working-class culture that included theater, magazines, books, newspapers, social clubs, and political parties dedicated to working-class life. However, over the years, this culture has weakened as the working class has become more involved with American culture in general.

There are several reasons why the working class is important to American labor history. First, the majority of Americans are working-class people, myths of a middle-class society notwithstanding. Although these people belong to the same class, it does not mean they always think and act the same way. They work in different industries and occupations, and they have different opinions, attitudes, and feelings. A second reason why the working class is important is that working-class life is imperiled in today's changing economic climate.

Many members of the working class fought for legislation that encouraged the establishment of Social Security, **minimum wages**, and occupational health and safety regulations, legislation from which all Americans benefit. As economic change continues, some analysts predict that **blue-collar** work in high-wage industrial jobs will become largely obsolete. Thus far, service-sector employment offers few of the **wage** and **benefit** comforts that labor unions struggled to attain. The transformation from a production to a service economy is unlikely to occur without social disruption, and it is possible that the future will involve disputes, even conflict, between the working class and those above them on the socioeconomic scale.

A final reason to understand the working class is that it has been and remains an important category of analysis for both scholars and activists. Most labor history is written from the assumption that the interests of the working class have been (and are) in opposition to those of the middle and upper classes. In sociological terms, most labor historians are conflict theorists, who see social change emerging from the clash between competing interests. The working class is the primary analytical tool for **socialist**, **communist**, and left-wing political theorists past and present. Karl Marx saw the working class—which he referred to as the "proletarians"—and their unions as a revolutionary force that would overthrow **capitalism** and construct a producer-based **utopia**. Marx did not anticipate advanced nonindustrial economies, thus neo-Marxists have expanded his original conception of the working class to encompass most wage-earners.

At its base, working class refers to power relationships. As long as the U.S. economy remains one in which profound gaps occur in wages, wealth, status, and decision-making authority, the working class will exist both in reality and as an analytical category.

Suggested Readings: Harry Braverman, "The Making of the U.S. Working Class," *Monthly Review*, vol. 46, no. 6 (November 1994); E. P. Thompson, *The Making of the English Working Class*, rev. ed., 1968; Michael Zweig, *The Working Class Majority: America's Best Kept Secret*, 2000.

Lisa J. Wells

Workingmen's Movement. Workingmen's Movement is the term used to identify unionization and third-party political agitation from 1828 through the Panic of 1837. It was not a unified movement, rather a catchall category to describe **working-class** political agitation that was strongest in eastern seaboard cities in the North.

In the 1820s, many **journeymen** began to transform traditional associations into trade unions. In 1827, Philadelphia carpenters struck for a ten-hour workday. That action failed, but the next year they and several other unions formed the Mechanics' Union of Trade Associations, considered by some historians as the first American labor federation. From it came the Workingmen's Party of Philadelphia, a model for other cities. Between 1828 and 1834, hundreds of **strikes** took place in eastern cities, scores of independent political parties formed, and at least sixty-eight **labor journals** were published, the most famous of which was New York City's *Working Man's Advocate*.

Many of the new parties were critical of both the Whigs and the Democrats, though in some places they allied with the latter. They operated under various names including the Workingmen's Party, the Farmer and Mechanics Society, and the Workingmen's Republican Association. Their platforms also varied, but most workingmen's parties called for land and tax reform, the passage of **lien laws**, free public education, the abolition of debtor prisons, shorter work hours, and strict regulations for banks, limited-liability corporations, and the use of labor-saving machinery. Many also adhered to the **labor theory of value**, the belief that the worth of any good or service is determined by the amount of labor put into it. All Workingmen, nicknamed "Workies," rejected Malthusian explanations for poverty and insisted that class privilege and unfair business practices caused privation. The "Workies" put forth a mixed bag of progressive, preindustrial, and agrarian values that was sometimes called **republicanism**.

Workingmen's parties competed for power throughout the Northeast and initially did very well. New York City sent a carpenter to the state legislature, Philadelphia elected twenty of its fifty-four Workingmen's candidates, and other cities elected Workies to a variety of municipal and state posts. Success proved fleeting, however, and by 1834 the movement was dead in

Spurred by long workdays imposed by management, such as outlined in this schedule of hours from the textile mills of the Boston Associates, the Workingmen's Movement of the 1830s included a ten-hour workday among its demands. © George Meany Memorial Archives/ Public Affairs Press.

most places. Decline came for many reasons. Coordinated efforts proved difficult because Workingmen leadership varied so greatly. In New York City, for example, **Thomas Skidmore**'s call for the state to seize and redistribute land struck George Henry Evans as so radical that he conspired with others to kick Skidmore out of the party. Another Workingmen's leader, Frances "Fanny" Wright, shocked Southerners and bigoted Northern workers with her attempts at forming a biracial community. Her views on sexual liberation were also widely parodied. Still other leaders, like **Robert Dale Owen**, were **utopian** thinkers whose plans proved unworkable. The Workies also generated religious controversy. Many of its leaders were freethinkers, and few shared the middle class's enthusiasm for the religious revivals of the Second Great Awakening. Critics often accused Workies of being anti-Christian, and this hurt their efforts to recruit workers for whom religion was important.

Mostly, though, the Workingmen were undone by employer opposition and weakening economic conditions. The parties drew much of their strength from nascent trade unions whose membership rolls were unstable due to high turnover. The movement was moribund by 1835, and the Panic of 1837 finished it. Many trade unions collapsed during the depression and would not revive until after the Civil War.

Suggested Readings: Philip Foner, *History of the American Labor Movement, Vol. I*, 1982; Edward Pessen, *Most Uncommon Jacksonians: Radical Leaders of the Early Labor Movement*, 1967; Sean Wilentz, *Chants Democratic: New York City and the Rise of the American Working Class, 1788–1850*, 1984.

Robert E. Weir

Workman's Compensation. Regulation of industrial safety began over 100 years ago in the late nineteenth century. At that time, the amount of money awarded after industrial accidents was based on who was at fault. However, even if the employer was at fault, the employer was often able to avoid payment and thereby leave the injured worker with nothing. It was clear that this system did not work and, as a result, a system of workman's compensation, also known as workers' compensation, was developed that eliminated fault as an issue. It was one of the first social-insurance programs in the United States, beginning in 1908 as part of the Federal Employees Compensation Act. In 1911, various states began to enact their own workman's compensation laws.

Every year, one out of ten workers in private industry is injured while working. The goal of workman's compensation is to alleviate the financial hardship of workers after an injury prevents them from working, as well as to make them more aware of injury and prevention costs. The system protects both the employer and the employee. Under workman's compensation, employers are obligated to pay their employees, or their families, benefits, as determined by the government, regardless of the cause of the injury. In turn, the employer is protected from being sued by the employee. The initial decision about whether to compensate workers is made by employers or insurance companies rather than the state workman's-compensation agencies. The state agencies will only intervene to resolve disputes.

Nearly 90 percent of all workers are covered by workman's compensation, which provides them with cash benefits, health care, and rehabilitation services in response to work-related injury and disease. Payments are provided in five benefits categories: (1) payment of medical expenses for injured workers;

(2) payment of temporary total disability to injured workers who temporarily cannot work, but are expected to fully recover; (3) payment of permanent partial disability to workers suffering from injuries that might affect their ability to work and support their families in the future; (4) payment of permanent total disability to workers permanently prevented from working; and (5) payment of burial and survival benefits to the families of workers killed in work-related accidents. Workman's compensation is important as it ensures that those injured on the job, or the families of those killed, receive adequate support.

Suggested Readings: John F. Burton, ed., *New Perspectives in Workers' Compensation*, 1988; James Robert Chelius, *Workplace Safety and Health: The Role of Workers' Compensation*, 1977; Price V. Fishback and Shawn Everett Kantor, *A Prelude to the Welfare State: The Origins of Workers' Compensation*, 2000.

Lisa J. Wells

Worksharing. Worksharing is a reduction in individual working hours so that more people can be employed. Worksharing was advocated in the United States during the Great Depression in the 1930s and over the last two decades in Europe as a method for reducing unemployment. It has also gained currency among women's organizations seeking greater flexibility for working mothers and among advocates for the elderly, who see worksharing as a way in which senior citizens can secure part-time employment. Government laws often encourage worksharing by requiring employers to pay an **overtime** premium for hours worked in excess of some standard.

The effectiveness of worksharing is controversial. If hourly **wage** rates are not increased when worksharing is implemented, weekly take-home pay will be reduced. If take-home pay levels are maintained, hourly labor costs will increase. This increase, along with the fixed per employee cost of **fringe benefits**, can reduce the number of new jobs created by a worksharing initiative. However, productivity increases accompanying a reduction in work hours can potentially offset these negative factors.

While worksharing is primarily advocated to reduce unemployment, a form of worksharing, job sharing, is offered by some organizations as a family-friendly benefit. Job sharing is an explicit division of one full-time job into two part-time jobs to allow workers to balance work and family responsibilities. Worksharing programs can also be part of a broader push for reduced working hours to improve workers' quality of life.

Suggested Readings: Anders Hayden, *Sharing the Work, Sparing the Planet: Work Time, Consumption, and Ecology*, 1999; Benjamin Hunnicutt, *Kellogg's Six-Hour Day*, 1996; Jennifer Hunt, "Has Work-Sharing Worked in Germany?" *Quarterly Journal of Economics* 114, no.1 (1999): 117–48.

John W. Budd

Work-to-Rule. The work-to-rule is a union pressure tactic employed in **contract** negotiations or a conflict about working conditions. It involves workers following company regulations exactly. In most workplaces, there are many rules that are outdated or ignored by both sides. A union may encourage members to follow archaic practices to slow production and service without violating the **collective bargaining** agreement. There are also many tasks that are routinely undertaken by employees, even though they are not specifically written into job descriptions or contracts. Employees refuse to undertake such tasks during a work-to-rule action. Such concerted actions can severely interrupt output and in some cases involve the public and politicians. For example, police officers might stop all vehicles going above a usually unenforceable minimum speed limit of twenty-five miles per hour, thus bringing an incensed citizenry into the negotiations. Bus drivers in Providence, Rhode Island, once used a regulation to inspect buses thoroughly to have off-duty union mechanics examine vehicles. This pulled several dozen buses off the road for various safety problems during the morning rush hour. In manufacturing facilities, work-to-rule can disrupt assembly by adhering to safety practices or interfering with delivery of parts. Teachers have effectively employed work-to-rule to jump-start stalled contract negotiations. By refusing to undertake tasks not covered by the contract—like coaching duties, helping students after hours, proctoring study halls, and so on—teachers stretch administrative personnel beyond their ability to cope effectively. Some experts in the field of labor-management relations charge that work-to-rule is a type of **strike** or **sabotage**, but is not legally defined as such as long as workers perform all assigned duties. The tactic continues to appear in different guises as the nature of work evolves.

Suggested Reading: Dan La Botz, A *Troublemaker's Handbook*, 1991.

Scott Molloy

World Trade Organization. *See General Agreement on Tariffs and Trade (GATT).*

Wurf, Jerome (Jerry) (May 18, 1919–December 10, 1981). Jerome Wurf, as head of the **American Federation of State, County, and Municipal Employees (AFSCME)**, was the voice for American public employees. When Wurf took over leadership of the AFSCME in 1964, the union had approximately 200,000 members. Under Wurf, the union grew to represent over a million public workers. The son of Sigmund Wurf, a textile jobber, and Lena (Tanenbaum) Wurf, Jerry (as he preferred to be known) moved from the Bronx to Brooklyn with his mother and her new husband following his father's death. In Brooklyn's James Madison High School, Wurf was challenged by his high school English teacher to avoid a failing grade by improving his communication skills. Wurf became involved in local political groups, which gave him an opportunity to develop his public speaking. He became active in the Young People's Socialist League (YPSL), which he later described as "the most important thing in my life" at the time. It was to the YPSL that Wurf ascribed his "moderate" radicalism, which he likened to that of his hero, **Eugene Debs**. Wurf particularly admired Debs's determination to never become "a zealot and [never to be] taken in by the **communists**." He praised Debs for remaining "an American man."

Wurf enrolled in New York University and eventually obtained a bachelor of arts degree, completing his studies in night school due to family financial circumstances. Following graduation, Wurf obtained a food-service job in a Brooklyn cafeteria. Prompted by unfavorable working conditions, he organized his fellow workers into Local 448 of the Food Checkers and Cashiers Union of the **Hotel and Restaurant Employees**. Wurf was so effective that the Yiddish-speaking owners referred to him as "Malach Hamoves" (the Angel of Death).

Young Wurf's effectiveness as an organizer drew the attention of Arnold S. Zander, whose AFSCME had grown from a single-state employees' union in Madison, Wisconsin, in 1932, to an **American Federation of Labor (AFL)**–chartered union. Zander hired Wurf in 1947 to organize an AFL competitor to the **Congress of Industrial Organizations (CIO)** Transport Workers' Union. When Wurf failed at this task, Zander assigned him to beef up AFSCME's New York City affiliate. Wurf was assisted by Mayor Robert Wagner's 1954 executive order recognizing city workers' rights to unionize. This

Jerry Wurf. © George Meany Memorial Archives.

pressured Park Commissioner Robert Moses, the planning guru of modern New York City, to consent grudgingly to a representation election. By 1958, New York City public workers had gained equality with their organized counterparts in the private sector, and District Council 37 elected Jerry Wurf as executive director in the following year.

In 1962, Wurf challenged his mentor, Arnold Zander, for the AFSCME presidency. Zander had invested union funds heavily in pricey housing developments while his union lagged in pay and benefit increases. Although he failed in 1962, by 1964, Wurf succeeded in dislodging Zander. Wurf sold off the housing developments, sold the union's national-headquarters building in Washington, D.C., and restructured the union leadership to fight off competitors and position the AFSCME for efficiency and growth. As president, Wurf discovered that the Central Intelligence Agency (CIA) had been using AFSCME's international connections with other unions to channel funds to anticommunist unionists in foreign countries. He terminated this arrangement and concentrated the union's efforts on bargaining gains for AFSCME members. In New York state, the AFSCME was instrumental in persuading the legislature to repeal the Condon-Wadlin Act, which required that striking public employees be dismissed.

With a significant African American membership, Wurf saw the importance of racial justice. Reverend Ralph Abernathy referred to him as a man "with a white skin but a black soul." On February 12, 1968, the largely African American members of the Memphis local walked off their jobs to protest racial discrimination. Twenty-two black sewer workers had been sent home without pay during a rainstorm, while white workers were allowed to remain on the job. Mass meetings, marches, and **boycotts** of white-owned businesses followed, with Wurf involved in strategic planning. Eventually he would be jailed for encouraging the work stoppage in violation of an injunction. On April 4, Reverend Martin Luther King, who had come to Memphis to support the strikers, was shot and killed. Shortly after Rev. King's assassination, city leaders acceded to union demands. Wurf compared the Memphis victory to classic labor battles of the past: **Homestead**; Hart, Schaffner, and Marx; and the General Motors Flint **sit-down strikes**.

During the 1970s, public employees, upset at their loss of purchasing power, flocked to the AFSCME, which briefly became the nation's fastest-growing union and the largest union in the AFL-CIO. In part this was a result of Wurf's active recruitment of women and African Americans, two groups often ignored by more traditional labor leaders. AFSCME's status assured that Wurf would be appointed to a vice presidency in the AFL-CIO, but his confrontational style and his open advocacy of positions counter to those supported by the AFL-CIO leadership would assure that his influence was less than would be expected from the leader of a large union. Wurf opposed American military involvement in Vietnam. He made President Richard Nixon's "enemies list," openly endorsed Senator George McGovern for the presidency of the United States in 1972, and he made no secret of his belief that AFL-CIO leadership had grown out of touch with ethnic minorities. The leadership, Wurf contended, was composed of elderly men, "products of an era and environment that is no longer," who had grown out of touch with their younger membership. Wurf feuded with AFL-CIO leadership over the formation of the Coalition of American Political Employees (CAPE), wherein Wurf allied with the **National Education Association**, an arch rival of the AFL-CIO's American Federation of Teachers (AFT). The AFT's **Albert Shanker** and Wurf were implacable enemies. Despite his differences with AFL-CIO leadership, Wurf publicly maintained his loyalty.

Wurf devoted his later years to national labor policy. He insisted on the importance of recognition by local government of the right of public employees to bargain collectively, while finding a way to avoid open confrontations between local government and public employees. Wurf saw the right of employees to **strike** or walk out as a fundamental right which could not be denied to a worker, yet he also saw that the exercise of that right by police officers, fire fighters, prison guards, and public-safety workers could create intolerable social chaos. Thus he argued strongly for compulsory **arbitration** which, he believed, should be extended to other public-sector employees. Jerry Wurf saw public-service workers as inherently conservative and reluctant to strike. As he once put it, "a guy whose been collecting garbage for twenty years is no militant but, when your employer is some elected official who wants to make a show of keeping down taxes and the worker is the guy who gets it in the neck, you do find him militant." During New York City's fiscal crisis of the 1970s, Wurf bitterly denounced demagogues who blamed the crisis on public employees. Wurf countered demagoguery with the fact that the average city employee at the time eked out a living on under $10,000 per year. Wurf argued for the creation of a leadership group of professional public managers who would bypass the political patronage system and bring efficiency and decent treatment to public employees. Under Wurf, the AFSCME became actively involved in public issues through its political office, Public Employees Organized to Promote Legislative Equality (PEOPLE), an organization not afraid to take outspoken positions on matters concerning public employees. Jerry Wurf died on December 10, 1981, survived by his wife of twenty-one years, Mildred (Kiefer), and their two children.

Suggested Reading: Joseph C. Goulden, *Jerry Wurf: Labor's Last Angry Man*, 1982.

James P. Hanlan

Y

Yablonski, Joseph A. (March 3, 1910–December 31, 1969). Joseph "Jock" Yablonski was a reform leader of the **United Mine Workers of America (UMWA)**. Yablonski was born in Pittsburgh, Pennsylvania, to a coal-mining family. His father died in the mines in 1933. At age fifteen, Yablonski entered the pits. He served in numerous UMWA posts from 1934 on, including a stint on the executive board from 1934 to 1942. He became president of Local 5 in 1958 and served until he was forced from office by UMWA national president W. A. "Tony" Boyle in 1966, when Yablonski supported reform candidates over Boyle and his cronies. By the mid-1960s, the UMWA had shed its former militancy in favor of a **business unionism** model. There were also allegations that union officials were corrupt and that the UMWA had ties to organized crime. Moreover, the gradual decline of the mining industry led to widespread **rank-and-file** discontent.

Yablonski allied himself with rank-and-file insurgents and announced his intention to challenge Boyle for the presidency. He was backed by consumer activist Ralph Nader and Washington, D.C., attorney Joseph Rauh, the vice chair of Americans for Democratic Action. He was also popular among the rank and file for his work with Labor's Non-Partisan League, and his efforts in getting the state of Pennsylvania to grant **workman's compensation** to **black-lung**-disease (pneumoconiosis) sufferers. Boyle was also unpopular because of his poor public relations handling of a 1968 mine disaster in which seventy-eight miners died, and he stood accused of embezzlement, questionable loans, and illegal campaign practices.

Boyle nonetheless defeated Yablonski. On December 31, 1969—just twenty-two days after the UMWA election—Yablonski, his wife, and a daughter were murdered in their Clarksville, Pennsylvania home. The crime received world-wide publicity, and suspicion centered on Boyle. Miners for Union Democracy, a rank-and-file movement, removed Boyle from the presidency in 1972 and elected Arnold Miller (1923–85), a former Yablonski supporter, in his stead. Boyle and several other officials were convicted of making illegal political contributions with union **pension** funds, and in 1974 Boyle was charged and convicted of Yablonski's murder. He died in prison in 1985. The UMWA—led by Rauh, Arnold Miller, Ed Sadlowski, Jerry Tucker, Yablonski's son, and others—carried on Yablonski's legacy and purged the UMWA of many of its abuses.

Suggested Readings: Joseph Finley, *The Corrupt Kingdom,* 1972; Elizabeth Levy, *Struggle and Lose, Struggle and Win,* 1987; Arthur Lewis, *Murder by Contract,* 1975.

Don Binkowski

Yellow-Dog Contract. The yellow-dog contract was an agreement signed by workers as a condition of employment in which they promised not to join a union during their term of employment with the company. In some cases, workers also had to sign affidavits that they had not previously belonged to a union. The term yellow-dog derives from a colloquial expression meaning an unworthy individual and is emblematic of the contempt in which unions and most workers held such **contracts**. The first known printed use of the term in a labor context is 1902, but it was probably used earlier than this.

Yellow-dog contracts were common in **company towns**, especially in coal-mining regions. Workers were threatened with firing and eviction from company housing for doing anything contrary to company policy. By the 1890s, widespread abuse led fifteen states to outlaw the use of yellow-dog contracts. However, such bans did little to deter the practice. Yellow-dog contracts were a centerpiece of the **National Civic Federation**'s 1903 **open-shop** drive, and they also factored prominently in so-called **American Plan** schemes in the 1920s, in which employers reinforced propaganda about the virtues of individual bargaining and self-reliance with yellow-dog contracts. A combination of the 1932 **Norris-La Guardia Act** and the 1935 **National Labor Relations Act** finally ended most uses of these contracts, although many workers in the 1980s complained that management imposed verbal forms of yellow-dog contracts.

Suggested Readings: Foster Rhea Dulles and Melvyn Dubofsky, *Labor in America,* 1993; Daniel Ernst, "The Yellow Dog Contract and Liberal Reform," *Labor History* vol. 30, no. 2 (1989); Joel Seidman, *The Yellow-Dog Contract,* 1932.

Robert E. Weir

Yeshiva Decision. *See National Labor Relations Board v. Yeshiva University.*

Appendix:
Labor Documents

1. American Federation of Labor-Congress of Industrial Organizations (AFL-CIO) Constitution: Preamble and Article II

*The **American Federation of Labor** and the **Congress of Industrial Organizations** merged in 1955 to create a labor federation of 15.5 million members. Its joint constitution is an elaborate document that lays out its objects and principles, as well as the duties of officers, procedural details of operating the AFL-CIO bureaucracy, collecting per capita taxes, settling disputes, and defining the relationship of affiliates to the federation.*

*Critics of the merger claim that the AFL-CIO is a bureaucratic **business union** that is inattentive to **rank-and-file** members and lacks the militancy to affect meaningful social and economic change. As the document below reveals, however, in principle the AFL-CIO is committed to equity, democracy, and improving the lives of working men and women. While it lacks the defiant spirit of the **Industrial Workers of the World's** Preamble or the utopian goals of the **Knights of Labor's** statement of principles, the AFL-CIO's constitution most certainly outlines a version of a just society. Quoted below are the preamble and Article II of the constitution, "Objects and Principles."*

PREAMBLE

The American Federation of Labor and Congress of Industrial Organizations is an expression of the hopes and aspirations of the working people of America. We resolve to fulfill the yearning of the human spirit for liberty, justice and community; to advance individual and associational freedom; to vanquish oppression, privation and cruelty in all their forms; and to join with all persons, of whatever nationality or faith, who cherish the cause of democracy and the call of solidarity, to grace the planet with these achievements.

We dedicate ourselves to improving the lives of working families, bringing fairness and dignity to the workplace and securing social equity in the Nation. We will prevail by building a strong, free and democratic labor movement.

We will organize workers into unions allied by common purposes and mutual reliance. We will recruit generations of organizers, amass resources to sustain their efforts and inspire workers to achieve dignity and security through organization and collective bargaining. We will generate broad understanding of the necessity of organizing among our members, our leaders and all unorganized workers.

We will give political voice to workers in the Nation. We will fight for an agenda for working families at all levels of government. We will assemble a broad progressive coalition for social and economic justice. We will create a political force within the labor movement that will speak forcefully and persuasively on the public issues that affect our lives.

We will enable workers to shape a changing global economy. We will speak for working people in the international marketplace, in the industries in which we are employed, and in the firms where we work. We will expand the role of unions to securing worker influence in all the decisions that affect our working lives, from capital investment to the quality of products and services to how work itself is organized.

We will establish unions as active forces in our communities. We will make the voices of working families heard in our neighborhoods. We will create vibrant state, local and community labor councils. We will strengthen the ties of labor with our allies. We will speak out effectively and creatively on behalf of all working Americans. . . .

ARTICLE II: OBJECTS AND PRINCIPLES

The objects and principles of this Federation are:

1. To aid workers in securing improved wages, hours and working conditions with due regard for the autonomy, integrity and jurisdiction of affiliated unions.

2. To aid and assist affiliated unions in extending the benefits of mutual assistance and collective bargaining to workers and to promote the organization of the unorganized into unions of their own choosing for their mutual aid, protection and advancement, giving recognition to the principle that both craft and industrial unions are appropriate, equal and necessary as methods of union organization.

3. To affiliate national and international unions with this Federation and to establish such unions; to form organizing committees and directly affiliated local unions and to secure their affiliation to appropriate national and international unions affiliated with or chartered by the Federation; to establish, assist and promote state and local central bodies composed of local unions of all affiliated organizations and directly affiliated local unions; to establish and assist trade departments composed of affiliated national and international unions and organizing committees.

4. To encourage all workers without regard to race, creed, color, sex, national origin, religion, age, disability or sexual orientation to share equally in the full benefits of union organization.

5. To secure legislation which will safeguard and promote the principle of free collective bargaining, the rights of workers, farmers and consumers, and the security and welfare of all the people and to oppose legislation inimical to these objectives.

6. To protect and strengthen our democratic institutions, to secure full recognition and enjoyment of the rights and liberties to which we are justly entitled, and to preserve and perpetuate the cherished traditions of our democracy.

7. To give constructive aid in promoting the cause of peace and freedom in the world and to aid, assist and cooperate with free and democratic labor movements throughout the world.

8. To preserve and maintain the integrity of each affiliated union in the organization to the end that each affiliate shall respect the established bargaining relationships of every other affiliate and that each affiliate shall refrain from raiding the established bargaining relationship of any other affiliate and, at the same time, to encourage the elimination of conflicting and duplicating organizations and jurisdictions through the process of voluntary agreement or voluntary merger in consultation with the appropriate officials of the Federation, to preserve, subject to the foregoing, the organizing jurisdiction of each affiliate.

9. To aid and encourage the sale and use of union made goods and union services through the use of the union label and other symbols; to promote the labor press and other means of furthering the education of the labor movement.

10. To protect the labor movement from any and all corrupt influences and from the undermining efforts of authoritarianism, totalitarianism, terrorism and all other forces that suppress individual liberties and freedom of association and oppose the basic principles of our democracy and of free and democratic unionism.

11. To safeguard the democratic character of the labor movement and to protect the autonomy of each affiliated national and international union.

12. While preserving the independence of the labor movement from political control, to encourage workers to register and vote, to exercise their full rights and responsibilities of citizenship, and to perform their rightful part in the political life of the local, state and national communities.

Source: AFL-CIO Constitution.

---

2. Anthracite Coal Strike of 1902: Response to a *New York Times* Letter by Mine Owners Spokesman George Baer

*The **Anthracite Coal Strike of 1902** became a classic confrontation between capital and labor. Eventually, President Theodore Roosevelt intervened to avoid the hardships that a winter without coal would bring to many Americans. The settlement that resulted exemplified what Roosevelt would call the "Square Deal" with mine owners, mineworkers, and the general public all gaining in the process and avoiding social and political upheaval. In the midst of the **strike**, George Baer, spokesman for the mine owners, responded to a letter in the New York Times and asserted what amounted to the divine right of capital. Baer's uncompromising stance, his assertion that God himself was on the side of the owners, and his defense of the rights of the wealthy proved unpalatable to the general public.*

WILKES BARRE, PA, Aug. 20, 1902—W. F. Clark, a photographer of this city, recently addressed a letter to President Baer of the Philadelphia and Reading

Railroad Company, appealing to him as a Christian to settle the miners' strike. The writer said if Christ were taken more into our business affairs there would be less trouble in the world, and that if Mr. Baer granted the strikers a slight concession they would gladly return to work and the President of the Philadelphia and Reading would have the blessing of God and the respect of the nation.

President Baer replied as follows:

> I see that you are evidently biased in your religious views in favor of the right of the working man to control a business in which he has no other interest than to secure fair wages for the work he does. I beg of you not to be discouraged. The rights and interests of the laboring man will be protected and cared for, not by the labor agitator, but by the Christian men to whom God in His infinite wisdom has given the control of the property interests of the country. Pray earnestly that the right may triumph, always remembering that the Lord God Omnipotent still reigns and that His reign is one of law and order, and not of violence and crime.

Source: The New York Times, August 21, 1902.

---

3. Black Workers after the Knights of Labor: July 1918 Article from *The Messenger*

*The decline of the **Knights of Labor** in the 1890s did not bode well for African American laborers. Although the **American Federation of Labor (AFL)** was founded in 1886, many of its constituent **craft unions** refused to accept black members. By the early twentieth century, some black leaders openly called upon black workers to **scab** upon white strikers to punish them for their racism. During the Progressive Era, cooler heads prevailed, and both black leaders and AFL officials at least broached the subject of organizing African Americans. But, except for a few select unions like the **United Mine Workers**, the AFL remained largely closed to African Americans well into the 1930s. On July 1, 1918, the following article appeared in the important African American journal The Messenger. Published in Harlem in New York City and associated with **A. Philip Randolph**, the future leader of the **Brotherhood of Sleeping Car Porters**, the article is both a plea for cooperation and a warning to white unionists.*

As workers, black and white, we all have one common interest, viz., the getting of more wages, shorter hours and better working conditions.

Black and white workers should combine for no other reason than that for which individual workers should combine, viz., to increase their bargaining power, which will enable them to get their demands.

Second, the history of the labor movement in America proves that the employing class recognizes no race lines. They will exploit a white man as readily as a black man. They will exploit women as readily as men. They will even go to the extent of coining the labor, blood and suffering of children into dollars. The introduction of women and children into the factories proves that capitalists are only concerned with profits and that they will exploit any race or class in order to make profits, whether they be black or white men, black or white women, or black or white children.

Third, it is apparent that every Negro worker or non-union man is a potential scab upon white union men and black union men.

Fourth, self-interest is the only principle upon which individual or groups will act if they are sane. Thus, it is idle and vain to hope or expect Negro workers out of work and who receive less wages when at work then white workers, to refuse to scab upon white workers when an opportunity presents itself.

Men will always seek to improve their condition. When colored workers, as scabs, accept the wages against which white workers strike, they (the Negro workers) have definitely improved their conditions.

That is the only reason why colored workers scab upon white workers or why non-union men scab upon white union men.

A scab who is ignorant of his class interest does not realize that it is necessary to sacrifice a temporary gain in order to secure a greater future gain which can only be secured through collective action.

Every member which is a part of the industrial machinery must be organized, if labor would win its demands. Organized labor cannot afford to ignore any labor factor of production which organized capital does not ignore.

Fifth, if the employers can keep the white and black dogs, on account of race prejudice, fighting over a bone; the yellow capitalist dog will get away with the bone—the bone, to which we refer, is profits. No union man's standard of living is safe as long as there is one man or woman who may be used as a scab.

Source: Philip Foner and Ronald Lewis, eds., *Black Workers: A Documentary History from Colonial Times to the Present* (Philadelphia: Temple University Press, 1989), pp. 354–55.

---

4. "Bread and Roses": Poem by James Oppenheim—1912

James Oppenheim (1882–1932) was inspired to write his poem, "Bread and Roses," by some of the **Lawrence textile strikers** *of 1912, who carried a banner reading "we want bread and roses too." Workers in Lawrence had walked off the job in response to pay cuts instituted by the American Woolen Company; the wool trust was the city's predominant employer. The poem was set to music by Caroline Kohlsaat and came to represent the goals of the women strikers: a life wherein both the necessities and the beauties of the world could be enjoyed by all. The Lawrence Textile Strike is thus sometimes known as the "bread and roses" strike.*

As we come marching, marching in the beauty of the day,
A million darkened kitchens, a thousand mill lofts gray,

Are touched with all the radiance that a sudden sun discloses,
For the people hear us singing: "Bread and roses! Bread and roses!"

As we come marching, marching, we battle too for men,
For they are women's children, and we mother them again.
Our lives shall not be sweated from birth until life closes;
Hearts starve as well as bodies; give us bread, but give us roses!

As we come marching, marching, unnumbered women dead
Go crying through our singing their ancient cry for bread.
Small art and love and beauty their drudging spirits knew.
Yes, it is bread we fight for—but we fight for roses, too!

As we come marching, marching, we bring the greater days.
The rising of the women means the rising of the race.
No more the drudge and idler—ten that toil where one reposes,
But a sharing of life's glories: Bread and roses! Bread and roses!

Source: Joyce L. Kornbluh, ed., *Rebel Voices: An I.W.W. Anthology* (Ann Arbor: University of Michigan Press, 1964), 195–96.

---

5. Cesar Chavez: "The Mexican-American and the Church"

*Cesar Chavez (1927–93) was an important voice for agricultural workers, especially Chicanos and other Latinos. Until his death, Chavez was the leading spokesperson for the **United Farm Workers of America (UFW)**, a union that sprang to public consciousness during the **grape boycott** of 1965 to 1970. One of the things that made Chavez effective was his deep understanding of the Chicano community in which he grew up. He was a fervent follower of the Roman Catholic religion, and was aware of the moral and political sway it held among Chicanos. Whenever he could, Chavez fostered ties between his union and his church. The following piece was written in 1968, during a fast Chavez held to pressure California growers into recognizing the UFW.*

THE MEXICAN-AMERICAN AND THE CHURCH

The place to begin is with our own experience with the Church in the strike which has gone on for thirty-one months in Delano. . . . [I]n Delano the church has been involved with the poor in a unique way which should stand as a symbol to other communities. . . . [W]hen we refer to the Church we should define the word a little. We mean the whole Church, the Church as an ecumenical body spread around the world, and not just its particular form in a parish in a local community. The Church we are talking about is a tremendously powerful institution in our society, and in the world. That Church is one form of the Presence of God on Earth, and . . . is a powerful moral and spiritual force which cannot be ignored by any movement. Furthermore, it is an organization with tremendous wealth. Since the Church is to be servant to the poor, it is our fault if that wealth is not channeled to help the poor in our world. In a small way we have been able, in the Delano strike, to work together with the Church . . . to bring some of its moral and economic power to bear on those who want to maintain the status quo, keeping farm workers in virtual enslavement. . . .

Some years ago . . . some of us . . . began to realize the powerful effect which the Church can have on the conscience of the opposition. In scattered instances, in San Jose, Sacramento, Oakland, Los Angeles and other places, priests would speak out loudly and clearly against specific instances of oppression, and in some cases, stand with the people who were being hurt. Furthermore, a small group of priests . . . began to pinpoint attention on the terrible situation of the farm workers in our state. At about that same time, we began to run into the California Migrant Ministry in the camps and field. They were about the only ones there, and a lot of us were very suspicious, since we were Catholics and they were Protestants.

However, they had developed a very clear conception of the Church. It was called to serve, to be at the mercy of the poor, and not to try to use them. After a while this made a lot of sense to us, and we began to find ourselves working side by side with them. In fact, it forced us to raise the question why OUR Church was not doing the same. We would ask, "Why do the Protestants come out here and help the people, demand nothing, and give all their time to serving farm workers, while our own parish priests stay in their churches, where only a few people come, and usually feel uncomfortable?" It was not until some of us moved to Delano and began working to build the National Farm Workers Association that we really saw how far removed from the people the parish Church was. . . . [W]e could not get any help at all from the priests of Delano. When the strike began, they told us we could not even use the Church's auditorium for . . . meetings. The farm workers' money helped build that auditorium! But the Protestants were there again, in the form of the California Migrant Ministry, and they began to help in little ways. . . .

[W]hen the strike started in 1965, most of our "friends" forsook us for a while. . . . But the California Migrant Ministry held a meeting with its staff and decided that the strike was a matter of life or death for farm workers everywhere, and that even if it meant the end of the Migrant Ministry they would turn over their resources to the strikers. The political pressure on the Protestant Churches was tremendous and the Migrant Ministry lost a lot of money. But they stuck it out, and they began to point the way to the rest of the Church. In fact, when 30 of the strikers were arrested for shouting "Huelga" [strike], 11 ministers went to jail with them. . . . Then the workers began to raise the question: "Why ministers? Why not priests? . . . " [S]lowly the pressure of the people grew . . . until finally we have in Delano a priest . . . who is there to help minister to the needs of farm workers.

Finally, our own Catholic Church has decided to recognize that we have our own peculiar needs, just as the growers have theirs. But outside of the local diocese, the pressure built up on growers to negotiate was tremendous. Though we were not allowed to have our own priest, the power of the ecumenical body of the Church was tremendous. The work of the Church, for example, in the Schenley, Di Giorgio, Perelly-Minetti strikes was fantastic. They applied pressure—and they mediated. When poor people get involved in a long conflict, such as a strike, or a civil rights drive, and the pressure increases each day, there is a deep need for spiritual advice. Without it we see families crumble, leadership weaken, and hard workers grow tired. And in such a situation the spiritual advice must be given by a friend, not by the opposition. What sense does it make to go to Mass on Sunday and reach out for spiritual help, and instead get sermons about the wickedness of your cause? That only drives one to question and to despair. The growers in Delano have their spiritual problems . . . we do not deny that. They have every right to have priests and ministers who serve their needs. BUT WE HAVE DIFFERENT NEEDS, AND SO WE NEEDED A FRIENDLY SPIRITUAL GUIDE. . . .

But the opposition raises a tremendous howl about this. They don't want us to have our spiritual advisors, friendly to our needs. Why is this? Why indeed except that THERE IS TREMENDOUS SPIRITUAL AND ECONOMIC POWER IN THE CHURCH. The rich know it, and for that reason they choose to keep it from the people. The leadership of the Mexican-American Community must admit that we have fallen far short in our task of helping provide spiritual guidance for our people. . . . For example, the Catholic Charities agencies of the Catholic Church has millions of dollars earmarked for the poor. But often the money is spent for food baskets for the needy instead of for effective action to eradicate the causes of poverty. The men and women who administer this money sincerely want to help their brothers. It should be our duty to help direct the attention to the basic needs of the Mexican-Americans in our society . . . needs which cannot be satisfied with baskets of food, but rather with effective organizing at the grass roots level.

Therefore, I am calling for Mexican-American groups to stop ignoring this source of power. It is not just our right to appeal to the Church to use its power effectively for the poor, it is our duty to do so. . . . Furthermore, we should be prepared to come to the defense of that priest, rabbi, minister, or layman of the Church, who out of commitment to truth and justice gets into a tight place with his pastor or bishop. It behooves us to stand with that man and . . . see to it that his rights of conscience are respected and that no bishop, pastor or other higher body takes that God-given, human right away. Finally, in a nutshell, what do we want the Church to do? . . . We ask for its presence with us, beside us, as Christ among us. We ask the Church to sacrifice with the people for social change, for justice, and for love of brother. We don't ask for words. We ask for deeds. We don't ask for paternalism. We ask for servanthood.

Source: TM/© 2003 the Cesar E. Chavez Foundation. www.chavezfoundation.org.

6. Coalition of Labor Union Women: Mission Statement

*Since 1974, the **Coalition of Labor Union Women (CLUW)** has fought to make certain that union women receive fair treatment and opportunities within the very organizations that are designed to liberate them. The CLUW formed after many decades in which male chauvinism was standard operating procedure for unions. Like millions of women in the culture at large, union women were inspired by the revitalization of the feminist movement in the 1960s. The CLUW's mission statement is a brief but poignant summary of the organization's aims. It also encapsulates the movement's broader concerns.*

The Coalition of Labor Union Women is America's only national organization for union women. Formed in 1974, CLUW is a nonpartisan organization within the union movement. The primary mission of CLUW is to unify all union women in a viable organization to determine our common problems and concerns and to develop action programs within the framework of our unions to deal effectively with our objectives. At its founding convention in Chicago, Illinois, CLUW adopted four basic goals of action: to promote affirmative action in the workplace; to strengthen the role of women in unions; to organize the unorganized women; and to increase the involvement of women in the political and legislative process. These goals continue to be the cornerstone of CLUW's activities as members speak out for equal pay, child and elder care benefits, job security, safe workplaces, affordable health care, contraceptive equity, and protection from sexual harassment and violence at work. . . .

Source: "Coalition of Labor Union Women," www.cluw.org.

7. Colored National Labor Union

*The **Colored National Labor Union (CNLU)** was largely the brainchild of African American ship caulker Isaac Myers. Myers convened a December 1860 meeting in his hometown of Baltimore to consider questions relating to black laborers. He did so mindful of the fact that the newly formed **National Labor Union (NLU)** was divided over the question of whether or not to admit black members, given that numerous affiliated unions barred African Americans. The issue of contract and coolie labor was a central concern for the early NLU. Myers may well have added this as a subtle appeal to white NLU leaders to recognize that white and black workers shared common interests and concerns. The CNLU and the NLU made overtures to each other, but differences ultimately undid a fragile alliance, and neither organization survived the Panic of 1873. Below is a call for a national convention of "Colored Men of the United States," which was published in* The Christian Recorder *on September 18, 1869. (Note: The seem-*

ingly random capitalization of words was common in eighteenth- and nineteenth-century documents and was done to call attention to key points.)

FELLOW CITIZENS:—At a State Labor Convention of the Colored Men of Maryland, held July 20, 1869, it was unanimously resolved a that a National Convention be called . . . to consider:

1st. The Present Status of Colored Labor in the United States and its Relationship to American Industry.

2d. To adopt such rules and devise such means as will systematically and effectively organize all the departments of said labor, and make it the more productive in its new Political relationship to Capital, and consolidate the Colored Workingmen of the several States to act in co-operation with our White Fellow-Workingmen . . . who are opposed to Distinction in the Apprenticeship Laws on account of Color. . . .

3d. To consider the question of the importation of Contract Coolie Labor, and to petition the Congress for the adoption of such Laws as will prevent its being a system of Slavery.

4th. And to adopt such other means as will best advance the interests of the Colored Mechanics and Workingmen of the whole country.

Fellow-Citizens: You cannot place too great an estimate upon the important objects this Convention is called upon to consider. . . . In the greater portion of the United States, Colored Men are excluded from the workshops on account of their *color*.

The laboring man in a large portion of Southern States, by a systematic understanding prevailing there, is unjustly deprived of the price of his labor, and in localities far removed from the Courts of Justice is forced to endure wrongs and oppressions worse than Slavery.

By falsely representing the laborers of the South, certain *interested* writers and journals are striving to bring Contract Chinese or Coolie Labor into popular favor there, thus forcing American laborers to work at Coolie wages or starve. . . .

Delegates will be admitted without regard to race or color. . . . It is hoped that all who feel an interest in the welfare and elevation of our race will take an active part in making the Convention a grand success. . . .

Source: Philip Foner and Ronald Lewis, eds., *Black Workers: A Documentary History from Colonial Times to the Present* (Philadelphia: Temple University, 1989), pp. 163–64.

---

8. Communist Manifesto (1848)

*Historians have debated the question of why American workers have been historically less committed to **socialist** and **communist** ideals than those in other indus-*

trialized nations. The reasons for this are complex, but the very question often misleads. While it is true that independent socialist or labor parties have often struggled in the United States, it does not mean that workers had no interest in such movements. From the 1870s through the red scare following World War I, consideration of Marxist ideals was among the options that American workers considered. Very often, communist organizers exerted great influence on labor organizations, even when their actual numbers were few. (This is especially the case inside the early **Congress of Industrial Organizations***.) For whatever faults they possessed, communists also played key roles in agitating for social change, were instrumental during the* **Popular Front***, and did much to publicize basic inequities in American society.*

The Communist Manifesto was published by Karl Marx and Friedrich Engels in 1848. It made its way to the United States through immigrants, then through the work of the First International Working Men's Association (1864), which in 1872, moved its headquarters to New York City. Socialist and communist influence waxed and waned, but legions of native-born and immigrant workers had at least passing knowledge of the manifesto and its central thesis: "The history of all hitherto existing society is the history of class struggles." This is also true of the document's stirring conclusion, quoted below. Its final line is a rallying cry for workers everywhere.

When, in the course of development, class distinctions have disappeared, and all production has been concentrated in the hands of a vast association of the whole nation, the public power will lose its political character. Political power, properly so called, is merely the organized power of one class for oppressing another. If the proletariat during its contest with the bourgeoisie is compelled by the force of circumstances to organize itself as a class, if, by means of a revolution, it makes itself the ruling class, and, as such, sweeps away by force the old conditions of production, then it will, along with these conditions, have swept away the conditions for the existence of class antagonisms and of classes generally, and will thereby have abolished its own supremacy as a class.

In the place of the old bourgeois society, with its classes and class antagonisms, we shall have an association in which the free development of each is the condition for the free development of all.

...the Communists everywhere support every revolutionary movement against the existing social and political order of things.

In all these movements they bring to the front ... the property question, no matter what its degree of development at the time.

Finally, they labor everywhere for the union and agreement of the democratic parties of all countries.

The communists disdain to conceal their views and aims. They openly declare that their ends can be obtained only by the forcible overthrow of all existing social conditions. Let the ruling classes tremble at a Communistic revolution. The proletarians have nothing to lose but their chains. They have a world to win.

WORKINGMEN OF ALL COUNTRIES, UNITE!

9. Comparable Worth: 1986 Minnesota Study by Sara Evans and Barbara Nelson

*One of the more controversial struggles of recent years has been the battle over comparable worth. The 1963 **Equal Pay Act** made it illegal, in most circumstances, to pay differing **wage** rates to employees doing the same job, if they have equal **seniority**. Women and minorities often found, however, that some employers sought to preserve traditional privileges—usually those of white males—by fudging on job classifications. For example, a woman doing filing and typing might be classified as a "secretary," while a man doing the same duties might be labeled an "executive assistant." Another way to perpetuate traditional discriminatory patterns is to reassign job duties so that, technically, two workers are doing different tasks when, in actuality, they are of comparable levels of expertise and difficulty. Comparable worth addresses such inequity by reclassifying work and pegging pay rates according to the skill required to produce it. To date, comparable-worth laws remain mostly local and state efforts.*

The excerpt below comes from a 1986 study done in Minnesota by Sara Evans and Barbara Nelson. It lays out the problem and offers a justification for considering comparable worth.

Wendy Robinson worked as an intro level secretary at the University of Minnesota at a time some years ago when there was a severe shortage of clerical workers. Interested in other opportunities, she would wander by the employment bulletin board in the basement of Morrill Hall to look at the jobs posted there. In the section labelled "clericals" there were "scads" of jobs, each of which had a lengthy description including requirements from three to five years of post-high-school education or experience, typing skills, shorthand, excellent command of grammar, and basic writing skills. The pay rate for such jobs, like her own, was $756 per month. One day she glanced over at the section of the bulletin marked "technical," where there was only one job posted. "Custodian," it read, "job requirement: eighth grade education, the ability to read and write, no experience." The starting salary, however, was $200 a month more than Wendy was making. . . .

Comparable worth or pay equity as it is often called, is the concept of providing equal pay for different jobs of equal value (i.e., jobs with similar scores along measures of skill, effort, responsibility, and working conditions). . . .

This type of analysis also takes into account race and ethnicity, looking to see if jobs held disproportionately by racial or ethnic minorities are paid less than equivalently valued jobs held primarily by whites. What is important to remember about comparable worth is that *only* equivalently evaluated jobs within a specific workplace are compared. Clerk typist salaries are not compared to doctors' salaries, and clerk typists working for the state of Minnesota are not compared with clerk typists working elsewhere. Comparable worth is an *internal* wage policy.

Why do most male jobs like delivery van drivers consistently get better pay than mostly female jobs like clerk typists? Among full time workers, why do white women make 64 cents, black women make 58 cents, Hispanic women make 54 cents, Black men make 74 cents, and Hispanic men make 71 cents, compared to every dollar made by white men? There are no easy answers. . . .

The problem of low wages for women and minorities is indeed broad and systematic. Opponents of public policies addressing wage rates cite the market system as the best mechanism for adjusting wages. Proponents point out that until the early 1960s it was perfectly legal and customary to pay women and men, and whites and minorities differently for exactly the same work, and market or no market that is precisely what was done. When women entered the teaching profession and factory work in the nineteenth century wages dropped. Employers argued that men had to support families and that women's income was secondary. The primacy of women's responsibilities for home and family meant that few considered them seriously as wage earners.

Not only did women and minorities receive lower pay, however. In addition they generally found jobs in separate sectors of the economy, jobs specifically for women or minorities. This was true in the 1820s when young white women entered newly opened textile mills, in the 1880s when white women dominated teaching in public schools, in the 1920s when they flocked into the new pink-collar ghetto of clerical work, and it is still true today.

Source: Sara Evans and Barbara Nelson "Comparable Worth in Minnesota: Implementing an Innovative Wage Policy," *Northwest Report* (Fall 1986): 18–21. Reprinted with permission.

---

10. Direct Action and Sabotage: Excerpt from May 1912 Article by Frank Bohn in *Solidarity*

Throughout the history of the labor movement, American labor leaders have quarreled over the use of violence to obtain their objectives, with some on the extreme left arguing that it is justifiable to use force against an oppressive state. The vast majority of leaders rejected violence, however, and asserted that such tactics only robbed unions of needed public support and/or justified harsh crackdowns on all labor movements, including those not engaged in illegal activities. Most of the violence associated with organized labor in the United States was done to, not by, workers.

*Those who criticized violence as a tactic had a point. Enemies of organized labor played upon various fears to break unions, often employing illegal methods of their own to do so. Few unions suffered as much repression as the **Industrial Workers of the World (IWW)**. Its own fiery concepts often came back to haunt it, especially the ideas of **direct action** and sabotage. IWW opponents claimed that the first idea stood for revolutionary violence and the second for wanton destruction of private property. Although a few hotheads occasionally expressed such views, the IWW's official position on these matters was quite different. In the passage below, IWW member Frank Bohn—who was also a committed **socialist**—explains what most early-twentieth-century workers meant by the terms. These definitions originally appeared in the May 18, 1912, issue of the IWW journal* Solidarity.

Direct Action: . . . By direct action is meant any action taken by workers directly at the point of production with a view to bettering their conditions. The organization of any labor union whatever is direct action. Sending the shop committee to demand of the boss a change of shop rules is direct action. To oppose direct action is to oppose labor unionism as a whole with all its activities. In this sense, the term has been used by those who made use of it down to the time of the late controversy. It was the misuse of this expression by the comrades who oppose class-labor unionism which has caused so much uneasiness in the Socialist Party. When we come to the question as to what direct action shall be taken and when and how—that is for the organization on the job to determine. For the Socialist Party to try to lay down rules for the conduct of unions or one union in this matter would be as ridiculous as for the Socialist Party to seek to determine what the workers shall eat for breakfast. It is the business of the Socialist Party to organize and conduct political education activity. . . .

Sabotage:—Sabotage means "strike and stay in the shop." Striking workers thus are enabled to draw pay and keep out scabs while fighting capitalists. Sabotage does not necessarily mean destruction of machinery or other property, although that method has always been indulged in and will continue to be used as long as there is a class struggle. More often it is used to advantage in a quieter way. Excessive limitation of output is sabotage. So is any obstruction of the regular conduct of the industry. Ancient Hebrews in Egypt practiced sabotage when they spoiled bricks. Slaves in the South practiced it regularly by putting stone and dirt in their bags of cotton to make them weigh heavier. An old cotton mill weaver in Massachusetts once told me that when baseball was first played, the boys in his mill stuck a bobbin in the running gear of the water wheel and so tied up the shop on Saturday afternoon that they could go and see the ballgame. . . . When the workers face a specific situation, they will very likely continue to do as their interests and intelligence dictate.

Source: Joyce Kornbluh, ed., *Rebel Voices: An I.W.W. Anthology* (Ann Arbor: University of Michigan Press, 1968), pp. 52–53.

---

11. Dodge Revolutionary Union Movement (D.R.U.M.): Excerpt of February 1971 Article in *Inner-City Voice*

African American workers had long lobbied and pressured white-dominated unions to recognize black workers as equal partners. By the mid-1960s, patience was growing thin both within the labor movement and in society at large. Many black activists associated with the civil-rights movement were attracted to the rising wave of militancy as embodied in organizations like the Black Panthers and the post-1965 Student Non-Violent Coordinating Committee. It was only a matter of time until militants espousing "black power" made their presence known in organized labor. In May 1968, the

*Dodge Revolutionary Union Movement (D.R.U.M.) was born, a radical black-labor caucus within the **United Auto Workers**. D.R.U.M. spawned numerous like-minded groups. The passage below appeared in Inner-City Voice, D.R.U.M.'s official newspaper in the greater Detroit area, in February 1971.*

Groups like D.R.U.M. engendered great fear with their fiery rhetoric. Like many groups emerging in the late 1960s, D.R.U.M.'s words were far more radical than its actions. In the end, one of the major accomplishments of militant groups was shaking up entrenched leaders and calcified organizations. Organized labor did not accede to D.R.U.M.'s most radical demands, but most unions began paying closer attention to African American concerns because of it.

Amidst the miserable conditions of a people whose legitimate struggle had for over 400 years been stifled by the forces of oppression rose the murmur of D.R.U.M. beats. D.R.U.M. beats could be heard in the wildcat strikes, and union elections at Dodge Main. . . . D.R.U.M. beats rapidly permeated to other plants; such as Eldon Gear and Axle, and Ford Rouge. As far away as Mahway, New Jersey (United Black Brothers) and Cambridge, Massachusetts (Polaroid Workers Revolutionary movements) similar beats could be heard.

The increased militancy on the part of black workers found both the bureaucratic unions and management unprepared. But, with great resilience on the part of these reactionary elements, they were able to a certain degree impede the tangible development of these black workers' movements, in 1970, toward the end of a two day union election held in Detroit at the U.A.W., workers who had served as voting challengers were forcibly removed from the union hall by union officials and the local police with three voting booths left open. As a result of this violation of election procedure the U.A.W. functionaries were able to maintain their strangle hold on the local.

Now the D.R.U.M. beats are sounding the tune of International Black Appeal. The International Black Appeal is a charitable fund apparatus, which is attempting to address itself to the problems of black, non-white, and poor white workers. It has five major areas of concern: (1) Emergency food and Health Centers; This component speaks firstly to the severe nature of hunger and incorrect diets of the black and poor people. . . . In addition, and equally important, we seek the immediate construction of medical neighborhood clinics which will provide immediate emergency relief. This would also identify and assist in developing drug centers to alleviate the problem as much as possible. (2) Labor strike [sic] and deals with the problems of black and poor workers' families who because of circumstances many times beyond their control, find the worker of the family is fired, laid off, or becomes severely ill. We want to address ourselves to the families of these needy workers and assist the worker in combating his problems (i.e. stamping out racism in plants, better work conditions, safety conditions, etc.). Families of the black and poor feel these problems in an economic and social order that's overflowing with racism and class preferences. (3) Legal Defense services: Black and poor people are the greatest victims of racism and unequal justice under the law. Here again, the problems of families are affected many times by the loss of the bread winner, inadequate or non-existent money for bail, equally little money for food, lawyers, etc. It is within this realm that the fund wishes to address itself. (4) Welfare system: Here the fund shall address itself to groups of organizations that attempt to make the welfare system and its agencies more responsive and cognizant to the needs of the black and poor communities. (5) Housing and Recreation: This field of endeavor is crucial to the black and poor people's areas. Many problems occur because of the inadequacy or lack of both these facilities. The fund shall seek out organizations to involve itself in combating these problems.

Albeit the I.B.A. is still in its initial stages, however black workers from many of the Detroit area plants have given it their full support. Already many of these workers have spent invaluable time working for I.B.A. . . . It is incumbent upon black and poor people to take an interest in the development of a program, which like no other program in the history of America is geared to operate in their interest. Black workers, especially, must make resolute their determination to insure that in 1971 D.R.U.M. BEATS WILL BE HEARD.

Source: "Drum Beats Will Be Heard," *Inner-City Voice* 3 (February 1971): 3. Reprinted with permission.

---

12. Edward Bellamy: Excerpts from *Looking Backward* (1888)

Few novels have had as much impact on society as Edward Bellamy's Looking Backward. *Some accounts claim that, among nineteenth-century works of fiction, only* Uncle Tom's Cabin *and* Ben-Hur *sold more copies.*

Edward Bellamy (1850–98) was a lifelong social reformer who was working as a newspaper journalist for the Springfield Union, near his home in Chicopee Falls, Massachusetts, at the time his novel was published in 1888. Looking Backward was an overnight success. It follows the fate of Julian West, an insomniac Boston Brahmin, who is put under hypnosis in 1887 and awakens in the year 2000. By then, the strife-torn Boston of his youth has been supplanted by an egalitarian utopia devoid of class strife. The book is essentially an extended lecture delivered by West's benevolent caretaker, Dr. Leete, who painstakingly explains how the utopia came to pass. (An appended Victorian romance enhanced the book's popularity.) The book resonated with Gilded Age audiences for its searing indictment of class conflict and deteriorating social conditions, and proved as popular among middle-class as among working-class readers. Within one year of the book's release, **Bellamyite Nationalist** *clubs sprung up around the nation, all of which were devoted to bringing Bellamy's fictive utopia into a working reality.*

Key to the utopia was the reorganization of labor. All productive, service, and distributive enterprises were controlled by the state, and all citizens were compelled to serve in the "Industrial Army" from ages twenty-one to forty-five. In the first passage below, Bellamy discusses how industry and commerce came to be rethought. In the second, he lays out the organization of the Industrial Army. In both cases, the speaker is Dr. Leete, and Julian West asks the questions.

Early in the last [nineteenth] century the evolution was completed by the final consolidation of the entire capital of the nation. The industry and commerce of the country, ceasing to be conducted by a set of irresponsible corporations and syndicates of private persons at their caprice and for their profit, were entrusted to a single syndicate representing the people, to be conducted in the common interest for the common profit. The nation, that is to say, organized as the one great business corporation in which all other corporations were absorbed; it became the one capitalist in the place of all other capitalists, the sole employer, the final monopoly in which all previous and lesser monopolies were swallowed up, a monopoly in the profits and economics of which all citizens shared. The epoch of trusts had ended in The Great Trust. In a word, the people of the United States concluded to assume the conduct of their own business, just as one hundred-odd years before they had assumed the conduct of their own government, organizing now for industrial purposes on precisely the same grounds that they had then organized for political purposes. . . .

Organization of labor under one direction was the complete solution of what was, in your day and under your system, just regarded as the insoluble labor problem. When the nation become the sole employer all the citizens, by virtue of their citizenship, became employees, to be distributed according to the needs of industry. . . .

The people were already accustomed to idea that the obligation of every citizen not physically disabled, to contribute his military services to the defense of the nation was equal and absolute. That it was equally the duty of every citizen to contribute his quota of industrial or intellectual services to the maintenance of the nation was equally evident, thought it was not until the nation became the employer of labor that citizens were able to render this sort of service with any pretence either of universality or equity. No organization of labor was possible when the employing power was divided among hundreds or thousands of individuals and corporations. . . .

It is regarded as so absolutely natural and reasonable that the idea of its being compulsory has ceased to be thought of. He would be thought to be a incredibly contemptible person who should need compulsion in such a case. . . .

"Is the term of service in this industrial army for life?" Oh, no; it both begins late and ends earlier than the average working period in your day. Your workshops were filled with children and old men but we hold the period of youth sacred to education, and the period of maturity, when the physical forces begin to flag, equally sacred to ease and agreeable relaxation. The period of industrial service is twenty-four years beginning at the close of the course of education at twenty-one and terminating at forty-five. After forty-five, while discharged from labor the citizen remains liable to special calls in case of emergencies. . . .

The fifteenth day of October of every year is what we call Muster Day, because those who have reached the age of twenty-one are then mustered into the industrial service, and at the same time those who, after twenty-four years' service, have reached the age of forty-five are honorably mustered out.

Source: Edward Bellamy, *Looking Backward* (New York: Signet, 1960), pp. 53–54, 57–58.

---

13. Eight-Hour Association: 1886 Appeal for Reduction in Working Hours

The quest for shorter working hours has long been a mainstay of the labor movement. In the early nineteenth century, factory workers customarily toiled twelve or more hours per day. By the Civil War, many workplaces had reduced the workday to ten hours, though longer days continued to prevail in many places. Post–Civil War leaders like **Ira Steward** *began to press Congress to legislate an eight-hour day and a veritable* **eight-hour movement** *emerged across the United States. The following document comes from the Eight-Hour Association, a Boston-based organization with a national presence, which was supported by various trade unions and the* **Knights of Labor***. Note that part of its appeal rests on opportunities for workers to improve themselves morally and intellectually. This is a clever appropriation of popular middle-class self-improvement schemes.*

This particular appeal appeared in **John Swinton***'s paper and was a prelude to the events that culminated in the* **Haymarket Square bombing** *in Chicago.*

The Eight-Hour Association asks for a reduction of all daily toil from ten hours to eight, for the reason that such reduction of time will give opportunity for two more men to work for every eight now employed. In other words, the work now performed by eight men will require ten men to achieve the same result. This will be twenty more men employed for every eighty, thus giving immediate, and for some years, constant labor to all who are willing and able to work.

That every one shall have steady employment at good wages, working eight hours daily, it is necessary that all agree and unite in this movement. In order for each workman to prosper it is essential that all other workmen prosper; because all people support each other by exchanging each others' production and services. Therefore everybody who has commodities or services for sale is interested in having everybody else have a sufficient income from his own earnings to make a mutual exchange. United action in this effort means not only strength but prosperity for all.

The advocates of eight hours for a day's labor advise all workers to take for this number of hours an eight hour price, allowing the law of supply and demand to regulate wages in the future. We fully believe that while merchants, manufacturers and all employers will be benefited, the wages for laborers will soon be higher than ever heretofore, for the following reasons: A reduction of one fifth of laboring time for all that work will make a reduction of one-fifth of all kinds of products in the near future, which will make proportionate scarcity. With scarcity will come advance in prices for every commodity, giving merchants and manufacturers a fair profit, and wage workers an advance in wages. Ere long, all being employed, the production will be as great as now, but, all earning wages, the consumption and demand will be greater than now, so that prices and wages will still continue better than at present.

Eight hours, instead of ten, means a gain of two hours each day—more than one day each week—*seventy-eight days a year!*—a time sufficient to enable every unlettered person to learn to read and write; time in which every foreigner can learn to speak the English language and familiarize himself with his political duty as an American citizen. The extra time thus gained in the year will afford every workingman not only a sufficient recreation, but opportunity to attend the State and county fairs, the National Exposition, and make a visit to the childhood home, with time to spare for a journey to Europe.

This appeal is in the interest of capital as well as labor. The plain facts are that the strikes, lockouts, business failures, general business depression throughout the world, overflowing prisons and poorhouses, are the result of the producing power of the country being far in excess of the practical ability to consume. We make, raise and produce more than we can readily eat, wear, or dispose of. This results, first, in a falling of prices; then a lowering of wages, succeeded by strikes and resistance of wage workers, and a final discharge of workmen into idleness. Then, as men are unable to buy, there is a great underconsumption, goods piling up on one side, while great want and destitution exist on the other. To remedy this, productive power, temporarily, must be lessened. To do this by destroying machinery is barbarous. It is wiser far to accomplish this result, and benefit all mankind, by lessening the hours in which machines and men labor in the work of production. . . .

The advantage of eight hours to the laboring classes will be: (1st) employment; (2d) steady employment; (3d) better wages; (4th) relief from anxiety that comes from idleness and poverty; (5th) an opportunity to lay aside the means for the purchase of a home; (6th) opportunity to see and get acquainted with the family by daylight; (7th) more time for intellectual improvement; (8th) a chance for outdoor recreation on the secular day, without being compelled to take Sunday for that purpose; (9th) the ability to obtain respectable dress and make a good appearance, whereby encouragement is given to attend church and social gatherings, resulting in intellectual, moral and spiritual improvement. . . .

To fully lay this matter before the people, through literature, discussion, lecture, sermon and study, we recommend Saturday, April 24, 1886, as a general holiday for the laboring classes, preparatory to inaugurating the Eight-Hour Movement seven days afterwards, on the first day of May.

In this effort we fervently invoke the aid of the press, the clergy, legislators, teachers, employers, and all persons in authority. Give us employment for the idle masses who are struggling for bread; give us a chance to send pauper and criminal back to shop, and field, and factory, where they may get an honest living; give us back again health and bloom for the sunken eyed, starving sewing-woman; give us homes for working people, and a chance to earn them; give us an honest opportunity for every human being to possess the reasonable comforts of life—GIVE US EIGHT HOURS!

Source: Paul Boller and Ronald Story, *A More Perfect Union: Documents in U.S. History*, vol. 2 (1992), pp. 45–48.

---

14. Emma Goldman: Excerpts from Her Autobiography

Few women have ever made middle-class citizens as nervous as **Emma Goldman** *(1869–1940). Goldman was born in Lithuania and immigrated to the United States when she was seventeen. She began attending* **socialist** *meetings while working as a factory worker in Rochester, New York. By the late 1880s, Goldman converted to* **anarchism**. *She saw the state as an oppressive force and advocated its violent overthrow. She was a dramatic and dynamic speaker who forcefully put forth anarchist precepts from any platform to which she gained access. A worldwide spate of anarchist bombings and assassinations from the 1880s on only added to the fears that Goldman engendered. In 1892, her lover, Alexander Berkman, attempted to murder Homestead Steel manager Henry Clay Frick. Goldman was assumed to have been involved, but there was no evidence linking her to Berkman's attempt. Likewise, prosecutors unsuccessfully sought to connect Goldman to President William McKinley's assassination in 1901. Goldman was deported in 1919 because of her opposition to the United States' entry into World War I.*

In the first passage below, Goldman articulates her intense dislike of governmental authority. It is excerpted from a public speech Goldman made in New York's Union Square, during a severe economic depression that began in 1893. The second excerpt reveals Goldman's take on the question of patriotism. Goldman was an internationalist who felt that shared social class was the true bond between peoples, not artificially constructed national identities. The latter she viewed as vehicles of social control emanating from an oppressive state. Both passages come from the first book of her two-volume autobiography, a rambling affair that is often more episodic than chronological, but which is filled with Goldman's passionate views on individualism, love, social conditions, and politics.

(Note: The reference to Cardinal Manning in the first passage is to Henry Edward Manning [1808–92], an English convert to Catholicism. He won renown for helping settle an 1889 London dockworkers' strike.)

"Men and women," I begin amidst sudden silence, "do you not realize that the State is the worst enemy you have? It is a machine that crushes you in order to sustain the ruling class, your masters. Like naïve children you put your trust in your political leaders. You make it possible for them to creep into your confidence, only to have them betray you to the first bidder. But even where there is no direct betrayal, the labour politicians make common cause with your enemies to keep you in leash, to prevent your direct action. The State is the pillar of capitalism, and it is ridiculous to expect any redress from it. Do you not see the stupidity of asking relief from Albany with immense wealth within a stone's throw from here? Fifth Avenue is laid in gold, every mansion is a citadel of money and power. Yet there you stand, a giant, starved and fettered, shorn of his strength. Cardinal Manning long ago proclaimed that 'necessity knows no law' and that 'the starving man has a right to share of his neighbour's bread.' Cardinal Manning was an ecclesiastic steeped in the traditions of the Church, which has always been on the side of the rich against the poor. But he had some humanity, and he knew that hunger is a compelling force. You, too, will have to learn that you have a right to share your neighbour's bread. Your neighbours—they have not only stolen your bread, but they are sapping your blood. They will go on robbing you, your children, and your children's children, unless you wake up, unless you become daring enough to demand your rights. Well, then, demonstrate before the palaces of the rich; demand work. If they do not give you work, demand bread. If they deny you both, take bread. It is your sacred right!"

Uproarious applause, wild and deafening, broke the stillness like a sudden storm. The sea of hands eagerly stretching out towards me seemed like the wings of white birds fluttering. . . .

[W]hat is patriotism? Is it the love of one's birthplace, the place of childhood recollections and hopes, dreams and aspirations? Is it the place where, in childlike naïveté, we used to watch the passing clouds and wonder why we, too, could not float so swiftly? The place where we used to count the milliard glittering stars, terror stricken lest each one an eye should be, piercing the very depths of our little souls? Is it the place where we would listen to the music of the birds and long to have wings to fly, even as they, to distant lands? Or the place where we would sit at Mother's knee, enraptured by tales of great deeds and conquests? In short, is it love for the spot, every inch representing dear and precious recollections of a happy, joyous, and playful childhood?

If that were patriotism, few American men of today could be called upon to be patriotic, since the place of play has been turned into factory, mill, or mine, while the deafening sounds of machinery have replaced the music of the birds. Nor can we hear any longer the tales of great deeds, for the stories our mothers tell today are but those of sorrow, tears, and grief.

What, then, is patriotism? "Patriotism, sir, is the last resort of scoundrels," said Dr. Johnson. Leo Tolstoy, the greatest anti-patriot of our times, defined patriotism as the principle that justifies the training of wholesale murderers; a trade that requires better equipment for the exercise of man killing than the making of such necessities as shoes, clothing, and houses; a trade that guarantees better returns and greater glory than that of the honest workingman.

Source: Emma Goldman *Living My Life, Volume One* (New York: Dover, 1970; reprint of 1931 original), pp. 122–23, 428–29.

15. Eugene V. Debs: Excerpts from His Statement Upon Sentencing for Violation of the Espionage Act, 1918

*Eugene V. Debs (1855–1926) came to national prominence with the **Pullman Strike** of 1894, which resulted in Debs's first imprisonment, for violating a court injunction. In the years after Pullman, Debs was active in **socialist** politics and ran for the presidency of the United States five times. In 1918, at the height of popular agitation to support World War I, Debs was arrested for making an antiwar speech in Canton, Ohio, in violation of the Espionage Act. Debs was tried, found guilty, and sentenced to serve ten consecutive one-year terms in the Atlanta federal penitentiary. When asked if he had anything to say to the court, Debs delivered this statement, in which he affirmed his ideals, expressed his belief in the need for social change, and insisted that a reorganized social order would eventually come about. During his imprisonment, Debs ran for the presidency again in 1920 and garnered almost a million popular votes. He was pardoned after the war by President Warren G. Harding.*

Your honor, years ago I recognized my kinship with all living beings, and I made up my mind that I was not one bit better than the meanest on earth. I said then, and I say now, that while there is a lower class, I am in it, while there is a criminal element, I am of it, and while there is a soul in prison, I am not free.

I listened to all that was said in this court in support and justification of this prosecution, but my mind remains unchanged. I look upon the Espionage Law as a despotic enactment in flagrant conflict with democratic principles and with the spirit of free institutions. . . .

Your Honor, I have stated in this court that I am opposed to the social system in which we live; that I believe in a fundamental change—but if possible by peaceable and orderly means. . . .

Standing here this morning, I recall my boyhood. At fourteen I went to work in a railroad shop; at sixteen I was firing a freight engine on a railroad. I remember all the hardships and privations of that earlier day, and from that time until now my heart has been with the working class. I could have been in Congress long ago. I have preferred to go to prison. . . .

I am thinking this morning of the men in the mills and factories; of the men in the mines and on the railroads. I am thinking of the women who for a paltry wage are compelled to work out their barren lives; of the little children who in this system are robbed of their childhood and in their tender years are seized in the remorseless grasp of Mammon and forced into the industrial dungeons, there to feed the monster machines while they themselves are being starved and stunted, body and soul. I see them dwarfed and diseased and their little lives broken and blasted because in this high noon of our twentieth-century Christian civilization money is still so much more important than the flesh and blood of childhood. In very truth gold is god today and rules with pitiless sway in the affairs of men.

In this country, the most favored beneath the bending skies—we have vast areas of the richest and most fertile soil, material resources in inexhaustible abundance, the most marvelous productive machinery on earth, and millions of eager workers ready to apply their labor to that machinery to produce an abundance for every man, woman, and child—and if there are still vast numbers of our people who are the victims of poverty and whose lives are an unceasing struggle all the way from youth to old age, until at last death comes to their rescue and stills their aching hearts and lulls these hapless victims to dreamless sleep, it is not the fault of the Almighty: it cannot be charged to nature, but it is due entirely to the outgrown social system in which we live, that ought to be abolished not only in the interest of the toiling masses but in the higher interest of all humanity. . . .

I believe, Your Honor, in common with all Socialists, that this nation ought to own and control its own industries. I believe, as all Socialists do, that all things that are jointly needed and used ought to be jointly owned—that industry, the basis of our social life, instead of being the private property of the few and operated for their enrichment, ought to be the common property of all, democratically administered in the interest of all. . . .

I am opposing a social order in which it is possible for one man who does absolutely nothing that is useful to amass a fortune of hundreds of millions of dollars, while millions of men and women who work all the days of their lives secure barely enough for a wretched existence.

This order of things cannot always endure. I have registered my protest against it. I recognize the feebleness of my effort, but fortunately I am not alone. There are multiplied thousands of others who, like myself, have come to realize that before we may truly enjoy the blessings of civilized life, we must reorganize society upon a Mutual and co-operative basis; and to this end we have organized a great economic and political movement that spreads over the face of all the earth.

There are today upwards of sixty millions of Socialists, loyal, devoted adherents to this cause, regardless of nationality, race, creed, color, or sex. They are all making common cause. They are spreading with tireless energy the propaganda of the new social order. They are waiting, watching, and working hopefully through all the hours of the day and the night. They are still in a minority. But they have learned how to be patient and to bide their time. They feel—they know, indeed—that the time is coming, in spite of all opposition, all persecution, when this emancipating gospel will spread among all the peoples, and when this minority will become the triumphant majority and, sweeping into power, inaugurate the greatest social and economic change in history.

In that day we shall have the universal commonwealth—the harmonious co-operation of every nation with every other nation on earth. . . .

Source: Eugene V. Debs, *Writings and Speeches* (New York: Hermitage Press, 1948).

---

16. Excluding Black Workers: 1902 Letter in *Locomotive Firemen's Magazine* and 1929 Article by Elmer Anderson Carter in *Opportunity*

Although labor unions have often been at the forefront of progressive change in the United States, they have had their share of blind spots as well. One of the worst of these has been race, especially as it pertains to African American workers. Many trade unions forbade black members well into the twentieth century, and some black leaders claim there are still prejudice barriers to overcome. Only a handful of organizations—most notably the **Knights of Labor**, *the* **United Mine Workers of America**, *and the* **Industrial Workers of the World**—*have consistently good records relating to black laborers, and there were plenty of ugly, racist incidents within even those organizations. The excerpts below highlight some of the challenges faced by black workers.*

The first letter appeared in a 1902 issue of the Locomotive Firemen's Magazine *and is in response to an appeal to accept black members, from a New Yorker named George Peters. It is important to realize that the response was typical and that the Firemen were no worse than many other trade unions, despite the fact that the rebuttal comes from a Southerner. Racism was pervasive, not regional.*

The second article contains Elmer Anderson Carter's blistering 1929 condemnation of the racial policies of the **American Federation of Labor**. *It appeared in* Opportunity *on November 7, 1929. Many of the same charges were echoed by* **A. Philip Randolph** *in a 1961 report to the American Federation of Labor-Congress of Industrial Organizations. Although the executive council refuted his charges, they resonated among many black workers.*

RESPONSE TO GEORGE H. PETERS

I have just read an article . . . entitled "The Negro and Organized Labor in the South." The brother's motives may be all right, but his article will receive a cup of very cold water in the South.

The Negro can organize on his own responsibility if he likes, but he can never affiliate with southern organizations of any kind. The firemen of the South have a great work to do . . . without crossing the color line and reaching out to Mr. "Burr Head," to assist him to a place of safety and security. . . .

What has the Negro done to merit recognition by the Firemen? The brother from New York says the Negro will accept his inferiority to the white man . . . but all southern men would laugh at the brother's ignorance of the Negro . . . for if he is given a foot, he tries to take a block. In many, many cases, he is thick headed and non-progressive, and when he goes to school for a couple of years he begins to think he knows it all, and it only makes a worthless fool of him. The southern man . . . draw(s) the line when it comes to taking him into our worthy order. . . .

Member of 522
Shreveport, LA

THE A.F.L. AND THE NEGRO

It has often been asserted that black workers have been slow in accepting the doctrines and methods of organized labor. . . . This apparent indifference of the black worker . . . has served to draw the fire of various officials of the American

Federation of Labor who, when accused of apathy to the fate of Negro labor, have replied . . . that the Negro worker was unorganizable. . . .

The recent convention of the American Federation of Labor . . . lacked much of being able to convince observers that it is the pillar of flame . . . to lead the black worker, or for that matter the white worker, out of the wilderness. Out of the thirty million workers in America less than three million are enrolled in the American Federation. . . .

Only in those occupations, generally semi-skilled or unskilled, which attract large numbers of Negroes, such as longshoremen, hod-carriers, common building laborers, or those in which Negroes enjoy a comparative monopoly, such as dining-car porters; or those in which Negro competition is able to cope . . . with the competition of white workers, as in the coal mining industry . . . has American organized labor made any real effort to enlist the black worker. . . . There are approximately 100,000 Negro workers who are affiliated with some form of labor organization, a remarkable number when one considers that the Negro not only is outside the pale of the skilled craft organizations, but also is compelled . . . to face the opposition of white labor, organized and unorganized, to gain a foothold in industry.

It is true that the American Federation of Labor has issued several lofty pronouncements to the effect that no discrimination because of race or color should govern admission to unions. It is also true that only eleven unions . . . specifically deny Negroes membership. But . . . even when racial prejudice does not operate . . . to keep Negroes put, craft limitations and restrictions achieve the same result. . . .

[T]here will be but little hope for the black worker in the American Federation of Labor as long as it is the so-called "aristocracy of labor," as long as it remains structurally a craft organization. . . .

Source: Philip Foner and Ronald Lewis, eds., *Black Workers: A Documentary History from Colonial Times to the Present* (Philadelphia: Temple University, 1989), pp. 255–56, 409–10.

---

17. Fair Wages: Excerpt from John L. Lewis's *The Miners' Fight for American Standards* (1925)

*One of the clearest statements ever uttered on **wages** was by **John L. Lewis**, who headed the **United Mine Workers of America (UMWA)** from 1920 to 1960 and was a founder of the **Congress of Industrial Organizations** and served as its president from 1935 to 1940. Before Lewis was such a well-known national figure, he penned* The Miners' Fight for American Standards *in 1925. The book's title is deliberate and strategic; Lewis wanted to show that what the UMWA wanted was in keeping with American values and aspirations. In the wake of the post–World War I crackdown on radicals, to say nothing of bloody capital/labor clashes involving coal miners in places like*

Matewan and *Blair Mountain*, *Lewis insisted that miners were loyal Americans seeking only a fair deal. Miners' Fight is, above all, a defense of prudent unionism. Lewis locates the desire for higher wages within the very logic of* **capitalism**.

Primarily the United Mine Workers of America insists upon the maintenance of the wage standards, guaranteed by the existing contractual relations in the industry, in the interests of its own membership. It is acting in that respect exactly as any other individual, organization, or corporation would do under like circumstances. The theory of our system of free enterprise is that the ultimate prosperity of all is best assured by the utmost endeavor of each to better his own condition. Trade unionism is an integral part of the existing system of industry first called by its critics capitalism. The word once used in reproach has in these times been adopted with pride by the advocates and defenders of the system, as was the case in regard to great religious sects and political parties, which adopted as badges of honor names first hurled at them as epithets.

Distrust and hostility toward the business system wane as it is becoming better understood how the general prosperity and individual and family welfare of modern peoples had been increased by the use of capital in production to multiply the productive power of man's labor, whether of hand or brain. Trade unionism is a phenomenon of capitalism quite similar to the cooperation. One is essentially a pooling of labor for purposes of common action in production and in sales. The other is a pooling of capital for exactly the same purposes. The economic aims of both are identical—gain. . . .

Source: John L. Lewis, *The Miners' Fight for American Standards* (Indianapolis: Bell Publishing Company, 1925), pp. 40–41.

---

18. Flint Sit-Down Strike: Excerpt of 1976 Interview of Genora Johnson Dollinger

One of the seminal events in American labor history was the 1936–37 **sit-down strike** *against General Motors (GM) in Flint, Michigan. Most analysts credit success at Flint as establishing the* **United Auto Workers (UAW)** *as a legitimate bargaining agent in the automotive industry. Still others claim that this strike virtually transformed the* **Congress of Industrial Organizations** *from a fledgling federation into a powerful rival to the established* **American Federation of Labor**. *For forty-four days, workers barricaded themselves inside the Chevrolet Number 1 and Fisher Body Number 2 buildings, key plants in GM's production. One estimate claims that 112,000 of the company's 150,000 employees were affected by the sit-down strike.*

The story of Flint usually centers on the men who stayed inside the factory, but they could not have held out were it not for the massive logistical and material support of the Women's Emergency Brigade. Women also placed their bodies and lives on the line in support of the strike. A key moment came on January 11, 1937, when GM tried to forcibly evict the sit-down strikers. First they cut off heat and power to Fisher Num-

ber 2, despite the sixteen-degree weather, then police rushed the plant. They were rebuffed by a fusillade of auto parts from occupying workers. As Victor Reuther, Roy Reuther, and Bob Travis arrived on the scene with a UAW sound truck, Genora Johnson took the microphone and exhorted the women of Flint to stand up for their husbands, boyfriends, and brothers. As the women surged, Flint police retreated, and the Battle of the Running Bulls ended in victory for the union. (Note: The term bull is a slang reference to police officers.)

In 1976, Genora Johnson Dollinger related the story to historian Sherna Gluck. This passage comes from Gluck's interview.

[W]e had the water hoses from the plant, and the hinges. . . . Those hinges were kind of heavy hinges. You know, the old car-door hinge was a different thing. And they got the big boxloads of them and they got them down to look so they could fire them from downstairs, and they were upstairs on the roof firing them, too. . . .

There was no hand-to-hand combat. [The police] . . . had rifle shot and buckshot. There was firebombs and those tear gas canisters. And we would run out and grab [those]—the men were much faster at that, and . . . they were better pitchers. . . . They'd get tear gas canisters and hurl them back. And the firebombs, they usually got those . . . but the timing on those was very important. . . .

So anyway, the sound car was down there, and we had Victor Reuther as the primary speaker. And then he would pull up other men, making their appeals, and this went on and on. It never dawned on me . . . to speak. In the first place, this was primarily a man's operation, and I'm down there helping out, although I never thought too much about men and women when we were right in the heart of a battle. . . . I'd never made any kind of a public speech over a microphone, and it—until [Victor Reuther] came back and told us. He said, "Well, we may have lost the battle. The war is not lost, but we may have lost this battle." And he gave us the idea that we had to prepare people for . . . this little defeat. And I said to him then, I said, "Well, Victor, why don't I speak over the . . . loudspeaker? . . . " And he says, "Well, we've got nothing to lose." He had great confidence . . . in women. . . . So that's when I got up to take the mike. And, again, there, you lose yourself. You go beyond yourself and think of the cause. And I was able to make my voice really ring out on that one because I knew that [sound system] battery was going down. We only had a few moments left. And so, that's when I appealed to the women of Flint. I bypassed everybody else . . . and went right to the women and told them what was happening. And that's when I said, "There are women down here, mothers of children," and I made it sound plural, because I knew that here was this gallantry that's always present in the hearts of men and other women that are going to come down and stand by women in such a situation. So that's when I said, "There are women down here, mothers of children, and I beg of you to come down here and stand with your husband, your loved ones . . . your brothers, and even your sweethearts," because we had a lot of couples . . . and I'd get their girlfriends.

And when I made that appeal, it was a strange thing. It was dark, too. But I could almost hear a hush. . . . I could hear a hush over that crowd the minute a woman's voice went over. It was startling, you know. All night long, they didn't know there was even a woman down there.

And as that happened, I thought I saw . . . car lights. Whatever it was in this darkness, we could see the action going on up [at Fisher Number 2]. . . . [M]aybe they were factory headlights or spotlights on us or . . . police lights. But I saw a first woman struggling, and I noticed that she had started to come down, and a cop grabbed her by the coat and she went right out of that coat. And this was in freezing weather. . . . There was ice on the . . . pavement and everything. And she just kept right on coming. And as soon as that happened, other women broke through, and again we had that situation where cops didn't want to fire into backs of women. And once they did that, the men came, naturally, and that was the end of the battle.

Source: Interview conducted by Sherna Gluck. © Feminist History Research Project, 1976. http://historymatters.gmu.edu/d/136/.

---

19. Forcing the Hand of the Fair Employment Practices Committee: Excerpt from November 1942 Article in *Survey Graphic* Magazine

As World War II loomed, African Americans found themselves in a precarious situation. Most of American society, North and South, was still deeply in the throes of Jim Crow systems that segregated whites and blacks. Good-paying jobs existed in the burgeoning defense industry, but most employers refused to hire black workers (often at the insistence of white labor unions). If work could be secured, it was often in jobs considered too degrading for white workers. The mobilization of large numbers of white workers—the armed forces remained segregated until after World War II— made it apparent that black labor would play an important part in America's defense efforts. **A. Philip Randolph** *seized upon the situation. Randolph put out a call for African Americans to march upon Washington, D.C., on July 1, 1941, to protest job and social discrimination. The prospect of tens of thousands of black citizens marching on the nation's Capitol at the same time efforts were afoot to counter fascism abroad forced the hand of President Franklin Roosevelt. In exchange for Randolph's agreement to call off the march, President Roosevelt issued Executive Order 8802, which created the* **Fair Employment Practices Committee (FEPC)**, *which mandated that all federal agencies, contractors, and job-training programs were to be free of religious or racial discrimination.*

The FEPC was an important first step, but hardly the panacea that cured racial discrimination. Randolph cagily kept the threat of a march on Washington alive, though most historians now believe that he was bluffing about the alleged numbers of African American marchers he could muster. Randolph nonetheless used his threat to keep demands for black equality alive. The piece from Randolph excerpted below appeared in the November 1942 issue of Survey Graphic *magazine.*

Though I have found no Negroes who want to see the United Nations lose this war, I have found many who, before the war ends, want to see the stuffing knocked out of white supremacy and of empire over subject peoples. American Negroes, involved as we are in the general issues of the conflict, are confronted not with a choice but with the challenge both to win democracy for ourselves at home and to help win the war for democracy the world over.

There is no escape from the horns of this dilemma. There ought not to be escape. For if the war for democracy is not won abroad, the fight for democracy cannot be won at home. If this war cannot be won for the white peoples, it will not be won for the darker races.

Controversially, if freedom and equality are not vouchsafed for the peoples of color, the war for democracy will not be won. Unless this double-barreled thesis is accepted and applied, the darker races will never whole-heartedly fight for the victory of the United Nations. That is why those familiar with the thinking of the American Negro have sensed his lack of enthusiasm, whether among the educated or uneducated, rich or poor, professional or non-professional, religious or secular, rural or urban, north, south, east or west. . . .

What are the reasons for this state of mind? The answer is: discrimination, segregation, Jim Crow. Witness the navy, the army, the air corps; and also government services at Washington. In many parts of the South, Negroes in Uncle Sam's uniform are being put upon, mobbed, sometimes even shot down by civilian and military police, and on occasion lynched. Vested political interests in race prejudice are so deeply entrenched that to them winning the war against Hitler is secondary to preventing Negroes from winning democracy for themselves. This is worth many divisions to Hitler and Hirohito. While labor, business, and farm are subjected to ceilings and floors and not allowed to carry on as usual, these interests trade in the dangerous business of race hate as usual.

When the defense program began and billions of taxpayers' money were appropriated for guns, ships, tanks, and bombs, Negroes presented themselves for work only to be given the cold shoulder. North as well as the South, and despite their qualifications, Negroes were denied skilled employment. Not until their wrath and indignation took the form of a proposed protest march on Washington, scheduled for July 1, 1941, did things begin to move in the form of defense jobs for Negroes. The march was postponed by the timely issuance (June 24, 1941) of the famous Executive Order No. 8802 by President Roosevelt. But this order and the President's Committee on Fair Public Practice, established there under, have as yet only scratched the surface by way of eliminating discriminations on account of race or color in war industry. Both management and labor unions in too many places in too many ways are still drawing the color line. . . .

PROGRAM OF THE MARCH ON WASHINGTON MOVEMENT

1. We demand, in the interest of national unity, the abrogation of every law which makes a distinction in treatment between citizens based on religion, creed, color, or national origin. This means an end to Jim Crow in education, in housing, in transportation and in every other social, economic, and political privilege; and especially, we demand, in the capital of the nation, an end to all segregation in public places and in public institutions.

2. We demand legislation to enforce the Fifth and Fourteenth Amendments guaranteeing that no person shall be deprived of life, liberty or property without due process of law, so that the full weight of the national government may be used for the protection of life and thereby may end the disgrace of lynching.

3. We demand the enforcement of the Fourteenth and Fifteenth Amendments and the enactment of the Pepper Poll Tax bill so that all barriers in the exercise of the suffrage are eliminated.

4. We demand the abolition of segregation and discrimination in the army, navy, marine corps, air corps, and all other branches of national defense.

5. We demand an end to discrimination in jobs and job training. Further, we demand that the F.E.P.C. be made a permanent administrative agency of the U.S. Government and that it be given power to enforce its decisions based on its findings.

6. We demand that federal funds be withheld from any agency which practices discrimination in the use of such funds.

7. We demand colored and minority group representation on all administrative agencies so that these groups may have recognition of their democratic right to participate in formulating policies.

8. We demand representation for the colored and minority racial groups on all missions, political and technical, which will be sent to the peace conference so that the interests of all people everywhere may be fully recognized and justly provided for in the post-war settlement.

Source: Philip Foner and Ronald Lewis, eds., *Black Workers: A Documentary History from Colonial Times to the Present* (Philadelphia: Temple University Press, 1989), pp. 527–30.

---

20. Forty Years in a Steel Mill: Studs Terkel Interviews Steelworker Steve Dubi

In 1972, Studs Terkel interviewed more than eighty Americans engaged in a wide variety of jobs about their work. Terkel called the resulting work a book about violence, both to body and to spirit. For many workers, he found the workday to be a struggle by the "walking wounded." Here Terkel talks with veteran Chicago steelworker Steve Dubi about his forty years in the steel mill. Dubi's discouragement is obvious, as is his pride in seeing his sons steer clear of work in the steel mills.

We're in Pullman, an industrial neighborhood on the far South Side of Chicago. It is a one-family dwelling, much like all the others on the block. He has lived in this area all his life. "I was born in the shadow of them steel mills." He has worked as an inspector at the South Works of U.S. Steel for forty years.

"I was hired in '29 as a water boy. I was sixteen. I had to be seventeen, but in those days they overlooked a little thing here, a little thing there. I worked for a year. Then came the Crash. I was rehired in June '33 and I've been inspecting ever since. I'm ready for retirement. But the home we live in isn't paid for yet. The car I'm driving isn't paid for yet. Nothing to show for forty years of work."

His wife is a licensed practical nurse who "works with geriatrics." They have two sons. Robert, a Vietnam war veteran, is married. He's in the field of sales. Their other son, Father Leonard Dubi, is one of the city's most renowned activist priests. As a passionate spokesman for the blue-collar community in which his parish is located, he has on numerous occasions challenged some of the city's most powerful men and institutions.

During the visit, as his weariness is evident, his wife joins the conversation.

When we were kids we thought the steel mill was it. We'd see the men comin' out, all dirty, black. The only thing white was the goggles over their eyes. We thought they were it, strong men. We just couldn't wait to get in there. When we finally did get in, we were sorry. (Chuckles.) It wasn't what it was cut out to be.

You're on your feet all day, on concrete. They lay the steel out on the skids. It's like a long horse, and they lay the steel across. You get your flashlight and you walk over it and you chalk it and mark the defect. You look for the defect in the steel. You watch the tolerances for lengths and thickness and what not. You have a chipper or a grinder to smooth it out. If it comes within the tolerance the customer allows, it's all right. If it goes too deep, you scrap the bar or recut it. When we broke in, the older men showed us what defects to look for. A crack in the bar is called a seam. Some would be wide open where you couldn't miss 'em. Some were real tight and you would have to look close. It's hard on the eyes. Oh, your eyes do get tired. I put some drops in my eyes.

I'm getting up in the age now where I can't take it any more. In my younger days I used to work eight hours, go out and play a doubleheader of softball, go out and drink a shot, and sleep it off (laughs), and go back to work in the morning. And not feel too much pain. (Sighs.) But now I can't take it any more. I'd like to retire. I think I've worked hard enough and long enough, but I still can't see my way out. I don't know if I'll make it. I got sore legs and a sore back, sore arms, arthritis, bursitis, and every other thing is catching up on me. (Laughs.)

Everyone looks forward to retirement, but there's a lot of 'em not makin' it. That's all they talk about is retirement. Where are you gonna go? What are you gonna do? And the poor soul never makes it. A lot of 'em, they're countin' the months instead of the years—and pass away. A lot of my friends are passed away already.

I can take it any time I want, but I won't be fifty-nine until December. I don't get on social security until I'm sixty-two. Why, that'll be another three years. I don't want to go just yet, but maybe I won't be able to take it any more. It's gettin' tougher. I'm not like a machine. Well, a machine wears out too sometimes.

And they're forcin' more work on ya. It's knockin' off men, makin' cutbacks here and there to save money. They've knocked off an awful lot of jobs. With the foreign imports of steel they're losin' money. That's what they say. I suppose in order to make a profit they have to cut somewhere. But I told 'em "After forty years of work, why do you take a man away from me? You're gonna force me into retirement." All of us were real angry. But there's nothin' we can do about it. What can I do? Quit?

I try not to take this home with me. I don't tell her nothin' about it. It'll cause her to worry. There's nothin' I can do about it. About four o'clock I'll sit down here and watch TV, maybe get my dinner on a TV table and I watch the finish of the ball game or the finish of a good movie. I'll sit back here and work the cross-word puzzle and read the sports news and I fall asleep. (Laughs.)

I had to ask [for] this coming Sunday off because I'm going to a golf outing. Otherwise I'd have had to work from three to eleven. They're working us twelve days in a row. When I'm workin' on the day shift I'll work Monday through Saturday, seven to three. The following week I'll be lined up on the three to eleven shift. It's a forty-hour week, but it's always twelve days in a row.

If they're in a slack time, they go down to one shift. You can't make any long-range plan. When we bought this house fourteen years ago, the real estate man wanted to sell me a lot more expensive house. I said no. With the job I have I don't know if I'll be workin' three, four months from now. We might go out on strike. We may go down to four days a week. Been like this all these years.

I got nothin' to show for it. I live in a home the bank has a mortgage on. (Laughs.) I own a car the finance people have the title to. (Laughs.) I don't know where they got the idea that we make so much. The lowest class payin' job there, he's makin' two dollars an hour if he's makin' that much. It starts with jobs class-1 and then they go up to class-35. But no one knows who that one is. Probably the superintendent. So they put all these class jobs together, divide it by the number of people workin' there, and you come up with a fabulous amount. But it's the big bosses who are makin' all the big money and the little guys are makin' the little money. You hear these politicians give themselves a thousand-dollar raise, and they scream when the steelworker asks for fifty cents an hour raise.

You pack your lunch, or you buy it at the vending machine. We used to have a canteen in there, but they cut that out. The vending machine is lousy. It hurts a man when he'll put his quarter or thirty-five cents in there for a can of vegetable soup and it takes the coin but don't kick anything out. There's no one there to open the machine and give him his quarter back or a can of food. (Laughs.) A lotta machines are broken that way. Every day it occurs.

You're not regarded. You're just a number out there. Just like a prisoner. When you report off you tell 'em your badge number. A lotta people don't know your name. They know you by your badge number. My number is 44–065. When your work sheet is sent in your name isn't put down, just your number. At the main office they don't know who 44–065 is. They don't know if he's black, white, or Indian. They just know he's 44–065.

Of course, there are accidents. They're movin' a lot of steel—a lot of crane movement and transfer buggy movement and switchin' and trucks. And there's machinery that straightens the bars and turning lathes. Always movement. You eat the dust and dirt and take all the different things that go with it. How you gonna grind a defect out of a bar without creating dust? How you can scarf the billet without makin' smoke? When a man takes off sick, he's got a chest cold, how do you know what he's got? A lot of people died, they just had a heart attack. Who knows what they die of?

We have to slog our way through dirt and smog and rain and slush to get to our place of work. From the mill gate to where I work is about a fifteen-, twenty-minute walk. In-between that you have puddles. We don't have a nice walkway with an overhead ramp. We don't have a shuttle bus. If it's raining, you walk through the rain. If it's snowin' or blowin', you're buckin' that snow and the wind. In the wintertime that wind is comin' off that lake, it's whippin' right into your face.

That place is not inside a building. It's just under a roof. There's no protection against the winds. They won't even plug up the holes to keep the draft off you. Even the snow comes through and falls on you while you're workin'. The roof is so leaky they should furnish you with umbrellas.

His wife murmurs: "He's sick all the time."

The union squawks about it, but if the steel mill don't fix it, what are you gonna do? The washrooms are in terrible shape. But when they get around to fixin' 'em, there's five hundred men usin' one bowl to sit on. The union's helped a great deal, but the steel mill is slow in comin' across with things like they should.

If I retire right now, I would make $350 a month. There's a woman across the street got a half a dozen kids and no husband, and she's probably gettin' five hundred dollars a month from ADC. She gets more money than I would right now after workin' for forty years. If I retire now, my insurance is dropped. I belong to this Blue Cross-Blue Shield insurance now. If I go on a pension, I would get dropped automatically. The day you retire, that's the day it's out.

I told my sons, "If you ever wind up in that steel mill like me, I'm gonna hit you right over your head. Don't be foolish. Go get yourself a schooling. Stay out of the steel mill or you'll wind up the same way I did." Forty years of hard work and what have I got to show for it? Nothing. I can't even speak proper. When you're a steelworker (laughs), you don't get to speak the same language that you would do if you meet people in a bank or a business office.

When I was going to school I really loved mechanical drawing. I really excelled in it in high school. I was gettin' good marks. But my dad died. Well, most of the children had saloon keepers and grocery store keepers, they had dads workin', and they were able to buy things. I felt embarrassed because I couldn't buy the proper paper. I would use the other side of someone else's discarded paper. I did love mechanical drawing and I was good at it. Well, I had to get a job. . . ."

I was hopin' Leonard would be a doctor. When he entered the seminary, I thought: Gee, what caused him to go in there? When he was an Andy Frain usher he was assigned to Holy Name and he got acquainted with a lot of priests there. A lot of the ushers were at the seminary. They probably influenced him. He's happy, so I'm happy for him. At first I wasn't sure he was gonna stay, 'cause he loved life too much. He loved everything, people and animals. (Muses) Maybe that's why he became a priest . . . (Trails off.)

In the past, it was strictly parish. They come out once a year to bless the house and shake the hand. But now, with the younger set, things have changed. All the priests are goin' without their collars and doin' a lot of things that the old-time priest would never think of doin'. I don't think they were allowed to.

Henrietta Dubi reflects: "I'll never forget those women, my neighbors, they were sittin' out on the porch and they couldn't understand why I'm grievin' that Leonard went into the seminary. They said, 'Oh, it's such an honor.' I said, 'Yes, but it's gonna be a hard life.' No freedom, no privileges. We could only see him once a month. I figured he was in prison. One day I said to him, 'Leonard, are you happy?' He said, 'I can't begin to tell you how happy I am. Please don't ask again. I chose this life and this is the life I'm going to lead.' When he was havin' his senior prom, I should have known then. Everything he was buying was black. It never dawned on me. The first time I seen Skid Row in my life was when my son took me down there. He said, 'I want to save people like this.' In a kidding way I said, 'These people are beyond saving.' He said, 'As long as there's breath in 'em, they can be saved.' I was sad and depressed when he first went in. I couldn't understand why. Now I'm very proud of him. I wish there were more like him to speak out, but some are afraid. We pray for him all the time."

Sometimes I worry about him. He takes on the real big shots. He might buck the wrong person. They've been shooting Presidents and senators. He could be shot at too—if he says the wrong thing or gets the wrong man angry. When you're foolin' around with a politician, why you got troubles. But he's for the people, he wants 'em to have a square deal. And I'm glad. If the people don't like what he's sayin', why that's too bad.

You know the big joke? When Len was an Andy Frain usher, he used to seat Mayor Daley in his box at Comiskey Park. Ten years later he's fightin' him on the Crosstown Expressway business and the county assessor's office. (Laughs.) When we first started visiting Leonard at the seminary we weren't even allowed to bring him a newspaper. He wasn't allowed to have a radio. It was so strict at that time. What amazes me now, I turn on the TV and I see him arguin' with the mayor. (Laughs.) Or the county assessor and them politicians. It's so different, it's fantastic.

When he started on this pollution against the steel mills, I told Leonard everybody knows the steel mill is polluting. How can you make steel without polluting? I'm not gonna bite the hand that feeds me. They been doing it for a hundred years. It could be cut down a great deal, I suppose, if they wanted—which they are trying to do. They're putting in a lot of new buildings. I don't know what they are, but they claim it's for ecology. Who knows?

This pollution business. He helped them people on the West Side where he lived. When we used to go to visit him it seemed you are going into a valley. It seemed you hit a fog bank. We learned later it was smog from the Edison plants. And he cleared it up. So we're for him one hundred percent. But this fightin' with the mayor and the aldermen, that scares me. (Laughs.)

Mrs. Dubi interjects: "When I see him on television, I run. There might be a nut in the audience who'll shoot."

She's scared. We're real proud of him. All my friends cut clippings out of the newspaper and bring 'em to me and they'll say, "Hey, I heard Leonard on the radio on my way to work." They'll tell me they're all for him. My sister was tellin' us the other day that her doctor was speakin' of a young priest who was doin' so much for the people in the neighborhood. She said, "That's my nephew." He said, "Gee, he's wonderful."

You know what I told him to start on next? He's fightin' for lower taxes, which is all right. And better livin' conditions, which is all right. And this road that he's against, it's all right. Like he said, they're gonna demolish a lotta homes, a lotta people are gonna be put out. So the next thing I want him to do is lower this age of retirement, social security to about sixty, so I can get out of the mill sooner. If they lowered the age to about sixty, maybe they'd get a year or two benefit out of the pension before they die.

Hard workin' never killed a man, they say. I say workin' in the steel mill is not like workin' in an air-conditioned office, where politicians and bankers sit on their fannies. Where you have to eat all that dust and smoke, you can't work hard and live a long life. You shouldn't be made to work till sixty-two or sixty-five to reap any benefit. We're paying social security, and most of us will never realize a penny from it. That's why they should give it to him at a younger age to let him enjoy a few years of the life he ruined workin' in the factory. I told him. "Leonard, you get to work on that next." (Laughs.)

Yeah, we're proud of Len. At least he's doin' somethin'. What have I done in my forty years of work? I led a useless life. Here I am almost sixty years old and I don't have anything to show for it. At least he's doing something for his people. I worked all my life and helped no one. What I'm happy about is that them two boys took my advice and stayed out of the steel mill. (Laughs.) We're a couple of dummies. We worked all our lives and we have nothing.

MRS. DUBI: You know what we have? We got two million dollars in our children. Even in this angered world, both these kids turned out good, right? So we're still winners. (To him) Even though we don't have the cash, Father, we don't have nothin' to retire with we still got two million dollars.

You gotta show it to me.

MRS. DUBI: You see him on TV, don't you?

No thanks to me. I had nothin' to do with makin' him what he is. I told you I am nothing. After forty years of workin' at the steel mill, I am just a number. I think I've been a pretty good worker. That job was just right for me. I had a minimum amount of education and a job using a micrometer and just a steel tape and your eyes—that's a job that was just made for me. But they don't appreciate it. They don't care. Bob worked in the mill a few months during a school vacation. He said, "I don't know how you done it all these years. I could never do it." I said, "I been tellin' you all your life never get into that mill." (Laughs.)

Source: Reprinted by permission of Donadio & Olson, Inc. Copyright © 1974 by Studs Terkel.

---

21. Founding of the American Federation of Labor (AFL): Excerpts from the AFL Call to Action (1886)

*The largest labor federation of the late nineteenth century was the **Knights of Labor**. The Knights, however, organized workers irrespective of their skill level, trade, race, ethnicity (except for Chinese), or gender. Its local assemblies often mixed workers from various walks of life. Some **craft unionists** disagreed with the Knights' catholic approach to organizing and felt that true solidarity could only be obtained among workers sharing the same skilled trades. Moreover, some resented what they perceived* *as the Knights of Labor's interference in matters pertaining to the trades. The Knights had many trade assemblies, but by the 1880s, it and national trade unions often found themselves embroiled in bitter battles over* **jurisdiction**, **strikes**—*which the Knights opposed—and numerous other tactics and issues. The Knights had an especially tumultuous relationship with the Cigar Makers International Union and two of its leaders,* **Adolph Strasser** *and* **Samuel Gompers**.

In May 1886, a "peace" conference between the Knights and trades unions ended acrimoniously, with the Knights of Labor claiming it was the only true repository of labor solidarity, while craft unions passed resolutions demanding that the Knights of Labor confine itself to unorganized and unskilled workers and leave all craft workers to their respective national and international unions. In December 1886, craft unionists met to transform a moribund craft federation, the Federation of Organized Trades and Labor Unions. It became the **American Federation of Labor (AFL)**. *The AFL's call to action is excerpted below.*

The time has now arrived to draw the bonds of unity much closer together between all the trades unions of America. We need an annual Trades Congress that shall have for its object:

1. The formation of trades unions and the encouragement of the trades union movement in America.
2. The organization of trades assemblies, trades councils or central labor unions in every city in America and the further encouragement of such bodies.
3. The founding of state trades assemblies or state labor congresses to influence state legislation in the interest of the working masses.
4. The establishment of national and international trades unions based upon the strict recognition of the autonomy of each trade, and the promotion and advancement of such bodies.
5. An American Federation of Alliance of all national and international trades unions to aid and assist each other and furthermore to secure national legislation in the interest of the working people and influence public opinion by peaceful and legal methods in favor of organized labor.
6. To aid and encourage the labor press of America and to disseminate tracts and literature on the labor movement. . . .
7. . . . Whereas the Knights of Labor have persistently attempted to undermine and disrupt the well-established trades unions [, have] organized and encouraged men who have proven untrue to their trade, false to the obligation of their union, embezzlers of moneys and expelled by many of the unions and conspiring to pull down the trades unions. . . .

Resolved: That we condemn the acts above recited and call upon all workingmen to join the unions of their respective trades and urge the formation of national and international unions and the centralization of all under one head, the American Federation of Labor.

Source: Norman Ware, The Labor Movement in the United States 1860–1895: A Study in Democracy *(1929; reprint; Gloucester: Peter Smith, 1959), pp. 294–97.*

22. Gilded Age Social Conditions: Testimony before the U.S. Senate Committee upon the Relations between Labor and Capital (1883)

The period from roughly the end of the Civil War to the turn of the twentieth century is often dubbed the "Gilded Age" by historians taking their lead from an eponymous 1873 novel by Mark Twain and Charles Dudley Warner. Although the decades following the Civil War saw the maturing of America's industrial revolution, a massive expansion of production, and the making of fabulous fortunes, it was marked also by a widening gap between rich and poor, labor strife, and deteriorating social relations. The underlying dross beneath the gilding was revealed to all during the traumatic railroad strikes that made up the **Great Labor Uprising** *of 1877. Moreover, though the economy grew, its pace was quite unstable, with periods of boom followed by equally dramatic depressions. The early 1880s saw one such economic downturn. In 1883, the United States Senate convened a Committee upon the Relations between Labor and Capital to investigate social and economic conditions. A parade of witnesses—industrialists, clerics, labor leaders, economists, financiers, health-care workers, and ordinary workers—offered testimony before the committee, which was chaired by Senator Henry W. Blair of New Hampshire.*

Two pieces of testimony are excerpted below. The first comes from Conrad Carl, a New York City tailor, who was questioned by Senators Blair and James L. Pugh of Alabama. The second comes from Dr. Timothy D. Stow, who shared his experiences of being a physician in the textile city of Fall River, Massachusetts.

TESTIMONY OF CONRAD CARL

Conrad Carl: During the time I have been here the tailoring business is altered in three different ways. Before we had sewing machines we worked piecework with our wives, and very often our children. We had no trouble then with our neighbors, nor with the landlord, because it was a very still business, very quiet; but in 1854 or 1855, and later, the sewing machine was invented and introduced, and it stitched very nicely, nicer than the tailor could do; and the bosses said: "We want you to use the sewing machine; you have to buy one." Many of the tailors had a few dollars in the bank, and they took the money and bought machines. Many others had no money, but must help themselves; so they brought their stitching, the coat or vest, to the other tailors who had sewing machines, and paid them a few cents for the stitching. Later, when the money was given out for the work, we found out that we could earn no more than we could without the machine; but the money for the machine was gone now, and we found that the machine was only for the profit of the bosses; that they got their work quicker, and it was done nicer. . . . The machine makes too much noise in the place, and the neighbors want to sleep, and we have to stop sewing earlier; so we have to work faster. We work now in excitement—in a hurry. It is hunting; it is not work at all; it is a hunt.

Senator Pugh: You turn out two or three times as much work per day now as you did in prior times before the war?—A. Yes, sir; two or three times as much; and we have to do it, because the wages are two-thirds lower than they were five or ten years back. . . .

Senator Blair: What proportion of them are women and what proportion men, according to your best judgment?—A. I guess there are many more women then men.

Q. The pay of women is the same as the pay of the men for the same quantity of work, I suppose?—A. Yes; in cases where a manufacturer—that is, a middleman—gets work from the shop and brings it into his store and employs hands to make it, women get paid by the piece also. If the manufacturer gets $.25 for a piece, he pays for the machine work on that piece so many cents to the finisher, and so many to the button-sewer—so much to each one—and what remains is to pay his rent and to pay for the machinery.

Q. What is your knowledge as to the amount that workers of that class are able to save from their wages?—A. I don't know any one that does save except those manufacturers.

Q. As a class, then, the workers save nothing?—A. No.

Q. What sort of house-room do they have? What is the character, in general, of the food and clothing which they are able to purchase with what they can make by their labor?—A. They live in tenement houses four or five stories high, and have two or three rooms.

Q. What is the character of their clothing?—A. They buy the clothing that they make—the cheapest of it.

Q. What about the character of food that they are able to provide for themselves?—A. Food? They have no time to eat dinner. They have a sandwich in the middle of the day, and in the evening when they go away from work it is the same, and they drink lager or anything they can get.

Q. They are kept busy all the time and have but little opportunity for rest?—A. Yes

Q. What is the state of feeling between the employers and their employees in that business? How do you workingmen feel towards the people who employ you and pay you?—A. Well, I must say the workingmen are discouraged. If I speak with them they go back and don't like to speak much about the business and the pay. They fear that if they say how it is they will get sent out of the shop. They hate the bosses and the foremen more than the bosses, and that feeling is deep.

Q. Why do they feel so towards the foremen?—A. They know that they do a wrong onto them; they know that.

Q. Do not the foremen act under the instruction of the bosses?—A. Well, it seems so.

Q. Could not the boss correct the wrong that the foreman does, if it is a wrong?—A. Well, when we complain that the foreman is so and so, the boss says, "Oh, I have nothing to do with it; I don't know; go to the foreman; it is the foreman's business." Then when we go to the foreman he says, "Oh, I can't pay more; these are my rules; if you don't like it, go to the boss."

Q. And when you do go to the boss he sends you back to the foreman?—A. Yes; he says, "I have nothing to do with this; that is my foreman's business; go to him." Therefore the workmen hate them both. . . .

Sen. Pugh: Then you are testifying here under the apprehension of punishment for what you have stated?—A. Well, I have no fear for anyone, you know, and if you think it is better that I say it, I do so.

Q. What is your feeling of restraint in testifying? What injury would you be subjected to for telling the truth? Would the workingmen in your business testify under a fear of being punished by their employers for telling the truth?—A. Yes. It is nothing but fear. . . .

Sen. Blair: Have you any objection to giving us the names of some of the bosses and foremen that you know, who control a large number of laborers of the class to which you belong? This committee desires to obtain such information as you can give in regard to the condition of the engaged trade, and if there is any attempt to punish you for giving such information I think you can find protection from the country, or from some source. We cannot compel you to give the information but we desire you to state, if you will, the names of some of the bosses and foremen, so that if they do not think proper to come here and speak for themselves the country will understand that you have told us the truth.—A. Now, sir, if I lose my work who can give me another work? I am an old man now, you know, and the young ones, they get work and they say, "He is an old man; what can he do? . . . "

TESTIMONY OF DR. TIMOTHY STOW

Sen. Blair: You are a physician?—A. Yes.

Q. You live at Fall River?—A. Yes.

Q. Won't you state how you happen to appear before the committee, what your object is in coming here, and at whose request you come; and then give us the benefit of any observations you choose to lay before us?—A. Mr. Robert Howard, of our city, called on me yesterday, and desired me to appear here today before your committee to give whatever testimony I could relating particularly to the physical and mental and perhaps the moral condition of the operatives and laboring classes of Fall River. I have made no notes, and I hardly know what your plan is; but I would as soon answer questions as to make any detailed statement.

Sen. Blair: We want to find out how the working people of Fall River are living and doing. You can tell us that in the way in which one gentleman would talk to another, the one understanding the subject and the other not understanding it. Just tell us the condition of the operatives there, in your own way, bearing in mind that we would rather have it without premeditation than as a prepared statement.

Stow: I have been in Fall River about eleven years. . . . As a physician and surgeon, of course, I have been brought into contact with all classes of people
there, particularly the laboring classes, the operatives of the city. . . .

As a class they are dwarfed physically. Of course there are exceptions to
that; some notable ones. On looking over their condition and weighing it
as carefully as I have been able to, I have come to the conclusion that the
character and quality of the labor which they have been doing in times
past, and most of them from childhood up, has been and is such as to bring
this condition upon them slowly and steadily.

They are dwarfed, in my estimation, sir, as the majority of men and
women who are brought up in factories must be dwarfed under the present
industrial system; because by their long hours of indoor labor and their hard
work they are cut off from the benefit of breathing fresh air, and from the
sights that surround a workman outside a mill. Being shut up all day long in
noise and in the high temperature of these mills, they become physically
weak.

Then, most of them are obliged to live from hand to mouth, or, at least,
they do not have sufficient food to nourish them as they need to be nour-
ished. Those things, together with the fact that they have to limit their
clothing supply—this constant strain upon the operative—all tend to
make him on the one hand uneasy and restless, or on the other hand to produce discouragement and recklessness. They make him careless in regard to
his own condition. All those things combined tend to produce what we
have in Fall River.

Now, first, as to the moral condition of the operatives of Fall River. I
think so far as crime is concerned we have quite as little crime there as in
any city of its size. We have a population rising on 50,000. There is a disposition at times, and under certain pressure, for some operatives to violate
the law, to pilfer, or something of that kind, and I think it grows out of not
what is called "pure cussedness," but a desire to relieve some physical want.
For instance, a man wants a coat and has not the means of earning it, and
he is out of employment, and being pinched with cold, and with no
prospect of getting employment, or of getting a coat by honest means, he
steals one. Or perhaps he steals food on the same principle.

But so far as crime is concerned, we have comparatively little. But what
I do say, and what has been on my mind ever since I came to Fall River,
with reference to operatives there, is the peculiar impress they seem to bear,
a sort of dejected, tired, worn-out, discouraged appearance, growing out of
the bad influences of long hours of labor, the close confinement of the
mills, the din of the machinery, their exclusion from social intercourse,
except at night.

And I think we can look for a solution of the problem which the country at large is endeavoring to solve—that with reference to the intemperate
habits of the laboring classes and the operatives—in those facts that I have
mentioned.

I have questioned many thoughtful men and women in regard to that I
have said, "Why is it that at night particularly you frequent the dram-

shops? Why is it that by day you drink; that you store enough even for the day in your houses?" The answer is, "Well, doctor, I tell you the fact is this, there is a sense of fatigue over us which we do not know how to overcome, and which we must overcome for the time being if we are to have any social qualities of an evening, and we can't do it without taking something which will bridge over the time and make us equal to the emergency of the evening or the occasion. . . ." But I have said, "How does this make you feel? You say you have been feeling fatigued in the evening and discouraged; that your future does not look bright; how do you feel when you get the liquor?" "Why," he will say, "it covers that all up; we lose all thought of that, and for the time being we feel well." And so they go on from day to day, and from night to night.

Now, after all, I do not know of many drunkards in Fall River, but this is true: the operative spends his five, ten, or fifteen, or twenty-five cents a night for liquor, and it is so much lost money to him, and yet he feels impelled to it, because he does not know how otherwise to adapt himself to the circumstances of the evening. . . .

Now, it is invariably the testimony of the more intelligent men and women in answer to the question, "Why do you persist in drinking?" "It makes us feel better; we are relieved of the ennui of life; we are relieved of mental depression for the time being, and after the evening's social engagements are over we get home and go to bed, and think nothing of it, and the next day resume our day's work." And so it goes on from day to day.

Now there are other things which hinge upon low wages and long hours of labor to demoralize the operative. For instance, his food. I think it is safe to say that the great mass of operatives there are forced to buy the cheapest food. They go to the meat stores and purchase joints, which, of course, made up into soup, generally makes good food, but it does not do to have soup all the time. Then they purchase the cheapest vegetables and endeavor to make the money go as far as it possibly will to supply their wants. But all that produces this condition: they lack that sort of nutrition which is essential to an increase of fiber and flesh, and to maintain that elasticity which they ought to have for the performance of a fair amount of labor. I think if the food of the operatives could be increased it would be better.

Q. You mean increased in quantity, quality, or both?—A. I mean both.

Q. You mean that they do not have enough to eat?—A. Many of them do not, they are limited in amount. I have occasion almost every day to see the manner in which the average operative has his table spread, and certainly it seems to me eminently proper that if it be within the scope of human legislation, or within the scope of the religion which men and women profess, to alleviate the condition of the laboring classes who are our producers, it should be done. . . .

Source: John Garraty, ed., *Labor and Capital in the Gilded Age: Testimony taken by the Senate Committee upon the Relations between Labor and Capital—1883* (Boston: Little, Brown, and Company, 1968), pp. 20–22, 30–33.

23. Grape Boycott: September 1965 Memo of Cesar Chavez

*The **grape boycott** from 1965 through 1970 was one of the most successful uses of the **boycott** tactic in U.S. labor history and a seminal event in transforming the **Agricultural Workers Organizing Committee** (AWOC) into the **United Farm Workers of America**. It was so successful that the **strike** that accompanied it is sometimes overlooked. Filipino and Chicano workers struck for humane working conditions and a living **wage**. **Cesar Chavez** and others were able to turn the strike into a nationwide boycott of California table grapes and wines. The following memo from Chavez was written on September 16, 1965, to rally support and boost the morale of workers in the Delano, California, region, the epicenter of the ongoing strike. His evocation of the Rev. Martin Luther King, Jr., was deliberate and genuine; Chavez knew and admired Rev. King. Soon the phrases "Viva La Causa" (Cause) and "Viva La Huelga" (Struggle) could be seen on banners, badges, and rally posters across the United States.*

"WE SHALL OVERCOME"

In a 400 square mile area halfway between Selma and Weedpatch, California, a general strike of farm workers has been going on for six weeks. The Filipinos, under AWOC, began the strike for a $1.40 per hour guarantee and a union contract. They were joined by the independent Farm Workers Association which has a membership of several thousand Mexican-Americans.

Filipino, Mexican-American and Puerto Rican workers have been manning picket lines daily for 41 days in a totally non-violent manner. Ranchers in the area, which include DiGiorgio Fruit, Schenley, and many independent growers, did not take the strike seriously at first. By the second or third week, however, they began taking another look—and striking back. Mechanized agriculture began picketing the pickets—spraying them with sulfur, running tractors by them to create dust storms, building barricades of farm machinery so that scabs could not see the pickets. These actions not only increased the determination of the strikers, but convinced some of the scabs that the ranchers were, in fact, less than human. Scabs quit work and the strike grew.

The growers hired security guards for $43 a day. They began driving their Thunderbirds, equipped with police dogs and rifles, up and down the roads. The people made more picket signs, drew in their belts, and kept marching. Production was down 30% and the growers began looking for more and more scabs. They went to Fresno and Bakersfield and Los Angeles to find them. They didn't tell the workers that they would be scab crews. The pickets followed them into every town and formed ad hoc strike committees to prevent scabbing. They succeeded in these towns. Within two weeks, only one bus, with half a dozen winos, escorted by a pearl gray Cadillac, drove into the strike zone.

A new plan was formed. The ranchers would advertise in South Texas and old Mexico. They bring these workers in buses and the workers are held in debt to the rancher before they even arrive in town. We have a new and more difficult task ahead of us with these scabs.

As our strike has grown, workers have matured and now know why and how to fight for their rights. As the strike has grown into a movement for justice by the lowest paid workers in America, friends of farm workers have begun to rally in support of LA CAUSA. Civil rights, church, student and union groups help with food and money.

We believe that this is the beginning of a significant drive to achieve equal rights for agricultural workers. In order to enlist your full support and to explain our work to you, I would like to bring some of our pickets and meet with you.

VIVA LA CAUSA Y
VIVA LA HUELGA

Cesar Estrada Chavez
General Director,
National Farm Workers Association

Source: TM/© 2003 the Cesar E. Chavez Foundation. www.chavezfoundation.org.

---

24. Immigrant Workers: Excerpt from a December 1881 Article by Elizabeth Buffum Chase in the *Labor Standard*

Between 1870 and 1910, more than twenty-one million immigrants poured into the United States. Many of them became the very bone and sinew of the economic expansion of post–Civil War America. Although many immigrants bettered their lives, it was usually difficult for the first generation. They were not only subject to intense nativist discrimination at the hands of those native-born groups who feared them, but also frequently found themselves toiling in some of the Gilded Age's worst sweatshops, factories, and mills.

The passage below was written by Elizabeth Buffum Chase, a suffragist, labor advocate, social reformer, and former abolitionist. It originally appeared in December 1881 in the Labor Standard, a working-class newspaper published in Fall River, Massachusetts. Fall River was dotted with numerous textile and shoe mills and owed its explosive late-nineteenth-century population growth to the influx of immigrant workers. Chase was rare among Gilded Age writers in that she posited that poverty was linked to social conditions rather than individual failings or ethnic characteristics. Here she defends the dignity of Irish, French Canadian, and Catholic immigrants.

Thus it is a fact, that a very large number of women and girls, from ten years old to forty or fifty are employed in the cotton and woolen mills of the northern and middle states of this country mostly in New England. It is, therefore, a subject of great concern as to what is their actual condition, and, what are the duties of other women toward them. Many of those born in England, Ireland, and Canada cannot read or write; and of those who have had a chance in our public schools most of them have gone to work so early that their schooling has been of the most rudimentary character, and is easily forgotten. They are excluded from the society of their own sex and outside of the factory by a variety of barriers—chief of which are their foreign birth or extraction, *their poverty*, their want of education, and the necessity that they should always be at work. [Emphasis in original] Two other causes also contribute to this large exclusion. These people are mostly Catholic in their religion, and this excludes them from Protestant companionship, and the other is, the growing tendency in our civilization toward class distinction.

Many of the operatives live a floating life. Unsettled from their native homes, the older members of the families never become truly nationalized anywhere; and the children grow up with the idea that they are an alien people. So, trifling circumstances and the hope of improving their condition lead them to move about, and this they continue unthrifty and poor; and whatever unfortunate results follow, they all bear with most hardship upon the women. On the contrary, those who remain in one place, if they cultivate habits of industry and sobriety, do constantly improve their circumstances and become more and more assimilated to the native inhabitants. But, with rare exceptions, they have brought with them the inherited improvidence, which comes from many generations in hopeless poverty under old world oppression.

Source: Labor Standard, December 10, 1881. Reprinted in Irwin Yellowitz, ed., *The Position of the Worker in American Society, 1865–1896* (Englewood Cliffs, N.J.: Prentice Hall, 1969), pp. 69–70.

---

25. Indentured Servant Contract (1627)

English colonists to the Americas often came under the illusion that Native Americans would willingly work for them. When persuasion and coercion of Native Americans proved unworkable, the colonies endured a labor crisis. To alleviate this, planters and investors turned to Great Britain's indigenous poor. Enclosure movements, industrialization, and increased agricultural yields conspired to create a large unemployed and underemployed group known as "sturdy beggars," who were deemed surplus labor within Great Britain. Thousands of these individuals were so poor they could not pay passage to the colonies. In exchange for transportation to the New World and basic sustenance, individuals agreed to work for their sponsor for a given number of years, customarily four to seven. In Virginia and elsewhere, individuals who completed their indentures were given land allotments, called headrights, to sustain themselves in the future. In the early days of Virginia, very few lived to collect their headrights, with death rates of over 50 percent per year typical into the mid-1620s. Most indentured servants died from a combination of malnutrition and overwork. By the time Richard Lowther arrived in 1627, tobacco had begun to rescue the colony financially and the death rate was dropping, but the indentured servant's lot was still a hard one.

Indentured servitude is an old European practice that was simply transplanted to the New World. The word indenture is an Anglicized version of the French dent, meaning tooth. Some contracts were written twice on a sheet of paper and then jaggedly torn apart in a toothlike pattern. The validity of the contract could be verified by matching the halves. The document below is typical of indenture contracts in seventeenth-century Virginia, although its language and spelling have been edited to make it more readable.

THIS WRITING INDENTED made the Last day of July . . . 1627 And in the Third year of the reign of our Sovereign Lord Charles by the Grace of God king of England Scotland France and Ireland Defender of the faith &c. between Richard Lowther of Broome in the Parish of Southwell [i.e., Southill] in the County of Bedford brewer of the one party and Edward Hurd Citizen and Iron monger of London of the other party witnesses that the said Richard Lowther . . . hired himself and . . . does Covenant and agree and bind himself to be remain and Continue the Covenant servant of him the said Edward Hurd his heirs and assigns to be by him or them sent and transported unto the Country and land of Virginia, in the parts beyond the Seas & to be by him or them employed upon his plantation there, for and during the space of Four years to begin at the feast day of St. Michael . . . now next coming during which said term the said Richard Lowther shall and will truly employ and endeavor himself to the utmost of his power knowledge and skill to do and perform true and faithful service unto the said Edward Hurd his heirs and assigns in for and concerning all such Labor and business as he or they shall think good to use and employ him the said Richard Lowther in, And shall and will be tractable and obedient as a good and a faithful servant ought to be in all such things as shall be Commanded him by the said Edward Hurd his heirs or assigns in Virginia aforesaid or elsewhere during the said term. IN CONSIDERATION whereof the said Edward Hurd for himself his executors administrators or assigns and for every of them do covenant promise and grant to and with the said Richard Lowther his heirs executors administrators and assigns . . . that . . . Edward Hurd his heirs executors administrators and assigns shall and will (at his and their own charges) not only transport and furnish out the said Richard Lowther to and for Virginia aforesaid and there find provide and allow unto him sufficient meat drink apparel and other necessaries for his livelihood and maintenance during the said term But also at the expiration of the said term shall and will grant assign and allot unto him the said Richard Lowther the quantity of Fifty acres of Land in Virginia aforesaid to hold to him his heirs and assigns for ever as in such Cases usual without fraud or Coven. . . .

Source: "Indentured Servant Contract." Virtual Jamestown. http://etext.lib.virginia.edu/etcbin/jamestown-browsemod?id=J1046.

26. An Insider's View of the Fair Employment Practices Committee: An Interview with Earl B. Dickerson

Born in Mississippi, Earl B. Dickerson (1891–1986) moved to Chicago at the age of fifteen. After obtaining a law degree from the University of Chicago, Dickerson rose to leadership of the country's largest African American–owned law firm, becoming known as "the dean of Chicago's black lawyers." Dickerson was active in Chicago and national politics, argued successfully before the Supreme Court for an end to restrictive real-estate covenants, and served on the **Fair Employment Practices Committee (FEPC)** *from 1941 to 1943. Established in wartime by President Franklin D. Roosevelt, the FEPC continued until 1946 when, against the recommendation of President Harry Truman, the Senate terminated the program. In this selection from the 1980s, Dickerson tells Studs Terkel about his experiences on the FEPC.*

Around 1940, '41, the war industries were set in motion: Lockheed, Boeing, all the rest. If this was a war to see that democracy prevails, preparations should involve all our people equally. Since blacks had been to a large extent excluded, A. Philip Randolph and Walter White planned a march on Washington. I knew both men intimately. To prevent this from happening, Mr. Roosevelt put forth Executive Order 8802. This set up the Fair Employment Practices Committee. I was one of the first named.

Because I was the only lawyer in this group, I was always sent out in advance of any hearing. With some investigators, I prepared the cases for the committee when it met.

One of the first hearings was here in Chicago at City Hall. It was a wonderful three days, examining these people from industry. I remember some fellow from LaGrange. It was one of these General Motors subsidiaries. We had him on the stand: "How many Negroes do you employ?" He replied, "One."

I distinctly remember the hearings in Los Angeles. I had gone out a week before the hearings with a couple of investigators. Lockheed had employed some twenty thousand people in the war effort. No Negroes. Not until the morning of the hearings did they employ any. I asked the head of personnel, "Are you familiar with the contents of Executive Order 8802?" He said yes. I said, "Do you have any Negroes in your employ?" He said yes. "How many do you have?" He said nine. I said, "In what department?" He said, "In the custodial department." That meant they were sweeping floors. (Wryly) Well, that was a beginning.

Another company, there were no black bricklayers. The reason given: one or two couldn't work alongside whites. They'd have to get enough to work one side of the building. Since they couldn't find that many, they'd employ none.

I distinctly remember the hearings in Birmingham. One of my colleagues on the committee, a southern newspaper publisher, called me on the phone a few days before the scheduled hearings: "Earl, perhaps you shouldn't go down there. There have been all sorts of threats." I said, "I want you to read Executive Order 8802 again. It says, 'the jurisdiction of this committee shall be in all states and territories of the United States.'" I had it before me. "The question I ask you now is, 'Is Birmingham within the jurisdiction of the United States?'" He said yes. I said, "That being the case, I'll be there."

When I got off the plane at Birmingham to walk to the terminal, a man about six feet four, a tall Caucasian, came to me and said, "Are you Mr. Earl B. Dickerson?" I said yes. He said, "I'm the United States marshal in this district and I have been requested by the Justice Department to protect you during your trip here." In those days, blacks couldn't stay in hotels in Birmingham. So he would come and pick me up each of those three days. And in the federal court, where the hearings were held, he stood beside me the whole three days.

There was another black fellow on the committee. He was very black and I'm sort of brown. The newspapers came out and described us as the black and brown babies from Chicago. That was around 1942.

You must remember Roosevelt had to be pushed. I had no personal relationship with President Roosevelt until he issued Executive Order 8802. It was June 25, 1941.

We had hearings in Washington, D.C., from time to time. The streetcar system did not employ blacks as motormen or conductors. This was during the war, and every day there were ads in the papers advertising for people to apply for jobs as motormen and conductors. The civil rights people there told blacks to apply for these jobs. They had no luck. We set a date for the hearings on this. I was the acting chairman at the time and prepared the case. It was in all the newspapers.

Just the day before the hearing, I got a call from a fellow named McIntyre. He was Roosevelt's secretary. He said, "We understand you are having hearings tomorrow. President Roosevelt has asked me to request that you postpone the hearings until some later date." I said that all the newspapers not only here but throughout the United States know about these hearings tomorrow. We have prepared the case, a noted lawyer from New York has come in, and it will be at Dumbarton Oaks. I said, "I can't go out to the public and postpone this case unless Mr. Roosevelt himself would tell me."

This was about one o'clock in the afternoon. He called me right back. "At two-thirty this afternoon, the President will meet with you in the White House." When I walked in the White House, Mrs. Mary McLeod Bethune was sitting just outside his office. She was the most influential black around, very close to Mrs. Roosevelt. I think Mrs. Roosevelt was one of the sparkplugs behind Executive Order 8802. After she hugged me, Mrs. Bethune said, "The President asked that I be in on this conversation."

Well, the President simply told me he wanted permission to defer the hearings. I said, "I'm just wondering why it is, Mr. President. He said, "I want it delayed until I return." I said, "Very well, Mr. President." Of course, the next morning we read about Mr. Roosevelt having flown to Yalta to meet with Churchill and Stalin.

Soon after this, Attorney General Francis Biddle came up with a proposal to reorganize the commission. All the members were reappointed except me. It was one of my major disappointments in life. I knew it was because I had been so aggressive. I had been the leader of all the agitation that went on in the committee.

What did they give as the reason?

They didn't have to, did they? Oh, they had hearings, but not the kind of aggressive ones I'd been pushing. Nobody ever criticized me. I was in all the newspapers throughout the country.

Roosevelt wanted to go slow. I was taking 'em too fast. When you talk about him, he was not unlike any other Caucasian in that position. The blacks had never challenged authority like that before, except for individuals. Here was a collective attack on the practices of the American people.

Do you know that my work on that committee has affected my life? Years later, when Governor Kerner appointed me as one of the first members of the Illinois Fair Employment Practices Committee, I had to be confirmed by the state senate. This fellow Broyles was chairman of the Illinois Un-American Activities Committee. On the day of the hearings, on the wall of that room, they had my files posted. My membership in the Soviet-American Friendship Committee, my membership in the National Lawyers' Guild—and all my activities on the Fair Employment Practices Committee. The fifteen Republicans voted no, the thirteen Democrats voted yes. I was not confirmed.

It was in World War Two—because it was so clear, it was against Hitler—that the blacks began to measure the rights they had as against the rights that the whites were given. Now I tell you, this measuring will never end. Not until they have the rights the others have.

Source: Reprinted by permission of Donadio & Olson, Inc. Copyright © 1974 by Studs Terkel.

---

27. Knights of Labor: Preamble and Platform to Their Constitution (1891)

The largest and most successful labor federation of the nineteenth century was the Noble and Holy Order of the **Knights of Labor (KOL)**. *The KOL was founded in 1869 and enjoyed its greatest strength in the mid-1880s, growing to perhaps as many as one million members by 1886. It quickly contracted from that plateau due to lost* **strikes**, *battles with rival unions, and internal dissension. Mostly, though, it faded due to the fierce counter assault of organized capital. The KOL was not a trade union battling just for improved wages, shorter hours, and better working conditions. As the preamble to its constitution shows, the KOL advocated revamping society along quite different lines than those which came to pass. The KOL's reform unionism produced a backlash in which some of the late nineteenth century's richest and most powerful corporate magnates decided to crush the organization at any cost*

The following document lays out the KOL's vision for reforming American society. The preamble and the first nine platform items were adopted in 1878, when the group held its first national convention. Additional agenda items were added after 1884. This document is a mature version of the platform from 1891. Comparing the KOL's goals with those of the **American Federation of Labor**, *which supplanted the Knights, suggests that the latter organization survived, in part, because its objectives* *meshed better with the capitalist forces that subdued the Knights. Some elements of the KOL platform remain progressive (and unrealized) to the present day.*

(Note: The five asterisks below stand for the Noble and Holy Order of the Knights of Labor. When the preamble was written, the KOL operated in total secrecy and even the organization's name was hidden from public view.)

The recent alarming development and aggression of aggregated wealth, which, unless checked, will invariably lead to the pauperization and hopeless degradation of the toiling masses, render it imperative, if we desire to enjoy the blessings of life, that a check should be placed upon its power and upon unjust accumulation, and a system adopted which will secure to the laborer the fruits of his toil; and as this much desired object can only be accomplished by the thorough unification of labor, and the united effort of those who obey the divine injunction that "In the sweat of thy brow shalt thou eat bread," we have formed the * * * * * with a view of securing the organization and direction, by co-operative effort, of the power of the industrial classes; and we submit to the world the object sought to be accomplished by our organization, calling upon all who believe in securing "the greatest good to the greatest number" to aid and assist us-

I. To bring within the folds of organization every department of productive industry, making knowledge a standpoint for action, and industrial and moral worth, not wealth, the true standard of individual and national greatness.

II. To secure to the toilers a proper share of the wealth that they create; more of the leisure that rightfully belongs to them; more societary advantages; more of the benefits, privileges, and emoluments of the world, all those rights and privileges necessary to make them capable of enjoying, appreciating, defending, and perpetuating the blessings of good government.

III. To arrive at the true condition of the producing masses in their educational, moral, and financial condition, by demanding from the various governments the establishment of bureaus of labor statistics.

IV. The establishment of co-operative institutions, productive and distributive.

V. The reserving of the public lands—the heritage of the people—for the actual settler; not another acre for railroads or speculators.

VI. The abrogation of all laws that do not bear equally upon capital and labor, the removal of unjust technicalities, delays, and discriminations in the administration of justice, and the adopting of measures providing for the health and safety of those engaged in mining, manufacturing, or building pursuits.

VII. The enactment of laws to compel chartered corporations to pay their employees weekly, in full, for the labor of the preceding week, in the lawful money of the country.

VIII. The enactment of laws giving mechanics and laborers a first lien on their work for their full wages.

  X. The abolishment of the contract system on national, state, and municipal work.

  X. The substitution of arbitration for strikes, whenever and wherever employers and employees are willing to meet on equitable grounds.

  XI. The prohibition of the employment of children in workshops, mines, and factories before attaining their fifteenth year.

  XII. To abolish the system of letting out by contract labor of convicts in our prisons and reformatory institutions.

  XIII. To secure for both sexes equal pay for equal work.

  XIV. The reduction of the hours of labor to eight per day, so that the laborers may have more time for social enjoyment and intellectual improvement, and be enabled to reap the advantages conferred by the labor-saving machinery which their brains have created.

  XV. To prevail upon governments to establish a purely national circulating medium, based upon the faith and resources of the nation, and issued directly to the people, without the intervention of any system of banking corporations, which money shall be a legal tender in payment of all debts, public or private.

Source: Journal of the Knights of Labor, June 4, 1891. (Nearly every edition of this paper printed the above document.)

28. The Lawrence Strike, 1912: Excerpt from the Autobiography of Big Bill Haywood

William D. (Big Bill) Haywood (1869–1928) led the Wobblies (Industrial Workers of the World) at the height of their most turbulent years. Haywood was known for his stirring rhetoric. Following the arrest of Joe Ettor and Arturro Giovanitti, Haywood personally took over leadership of the Lawrence strike. In his autobiography, Haywood gave the following account of the IWW's one great eastern victory: the Lawrence, Massachusetts, textile strike of 1912. In 1918, Haywood was convicted of violating the Espionage Act during World War I. He eventually fled the country and died in exile.

I pointed out that although the I.W.W. would not affiliate with any political party, this action did not make them anti-political; that I was as much a Socialist as any other member of the Socialist Party. I remember that after the meeting, Hubert Harrison, a colored man, said to me that while Douglas had won the debate, Lincoln had carried the country. I took this to mean that Hillquit had won the debate, but the workers of the nation were with me.

This meeting was attended by many leading members of the I.W.W. Ettor, Giovanitti, Gurley Flynn, and Jim Thompson were there. Ettor had just received a telegram from the Italians of Lawrence, Massachusetts, asking him to come there, as there was going to be a strike of the textile workers. Ettor left for Lawrence at once and in a few days I got a telegram from him asking me to come and help him with the strike.

When I got to Lawrence, Ettor had the situation well in hand. There was a General Strike Committee organized, composed of one or more members from every mill or large department of the mills that were on strike.

The legislature of Massachusetts had passed a law reducing the hours of labor in the textile industry from fifty-six to fifty-four a week. The cotton and woolen companies announced that when this law went into effect wages would be reduced in proportion. The workers declared that wages were already lower than they should be. The average weekly wage was eight dollars and seventy-six cents, the women getting an average of only seven dollars and forty-two cents. This was the average for all workers, including the skilled. The average for the workers who conducted this strike was six dollars a week. These wages were only for time at work; there were no vacations, and all the holidays were deducted from the weekly pay. It was impossible to bring up families on such wages. The workers went on strike.

It was a strike against all the mills, and every worker, except a few of the most skilled, took part in the struggle. The strikers demanded a fifty-four hour week, a fifteen per cent increase in pay, double pay for overtime, abolition of all bonus or premium systems, and no discrimination against workers for activities during the strike.

The Lawrence strike grew, until by the latter part of January, 1912, there were twenty-five thousand workers taking part in it. They were of about twenty-eight different nationalities and spoke forty-five different dialects. The entire textile industry of Lawrence and vicinity was closed down tight.

On my arrival in Lawrence a reception committee met me, composed of ten or fifteen thousand strikers. A parade was formed as we marched to the common, as the public park of every New England town is called. This, the *Lawrence Tribune* said, was the greatest demonstration ever accorded a visitor to Lawrence. On the common I spoke to the strikers.

I spoke many times to the strikers, and left Lawrence to go out and raise funds and create sympathy for the strike, until on February second, Ettor and Giovanitti were arrested under a framed-up charge of murder. Anna LaPiza, an Italian girl striker, had been killed by a policeman, but the charge was laid against the leaders of the strike. I returned at once to Lawrence and became chairman of the strike committee, which was composed of fifty-six members. Back of these were another fifty-six members ready to take the places of the strike committee if any arrests were made.

A writer in the *Outlook*, a conservative weekly which reported the strike, said

> Haywood does not want unions of weavers, unions of spinners, unions of loom-fixers, unions of woolsorters, but he wants one comprehensive union of all textile workers, which in time will take over the textile factories, as the steelworkers will take over the steel mills and the railway workers the railways. Haywood interprets the class conflict literally as a war which is always on, which becomes daily more bitter and uncompromising, which can end only with the conquest of capitalistic society by proletarians or wage workers, organized industry by industry.
>
> Haywood places no trust in trade agreements, which, according to his theory, lead merely to social peace and "put the workers to sleep." Let the employer lock out his men when he pleases, and let the workmen strike when they please. He is opposed to arbitration, conciliation, compromise; to sliding scales, profit sharing, welfare work; to everything, in short, which may weaken the revolutionary force of workers. He does not ask for the closed shop or the official recognition of the union, for he has no intention of recognizing the employer. What he desires is not a treaty or industrial peace between the two high contracting parties, but merely the creation of a proletarian impulse which will eventually revolutionize society. Haywood is a man who believes in men, not as you and I believe in them, but fervently, uncompromisingly, with an obstinate faith in the universal good-will and constancy of the workers worthy of a great religious leader. That is what makes him supremely dangerous.

To the Legislative Committee which came to Lawrence I showed pay envelopes of the workers—six dollars and ninety-nine cents, five dollars and forty-five cents, six-thirty, and so on. I showed them, printed on the envelope marked five forty-five, advice about saving money, and the advertisement of the local bank. Five forty-five for a week's work—and advice about saving thrown in free! This was adding insult to injury indeed! The old man who had given me this particular envelope was an old-time employee of the mill, who should have been pensioned long before, after a life-time in the mill. Instead he had been reduced and reduced as he grew less active, until he was plugging along as a wool-sorter on five dollars and forty-five cents a week.

I knew the investigation would result in nothing; but it was good publicity.

After the arrest of Ettor and Giovanitti a demand was made for their release on bail. These men had been charged with being accessories to the death of Anna LaPiza, although nineteen witnesses had seen Policeman Beloit murder the girl. Ettor and Giovanitti were refused bail and held in jail for seven months.

Elizabeth Gurley Flynn, the leading woman organizer of the I.W.W., gave splendid service at Lawrence, speaking to the strikers, and also at meetings outside the strike district, raising money for the relief fund and for the defense of prisoners.

We were sending the children of strikers to sympathizers in other cities, to be cared for during the strike. Some of the groups of children were large and attracted a good deal of attention and sympathy. One day when a group was to be sent away, the militia formed a cordon around the depot and the police attempted to prevent the children getting on the train. When one of these big burleys would lay his hand on a child, of course it would scream, and its mother would fly to the rescue of her captive young. There was a turmoil in the station between the policemen and the fighting women. They stopped the children leaving this day, but they never attempted it a second time.

One morning on the picket line a Syrian boy, who belonged to the strikers fife and drum corps, was stabbed in the back with a bayonet. He died soon after being taken to the hospital.

Not only the local police force was used against the strikers, but police from other cities, the state police, and the state militia had been called in. These organized forces used the mills as their barracks.

The women strikers were as active and efficient as the men, and fought as well. One cold morning, after the strikers had been drenched on the bridge with the firehose of the mills, the women caught a policeman in the middle of the bridge and stripped off his uniform, pants and all. They were about to throw him in the icy river, when other policemen rushed in and saved him from the chilly ducking.

We appealed to Congressman Victor Berger for an investigation of the Lawrence strike, and through this Socialist congressman's efforts, a hearing was arranged before the Rules Committee of the House, in Washington, D.C. When we got news of this, the General Strike Committee decided to send sixteen witnesses to Washington, all boys and girls under sixteen years of age. One of them was a little girl whose hair had been caught in a machine and her scalp torn from her head. These child workers from the mills were able to picture their working conditions and their home life, and we felt convinced of their ability to explain why they and twenty-five thousand others were striking in the textile center of Lawrence and adjacent towns. Margaret Sanger, who afterward became famous for her campaigns for birth control, went with the children to Washington.

On the day of their arrival there, the boys and girls appeared before the Rules Committee. Samuel Gompers was present presumably in the interests of the A. F. of L. He was called as a witness, and condemned the strike and its leaders. Suddenly a childish voice rang out:

"You old son-of-a-bitch! You're telling a god-damned lie!"

It was a Polish boy who had interrupted Gompers. The chairman of the Committee rapped vigorously with his gavel and, looking sternly at the boy, said

"Young man, that sort of language will not be tolerated here. Do not attempt it again!"

"It's the only kind of language I know," answered the boy, "and I'm not a-goin' to let that guy lie about us and get away with it!"

This incident is not reported in Gompers' *Seventy Years of Life and Labor.*

A newspaper reporter at the hearing remarked that "here was presented the old and the new of the labor movement."

When the committee in Lawrence heard that Gompers was taking part in the hearing, they decided to send me down to Washington to help the children who were representing the strikers, if they should need help. But the children had told everything about conditions in the mills, even to being compelled to buy drinking water.

The arranging of this hearing was not the only time that Victor Berger had responded to requests of the I.W.W. On a previous occasion I had appealed to him, when Federal Judge Hanford of Seattle had denied men citizenship because they belonged to the I.W.W. Hanford lost his job as a result of Berger's investigation.

The newspapers had a staff of reporters in Lawrence to cover the strike. Many of them were of the usual type; one told me that he was the man who had concocted the scheme for my arrest in Yakima, in order to test the anti-cigarette law and to make a good story that he could sell.

Gertrude Marvin was reporting for the *Boston American*. She came to me for an interview and got it. When the story was finished, she thought she had something good for her paper, but the managing editor remarked, as he threw it in the wastebasket

"That big two-fisted thug has put it all over you!"

Miss Marvin resigned and went to work for the I.W.W. in Lawrence, doing publicity work for the strike. Later she was engaged by the United Press to assist Marlen Pew. The stories these two sent out about the strike were so thoroughly appreciated by the papers subscribing to the United Press that these papers sent hundreds of letters from all over the country commending the stories. I saw these letters posted up all over the walls of the United Press' New York office.

The managing editor of the *Boston American* finally came to Lawrence and asked Gertrude Marvin to arrange an interview with me. After a long talk with me, he told her that he knew that he had made a mistake in throwing away that story.

I was speaking one night to a meeting made up almost entirely of Polish workers, when two Italian women came into the hall and were brought to the platform. The younger of the two said to me, "To-morrow morning man no go on picket line. All man, boy stay home, sleep. Only woman, girl on picket line to-morrow morning. Soldier and policeman no beat woman, girl. You see—" turning to her companion, she said, "I got big belly, she too got big belly. Police-man no beat us. I want to speak to all woman here."

I presented her to the assembled strikers and told them what she had said to me. Then she spoke herself, in plaintive voice reciting her message, and all agreed that next morning no men or boys should be on the picket line.

The women were out in full force, many of them pregnant mothers. Horrible to relate, the little Italian woman who had organized the women pickets, and another woman, Bertha Crouse, were so terribly beaten by the police that they gave premature birth to their babies and nearly died themselves.

Later a gang of gunmen was brought in. One night they went to the room of Jim Thompson, I.W.W. organizer and prominent figure in the steel strike. When he opened the door the crowd pushed in. Several shots were fired, but Thompson, a big man, was able to force his way out of the room, and ran naked to an adjoining harness shop. He had severe contusions on the head, but no other injuries. A stranger's gun and hat were found in his room, but there was no effort made by the Lawrence police to discover the culprits; they probably knew who they were.

Besides the mass picket line every day, there were many parades. One day sympathizers from Boston joined with the strikers in parade, carrying a banner inscribed

"Arise! Slaves of the World! No God! No Master!"
  "One for all and all for one!"

This was answered by a parade called by the mill owners, which included some of the priests and ministers, the business men, and most of the public school children, although their parents were strikers. Across the principal street a banner was stretched, reading

"For God and Country!"
  "The stars and stripes forever!"
  "The red flag never!"

A protest against the I.W.W., its principles and methods! A mad wave of patriotism came over the business element, and for a time they all wore little American flags in their buttonholes to the great satisfaction of the flag-manufacturers.

The mill owners were becoming desperate, and they resorted to the trick of planting dynamite where it would be found and charged to the strikers. But being on the alert, the workers discovered that the dynamite had been planted by the coroner of the county. This coroner, tool of the textile trust, was arrested, convicted, and fined five hundred dollars. Later a high official of the American Woolen Company committed suicide. It was rumored that he, too, had had something to do with the planted dynamite.

There were many hundreds of workers arrested during the strike. The United States Commissioner of Labor, in his report on the strike, cites three hundred and fifty-five arrests, but this makes no mention of the many hundreds thrown into jail and held for a time, and then released without a hearing or record. A man by the name of Caruso had been arrested later, on the same charge as Ettor and Giovanitti.

The United Textile Workers which belonged to the A. F. of L., and the Loom Fixers, most of them having no work on account of the strike, decided to go on strike themselves. They started a relief fund and sent out appeals. It has always been my opinion that most of the money, clothes and other supplies that they gathered in were intended by the donors for the great mass of the strikers. These skilled workers received the same proportional increase in pay, in the settlement, notwithstanding the fact that they had been scabbing during the early part of the strike, and grafting during the later.

The I.W.W. was active in every textile center that we could reach. The blaze in Lawrence had spread, and when the strike was settled, two hundred and fifty thousand other textile workers received a small increase in wages.

The strike committee had its last meeting after a sub-committee had gone to Boston and made a settlement with William Wood of the American Woolen Company. The report of the sub-committee was received with long cheers. The strike was off, if the settlement should prove satisfactory to the majority of the workers of all the mills involved, and there was no reason to suppose they would not be satisfied. I appealed to the committee and the strikers that filled the hall, to hold their union together, as there would be a time when they would have to strike again, if Ettor and Giovanitti were not released from prison. I helped twenty-three members of the strike committee to climb up on the platform. They were all of different nationalities, and we sang the *International* in as many different tongues as were represented on the strike committee.

When the strike was settled, early in March, it was a sweeping victory for the workers. Hours of labor were reduced, wages were increased from five to twenty per cent, with increased compensation for overtime, and there was to be no discrimination against any person who had taken part in the strike. The strike had been a magnificent demonstration of solidarity, and of what solidarity can do for the workers.

Jim Thompson, Grover Perry, Gurley Flynn, Bill Trautmann, and other I.W.W. organizers, including myself, went on the road to raise funds for the approaching murder trial of Ettor, Giovanitti, and Caruso.

Source: William D. Haywood, *The Autobiography of Big Bill Haywood* (New York: International Publishers, 1929), 246–53.

---

29. Life in Lowell, Massachusetts: Boarding House and Factory Rules for the Hamilton Manufacturing Company (1848)

Textiles were the first American industry to experiment with mass-production techniques. The most famous nineteenth-century industrial city was Lowell, Massachusetts. By 1836, Lowell was one of the largest industrial cities in the world, with twenty mills employing nearly 7,000 workers. Lowell was also a **company town** *with most of the businesses, boarding houses, and infrastructure owned by a consortium known as the Boston Associates. The vast majority of Lowell's workforce was young women, especially those drawn from New England farms. Although economically depressed*

*New England farmers certainly welcomed the income that their daughters could earn in Lowell, they also sought assurances that mill operators would safeguard their daughters' morality. What evolved in Lowell—and in many other nineteenth-century workplaces—was a form of **paternalism** that blended prevailing moral and gender constructs with employer desires to create a pliant and disciplined workforce.*

The first document illustrates moral concerns, while the second is more authoritarian.

BOARDING HOUSE RULES OF THE HAMILTON MANUFACTURING COMPANY: 1848

The tenants of the boarding-houses are not to board, or permit any part of their houses to be occupied by any person, except those in the employ of the company, without special permission.

They will be considered answerable for any improper conduct in their houses, and are not to permit their boarders to have company at unreasonable hours.

The doors must be closed at ten o'clock in the evening, and no person admitted after that time, without some reasonable excuse.

The keepers of the boarding-houses must give an account of the number, names and employment of their boarders, when required, and report the names of such as are guilty of any improper conduct, or are not in the regular habit of attending public worship.

The buildings, and yards about them, must be kept clean and in good order; and if they are injured, other-wise than from ordinary use, all necessary repairs will be made, and charged to the occupant.

The sidewalks, also, in front of the houses, must be kept clean, and free from snow, which must be removed from them immediately after it has ceased falling; if neglected, it will be removed by the company at the expense of the tenant.

It is desirable that the families of those who live in the houses, as well as the boarders, who have not had the . . . pox, should be vaccinated, which will be done at the expense of the company, for such as wish it.

Some suitable chamber in the house must be reserved, and appropriated for the use of the sick, so that others may not be under the necessity of sleeping in the same room.

JOHN AVERY, Agent.

FACTORY RULES FOR THE HAMILTON MANUFACTURING COMPANY: 1848

The overseers are to be always in their rooms at the starting of the mill, and not absent unnecessarily during working hours. They are to see that all those employed in their rooms, are in their places in due season, and keep a correct account of their time and work. They may grant leave of absence to those employed under them, when they have spare hands to supply their places, and not otherwise, except in cases of absolute necessity.

All persons in the employ of the Hamilton Manufacturing Company, are to observe the regulations of the room where they are employed. They are not to be absent from their work without the consent of the over-seer, except in cases of sickness, and then they are to send him word of the cause of their absence.

They are to board in one of the houses of the company and give information at the counting room, where they board, when they begin, or, whenever they change their boarding place; and are to observe the regulations of their boarding-house.

Those intending to leave the employment of the company, are to give at least two weeks' notice thereof to their overseer.

All persons entering into the employment of the company, are considered as engaged for twelve months, and those who leave sooner, or do not comply with all these regulations, will not be entitled to a regular discharge.

The company will not employ any one who is habitually absent from public worship on the Sabbath, or known to be guilty of immorality.

A physician will attend once in every month at the counting-room, to vaccinate all who may need it, free of expense.

Any one who shall take from the mills or the yard, any yarn, cloth or other article belonging to the company, will be considered guilty of stealing and be liable to prosecution.

Payment will be made monthly, including board and wages. The accounts will be made up to the last Saturday but one in every month, and paid in the course of the following week.

These regulations are considered part of the contract, with which all persons entering into the employment of the Hamilton Manufacturing Company, engage to comply.

JOHN AVERY, Agent.

Source: Illinois Labor History Society, http://www.kentlaw.edu/ilhs/lowell.html.

---

30. Molly Maguires: Excerpts from an 1894 Article by Cleveland Moffet in *McClure's Magazine*

*The case of the **Molly Maguires** is one of the more perplexing ones facing students of American labor history. Nineteen men were eventually hanged for involvement in what was supposedly a clandestine Irish and Irish American terrorist organization responsible for disorder and murders in coal mining regions of northeast Pennsylvania between 1870 and 1876. It has never been definitively proven that such an organiza-*

tion actually existed. Most of the testimony that condemned alleged Mollies came from **Pinkerton** *agent James McParland, who supposedly infiltrated the Molly Maguires.*

Critics of the verdict claim that the organization was a fiction invented by coal and railroad barons as an excuse for crushing a legitimate trade-union movement that threatened to loosen the autocratic grip of mine owners, who kept workers toiling in **company towns** *as impoverished chattel. They also point out that McParland was exposed as a pathological liar in a twentieth-century case involving the Western Federation of Miners, in which* **William Haywood** *and others were acquitted.*

The passage below recounts McParland's exploits on behalf of the Pinkertons. It was written by acclaimed journalist Cleveland Moffett for McClure's Magazine, a publication popular among the Gilded-Age middle class.

Some twenty years ago five counties in eastern Pennsylvania were dominated, terrorized, by a secret organization, thousands strong, whose special purpose was to rob, burn, pillage, and kill. Find on the map that marvelous mineral country, as large as Delaware, which lies between the Blue Mountains on the south and the arm of the Susquehanna on the north, and there you will see what was the home of these banded outlaws, the merciless Molly Maguires. . . .

The origin and development of the Molly Maguires will always present a hard problem to the social philosopher, who will, perhaps, find some subtle relation between crime and coal. One understands the act of an ordinary murderer who kills from greed, or fear, or hatred; but the Molly Maguires killed men and women with whom they had had no dealings, against whom they had no personal grievances, and from whose death they had nothing to gain, except, perhaps, the price of a few rounds of whiskey. They committed murders by the score, stupidly, brutally. . . . The men who decreed these monstrous crimes did so for the most trivial reasons—a reduction in wages, a personal dislike, some imagined grievance of a friend. These were sufficient to call forth an order to burn a house where women and children were sleeping, to shoot down in cold blood an employer or fellow workman, to lie in wait for an officer of the law and club him to death. In . . . trial of one of them, Mr. Franklin B. Gowen described the reign of these ready murderers as a time "when men retired to their homes at eight or nine o'clock in the evening and no one ventured beyond the precincts of his own door; when every man engaged in any enterprise of magnitude, or connected with industrial pursuits, left his home in the morning with his hand upon his pistol, unknowing whether he would again return alive; when the very foundations of society were being overturned."

In vain the officials of the Philadelphia and Reading and Lehigh Valley Railroads . . . offered thousands of dollars in rewards for the apprehension of the criminals. In vain Archbishop Wood, of Philadelphia fought the Molly Maguires with the whole power of the Catholic Church. . . . In vain, reputable citizens in almost every town, formed and armed committees of vigilantes who were to take the law into their own hands, inasmuch as the forces of the law were paralyzed. All was of no avail; public offices remained in the hands of ruffians; the same fierce crimes persisted; people were assaulted, robbed, and murdered with increasing frequency. . . .

In 1873, Mr. Franklin B. Gowen, then President of the Philadelphia and Reading Railroad, took counsel with Allan Pinkerton in regard to the matter. "It was owing to Mr. Gowen," says Mr. Robert A. Pinkerton in a recent letter, "that the Molly Maguire organization was broken up. . . ." [I]n order to protect its interests, and its employees, and the managers and superintendents of the mines . . . [Gowen] consulted Mr. Allan Pinkerton. "I have the very man for you," said Allan Pinkerton . . . James McParland.

A few weeks after the interview between Mr. Gowen and Mr. Pinkerton, James McParland was announced to have sailed for Europe on an important mission. Only two men in the country knew that he had really set out for the terrorized region, with instructions to run down these Molly Maguire bandits. . . . After some weeks of reconnoitering on foot through the coal regions, the young detective arrived in Pottsville, where he established himself in a boarding-house kept by a Mrs. O'Regan. There he met a man named Jennings, who volunteered to show him the sights of the city that same night. Passing a noisy drinking-place called the Sheridan House, McKenna, for that was McParland's assumed name, proposed going in. Jennings warned him as he valued his life never to cross the threshold of that place. "It's kept by Pat Dormer," he said, "the big body-master of the Molly Maguires. . . ."

[McKenna slowly ingratiated himself with Dormer, then moved to Shenandoah, where he met "Muff" Lawler, the Molly Maguires body-master for that region, whose life he saved in a barroom dispute.] . . . [H]e made the acquaintance of most of the prominent Mollys, including Jack Kehoe, of Girardville, and "Yellow Jack" Donahue, both of whom were afterwards hanged on his testimony. Everywhere he found that his reputation had preceded him, and he was received by all the Mollys with the respect which ruffians never fail to pay men whom they regard as greater ruffians than themselves. At each new stopping place he came into possession of new secrets touching crimes of the order already committed, and others that were planning, all of which he reported day by day to Allan Pinkerton. . . .

He learned that the number of Molly Maguires in the five counties had been much exaggerated in the popular mind, through fear, and that there were not really more than three or four thousand active members of the organization, whereas it had been reported through the State that there were ten times that many. McKenna saw, however, that it was impossible to exaggerate the desperate character of these men. He found that each county was governed by a "county delegate," his territory being divided into districts, or "patches," each under a "body-master" or chief officer, who gave out the signs and pass-words to trusted members, and ordered the execution of crimes that had been decided upon. In nearly every case the body-master was the keeper of a saloon near one of the shafts, slopes, or drifts. . . . If any superintendent dared to refuse the request of a body-master to hire or discharge any man, with or without reason, that superintendent's life was as good as forfeited. "Bosses" were in the same way constrained to give Mollys the best jobs—that is, the easiest—and in case of their failure to do so they were promptly made an example of with clubs or revolvers. Before killing a superintendent or a colliery "boss," the body-master would usually serve him with a "coffin notice," a roughly written warning, bearing crudely drawn knives and revolvers, and a large coffin in the center. Woe to the man who allowed such a notice to go unheeded! In nearly every instance he was shot or clubbed to death within a few days by unknown assailants. . . .

Early in July, 1875, while McKenna was still in Shenandoah, acting as a body-master, a shocking murder was committed by Molly Maguires at the town of Tamaqua . . . the east. The victim was Franklin B. Yost, a policeman, and a man who had served honorably in the civil war, and a most peaceful and worthy citizen. Hurrying to the scene of the crime, McKenna addressed himself to "Powder Keg" Carrigan, the body-master of that patch. . . .

McKenna was not long in learning that "Powder Keg" himself was the man at whose instigation the murder had been committed. Carrigan explained to him that they had killed the wrong man, his grievance having been not against Yost, but against another policeman, Bernard McCarron, who had aroused "Powder Keg's" enmity years before by frequently arresting him for disorderly conduct. Carrigan nursed the memory of this treatment, and when he had became a body-master at once proceeded to arrange for the killing of McCarron. Having applied to Alexander Campbell, the body-master of Landsford, Carbon County . . . for two men to do a "clean job," he brought the men to a retired spot on McCarron's beat. Later in the night, when a policeman passed by, the two men shot him, according to orders, and then started for their homes. But on that night McCarron had exchanged beats with Yost, who accordingly came to a violent death, although neither the Mollys nor anyone else in the region had any but kind feelings toward him. Carrigan showed McKenna the revolver, a weapon of thirty-two caliber, with which the policeman had been killed, and explained that it had been borrowed from a Molly named Roarity by the two men, Hugh McGehan and James Doyle, who with others had done the murder. McGehan was the man who fired the fatal shot. McKenna secured the names of every man concerned in the crime, and ultimately, on his evidence, it was punished by the hanging, in Pottsville, of Hugh McGehan, Thomas Duffy, James Roarity, James Carl, and James Doyle.

. . . Following closely upon the murder of Yost, there came in August, 1875, a "Bloody Saturday," as it was called by the Mollys, when they killed on that one day, Thomas Guyther, a justice of the peace, at Gerardville, and, at Shenandoah, Gomer James, the same whose life had been saved a few weeks before by McKenna's intervention. James was a desperado himself, having some time before, while drunk, shot down an Irishman named Cosgrove, and this offense the Mollys had sworn to avenge. . . . The Shenandoah firemen were giving a banquet in a public hall, and Gomer James was serving as bartender. A little before midnight, when the gaiety was at its height, Thomas Hurler left his mother, who was sitting on a bench near the bar, and going up to James ordered a glass of beer. James served him promptly, whereupon Hurley threw down a nickel, and lifting the glass in his left hand, pretended to drain it. but he held a pistol, ready cocked, in the right-hand pocket of his sack coat, and while the glass was at his lips, he pulled the trigger. Then, quite unconcerned, he finished his beer, and affected to join in a search for the murderer. . . .

. . . Toward the end of 1875, the strain under which McParland had been working for eighteen months began to tell upon him and he appealed to Allan Pinkerton to be allowed to strike the final blow. . . . Allan Pinkerton and his assistants . . . concluded that the evidence McParland had secured was sufficient, and steps were forthwith taken to close in on the murderers. McParland had still, however; many dangers to face; first from fellow members of the order who were beginning to believe he had played them false, and then from outraged citizens, who regarded him as a monster of crime whose unceremonious killing would be a service to the State. One night, in Tamaqua, bands of armed men searched for him from house to house until morning, and would certainly have discovered and lynched him, had he not, by pretending to fall into a drunken sleep, succeeded in remaining all night in the house of a respectable citizen who was not suspected of harboring him. . . .

Jack Kehoe, the county delegate whose influence in the order was very great, was now busily reporting his suspicion that "James McKenna" was a detective. To meet this danger McParland boldly went straight to Kehoe, accused him of treachery and demanded an immediate investigation. As county delegate, Kehoe instructed McKenna, who was at that time county secretary, to write notices to all the body-masters in the county to meet at Shenandoah at a given date, to conduct the investigation. He was writing the notices in a room over Kehoe's saloon, where Mrs. Kehoe was sewing, when Kehoe came in suddenly with a glass of soda for his wife, and a hot whiskey for McKenna. Having placed the two glasses on the table, he left the room. . . . As soon as he had gone, Mrs. Kehoe, who was a good woman at heart, and devoted to McKenna, took up the hot whiskey, threw it into the stove, and then burst into tears. . . . It is certain that the whiskey was poisoned. A second attempt to poison McKenna was made the day before his trial at Shenandoah. He was lifting the drugged glass to his lips when an instinctive suspicion moved him to set it down.

On the day of the trial Jack Kehoe did not appear. He was expecting that there would be no trial; for he had engaged sixteen men to murder McKenna, and had even advanced several of them twenty-five dollars each for the service.

McKenna's life was probably saved by the personal devotion of a Molly Maguire named Frank McAndrew, who told him of the plot to kill him, and swore to stand true to him. . . . By McAndrew's aid he stole away and returned to Philadelphia, where he was warmly welcomed by Allan Pinkerton and the president of the Philadelphia and Reading Railroad, Mr. Gowen. . . . And here the services of McParland (alias McKenna) as a detective in the Molly Maguire cases ended; but he had still a most important service to render as a witness. . . .

. . . [O]n May 6, 1876 a number of arrests were made, [and] the trials that followed were highly dramatic. Held as they were at the very center of the lawless district, there was more or less danger that persons engaged in them would themselves suffer the fraternity's vengeance. The result of the trials—which is to say the result of McParland's dangerous investigations and subsequent testimony—was the complete extermination of the order of Molly Maguires. A score or more of the desperadoes were condemned to longer or shorter terms in the penitentiary. Nineteen were hanged. Among the latter was Jack Kehoe, who had been among the first to suspect McParland of being a detective, and had expended all his power and ingenuity to get him killed and well out of the way.

Source: Cleveland Moffett, "The Overthrow of the Molly Maguires," *McClure's Magazine,* 1894; Ohio State University, Department of History, http://www.history.ohio-state.edu/projects/coal/ MollyMaguire/mollymaguires.htm.

31. National Labor Relations (Wagner) Act (1935)

The National Labor Relations Act (Wagner-Connery Act) established the right of workers to organize unions of their own choosing, free from employer coercion, and established the obligation of employers to recognize such unions and bargain in good faith with them. Senator Robert Wagner (D-N.Y.) drew upon his experience as chairman of the National Labor Board, established under the **National Industrial Recovery Act***, to draft this legislation. The* **National Labor Relations Act** *(NLRA) established a National Labor Relations Board to oversee the rights and obligations of employees and employers as established under the act. Additionally, the NLRA defined unfair labor practices on the part of employers. In 1937, the Supreme Court upheld this legislation, and it has remained the foundation of American labor law to the present day.*

FINDINGS AND POLICY

Sec. I. The denial by employers of the right of employees to organize and the refusal by employers to accept the procedure of collective bargaining lead to strikes and other forms of industrial strife or unrest, which have the intent or the necessary effect of burdening or obstructing commerce by (a) impairing the efficiency, safety, or operation of the instrumentalities of commerce; (b) occurring in the current of commerce; (c) materially affecting, restraining, or controlling the flow of raw materials or manufactured or processed goods from or into the channels of commerce, or the prices of such materials or goods in commerce; or (d) using diminution of employment and wages in such volume as substantially to impair or disrupt the market for goods flowing from or into the channels of commerce.

The inequality of bargaining power between employees who do not possess full freedom of association or actual *liberty* of contract, and employers who are organized in the corporate or other forms of ownership association substantially burdens and affects the flow of commerce, and tends to aggravate recurrent business depressions, by depressing wage rates and the purchasing power of wage earners in industry and by preventing the stabilization of competitive wage rates and working conditions within and between industries.

Experience has proved that protection by law of the right of employees to organize and bargain collectively safeguards commerce from injury, impairment, or interruption, and promotes the flow of commerce by removing certain recognized sources of industrial strife and unrest, by encouraging practices fundamental to the friendly adjustment of industrial disputes arising out of differences as to wages, hours, or other working conditions, and by restoring equality of bargaining power between employers and employees.

It is hereby declared to be the policy of the United States to eliminate the causes of certain substantial obstructions to the free flow of commerce and to mitigate and eliminate these obstructions when they have occurred by encouraging the practice and procedure of collective bargaining and by protecting the exercise by workers of full freedom of association, self-organization, and designation of representatives of their own choosing, for the purpose of negotiating the terms and conditions of their employment. . . .

NATIONAL LABOR RELATIONS BOARD

Sec. 3. (a) There is hereby created a board, to be known as the "National Labor Relations Board," which shall be composed of three members, who shall be appointed by the President, by and with the advice and consent of the Senate. One of the original members shall be appointed for a term of one year, one for a term of three years, and one for a term of five years, but their successors shall be appointed for terms of five years each, except that any individual chosen to fill a vacancy shall be appointed only for the unexpired term of the member whom he shall succeed. The President shall designate one member to serve as chairman of the Board. Any member of the Board may be removed by the President, upon notice and hearing, for neglect of duty or malfeasance in office, but for no other cause. . . .

Sec. 4. (a) Each member of the Board shall receive a salary of $10,000 a year, shall be eligible for reappointment, and shall not engage in any other business, vocation, or employment. . . . The Board may establish or utilize such regional, local, or other agencies, and utilize such voluntary and uncompensated services, as may from time to time be needed. . . .

Sec. 6. (a) The Board shall have authority from time to time to make, amend, and rescind such rules and regulations as may be necessary to carry out the provisions of this Act. Such rules and regulations shall be effective upon publication in the manner which the Board shall prescribe.

RIGHTS OF EMPLOYEES

Sec. 7. Employees shall have the right of self-organization, to form, join, or assist labor organizations, to bargain collectively through representatives of their own choosing, and to engage in concerted activities, for the purpose of collective bargaining or other mutual aid or protection.

Sec. 8. It shall be an unfair labor practice for an employer

(1) To interfere with, restrain, or coerce employees in the exercise of the rights guaranteed in section 7.

(2) To dominate or interfere with the formation or administration of any labor organization or contribute financial or other support to it: *Provided,* That subject to rules and regulations made and published by the Board pursuant to section 6 (a), an employer shall not be prohibited from permitting employees to confer with him during working hours without loss of time or pay.

(3) By discrimination in regard to hire or tenure of employment or any term or condition of employment to encourage or discourage membership in any labor organization: *Provided*, That nothing in this Act, or in the National Industrial Recovery Act (U.S. C., Supp. VII, title 15, secs. 701–712), as amended from time to time, or in any code or agreement approved or prescribed thereunder, or in any other statute of the United States, shall preclude an employer from making an agreement with a labor organization (not established, maintained, or assisted by any action defined in this Act as an unfair labor practice) to require as a condition of employment membership therein, if such labor organization is the representative of the employees as provided in section 9 (a), in the appropriate collective bargaining unit covered by such agreement when made.

(4) To discharge or otherwise discriminate against an employee because he has filed charges or given testimony under this Act.

(5) To refuse to bargain collectively with the representatives of his employees, subject to the provisions of Section 9 (a).

REPRESENTATIVES AND ELECTIONS

Sec. 9. (a) Representatives designated or elected for the purposes of collective bargaining by the majority of the employees in a unit appropriate for such purposes, shall be the exclusive representatives of all the employees in such unit for the purposes of collective bargaining in respect to rates of pay, wages, hours of employment, or other conditions of employment: *Provided*, That any individual employee or a group of employees shall have the right at any time to present grievances to their employer.

(b) The Board shall decide in each case whether, in order to insure to employees the full benefit of their right to self-organization and to collective bargaining, and otherwise to effectuate the policies of this Act, the unit appropriate for the purposes of collective bargaining shall be the employer unit, craft unit, plant unit, or subdivision thereof.

(c) Whenever a question affecting commerce arises concerning the representation of employees, the Board may investigate such controversy and certify to the parties, in writing, the name or names of the representatives that have been designated or selected. In any such investigation, the Board shall provide for an appropriate hearing upon due notice, either in conjunction with a proceeding under section 10 or otherwise, and may take a secret ballot of employees, or utilize any other suitable method to ascertain such representatives.

(d) Whenever an order of the Board made pursuant to section 10 (c) is based in whole or in part upon facts certified following an investigation pursuant to subsection (c) of this section, and there is a petition for the movement or review of such order, such certification and the record of such investigation shall be included in the transcript of the entire record required to be filed under subsections 10 (e) or 10 (f), and thereupon the decree of the court enforcing, modifying, or setting aside in whole or in part the order of the Board shall be made and entered upon the pleadings, testimony, and proceedings set forth in such transcript.

PREVENTION OF UNFAIR LABOR PRACTICES

Sec. 10. (a) The Board is empowered, as hereinafter provided, to prevent any person from engaging in any unfair labor practice (listed in section 8) affecting commerce. This power shall be exclusive, and shall not be affected by any other means of adjustment or prevention that has been or may be established by agreement, code, law, or otherwise.

(b) Whenever it is charged that any person has engaged in or is engaging in any such unfair labor practice, the Board, or any agent or agency designated by the Board for such purposes, shall have power to issue and cause to be served upon such person a complaint stating the charges in that respect, and containing a notice of hearing before the Board or a member thereof, or before a designated agent or agency, at a place therein fixed, not less than five days after the serving of said complaint. Any such complaint may be amended by the member, agent, or agency conducting the hearing or the Board in its discretion at any time prior to the issuance of an order based thereon. The person so complained of shall have the right to file an answer to the original or amended complaint and to appear in person or otherwise and give testimony at the place and time fixed in the complaint. In the discretion of the member, agent or agency conducting the hearing of the Board, any other person may be allowed to intervene in the said proceeding and to present testimony. In any such proceeding the rules of evidence prevailing in courts of law or equity shall not be controlling.

(c) The testimony taken by such member, agent or agency or the Board shall be reduced to writing and filed with the Board. Thereafter, in its discretion, the Board upon notice may take further testimony or hear argument. If upon all the testimony taken the Board shall be of the opinion that any person named in the complaint has engaged in or is engaging in any such unfair labor practice, then the Board shall state its findings of fact and shall issue and cause to be served on such person an order requiring such person to cease and desist from such unfair labor practice, and to take such affirmative action, including reinstatement of employees with or without back pay, as will effectuate the policies of this Act. Such order may further require such person to make reports from time to time showing the extent to which it has complied with the order. If upon all the testimony taken the Board shall be of the opinion that no person named in the complaint has engaged in or is engaging in any such unfair labor practice, then the Board shall state its findings of fact and shall issue an order dismissing the said complaint. . . .

(e) The Board shall have power to petition any circuit court of appeals of the United States, or if all the circuit courts of appeals to which application may be made are in vacation, any district court of the United States, within any circuit or district, respectively, wherein the unfair labor practice in question occurred or wherein such person resides or transacts business, for the enforcement of such order and for appropriate temporary relief or restraining order, and shall certify and file in the court a transcript of the entire record in the proceeding, including the pleadings and testimony upon which such order was entered and the findings and order of the Board. Upon such filing, the court shall cause notice thereof to be served upon such person, and thereupon shall have jurisdiction of the proceeding and of the question determined therein, and shall have power to grant such temporary relief or restraining order as it deems just and proper, and to make and enter upon the pleadings, testimony, and proceedings set forth in such transcript a decree enforcing, modifying, and enforcing as so modified, or setting aside in whole or in part the order of the Board. . . .

Source: U.S. Statutes at Large, vol. XLIX.

---

32. Persecution of the Industrial Workers of the World: "Big Bill" Haywood's Description of the 1919 Murder of Wesley Everest

*The **Industrial Workers of the World (IWW)** was one of the most colorful and overtly radical labor organizations to appear on American soil. Because the IWW openly espoused the destruction of the **wage** system, it engendered great opposition. For most of its most active period—roughly 1907 to 1919—the IWW's own revolutionary rhetoric contributed to the ferocity with which organized capital sought to silence the group. Fears of revolution and sabotage were used by IWW enemies to justify crackdowns of dubious legality. For all the IWW's fiery words, far more violence was done to IWW members than by them. Persecutions of IWW members intensified once the United States entered World War I. The IWW viewed the war as a capitalist struggle and many of its leaders encouraged workers to avoid taking part in it. Official raids took place, and quasi-legal vigilante actions proliferated.*

*One of the worst of the latter took place in Centralia, Washington, in 1919, where the American Legion and local citizens, encouraged by timber barons, targeted IWW organizers and took it upon themselves to destroy the town's IWW labor hall. That raid led to the lynching of Wesley Everest. Everest is one of the three most-famed martyrs of the early IWW, and joined a pantheon also occupied by Frank Little, who was killed by a Montana mob in 1917, and songwriter **Joe Hill**, who was executed for murder in 1915. The story of Everest's martyrdom is told by famed IWW organizer **William "Big Bill" Haywood**.*

On November 11th, 1919, a parade of American Legion men and assorted patriots was held. At the meeting to "deal with the I.W.W." . . . a secret plot was concocted among the Lumber Trust leaders to mob the I.W.W. Hall, leading the paraders into the attack.

At the moment agreed upon, the leaders cried out upon signal from a man on horseback, "Let's go-o-o! At 'em boys!" and the door of the hall was smashed in, some entering, when a rain of bullets came from within, halting the attack and leaving two attackers dead and several wounded. Some of the mob carried ropes, evidently ready to lynch the union men. . . .

But the hall was surrounded and the attackers gained entrance in force, seizing the few workers there, with the exception of one man, Wesley Everest. Leaving the hall by the rear door he broke through the mob and made for the river, rifle bullets of his prepared assassins zipping around him. With the ammunition, he stopped to reload, reached the river and tried to ford it. Failing because of its depth, he came back to shore and shouted his readiness to surrender to any constituted authority.

The mob paid no attention and came on, firing as they came, until Everest saw there was no hope of ceasing the fight and resumed with firing. This halted the mob but one man came on, armed and firing. With his last cartridge Everest shot this fellow, Dale Hubbard, nephew of the chief conspirator. Everest was seized by the mob.

On the way to the jail he was beaten, kicked and cursed. With a rifle-butt his front teeth were knocked out. A rope was thrown round his neck, but with characteristic defiance he told them, "You haven't got the guts to lynch a man in the daytime."

Night came. Maimed and bleeding in a cell next to his fellow workers, lay Everest. At a late hour the lights of the city suddenly were extinguished. The jail door was smashed. No one tried to stop the lynchers. Staggering erect, Everest said to the other prisoners: "Tell the boys I died for my class."

A brief struggle. Many blows. A sound of dragging. The purring of high-powered cars. Again the lights came on. The autos reached the bridge over the Chehalis River. A rope was tied to the steel framework and Everest with a noose around his neck was brutally kicked from the bridge. After a pause he was hauled up, and it being found that he had some life left, a longer rope was used and the brutal process repeated. Again hauled up, the ghouls again flung the body over. An auto headlight was trained on the body disclosing that some sadist, more degenerate than the rest, had ripped Everest's sexual organs almost loose from his body with some sharp instrument during the auto trip to the bridge.

Finally, after riddling the body with bullets, it was cut loose and let fall in the river later to be found, a sodden, ghastly thing, taken back to the jail where it was placed in view of Everest's friends there in prison and at last buried in an unmarked grave.

Source: William Haywood, *The Autobiography of Big Bill Haywood* (1929; reprint New York: International Publishers, 1966), pp. 355–56.

33. Principles of Scientific Management: Excerpt from Frederick Winslow Taylor's *Shop Management*, 1911

*Frederick Winslow Taylor (1856–1915) was known as the "father" of scientific management. Taylor utilized time-motion studies to analyze the work process. Using incentive pay, Taylor aimed to coordinate human efforts with the maximum efficiency of production. Taylor's system of work measurement, work design, and production control transformed the nature of American industrial production. Taylor believed that the key to higher **wages** and higher profits, simultaneously, was to increase productivity. With increased wages, hence increased worker satisfaction, it was believed that the incentive to join unions would be lessened. **Taylorism**, as Taylor's "brand" of scientific management came to be known, achieved great popularity in the first two decades of the twentieth century. In this 1911 publication, Taylor explains his system.*

INTRODUCTION

President Roosevelt, in his address to the Governors at the White House, prophetically remarked that "The conservation of our national resources is only preliminary to the larger question of national efficiency."

The whole country at once recognized the importance of conserving our material resources and a large movement has been started which will be effective in accomplishing this object. As yet, however, we have but vaguely appreciated the importance of "the larger question of increasing our national efficiency."

We can see our forests vanishing, our water-powers going to waste, our soil being carried by floods into the sea; and the end of our coal and our iron is in sight. But our larger wastes of human effort, which go on every day through such of our acts as are blundering, ill-directed, or inefficient, and which Mr. Roosevelt refers to as a lack of "national efficiency," are less visible, less tangible, and are but vaguely appreciated.

We can see and feel the waste of material things. Awkward, inefficient, or ill-directed movements of men, however, leave nothing visible or tangible behind them. Their appreciation calls for an act of memory, an effort of the imagination. And for this reason, even though our daily loss from this source is greater than from our waste of material things, the one has stirred us deeply, while the other has moved us but little.

As yet there has been no public agitation for "greater national efficiency," no meetings have been called to consider how this is to be brought about. And still there are signs that the need for greater efficiency is widely felt.

The search for better, for more competent men, from the presidents of our great companies down to our household servants, was never more vigorous than it is now. And more than ever before is the demand for competent men in excess of the supply.

What we are all looking for, however, is the ready-made, competent man; the man whom some one else has trained. It is only when we fully realize that our duty, as well as our opportunity, lies in systematically cooperating to train and to make this competent man, instead of in hunting for a man whom some one else has trained, that we shall be on the road to national efficiency.

In the past the prevailing idea has been well expressed in the saying that "Captains of industry are born, not made" and the theory has been that if one could get the right man, methods could be safely left to him. In the future it will be appreciated that our leaders must be trained right as well as born right, and that no great man can (with the old system of personal management) hope to compete with a number of ordinary men who have been properly organized so as efficiently to cooperate.

In the past the man has been first; in the future the system must be first. This in no sense, however, implies that great men are not needed. On the contrary, the first object of any good system must be that of developing first-class men; and under systematic management the best man rises to the top more certainly and more rapidly than ever before.

This paper has been written:

First. To point out, through a series of simple illustrations, the great loss which the whole country is suffering through inefficiency in almost all of our daily acts.

Second. To try to convince the reader that the remedy for this inefficiency lies in systematic management, rather than in searching for some unusual or extraordinary man.

Third. To prove that the best management is a true science, resting upon clearly defined laws, rules, and principles, as a foundation. And further to show that the fundamental principles of scientific management are applicable to all kinds of human activities, from our simplest individual acts to the work of our great corporations, which call for the most elaborate cooperation. And, briefly, through a series of illustrations, to convince the reader that whenever these principles are correctly applied, results must follow which are truly astounding.

This paper was originally prepared for presentation to The American Society of Mechanical Engineers. The illustrations chosen are such as, it is believed, will especially appeal to engineers and to managers of industrial and manufacturing establishments, and also quite as much to all of the men who are working in these establishments. It is hoped, however, that it will be clear to other readers that the same principles can be applied with equal force to all social activities: to the management of our homes; the management of our farms; the management of the business of our tradesmen, large and small; of our churches, our philanthropic institutions, our universities, and our governmental departments.

CHAPTER I: FUNDAMENTALS OF SCIENTIFIC MANAGEMENT

The principal object of management should be to secure the maximum prosperity for the employer, coupled with the maximum prosperity for each employee. The words "maximum prosperity" are used, in their broad sense, to mean not only large dividends for the company or owner, but the development of every branch of the business to its highest state of excellence, so that the prosperity may be permanent.

In the same way maximum prosperity for each employee means not only higher wages than are usually received by men of his class, but, of more importance still, it also means the development of each man to his state of maximum efficiency, so that he may be able to do, generally speaking, the highest grade of work for which his natural abilities fit him, and it further means giving him, when possible, this class of work to do.

It would seem to be so self-evident that maximum prosperity for the employer, coupled with maximum prosperity for the employee, ought to be the two leading objects of management, that even to state this fact should be unnecessary. And yet there is no question that, throughout the industrial world, a large part of the organization of employers, as well as employees, is for war rather than for peace, and that perhaps the majority on either side do not believe that it is possible so to arrange their mutual relations that their interests become identical.

The majority of these men believe that the fundamental interests of employees and employers are necessarily antagonistic. Scientific management, on the contrary, has for its very foundation the firm conviction that the true interests of the two are one and the same; that prosperity for the employer cannot exist through a long term of years unless it is accompanied by prosperity for the employee, and vice versa; and that it is possible to give the workman what he most wants high wages and the employer what he wants a low labor cost—for his manufactures.

It is hoped that some at least of those who do not sympathize with each of these objects may be led to modify their views; that some employers, whose attitude toward their workmen has been that of trying to get the largest amount of work out of them for the smallest possible wages, may be led to see that a more liberal policy toward their men will pay them better; and that some of those workmen who begrudge a fair and even a large profit to their employers, and who feel that all of the fruits of their labor should belong to them, and that those for whom they work and the capital invested in the business are entitled to little or nothing, may be led to modify these views.

No one can be found who will deny that in the case of any single individual the greatest prosperity can exist only when that individual has reached his highest state of efficiency; that is, when he is turning out his largest daily output. The truth of this fact is also perfectly clear in the case of two men working together.

To illustrate: if you and your workman have become so skillful that you and he together are making two pairs of shoes in a day, while your competitor and his workman are making only one pair, it is clear that after selling your two pairs of shoes you can pay your workman much higher wages than your competitor who produces only one pair of shoes is able to pay his man, and that there will still be enough money left over for you to have a larger profit than your competitor.

In the case of a more complicated manufacturing establishment, it should also be perfectly clear that the greatest permanent prosperity for the workman, coupled with the greatest prosperity for the employer, can be brought about only when the work of the establishment is done with the smallest combined expenditure of human effort, plus nature's resources, plus the cost for the use of capital in the shape of machines, buildings, etc. Or, to state the same thing in a different way: that the greatest prosperity can exist only as the result of the greatest possible productivity of the men and machines of the establishment that is, when each man and each machine are turning out the largest possible output; because unless your men and your machines are daily turning out more work than others around you, it is clear that competition will prevent your paying higher wages to your workmen than are paid to those of your competitor. And what is true as to the possibility of paying high wages in the case of two companies competing close beside one another is also true as to whole districts of the country and even as to nations which are in competition. In a word, that maximum prosperity can exist only as the result of maximum productivity. Later in this paper illustrations will be given of several companies which are earning large dividends and at the same time paying from 30 per cent to 100 per cent higher wages to their men than are paid to similar men immediately around them, and with whose employers they are in competition. These illustrations will cover different types of work, from the most elementary to the most complicated. If the above reasoning is correct, it follows that the most important object of both the workmen and the management should be the training and development of each individual in the establishment, so that he can do (at his fastest pace and with the maximum of efficiency) the highest class of work for which his natural abilities fit him.

These principles appear to be so self-evident that many men may think it almost childish to state them. Let us, however, turn to the facts, as they actually exist in this country and in England. The English and American peoples are the greatest sportsmen in the world. Whenever an American workman plays baseball, or an English workman plays cricket, it is safe to say that he strains every nerve to secure victory for his side. He does his very best to make the largest possible number of runs. The universal sentiment is so strong that any man who fails to give out all there is in him in sport is branded as a "quitter," and treated with contempt by those who are around him. When the same workman returns to work on the following day, instead of using every effort to turn out the largest possible amount of work, in a majority of the cases this man deliberately plans to do as little as he safely can—to turn out far less work than he is well able to do—in many instances to do not more than one-third to one-half of a proper day's work. And in fact if he were to do his best to turn out his largest possible day's work, he would be abused by his fellow-workers for so doing, even more than if he had proved himself a "quitter" in sport. Under working, that is, deliberately working slowly so as to avoid doing a full day's work, "soldiering," as it is called in this country, "hanging it out," as it is called in England, "ca' cannie," as it is called in Scotland, is almost universal in industrial establishments, and prevails also to a large extent in the building trades; and the writer asserts without fear of contradiction that this constitutes the greatest evil with which the working-people of both England and America are now afflicted. It will be shown later in this paper that doing away with slow working and "soldiering" in all its forms and so arranging the relations between employer and employee that each workman will work to his very best advantage and at his best speed, accompanied by the intimate cooperation with the management and the help (which the workman should receive) from the management, would result on the average in nearly doubling the output of each man and each machine. What other reforms, among those which are being discussed by these two nations, could do as much toward promoting prosperity, toward the diminution of poverty, and the alleviation of suffering? America and England have been recently agitated over such subjects as the tariff, the control of the large corporations on the one hand, and of hereditary power on the other hand, and over various more or less socialistic proposals for taxation, etc. On these subjects both peoples have been profoundly stirred, and yet hardly a voice has been raised to call attention to this vastly greater and more important subject of "soldiering," which directly and powerfully affects the wages, the prosperity, and the life of almost every working-man, and also quite as much the prosperity of every industrial establishment in the nation.

The elimination of "soldiering" and of the several causes of slow working would so lower the cost of production that both our home and foreign markets would be greatly enlarged, and we could compete on more than even terms with our rivals. It would remove one of the fundamental causes for dull times, for lack of employment, and for poverty, and therefore would have a more permanent and far-reaching effect upon these misfortunes than any of the curative remedies that are now being used to soften their consequences. It would insure higher wages and make shorter working hours and better working and home conditions possible.

Why is it, then, in the face of the self-evident fact that maximum prosperity can exist only as the result of the determined effort of each workman to turn out each day his largest possible day's work, that the great majority of our men are deliberately doing just the opposite, and that even when the men have the best of intentions their work is in most cases far from efficient? There are three causes for this condition, which may be briefly summarized as:

First. The fallacy, which has from time immemorial been almost universal among workmen, that a material increase in the output of each man or each machine in the trade would result in the end in throwing a large number of men out of work.

Second. The defective systems of management which are in common use, and which make it necessary for each workman to soldier, or work slowly, in order that he may protect his own best interests.

Third. The inefficient rule-of-thumb methods, which are still almost universal in all trades and in practicing which our workmen waste a large part of their effort.

This paper will attempt to show the enormous gains which would result from the substitution by our workmen of scientific for rule-of-thumb methods.

To explain a little more fully these three causes:

First. The great majority of workmen still believe that if they were to work at their best speed they would be doing a great injustice to the whole trade by throwing a lot of men out of work, and yet the history of the development of each trade shows that each improvement, whether it be the invention of a new machine or the introduction of a better method, which results in increasing the productive capacity of the men in the trade and cheapening the costs, instead of throwing men out of work make in the end work for more men.

The cheapening of any article in common use almost immediately results in a largely increased demand for that article. Take the case of shoes, for instance. The introduction of machinery for doing every element of the work which was formerly done by hand has resulted in making shoes at a fraction of their former labor cost, and in selling them so cheap that now almost every man, woman, and child in the working-classes buys one or two pairs of shoes per year, and wears shoes all the time, whereas formerly each workman bought perhaps one pair of shoes every five years, and went barefoot most of the time, wearing shoes only as a luxury or as a matter of the sternest necessity. In spite of the enormously increased output of shoes per workman, which has come with shoe machinery, the demand for shoes has so increased that there are relatively more men working in the shoe industry now than ever before.

The workmen in almost every trade have before them an object lesson of this kind, and yet, because they are ignorant of the history of their own trade even, they still firmly believe, as their fathers did before them, that it is against their best interests for each man to turn out each day as much work as possible.

Under this fallacious idea a large proportion of the workmen of both countries each day deliberately work slowly so as to curtail the output. Almost every labor union has made, or is contemplating making, rules which have for their object curtailing the output of their members, and those men who have the greatest influence with the working-people, the labor leaders as well as many people with philanthropic feelings who are helping them, are daily spreading this fallacy and at the same time telling them that they are overworked. A great deal has been and is being constantly said about "sweat-shop" work and conditions. The writer has great sympathy with those who are overworked, but on the whole a greater sympathy for those who are under paid. For every individual, however, who is overworked, there are a hundred who intentionally underwork—greatly under-work—every day of their lives, and who for this reason deliberately aid in establishing those conditions which in the end inevitably result in low wages. And yet hardly a single voice is being raised in an endeavor to correct this evil.

As engineers and managers, we are more intimately acquainted with these facts than any other class in the community, and are therefore best fitted to lead in a movement to combat this fallacious idea by educating not only the work-men but the whole of the country as to the true facts. And yet we are practically doing nothing in this direction, and are leaving this field entirely in the hands of the labor agitators (many of whom are misinformed and mis-guided), and of sentimentalists who are ignorant as to actual working conditions.

Second. As to the second cause for soldiering—the relations which exist between employers and employees under almost all of the systems of management which are in common use—it is impossible in a few words to make it clear to one not familiar with this problem why it is that the ignorance of employers as to the proper time in which work of various kinds should be done makes it for the interest of the workman to "soldier."

The writer therefore quotes herewith from a paper read before The American Society of Mechanical Engineers in June, 1903, entitled "Shop Management," which it is hoped will explain fully this cause for soldiering:

This loafing or soldiering proceeds from two causes. First, from the natural instinct and tendency of men to take it easy, which may be called natural soldiering. Second, from more intricate second thought and reasoning caused by their relations with other men, which may be called systematic soldiering. There is no question that the tendency of the average man (in all walks of life) is toward working at a slow, easy gait, and that it is only after a good deal of thought and observation on his part or as a result of example, conscience, or external pressure that he takes a more rapid pace. There are, of course, men of unusual energy, vitality, and ambition who naturally choose the fastest gait, who set up their own standards, and who work hard, even though it may be against their best interests. But these few uncommon men only serve by forming a contrast to emphasize the tendency of the average. This common tendency to "take it easy" is greatly increased by bringing a number of men together on similar work and at a uniform standard rate of pay by the day.

Under this plan the better men gradually but surely slow down their gait to that of the poorest and least efficient. When a naturally energetic man works for a few days beside a lazy one, the logic of the situation is unanswerable. "Why should I work hard when that lazy fellow gets the same pay that I do and does only half as much work?"

A careful time study of men working under these conditions will disclose facts which are ludicrous as well as pitiable.

To illustrate: The writer has timed a naturally energetic workman who, while going and coming from work, would walk at a speed of from three to four miles per hour, and not infrequently trot home after a day's work. On arriving at his work he would immediately slow down to a speed of about one mile an hour. When, for example, wheeling a loaded wheelbarrow, he would go at a good fast pace even uphill in order to be as short a time as possible under load, and immediately on the return walk slow down to a mile an hour, improving every opportunity for delay short of actually sitting down. In order to be sure not to do more than his lazy neighbor, he would actually tire himself in his effort to go slow.

These men were working under a foreman of good reputation and highly thought of by his employer, who, when his attention was called to this state of things, answered: "Well, I can keep them from sitting down, but the devil can't make them get a move on while they are at work."

The natural laziness of men is serious, but by far the greatest evil from which both workmen and employers are suffering is the systematic soldiering which is almost universal under all of the ordinary schemes of management and which results from a careful study on the part of the workmen of what will promote their best interests.

The writer was much interested recently in hearing one small but experienced golf caddy boy of twelve explaining to a green caddy, who had shown special energy and interest, the necessity of going slow and lagging behind his man when he came up to the ball, showing him that since they were paid by the hour, the faster they went the less money they got, and finally telling him that if he went too fast the other boys would give him a licking.

This represents a type of systematic soldiering which is not, however, very serious, since it is done with the knowledge of the employer, who can quite easily break it up if he wishes.

The greater part of the systematic soldiering, however, is done by the men with the deliberate object of keeping their employers ignorant of how fast work can be done.

So universal is soldiering for this purpose that hardly a competent workman can be found in a large establishment, whether he works by the day or on piece work, contract work, or under any of the ordinary systems, who does not devote a considerable part of his time to studying just how slow he can work and still convince his employer that he is going at a good pace.

The causes for this are, briefly, that practically all employers determine upon a maximum sum which they feel it is right for each of their classes of employees to earn per day, whether their men work by the day or piece.

Each workman soon finds out about what this figure is for his particular case, and he also realizes that when his employer is convinced that a man is capable of doing more work than he has done, he will find sooner or later some way of compelling him to do it with little or no increase of pay.

Employers derive their knowledge of how much of a given class of work can be done in a day from either their own experience, which has frequently grown hazy with age, from casual and unsystematic observation of their men, or at best from records which are kept, showing the quickest time in which each job has been done. In many cases the employer will feel almost certain that a given job can be done faster than it has been, but he rarely cares to take the drastic measures necessary to force men to do it in the quickest time, unless he has an actual record proving conclusively how fast the work can be done.

It evidently becomes for each man's interest, then, to see that no job is done faster than it has been in the past. The younger and less experienced men are taught this by their elders, and all possible persuasion and social pressure is brought to bear upon the greedy and selfish men to keep them from making new records which result in temporarily increasing their wages, while all those who come after them are made to work harder for the same old pay.

Under the best day work of the ordinary type, when accurate records are kept of the amount of work done by each man and of his efficiency, and when each man's wages are raised as he improves, and those who fail to rise to a certain standard are discharged and a fresh supply of carefully selected men are given work in their places, both the natural loafing and systematic soldiering can be largely broken up. This can only be done, however, when the men are thoroughly convinced that there is no intention of establishing piece work even in the remote future, and it is next to impossible to make men believe this when the work is of such a nature that they believe piece work to be practicable. In most cases their fear of making a record which will be used as a basis for piece work will cause them to soldier as much as they dare.

It is, however, under piece work that the art of systematic soldiering is thoroughly developed; after a workman has had the price per piece of the work he is doing lowered two or three times as a result of his having worked harder and increased his output, he is likely entirely to lose sight of his employer's side of the case and become imbued with a grim determination to have no more cuts if soldiering can prevent it. Unfortunately for the character of the workman, soldiering involves a deliberate attempt to mislead and deceive his employer, and thus upright and straightforward workmen are compelled to become more or less hypocritical. The employer is soon looked upon as an antagonist, if not an enemy, and the mutual confidence which should exist between a leader and his men, the enthusiasm, the feeling that they are all working for the same end and will share in the results is entirely lacking.

The feeling of antagonism under the ordinary piece-work system becomes in many cases so marked on the part of the men that any proposition made by their employers, however reasonable, is looked upon with suspicion, and soldiering becomes such a fixed habit that men will frequently take pains to restrict the product of machines which they are running when even a large increase in output would involve no more work on their part.

Third. As to the third cause for slow work, considerable space will later in this paper be devoted to illustrating the great gain, both to employers and employees, which results from the substitution of scientific for rule-of-thumb methods in even the smallest details of the work of every trade. The enormous saving of time and therefore increase in the output which it is possible to effect through eliminating unnecessary motions and substituting fast for slow and inefficient motions for the men working in any of our trades can be fully realized only after one has personally seen the improvement which results from a thorough motion and time study, made by a competent man.

To explain briefly: owing to the fact that the workmen in all of our trades have been taught the details of their work by observation of those immediately around them, there are many different ways in common use for doing the same thing, perhaps forty, fifty, or a hundred ways of doing each act in each trade, and for the same reason there is a great variety in the implements used for each class of work. Now, among the various methods and implements used in each element of each trade there is always one method and one implement which is quicker and better than any of the rest. And this one best method and best implement can only be discovered or developed through a scientific study and analysis of all of the methods and implements in use, together with accurate, minute, motion and time study. This involves the gradual substitution of science for rule of thumb throughout the mechanic arts.

This paper will show that the underlying philosophy of all of the old systems of management in common use makes it imperative that each workman shall be left with the final responsibility for doing his job practically as he thinks best, with comparatively little help and advice from the management. And it will also show that because of this isolation of workmen, it is in most cases impossible for the men working under these systems to do their work in accordance with the rules and laws of a science or art, even where one exists.

The writer asserts as a general principle (and he proposes to give illustrations tending to prove the fact later in this paper) that in almost all of the mechanic arts the science which underlies each act of each workman is so great and amounts to so much that the workman who is best suited to actually doing the work is incapable of fully understanding this science, without the guidance and help of those who are working with him or over him, either through lack of education or through insufficient mental capacity. In order that the work may be done in accordance with scientific laws, it is necessary that there shall be a far more equal division of the responsibility between the management and the workmen than exists under any of the ordinary types of management. Those in the management whose duty it is to develop this science should also guide and help the workman in working under it, and should assume a much larger share of the responsibility for results than under usual conditions is assumed by the management.

The body of this paper will make it clear that, to work according to scientific laws, the management must take over and perform much of the work which is now left to the men; almost every act of the workman should be preceded by one or more preparatory acts of the management which enable him to do his work better and quicker than he otherwise could. And each man should daily be taught by and receive the most friendly help from those who are over him, instead of being, at the one extreme, driven or coerced by his bosses, and at the other left to his own unaided devices.

This close, intimate, personal cooperation between the management and the men is of the essence of modern scientific or task management.

It will be shown by a series of practical illustrations that, through this friendly cooperation, namely, through sharing equally in every day's burden, all of the great obstacles (above described) to obtaining the maximum output for each man and each machine in the establishment are swept away. The 30 per cent to 100 per cent increase in wages which the workmen are able to earn beyond what they receive under the old type of management, coupled with the daily intimate shoulder to shoulder contact with the management, entirely removes all cause for soldiering. And in a few years, under this system, the workmen have before them the object lesson of seeing that a great increase in the output per man results in giving employment to more men, instead of throwing men out of work, thus completely eradicating the fallacy that a larger output for each man will throw other men out of work.

It is the writer's judgment, then, that while much can be done and should be done by writing and talking toward educating not only workmen, but all classes in the community, as to the importance of obtaining the maximum output of each man and each machine, it is only through the adoption of modern scientific management that this great problem can be finally solved. Probably most of the readers of this paper will say that all of this is mere theory. On the contrary, the theory, or philosophy, of scientific management is just beginning to be understood, whereas the management itself has been a gradual evolution, extending over a period of nearly thirty years. And during this time the employees of one company after another, including a large range and diversity of industries, have gradually changed from the ordinary to the scientific type of management. At least 50,000 workmen in the United States are now employed under this system; and they are receiving from 30 per cent to 100 per cent higher wages daily than are paid to men of similar caliber with whom they are surrounded, while the companies employing them are more prosperous than ever before. In these companies the output, per man and per machine, has on an average been doubled. During all these years there has never been a single strike among the men working under this system. In place of the suspicious watchfulness and the more or less open warfare which characterizes the ordinary types of management, there is universally friendly cooperation between the management and the men.

Several papers have been written, describing the expedients which have been adopted and the details which have been developed under scientific management and the steps to be taken in changing from the ordinary to the scientific type. But unfortunately most of the readers of these papers have mistaken the mechanism for the true essence. Scientific management fundamentally consists of certain broad general principles, a certain philosophy, which can be applied in many ways, and a description of what any one man or men may believe to be the best mechanism for applying these general principles should in no way be confused with the principles themselves.

It is not here claimed that any single panacea exists for all of the troubles of the working-people or of employers. As long as some people are born lazy or inefficient, and others are born greedy and brutal, as long as vice and crime are with us, just so long will a certain amount of poverty, misery, and unhappiness be with us also. No system of management, no single expedient within the control of any man or any set of men can insure continuous prosperity to either workmen or employers. Prosperity depends upon so many factors entirely beyond the control of any one set of men, any state, or even any one country, that certain periods will inevitably come when both sides must suffer, more or less. It is claimed, however, that under scientific management the intermediate periods will be far more prosperous, far happier, and more free from discord and dissension. And also, that the periods will be fewer, shorter and the suffering less. And this will be particularly true in any one town, any one section of the country, or any one state which first substitutes the principles of scientific management for the rule of thumb.

That these principles are certain to come into general use practically throughout the civilized world, sooner or later, the writer is profoundly convinced, and the sooner they come the better for all the people.

Source: Frederick Winslow Taylor, *Shop Management* (New York: Harper & Brothers, 1911).

---

34. Excerpts from Henry George's *Progress and Poverty* (1879)

*It would be nearly impossible to exaggerate the impact that **Henry George** had on the thinking of late-nineteenth-century workers and reformers. The 1879 publication of* Progress and Poverty *caused an overnight sensation. In it, George rejects the popular Malthusianism and **Social Darwinism** of his day that posited that poverty was the result of a natural struggle for resources in which the fittest rose to the top of the economic heap. George attacked Malthusian assumptions at their core and demonstrated that the causes of poverty were rooted in unfair advantages in the way that tax policies, rents, and social improvements were allocated. In particular, George felt that social improvements and a steep decline in the availability of land had led to steep increases in the value of the latter. George targeted land speculators and others holding "idle" lands and argued that the state should abolish all taxes except for a "single tax" on unimproved land, which would be used by the state for all its needs, including alleviating poverty. Unimproved land would be taxed at its full value, thereby discouraging speculation, making more land available, and encouraging development that would benefit all of society.*

*George's theories are rooted in agrarian ideals and, like most panaceas, were criticized for being overly simplistic or impractical. Millions of people around the world disagreed and formed single-tax associations. Whatever one thinks of George's theories, he deserves credit for exposing the illogic of Social Darwinism. The popularity of his views may also help explain why imported ideas—like **socialism**, communism, and **anarchism**—held relatively less sway in the United States than they did elsewhere.*

In the two passages below, George lays out "The True Remedy" to society's problems, then explains "How Equal Rights to the Land May Be Asserted and Secured." [All emphasis in original]

We have traced the unequal distribution of wealth which is the curse and menace of modern civilization to the institution of private property in land. We have seen that so long as this institution exists no increase in productive power can permanently benefit the masses but, on the contrary, must tend still further to depress their condition. We have examined all the remedies, short of the abolition of private property in land . . . and have found them all inefficacious or impracticable.

There is but one way to remove an evil—and that is, to remove its cause. Poverty deepens as wealth increases, and wages are forced down while productive power grows, because land which is the source of all wealth and the field of all labor, is monopolized. To extirpate poverty, to make wages what justice commands they should be . . . we must therefore substitute for the individual ownership of land a common ownership. . . . *We must make land common property.* . . .

But a question of method remains. How shall we do it? . . .

I do not propose either to purchase or confiscate private property in land. The first would be unjust; the second needless. Let the individuals who now hold it still retain . . . possession of what they are pleased to call *their* land. Let them continue to call it *their* land. Let them buy and sell, and bequeath and devise it. . . . *It is not necessary to confiscate land; it is only necessary to confiscate rent.* . . .

What I, therefore, propose, as the simple yet sovereign remedy, which will raise wages, increase the earnings of capital, extirpate pauperism, abolish poverty, give remunerative employment to whomever wishes it, afford free scope to human powers, lessen crime, elevate morals . . . purify government, and carry civilization to yet nobler heights, is—*to appropriate rent by taxation.* . . .

Now, insomuch as the taxation of rent, of land values, must necessarily be increased just as we abolish other taxes, we may put forth the proposition into practical form by proposing—

To abolish all taxation save that upon land values. . . .

Source: Henry George, *Progress and Poverty: An Inquiry Into the Cause of Industrial Depressions and of Increase of Want with Increase of Wealth* (New York: Walter J. Black, 1942 reprint), pp. 274, 338, 340–41.

---

35. Pullman, Illinois, a Company Town: Excerpt from U.S. Strike Commission Report on the Chicago Strikes of June and July 1894

*The Pullman **boycott** of 1894 was one of the most famed clashes of **capital** and labor in American labor history. The violence associated with it, the wholesale abuse of injunctions, and the dramatic leadership of **Eugene Debs** notwithstanding, the boycott and **strike** shocked many Americans because Pullman, Illinois, was considered by many to be a model town. It was built by George Pullman, whose initial goal was to build a workers' town to surround the factories wherein his railroad sleeper and bag-*

gage cars were produced. Pullman's artificial lake, its grand hotel, its leafy boulevards, and its neat houses attracted tourists and some hailed him as a social reformer.

*But, Pullman quickly betrayed the underlying illogic of **company towns**. As a corporate-owned enterprise, Pullman was part of the same for-profit system as the ever-looming factories in its midst. Rents, utilities, store prices, and rail service were more expensive than those in nearby Chicago, and many workers also resented the degree of social and cultural control demanded by the moralistic Pullman. Like most company towns, Pullman unraveled due to economic pressures. The Panic of 1893 exacerbated an already tense situation. **Wage** cuts were bad enough, but increased rents and other costs within the Pullman-owned town pushed many workers to desperation. In 1895, a special government commission on Pullman rents issued a critical report of how the town of Pullman operated. It is excerpted below:*

If we exclude the aesthetic and sanitary features at Pullman, the rents there are from twenty to twenty-five per cent higher than rents in Chicago or surrounding towns for similar accommodations. The aesthetic features are admired by visitors, but have little money value to employees, especially when they lack bread. The company aims to secure six per cent upon the cost of its tenements, which cost includes a proportionate share for paving, sewerage, water, parks, etc. It claims now to receive less than four per cent. . . . The company makes all repairs and heretofore has not compelled tenants to pay for them. Under the printed leases, however, which tenants must sign, they agree to pay for all repairs which are either necessary (ordinary wear and damages by the elements not excepted) or which the company *chooses* to make.

The company's claim that the workmen need not hire its tenements and can live elsewhere if they choose is not entirely tenable. The fear of losing work keeps them in Pullman as long as there are tenements unoccupied, because the company is supposed, as a matter of business, to give preference to its tenants when work is slack. The employees, believing that a tenant at Pullman has this advantage, naturally feel some compulsion to rent at Pullman, and thus to stand well with management. Exceptional and necessary workmen do not share this feeling to the same extent and are more free to hire or own homes elsewhere. While reducing wages the company made no reduction in rents. Its position is that the two matters are distinct, and that none of the reasons urged as justifying wage reduction by it as an employer can be considered by the company as a landlord.

The company claims that it is simply legitimate business to use its position and resources to hire in the labor market as cheaply as possible and at the same time to keep rents up regardless of what wages are paid to its tenants or what similar tenements rent for elsewhere; to avail itself to the full extent of business depression and completion in reducing wages, and to disregard these same conditions as to rents. No valid reason is assigned for this position except simply that the company has the power and the legal right to do it.

Source: U.S. Strike Commission, *Report on the Chicago Strikes of June–July, 1894* (U.S. Government Printing Office, 1895), xxxv–xxxvi. Reprinted in Leon Litwack, *The American Labor Movement* (Englewood Cliffs, N.J.: Prentice-Hall, 1962), pp. 20–21.

36. Pullman Strike: Another Excerpt from the U.S. Strike Commission Report

*The U.S. Strike Commission reported on the Pullman Strike to the House of Representatives in 1894. The Pullman Strike was prompted by George Pullman's repeated reductions in **wages** of his workers, while he simultaneously refused to cut fees charged to those workers who rented their homes in his **company town**. The Pullman Strike brought **Eugene V. Debs**, leader of the **American Railway Union**, to national prominence. It also set unfortunate precedents for the use of injunctions in labor disputes, as well as for the employment of federal troops. Troops were sent to Chicago by President Grover Cleveland at the urging of his Attorney General Richard Olney, formerly an attorney associated with the railway operators.*

Mr. President and Brothers of the American Railway Union: We struck at Pullman because we were without hope. We joined the American Railway Union because it gave us a glimmer of hope. Twenty thousand souls, men, women, and little ones, have their eyes turned toward this convention today, straining eagerly through dark despondency for a glimmer of the heaven-sent message you alone can give us on this earth.

In stating to this body our grievances it is hard to tell where to begin. You all must know that the proximate cause of our strike was the discharge of two members of our grievance committee the day after George M. Pullman, himself, and Thomas H. Wickes, his second vice-president, had guaranteed them absolute immunity. The more remote causes are still imminent. Five reductions in wages, in work, and in conditions of employment swept through the shops at Pullman between May and December, 1893. The last was the most severe, amounting to nearly thirty per cent, and our rents had not fallen. We owed Pullman $70,000 when we struck May 11. We owe him twice as much today. He does not evict us for two reasons: One, the force of popular sentiment and public opinion; the other because he hopes to starve us out, to break the back of the American Railway Union, and to deduct from our miserable wages when we are forced to return to him the last dollar we owe him for the occupancy of his houses.

Rents all over the city in every quarter of its vast extent have fallen, in some cases to one-half. Residences, compared with which ours are hovels, can be had a few miles away at the price we have been contributing to make a millionaire a billionaire. What we pay $15 for in Pullman is leased for $8 in Roseland; and remember that just as no man or woman of our 4,000 toilers has ever felt the friendly pressure of George M. Pullman's hand, so no man or woman of us all has ever owned or can ever hope to own one inch of George M. Pullman's land. Why, even the very streets are his. His ground has never been platted of record, and today he may debar any man who has acquiring rights as his tenant from walking in his highways. And those streets; do you know what he has named them? He says after the four great inventors in methods of transportation. And do you know what their names are? Why, Fulton, Stephenson, Watt, and Pullman.

Water which Pullman buys from the city at 8 cents a thousand gallons he retails to us at 500 per cent advance and claims he is losing $400 a month on it. Gas which sells at 75 cents per thousand feet in Hyde Park, just north of us, he sells for $2.25. When we went to tell him our grievances he said we were all his "children."

Pullman, both the man and the town, is an ulcer on the body politic. He owns the houses, the schoolhouses, and churches of God in the town he gave his once humble name. The revenue he derives from these, the wages he pays out with one hand—the Pullman Palace Car Company, he takes back with the other—the Pullman Land Association. He is able by this to bid under any contract car shop in this country. His competitors in business, to meet this, must reduce the wages of their men. This gives him the excuse to reduce ours to conform to the market. His business rivals must in turn scale down; so must he. And thus the merry war—the dance of skeletons bathed in human tears—goes on, and it will go on, brothers, forever, unless you, the American Railway Union, stop it; end it; crush it out.

Source: U.S. Congress, House of Representatives, U.S. Strike Commission, *Report on the Chicago Strike* (Washington: U.S. Government Printing Office, 1895).

---

37. Real-Life Rosie the Riveter: Excerpt of Augusta Clawson's Experiences as a World War II Shipyard Worker

World War II abruptly ended the Great Depression. Almost overnight, the labor surplus disappeared and demand for female labor skyrocketed, as men joined the military. Before the war, women made up about 25 percent of the workforce; by 1945, they were around 38 percent. In raw numbers, the number of working women jumped from around fourteen million in 1940, to more than twenty million by early 1945. Women not only worked in larger numbers, they also entered skilled occupations once closed to them, such as welding, precision-parts grinding, and riveting. The famed "Rosie the Riveter" campaign was part of an overall government and industry program to encourage women to tackle what was before considered "men's work."

Millions of women heeded the call and, in many locales, surpassed the output in divisions once reserved for male workers. Although postwar propaganda and mass firings either convinced or coerced women to surrender their jobs to returning male veterans, real-life Rosie the Riveters altered the American labor force. Short-term drops in female employment quickly reversed and women reentered the job market in ever-

increasing numbers, albeit usually not in the skilled, high-paying jobs they held during World War II.

Breaking male preserves during the war was more than just learning a craft; it also involved significant shifts in self-perception, confidence, and values. Again, many of these persisted long after women left the defense plants. Augusta Clawson left a government job to work in a shipyard in Oregon during the war. Some of her experiences are recounted below.

I, who hate heights, climbed stair after stair after stair till I thought I must be close to the sun. I stopped in the top deck. I who, hate confined spaces, went through narrow corridors, stumbling my way over rubber coated leads—dozens of them, scores of them, even hundreds of them. I went into a room about four feet by ten where two shipfitters, a shipfitter's helper, a chipper, and I all worked. I welded in the poop deck lying on the floor while another welder spattered sparks from the ceiling and chippers like giant woodpeckers shattered our eardrums. I, who've taken welding, and have sat at a bench welding flat and vertical plates, was told to weld braces along a baseboard below a door opening. On these a heavy steel door was braced while it was hung to a fine degree of accuracy. I welded more braces along the side, and along the top. I did overhead welding, horizontal, flat, vertical. I welded around curved hinges which were placed so close to the side wall that I had to bend my rod in a curve to get it in. I made some good welds and some frightful ones. But now a door in the poop deck of an oil tanker is hanging, four feet by six of solid steel, by my welds. Pretty exciting! . . .

I talked with Joanne, a very attractive brunette who had previously been a waitress in Atlantic City. She came West when her husband came for a job. She, like the other waitresses, preferred welding because you "don't have to take so much from the public. . . ."

I had a good taste of summer today, and I am convinced that it is going to take backbone for welders to stick to their jobs through the summer months. It is harder on them than on any of the other workers—their leathers are so hot and heavy, they get more of the fumes, and their hoods become instruments of torture. There were times today when I'd have to stop in the middle of a tack and push my hood back just to get a breath of fresh air. It grows unbearably hot under the hood, my glasses fog and blur my vision, and the only thing to do is to stop. . . .

Yet the job confirmed my strong conviction—I have stated it before—what exhausts the woman welder is not the work, nor the heat, nor the demands upon physical strength. It is the apprehension that arises from inadequate skill and consequent lack of confidence; and this can be overcome by the right kind of training. I've mastered tacking now, so that no kind bothers me. I know I can do it if my machine is correctly set, and I have learned enough of the vagaries of machines to be able to set them. And so, in spite of the discomforts of climbing, heavy equipment, and heat, I enjoyed the work today because I could do it. . . .

Source: From *Shipyard Diary of a Woman Welder* by Augusta Clawson, illustrated by Boris Givotovsky, copyright 1944 by Penguin Books Inc. Used by permission of Viking Penguin, a division of Penguin Group (USA) Inc.

38. *Rerum Novarum*: Excerpts from Bull Issued by Pope Leo XIII in 1891

Rerum Novarum was a landmark papal encyclical issued by Leo XIII in 1891 that paved the way for Roman Catholic workers to join labor unions without fear of reprisal from their spiritual confessors. The Catholic Church had troubled relations with organized labor in the period immediately following the Civil War. Many unions operated in secrecy and/or required workers to swear oaths the church found objectionable. Moreover, the **Molly Maguire** *agitations of the 1870s involved large numbers of Irish Catholics, a public relations nightmare for a church that was already distrusted by nativists and other bigots. The Holy See also disapproved of most of the radical economic and political theories of the day. Catholic workers nonetheless joined unions, and some were forced out of the church. The spectacular rise of the* **Knights of Labor** *altered matters considerably, with officials like James Cardinal Gibbons warning the Vatican that forcing workers to choose between union and church imperiled the latter.*

The modern reader will no doubt notice the extreme caution of Leo XIII's language. That said, Rerum Novarum *marks a dramatic change in direction. Subsequent encyclicals, like* Quadragesimo Anno *(1931) and* Laborem Exercens *(1981) have further clarified church doctrines on labor.*

RIGHTS AND DUTIES OF CAPITAL AND LABOR

That the spirit of revolutionary change, which has long been disturbing the nations of the world, should have passed beyond the sphere of politics and made its influence felt in the cognate sphere of practical economics is not surprising. The elements of the conflict now raging are unmistakable, in the vast expansion of industrial pursuits and the marvelous discoveries of science; in the changed relations between masters and workmen; in the enormous fortunes of some few individuals, and the utter poverty of the masses; the increased self reliance and closer mutual combination of the working classes; as also, finally, in the prevailing moral degeneracy. The momentous gravity of the state of things now obtaining fills every mind with painful apprehension; wise men are discussing it. . . .

2. . . . The discussion is not easy, nor is it void of danger. It is no easy matter to define the relative rights and mutual duties of the rich and of the poor, of capital and of labor. . . .

3. In any case we clearly see . . . that some opportune remedy must be found quickly for the misery and wretchedness pressing so unjustly on the majority of the working class. . . . [B]y degrees it has come to pass that working men have been surrendered, isolated and helpless, to the hardheartedness of employers and the greed of unchecked competition. The mischief has been

increased by rapacious usury, which, although more than once condemned by the Church, is nevertheless . . . still practiced by covetous and grasping men. To this must be added that the hiring of labor and the conduct of trade are concentrated in the hands of comparatively few; so that a small number of very rich men have been able to lay upon the teeming masses of the laboring poor a yoke little better than that of slavery itself.

4. To remedy these wrongs the socialists, working on the poor man's envy of the rich, are striving to do away with private property, and contend that individual possessions should become the common property of all, to be administered by the State or by municipal bodies. . . . But their contentions are so clearly powerless to end the controversy that were they carried into effect the working man himself would be among the first to suffer. They are, moreover, emphatically unjust. . . .

5. . . . when a man engages in remunerative labor, the impelling reason and motive of his work is to obtain property, and thereafter to hold it as his very own. . . . Socialists, therefore, by endeavoring to transfer the possessions of individuals to the community at large, strike at the interests of every wage earner, since they would deprive him of the liberty of disposing of his wages, and thereby of all hope and possibility of increasing his resources and of bettering his condition in life. . . .

15. . . . The door would be thrown open to envy, to mutual invective, and to discord; the sources of wealth themselves would run dry, for no one would have any interest in exerting his talents or his industry; and that ideal equality about which they entertain pleasant dreams would be in reality the leveling down of all to a like condition of misery and degradation. Hence, it is clear that the main tenet of socialism, community of goods, must be utterly rejected. . . . The first and most fundamental principle, therefore, if one would undertake to alleviate the condition of the masses, must be the inviolability of private property. . . .

20. Of these duties, the following bind the proletarian and the worker: fully and faithfully to perform the work which has been freely and equitably agreed upon; never to injure the property, nor to outrage the person, of an employer; never to resort to violence in defending their own cause, nor to engage in riot or disorder; and to have nothing to do with men of evil principles, who work upon the people with artful promises of great results, and excite foolish hopes which usually end in useless regrets and grievous loss. The following duties bind the wealthy owner and the employer: not to look upon their work people as their bondsmen, but to respect in every man his dignity as a person ennobled by Christian character. They are reminded that, according to natural reason and Christian philosophy, working for gain is creditable, not shameful, to a man, since it enables him to earn an honorable livelihood; but to misuse men as though they were things in the pursuit of gain, or to value them solely for their physical powers—that is truly shameful and inhuman. . . . Furthermore, the employer must never tax his work people beyond their strength, or employ them in work unsuited to their sex and age. His great and principal duty is to give every one what is just. . . . To defraud any

one of wages that are his due is a great crime which cries to the avenging anger of Heaven. . . . Lastly, the rich must religiously refrain from cutting down the workmen's earnings, whether by force, by fraud, or by usurious dealing. . . .

39. When work people have recourse to a strike and become voluntarily idle, it is frequently because the hours of labor are too long, or the work too hard, or because they consider their wages insufficient. The grave inconvenience of this . . . should be obviated by public remedial measures; for such paralyzing of labor not only affects the masters and their work people . . . but is extremely injurious to trade and to the general interests of the public; moreover, on such occasions, violence and disorder are generally not far distant. . . . The laws should forestall and prevent such troubles from arising. . . .

40. The working man, too, has interests in which he should be protected by the State; and first of all, there are the interests of his soul. . . . No man may with impunity outrage that human dignity which God Himself treats with great reverence, nor stand in the way of that higher life which is the preparation of the eternal life of heaven. . . .

41. From this follows the obligation of the cessation from work and labor on Sundays and certain holy days. . . .

42. If we turn not to things external and material, the first thing of all to secure is to save unfortunate working people from the cruelty of men of greed, who use human beings as mere instruments for money-making. . . . Daily labor, therefore, should be so regulated as not to be protracted over longer hours than strength admits. . . . In all agreements between masters and work people there is always the condition expressed or understood that there should be allowed proper rest for soul and body. . . .

45. Let the working man and the employer make free agreements, and in particular let them agree freely as to the wages; nevertheless, there underlies a dictate of natural justice more imperious and ancient than any bargain between man and man, namely, that wages ought not to be insufficient to support a frugal and well-behaved wage-earner. If through necessity or fear of a worse evil the workman accept harder conditions because an employer or contractor will afford him no better, he is made the victim of force and injustice. . . .

48. In the last place, employers and workmen may of themselves effect much, in the matter We are treating, by means of such associations and organizations as afford opportune aid to those who are in distress, and which draw the two classes more closely together. . . .

49. The most important of all are workingmen's unions. . . .

58. . . . The offices and charges of the society should be apportioned for the good of the society itself . . . It is most important that office bearers be appointed with due prudence and discretion, and each one's charge carefully mapped out, in order that no members may suffer harm. The common funds must be administered with strict honesty. . . . Among the several purposes of a society, one should be to try to arrange for a continuous supply of work at all

times and seasons; as well as to create a fund out of which the members may be effectually helped in their needs, not only in the cases of accident, but also in sickness, old age, and distress. . . .

Given at St. Peter's in Rome, the fifteenth day of May, 1891, the fourteenth year of Our pontificate.

LEO XIII

---

39. Social Darwinism: Excerpt from Rev. Henry Ward Beecher's "Bread-and-Water" Sermon (1877)

Railroad **strikes** *associated with the* **Great Labor Uprising** *of 1877 badly frightened middle-class Americans not yet recovered from the Civil War, which had ended a scant dozen years earlier. The violence, property destruction, and loss of life led some nervous bourgeois members of society to fear a revolution was brewing, perhaps on a scale of that of the 1871 Paris Commune. Most middle-class publications and public figures spoke out against the strike. A few, like the Rev. Henry Ward Beecher, articulated views associated with* **Social Darwinism**, *a philosophy that attempted to explain the unequal distribution of wealth through a social application of Charles Darwin's biological theories of natural selection.*

At the height of tension during the summer of 1877, the Rev. Beecher took to his pulpit in New York's Plymouth Church and delivered what became known as the "bread-and-water" sermon. Beecher was among the era's best-known Protestant ministers. He was the son of a famed family of preachers, and the brother of Catherine Beecher and Harriet Beecher-Stowe. The Rev. Beecher may well have been using some poorly considered levity to try to break the solemn fear-induced mood, but his remarks were published in the New York Times *and circulated broadly. These remarks became shorthand for workers wishing to express their contempt for middle-class hypocrisy, and they made Beecher one of the Gilded Age's most reviled figures among the working class. They embody the ultimate logic of unbridled Social Darwinian thought.*

(Note: The Times *reported that laughter accompanied many of Beecher's comments.)*

What right had the workmen, the members of those great organizations, to say to any one, "You shall not work for wages which we refuse." They had a perfect right to say to employers, "We shall not work for you," but they had no right to tyrannize over their fellowmen. They had put themselves in an attitude of tyrannical opposition to all law and order and they could not be defended. The necessities of the great railroad companies demanded that there should be reduction of wages. There must be continual shrinkage until things come back to the gold standard, and wages, as well as greenbacks, provisions and property, must share in it. It was true that $1 a day was not enough to support a man and five children, if a man would insist on smoking and drinking beer. Was not a dollar a day enough to buy bread? Water costs nothing. Men cannot live by bread alone, it is true; but the man who cannot live on bread and water is not fit to live. When a man is educated away from the power of self-denial, he is falsely educated. A family may live on good bread and water in the morning, water and bread at midday, and good water and bread at night. Such may be called the bread of affliction, but it was fit that man should eat of the bread of affliction. Thousands would be very glad of a dollar a day, and it added to the sin of the men on strike for them to turn and say to those men, "You can do so, but you shall not." There might be special cases of hardships, but the great laws of political economy could not be set at defiance.

Source: The New York Times, 23 July 1877.

---

40. "Solidarity Forever": Ralph Chaplin's American Labor Anthem (1915)

*"Solidarity Forever" is the de facto official anthem of the American labor movement. It was penned by Ralph Chaplin (1887–1961), a member of the **Industrial Workers of the World (IWW)**, in 1915. Chaplin claimed the inspiration came to him while he was editing a labor journal during a Kanawha Valley, West Virginia, coal **strike**, although he did not write out the lyrics until he was living in Chicago. Like many labor songwriters, Chaplin chose an already familiar tune, "John Brown's Body," which by then had been appropriated for an even-more-famed song, "The Battle Hymn of the Republic."*

*"Solidarity Forever" appeared in the IWW journal, Solidarity, in January 1915, and became an immediate favorite of American workers. Although its writer was a radical IWW member and that organization was brutally suppressed during and after World War I, by the 1920s it carried less ideological baggage than two alternatives popular in the international labor movement, "The Marseillaise," and "The Internationale." Chaplin's song became standard fare even among conservative craft unionists in the **American Federation of Labor**, many of whom sang it oblivious of its IWW origins. It remains the best-known labor song in the United States.*

When the union's inspiration through the workers' blood shall run,
There can be no power greater anywhere beneath the sun;
Yet what force on earth is weaker than the feeble strength of one,
But the union makes us strong.

CHORUS:

Solidarity forever,
Solidarity forever,

Solidarity forever,
For the union makes us strong.

Is there aught we hold in common with the greedy parasite,
Who would lash us into serfdom and would crush us with his might?
Is there anything left for us but to organize and fight?
For the union makes us strong.

It is we who plowed the prairies; built the cities where they trade;
Dug the mines and built the workshops, endless miles of railroad laid;
Now we stand outcast and starving midst the wonders we have made;
But the union makes us strong.

All the world that's owned by idle drones is ours and ours alone.
We have laid the wide foundations; built it skyward stone by stone.
It is ours, not to slave in, but to master and to own.
While the union makes us strong.

They have taken untold millions that they never toiled to earn,
But without our brain and muscle not a single wheel can turn.
We can break their haughty power, gain our freedom when we learn
That the union makes us strong.

In our hands is placed a power greater than their hoarded gold,
Greater than the might of armies, magnified a thousand-fold.
We can bring to birth a new world from the ashes of the old
For the union makes us strong.

Source: Copyright © 1973 by Monthly Review Press. Reprinted by permission of Monthly Review Foundation.

---

41. Steel Workers: Excerpt from John Fitch's *The Steel Workers,* 1910

John Fitch was a student of John R. Commons, the pioneering labor historian. Fitch spent over a year, in 1907 and 1908, interviewing and observing steel workers in Pittsburgh, where 80,000 workers were employed by the steel companies that dominated every aspect of community life. The result of Fitch's work was The Steel Workers *(1910), one of the six volumes of the famous Pittsburgh Survey (1909–14), an attempt to carefully document life in an American industrial city from a social science perspective. In the selection reproduced here, Fitch observes the importance of the saloons in the lives of workers and the way in which the steel companies promoted the interests of the saloons.*

Thus it was that my residence in the mill towns brought it home to me that three institutions organized to promote enjoyment and progress are not, in these communities, exerting their proper influence. As was shown in an earlier chapter, the schedule of hours does not permit the home and the library to fulfill their natural functions. We have now seen how lethargy within and pressure without are tending to nullify or misdirect the influence of the church.

But this does not mean that the workingmen in the mill towns have no opportunity whatever for pleasure or society. It is only the moral and intellectual forces that are insulated. Young men who work in the mills cannot have their spirits utterly dampened by a long working day, and they often take trouble to dress for an evening's entertainment or to meet their friends socially. This does not last long, for youth itself is not long-lived in the steel mills; but whether young or old, men cannot thus easily be deprived of the social instinct. It is essential that they should meet together somehow and somewhere in fellowship and in relaxation from their work. The saloon and the lodge remain as the social centers for the steel workers.*

There are other reasons, to be sure, than the desire to mingle with one's fellows, for the popularity of the saloon; drinking is traditional among iron and steel workers. But there is no doubt that the craving for companionship is one of the strongest reasons for its hold upon a community of workingmen. The nature of mill work is such as to make the saloon habit one of the most natural ones in the world. Practically every man is affected by the heat even if he does not have a "hot job." The whole atmosphere is such as to induce perspiration and enhance thirst. All the workers drink water in great quantities as long as they are in the mill. Sometimes a man drinks too much, so that he leaves at the end of a day's work feeling half nauseated. Such a man steps into a saloon for a glass of something to set his stomach right. Or if a man does not overdrink during the day, he is still chronically thirsty, and it is to satisfy a real longing for drink that he stops for his beer. The dust of the mills, too, that the men have been breathing for twelve hours, sends another quota to their beer or whiskey to clear out their throats. Then comes the largest contingent of all, the men wearied with the heat and the work, some almost overcome and dragging their feet. These feel the necessity of a stimulant, and they get it day after day, regardless of the waste of physical and nervous energy involved in keeping themselves keyed up to their work by an artificial aid. I do not think I am far wrong when I say that a large majority of steel workers sincerely believe that the regular use of alcoholic drinks is essential to keep them from breaking down. It is seldom a pleasure-seeking crowd that fills the saloons after the whistle has blown at the end of a turn. The men line up at the bar, each one taking one drink and paying for it himself. The first line of men put down their glasses and leave, and the bar is filled again with a second group. There are very few who take more than one drink on coming from the mill.

There is more conviviality on Saturday nights and after pay days than on an ordinary midweek night. Then is the time the men relax; then the treating is done. The saloon becomes a social center and the men find the fellowship that they crave. It is a following of the line of least resistance that makes the saloon supplant all better forms of social life. A man does not need to change his clothing and get a shave before he is made welcome here. He may come covered with the grime of the mill and not feel out of place. In slack times, when the mills are not running, the saloon becomes a regular meeting place, and men go there primarily for companionship, the drinking becoming secondary. Ordinarily one does not see very much drunkenness. The men want to be fit for work the next day. On the eve of a holiday some will go too far, but these are most likely to be the unskilled workmen. The only men whom I found in a state of intoxication when I looked for them at their homes were blast furnace men—men who had been working for months without a holiday or a Sunday. The men I refer to had had a brief holiday and they spent it in the only way they knew. The better class of steel workers, who view their fellows with a sympathetic eye, explain the holiday intoxication of a certain element in the industry as a logical result of steady work and the long day. After weeks and months of work, twelve hours a day, and no holidays, a man gets far behind in his accumulation of the pleasure that he feels to be his due. When a holiday comes it is all too short to collect the overdue bill; pleasure of a concentrated sort must be sought in order to make up for lost time.

As a result of all these cumulative promptings, the saloons take more of the steel worker's money than do many of the legitimate business interests of the mill towns. During 1907 there were 30 saloons in Duquesne, a mill town of 10,000 or 12,000 population. I was told in 1908, by one who was in a position to know, that the leading saloonkeeper in this borough drew from the bank, regularly, every two weeks, just before pay day, between $200 and $300 to be used as change in anticipation of the bills of large denomination that would be handed over the bar. Braddock, where the Edgar Thomson steel works are located, had in 1907, 65 saloons. Braddock and North Braddock together had a population of about 25,000. I was told that a considerably larger sum was required for change on pay days here than in Duquesne, the average to each saloon being $500, making over $30,000 in all. I cannot vouch for the truth of this statement—it was a report which reached me indirectly and may be only an expression of some one's opinion and not based on facts. But information in regard to the situation in McKeesport in 1906 came to me through such channels that there can be little doubt as to its accuracy. McKeesport had about 40,000 people in 1906, and 69 saloons. On the Thursdays preceding the semi-monthly pay days, which fall on Fridays and Saturdays, the three leading saloonkeepers of the city were accustomed to draw from their bank accounts from $1200 to $1500 each in dollar bills and small denominations, to be used as change. Other saloonkeepers drew varying amounts, and the totals thus drawn each fortnight footed up to $60,000. On the Mondays after pay days the saloonkeepers usually deposited double the amount drawn. These periodic leaps in deposits never failed to coincide with pay days, and the inevitable conclusion is that about $60,000 of the steel workers' wages were regularly expended in the saloons within the two days. If this seems overdrawn, let me cite the case of George Holloway, who was blacklisted in 1901 after leading a strike in the Wood plant of the American Sheet and Tin Plate

Company in McKeesport. With what was generally understood to be borrowed funds—for Holloway was left almost penniless by the strike—he started a saloon in McKeesport. I saw and talked with him in the fall of 1907, and he told me that in 1905, four years from the time of entering business, he had sold out. He has established a son in a saloon in the west, and with the rest of his family he is now living in McKeesport on the income of his investments, a retired capitalist.

The liquor situation in an American town bears a very direct relation to the political life. This is true in these boroughs. In earlier chapters we have seen how the steel companies deny the employees the right to organize in unions. In spite of this, the situation is not hopeless so long as the workingman is secure in his possession of the ballot. It is commonly understood that the United States Steel Corporation is the dominant force in politics in the mill towns, except in McKeesport, where authority seems to be divided with the brewing interests.**

Repeatedly I was told that workmen have been discharged at Duquesne for refusing to vote the way the company wished. I was told by one employee that he had been called into the office of his superintendent and remonstrated with working against the company ticket, and an indirect threat was made of discharge. I was told by men of unimpeachable standing in Braddock, who were not steel works employees, that in the spring of 1908, preceding the May primaries, men were induced to vote for the candidates favored by the Corporation by promises of a resumption in industry if the right men were nominated. But the most damaging testimony that I received regarding the interference of the Steel Corporation in politics came from a source clearly authoritative.

For obvious reasons I cannot give my informant's name. "A short time before the primaries of May, 1908," he said, "orders came from the New York office of the United States Steel Corporation, to the general superintendent of the Edgar Thomson plant at Braddock, directing him to order the department superintendents to line up their employees for the Penrose candidates for the legislature. The general superintendent called a meeting of the department superintendents and delivered the orders. This created considerable dismay, for local option was an issue in the primaries and the Penrose candidates were opposed to local option. Some of the superintendents were already prominently identified with the local option party and had been assisting in organizing the campaign. How they could with honor or self-respect abandon the issue at this point was not clear to the officials. But the answer to the objections was clear and to the point. They were told that their first duties were to the Corporation. They must, accordingly, break any or all promises and work for Penrose, because the United States Steel Corporation needed him in the Senate."

After this information had come to me, I received other corroborative testimony. I had a talk with a man who had been prominent in the local option campaign previous to the primaries of 1908 at Braddock. I wrote down what he said, and after he had read my manuscript he indorsed every word. His statement was as follows:

The most damnable feature of the whole campaign was the attitude of the United States Steel Corporation. There is not such a perfect political organization in the country as the steel trust. They aim to control the politics of every borough and town where their works are located, and usually they do control. They plan their campaigns far in advance; they are laying their wires now to control the borough council three years ahead. You ought to see the way they line up their men at the polls and vote them by thousands. What does a secret ballot amount to? In every ward in this borough the steel works employees are in the majority. There are two or three foremen in nearly every ward, and it is up to them to round up the vote. If there are not enough foremen in a ward, they send them over from the next ward to help out. Naturalized foreigners can be handled easily, but so can men of three and four generations of American blood. These men have been so long dominated by the Corporation that they dare not disobey. They have a sort of superstitious feeling that somehow the boss will know if they vote wrong. And the workingmen are not the only ones that can be managed. Before the May primaries we perfected an organization in this borough to fight for local option. Several of the foremen and assistant superintendents in the mills were among our most active workers. Some of them helped in the speaking campaign. One day an order came that the thing must stop. The United States Steel Corporation needs to have Boies Penrose in the Senate, and the political life of Penrose is bound up with the liquor interests of the state. So a blow to liquor is a blow to Penrose, and the steel trust cannot have that. So the superintendents and foremen were ordered to line up their men for Penrose and the saloon. One young man who had been speaking in the campaign refused to stop, and he was called into the office and plainly told that he must either quit local option or quit the mills. That was not unusual though. The bread and butter argument is always used. As a result, the local optionists were badly broken up. The speaking campaign practically stopped and men whom we had counted on and who had been with us, actually turned around and made a show at least of opposing local option. Then the company gave it out that if the Penrose candidates to the legislature were nominated, the mill would be likely to resume operations, and the men who had been idle half or two-thirds of the time since October, clutched at that half promise like drowning men.

It is probably unnecessary to add that Penrose carried Allegheny County.

*For description of the fraternal orders see *Homestead: The Households of a Mill Town*, by Margaret F. Byington.

**In McKeesport, during the strike of 1901, when the threat was made that the Dewees Wood plant would be dismantled on account of the alleged hostility of the people of the town, the mayor issued a statement in which he charged that the property of the Steel Corporation in this city was assessed at 40 per cent of its market value, while the houses of the citizens were assessed at 70 per cent. (*Outlook*, August 17, 1901, p. 889.)

Source: John A. Fitch, *The Steelworkers* (New York: Russell Sage Foundation, 1910).

42. Stella Nowicki: Interview with a Meatpacking Plant Worker, 1973

In 1973, Alice and Staughton Lynd conducted a series of interviews with rank-and-file workers, not union leaders, but Midwestern men and women who worked on the job and were active in organizing unions, some in the 1930s and some in the post–World War II period. Stella Nowicki moved to Chicago from the family farm in 1933 and worked in the cook room at the Armour meatpacking plant. Here she tells of the excitement of her involvement in the **Congress of Industrial Organizations (CIO)** *during the height of its power and through the purge of the radicals after the war.*

The union mushroomed; it spread. The union had a certain vitality about it that was just tremendous. We had many problems but they were all problems of growth. We tried to make sure that there were both Negroes and whites as officers, stewards, etc., in all the locals. There were people vying for jobs—they wanted to be leaders of this union. It was a marvelous time.

For a long time I fought dishonesty within my local. There were some guys who would pocket the dues money. I would debate them on the union floor. Many times I was the only female there.

The women felt the union was a man's thing because once they got through the day's work they had another job. When they got home they had to take care of their one to fifteen children and the meals and the house and all the rest, and the men went to the tavern and to the meetings and to the racetrack and so forth. The fellows were competing for positions and the women didn't feel that that was their role. They were brainwashed into thinking that this union was for men.

The union didn't encourage women to come to meetings. They didn't actually want to take up the problems that the women had. I did what I could to get the women to come to the meetings but very few came—only when there was a strike. I tried to make the meetings more interesting than just a bunch of guys talking all evening.

We organized women's groups, young women's groups. They liked to dance and I loved to dance so we went dancing together and I talked to them about the union. The women were interested after a while when they saw that the union could actually win things for them, bread and butter things.

We talked about nurseries. In World War II we finally did get some because women were needed in greater quantities than ever before in the factories. But the unions had so many things they had to work for—the shorter work day, improved conditions—so many things that they couldn't worry about these things in relation to women.

Later on, during the war, there was one department where I got the women but couldn't get the guys in. They hung out in the tavern and so I went there and started talking with them. I didn't like beer, but I'd drink ginger ale and told them to show me how to play pool. I learned to play pool and I got the men into the union. I did what they did. I went into the taverns. I became a bowler and I joined the league. The only thing I didn't do is rejoin the Catholic Church.

I was on the grievance committee and I was on the Swift nationwide negotiating team. Before I left, there were a whole number of job evaluations. It was one of the things we fought for on the wage policy committees. I remember talking with Helstein (president of UPWA) in the national office one day and saying that I thought there should be a study made of jobs, especially for women, because I didn't see that a job had a sex. He said that it was a very interesting idea and that maybe I could do something about it. But I wasn't equipped to go into research, nor did I have the time even if I were. Later on they set up a Women's Department and did it.

There were only so many things that we could do and there were so many big things, we couldn't handle everything. You'd have to have socialism.

About socialism, you didn't talk about socialism per se. You talked about issues and saw how people reacted. You talked about how one could attain these things. The only time I ever heard anyone from the union talk about socialism outside of the small meetings was the head of another CIO local, a Scotsman. After negotiations and they didn't get all they wanted, the guys were turning down the contract. He said, "Look, you bunch of bastards, you're not going to get all of this stuff, not until you have socialism." That's the way he put it to them and I thought it was great. "This is a limited contract under capitalism." I think the workers got the message. It all depends what your relationship is to the people you are talking with.

If you are an honest leader, recognized and supported by the workers, you could raise and talk about issues. You couldn't talk about socialism and what it meant in an abstract sense. You had to talk about it in terms of what it would mean for that person. We learned that you can't manipulate people but that you really had to be concerned with the interests and needs of the people. However, you also had to have a platform—a projection of where you were going.

At certain times we felt that the union wasn't enough. We worked in the stockyards with blacks but when we came home, we went to lily-white neighborhoods and the blacks went to their ghetto. How were we going to bridge that? There was unemployment and people were being laid off. There were many young people who didn't get jobs. There was no concern on the part of anyone, the city fathers, the church, the union and others, about the needs of young people and places to play. What are unemployed young people going to do? There were a bunch of young people—I was twenty-four or so—and we felt that our needs were not being met by the union.

The Yards YCL group got together and talked about getting more playgrounds for baseball, basketball and so forth. One of the things that we felt we should do was fight to get blacks into professional baseball. I remember being part of the delegation that went to see Fitzpatrick, who was chairman of the

Central Labor Council, about labor exerting its influence to get blacks on organized professional baseball teams. It was one of the initial things our union did.

We tried to show the community that the union was concerned about the welfare of the young people. We raised the problems of youth; we raised the problems of women; we raised the problem of inequality. We tried through the National Youth Act to get some funds to set up facilities for young people in the community. We had to find ways to attract youth and women and keep all these people within the union.

We asked the union to back us up in calling a community conference to set up a council, a Back of the Yards Youth Council, which would be concerned about these kinds of things in the community. The union said OK. They gave us their blessings. We went ahead and we did it. Actually there were three of us young women who did it.

We had a successful conference. The place wasn't big enough, it was such a turn-out—young people from about 18 to about 25 from the neighborhood.

The man who really organized some massive youth activities was Bishop Shiel. I think he was the first major churchman to recognize the CIO. The first time this bishop of the Catholic Church accepted to come to a CIO meeting, it was historic.

Remember that the CIO didn't have bargaining rights in the different plants yet. This was 1938, '39, '40. We were in the organizational stage and there was tremendous ferment. There were strikes. There were beatings. There were people being fired and laid off and there were test cases in the NLRB [National Labor Relations Board]. There was picketing going on.

The AFL was opposing it. During the early organizing meetings they sent goons with guns to threaten individuals to scare them so they would not organize. Twice they shot at Herb March.

But you had this sense that people were ready come hell or high water to get together, to protect each other, and come into the union. It did happen that people were fired but when people were fired the whole department just closed down. People refused to work until this person was put back. They had this feeling of solidarity, this sense, because they knew that if the company could get by with doing it to one they could do it to another, maybe me.

By the 1940s, we had meetings on every issue where we would call on the workers to come out. The union would come around with their sound truck and everybody would come to the CIO corners in the Yards. The butchers would all come out with their boots and their bloody white smocks. Thousands and thousands of people would show up for meetings right there in the middle of the stockyards at noontime. Even people who were not in the union would come out.

There would be an issue a day, just about. The Armour Plant, Local 347, would have meetings on Wednesday. Friday was payday so it was sacrosanct and there were no meetings. Tuesday was our day. Wilson's on Thursday. Then for some overall issue we'd have everybody come out. There would be so many people coming that the companies would protest to the union—we had half hour lunch breaks and we would stay out for an hour. The companies never did a thing about it because the turnout was that tremendous and massive.

The union leadership would be negotiating within a particular plant on a grievance and the agreement was that if they hadn't received word that the matter was settled by a certain time, the department would walk out. The beef kill at Armour's stopped so many times! They were the best organized and most militant. (These were blacks, by the way.) And if this department went down, the whole plant went down. The kill floors were the key floors. This was true all over. The beef kill was the most important because more beef was killed; then the hog kill, then the sheep.

We participated in all sorts of things beyond just our own industry.

At that time there were no black bus drivers. Bus and streetcar driver jobs were considered very good-paying jobs and our union promoted the idea of having blacks work as streetcar and bus conductors.

The contract and recognition were the thing that everybody wanted. Armour's was the plant with the greatest concentration of people and the union came to be recognized there in 1941. Wilson went before our plant did. Swift's had to have two elections and it was the toughest. We won there during the war, I think in '42. We didn't have the militancy in the Swift plant that we did elsewhere. The Swift Company bought off many guys. Later on we found out that some of the white leaders were paid agents because they testified before the House Committee on Un-American Activities on a lot of us. They were stool pigeons.

I worked in the yards during the war because I thought that it was my patriotic duty. It was part of the thinking of everybody within unions that you just couldn't quit. We even tried to get people to produce more in our zeal to support the war effort. Besides, I had all this seniority and all this history. Then I got frozen on the job. There was a job freeze because white workers were leaving the industry to go to higher-paid jobs in defense plants.

No-strike was part of the deal. The men in the union felt that the company was making all kinds of money on the war and the workers weren't. During that time there were slow-ups and workers who didn't join the union were ostracized. Grievances were hung up without being settled or turned down because the company knew we couldn't do anything. We knew that the company took advantage of the war in a whole number of situations.

I left packing in 1945. With recognition and with the war ending, certain changes took place within the union itself and within the union officialdom. Soon after, a whole group of radical CIO unions were kicked out of the CIO and the McCarthy period set in. I think this ended that era. It was a privilege and a wonderful experience to participate in the excitement of those times.

Source: Alice and Staughton Lynd, eds., *Rank and File: Personal Histories by Working-Class Organizers* (Boston: Beacon Press, 1974).

43. Strikes: Excerpts from Samuel Gompers's Testimony before a U.S. House Committee upon the Relations between Labor and Capital (1899)

*Strikes have long been the hallmark of clashes between capital and labor. To leaders like **Samuel Gompers** of the **American Federation of Labor (AFL)**, the right to withhold labor was the primary weapon that workers could use in their struggle to obtain higher **wages**, shorter working hours, and better conditions. The AFL actively defended the right to **strike**, unlike earlier labor federations like the **National Labor Union** and the **Knights of Labor**, whose leaders felt strikes should only be undertaken as a last resort, and only if strict conditions prevailed that made success likely. (See Document Number 46, **Terence V. Powderly**, on strikes.)*

The passage below excerpts Gompers's 1899 testimony before a House of Representatives committee on capital-labor relations. In it, he defends strikes.

The working people find that improvements in the methods of production and distribution are constantly being made, and unless they occasionally strike, or have the power to enter upon a strike the improvements will all go to the employer and all the injuries to the employees. A strike is an effort on the part of the workers to obtain some of the improvements that have occurred resultant from the bygone and present genius of our intelligence, of our mental progress. We are producing wealth today at a greater ratio than ever in the history of mankind and a strike on the part of workers is, first against deterioration in their condition, and, second, to be participants in some of the improvements. Strikes are caused from various reasons. The employer desires to reduce wages and lengthen hours of labor, while the desire on the part of the employees is to obtain shorter hours of labor and better wages, and better surroundings. Strikes establish or maintain the rights of the unionism; that is, to establish and maintain the organization by which the rights if the workers can be the better protected and advanced against the little forms of oppression, sometimes economical, sometimes political—the effort on the part of employers to influence and intimidate workmen's political preferences; strikes against victimization; activity in the cause of the workers against the blacklist. . . .

It required 40,000 people in the city of New York in my own trade [cigar making] in 1877 to demonstrate to the employers that we had the right to be heard in our own defense of our trade, and an opportunity to be heard in our own interests. It cost the miners of the country, in 1897, sixteen weeks of suffering to secure a national conference and a national agreement. It cost the railroad brotherhoods long months of suffering, many of them sacrificing their positions, in the railroad strike of 1877, and in the Chicago, Burlington, and Quincy strike, of the same year, to secure from the employers the right to be heard through committees, their representatives—that is, their committee of the organization to secure these rights. Workmen have had to stand the brunt of the suffering. The American

Republic was not established without some suffering, without some sacrifice, and no tangible right has yet been achieved in the interest of the people unless it has been secured by the sacrifices and persistency. After a while we become a little more tolerant to each other and recognize all have rights; get around the table and chaff each other and recognize that they were not so reasonable in the beginning. Now we propose to meet and discuss our interests, and if we can not agree we propose in a more reasonable way to conduct our contests, each to decide how to hold out and bring the other one to terms. . . . A strike on the part of the workmen is to close production and compel better terms and more rights to be acceded to the producers. The economic results of strikes to workers have been advantageous. Without strikes their rights would not have been considered. It is not that workmen or organized labor desires the strike, but it will tenaciously hold the right to strike. We recognize that peaceful industry is necessary to successful civilized life, but the right to strike and the preparation to strike is the greatest preventative to strikes. If the workmen were to make up their minds tomorrow that they would under no circumstances strike, the employers would do all the striking for them in the way of lesser wages and longer hours of labor.

Source: Testimony of Samuel Gompers, November 29, 1899, U.S. Congress, House, *Report of the Industrial Commission on the Relations and Conditions of Capital and Labor Employed in Manufactures and General Business* (Washington: U.S. Government Printing Office, 1901), VII pp. 605–9. Reprinted in Leon Litwack, *The American Labor Movement* (Englewood Cliffs, N.J.: Prentice-Hall, 1962), pp. 34–35.

---

44. Sweatshops: Excerpt from Louis Levine's Description of Turn-of-the-Century Abuses in Garment-Industry Sweatshops

*The battle to regulate **sweatshops** is one of the oldest and most enduring struggles facing American organized labor. The term first appeared in the United States in the 1860s, though complaints resonated long before. For most of the eighteenth and nineteenth centuries, there were few regulations governing the safety and sanitary conditions under which laborers toiled, and the very definition of what constituted a "sweatshop" was open to broad interpretation. In general, a sweatshop was an inordinately cramped and unhealthy workplace in which laborers toiled long hours at monotonous jobs for very low pay. These workplaces often appeared in run-down buildings with poor ventilation and light. Frequently, they were also dangerous, as driven home during such horrible episodes as the 1911 **Triangle factory fire**. The garment industry was marked by some of the worst sweatshop abuses, as is revealed in the passage below from Louis Levine, the official historian for the early **International Ladies' Garment Workers' Union**. Cigarmakers and assembly workers also complained of sweatshop conditions.*

Although laws regulate current practices and the classic sweatshop has receded from public consciousness, many labor advocates charge that sweatshops are still alive, especially in large cities where immigrant labor—much of it undocumented or illegal—

continues to toil in the sort of Dickensian conditions described by Levine. This excerpt comes originally from Louis Levine's The Women Garment Workers *(New York: B. W. Hebsch, 1924).*

The three main features of the sweat-shop have been described as unsanitary conditions, excessively long hours, and extremely low wages. The shops were generally located in tenement houses. As a rule, one of the rooms of the flat in which the contractor lived was used as a working place. Sometimes work would be carried on all over the place in the bedroom as well as in the kitchen. Even under the best conditions this would have made for living and working in grime and dirt. But the conditions were not of the best. . . . Investigations showed that about one out of every three persons whose living quarters were examined "slept in unventilated rooms without windows." One can imagine what happened when these "homes" were also turned into shops and became home and workshop at the same time.

A writer who made a valiant fight against the evils of the tenement house and of the sweat-shop, gives a graphic description of the district in New York City where the sweat-shops were situated.

. . . "Take the Second Avenue Elevated," he writes, "and ride up half a mile through the sweaters' district. Every open window of the big tenements, that stand like a continuous brick wall on both sides of the way, give you a glimpse of one of these shops as the train speeds by. Men and women bending over their machines or ironing clothes at the window, half-naked. . . . The road is like a big gangway through an endless workroom where vast multitudes are forever labouring [sic]. Morning, noon, night, it makes no difference; the scene is always the same." Not only insides of the tenements were turned into work places. "It is not unusual," reported the New York State factory inspector, "when the weather permits to see the balconies of the fire escapes occupied by from two to four busy workmen. The halls and roofs are also utilized for workshop purposes very frequently." The same factory inspector describes one of the many sweatshops which he visited. This particular one, which was typical of others, was that "of a cloakmaker, who used one room for his shop, while the other three rooms were supposed to be used for domestic purposes only, his family consisting of his wife and seven children. In the room adjoining the shop, used as the kitchen, there was a red-hot stove, two tables, a clothes rack, and several piles of goods. A woman was making bread on a table upon which there was a baby's stocking, scraps of cloth, several old tin cans, and a small pile of unfinished garments. In the next room was an old woman with a diseased face walking the floor with a crying child in her arms."

In the "outside" shops, the working hours were eighty-four per week. But besides "regular" hours, there was "overtime" in both the "inside" and "outside" shops, and in addition many of the workers "took material home and worked until two and three o'clock in the morning." It was quite common to work fifteen and sixteen hours a day, from five in the morning to nine at night, and in the busy season many frequently worked all night. "If you look into the streets any morning," wrote an investigator of conditions in New York City, "at four o'clock you will see them full of people going to work. They rouse themselves at three o'clock and are often at their machines at four. The latest is sure to be there by five. The general time is five o'clock all year round in good times, winter and summer, and if the boss will give them gaslight, some will go even earlier than three o'clock." Old-timers in the industry are fond of telling to-day about the over-zealous workers of those days, cloak pressers and operators, who saved time and rent by sleeping on "bundles" in the shop between working. It was a current saying that one could always do with a little more work by "borrowing a couple hours from the following days." No wonder the industry, and especially the cloak making trade, early acquired the sad distinction of being the "worst-driven trade in the matter of hours in the season."

Source: Rosalyn Baxandall and Linda Gordon, eds., *America's Working Women: A Documentary History 1600 to the Present* (New York: W. W. Norton, 1995), pp. 91–93.

---

45. Taft-Hartley Labor Relations Act (1947)

*Among labor union members and advocates, the 1947 **Taft-Hartley Act** is the single most unpopular piece of labor legislation ever passed in the United States. Its passage was hailed by supporters as a needed corrective to the **National Labor Relations Act (NLRA)** and defended as restoring balance to relations between capital and labor. Critics claim it so tilted the balance in favor of employers as to negate vast sections of the NLRA.*

*Passage of the bill took place as Republicans regained control of Congress in 1946, after many years of backbench sniping against Franklin Roosevelt's New Deal policies. It is named for Ohio Senator Robert Taft and New Jersey Representative Fred Hartley, the Republicans who coauthored the bill. President Harry Truman vetoed the Taft-Hartley Act, but Congress overrode that veto. Unions have repeatedly lobbied for its repeal, as yet to no avail. The excerpts below outline some of the act's key provisions, including controversial passages outlining **unfair labor practices** on the part of unions, the requirement that union officials sign anticommunist affidavits, the outlawing of secondary **boycotts**, mandated "cooling-off" periods, forbidding **strikes** among government employees, and curtailing union political action committees.*

Section 7. Employees shall have the right to self-organization, to form, join, or assist labor organizations, to bargain collectively through representatives of their own choosing, and to engage in other concerted activities for the purpose of collective bargaining or other mutual aid or protection, and shall also have the right to refrain from any or all of such activities except to the extent that such right may be affected by an agreement requiring membership in a labor organization as a condition of employment. . . .

Section 8. (a) It shall be an unfair labor practice for an employer—

(1) to interfere with, restrain, or coerce employees in the exercise of the rights guaranteed in section 7;

(2) to dominate or interfere with the formation or administration of any labor organization or contribute financial or other support to it. . . .

(3) by discrimination in regard to hire or tenure of employment or any term or condition of employment to encourage or discourage membership in any labor organization. . . .

(4) to discharge or otherwise discriminate against an employee because he has filed charges or given testimony under this Act;

(5) to refuse to bargain collectively with the representatives of his employees. . . .

It shall be an unfair labor practice for a labor organization or its agents—

(1) to restrain or coerce employees in the exercise of the rights guaranteed in section 7: Provided (A)That this paragraph shall not impair the right of a labor organization to prescribe its own rules with respect to the acquisition or retention of membership therein- or (B) an employer in the selection of his representatives for the purposes of collective bargaining or the adjustment of grievances;

(2) to cause or attempt to cause an employer to discriminate against an employee . . . or to discriminate against an employee with respect to whom membership in such organization has been denied or terminated on some ground other than his failure to tender the periodic dues and the initiation fees uniformly required as a condition of acquiring or retaining membership;

(3) to refuse to bargain collectively with an employer. . . .

(4) to engage in, or to induce or encourage the employees of any employer to engage in, a strike or a concerted refusal in the course of their employment to use, manufacture, process, transport, or otherwise handle or work on any goods, articles, materials, or commodities or to perform any services, where an object thereof is: (A) forcing or requiring any employer or self-employed person to join any labor or employer organization or any employer or other person to cease using, selling, handling, transporting, or otherwise dealing in the products of any other producer, processor, or manufacturer, or to cease doing business with any other person; (B) forcing or requiring any other employer to recognize or bargain with a labor organization as the representative of his employees unless such labor organization has been certified as the representative of such employees . . . (C) forcing or requiring any employer to recognize or bargain with a particular labor organization as the representative of his employees if another labor organization has been certified as the representative of such employees . . . (D) forcing or requiring any employer to assign particular work to employees in a particular labor organization or in a particular trade, craft, or class rather than to employees in another labor

organization or in another trade, craft, or class, unless such employer is failing to conform to an order or certification of the Board determining the bargaining representative for employees performing such work. . . .

(5) to require of employees covered by an agreement . . . as a condition precedent to becoming a member of such organization, of a fee in an amount which the Board finds excessive or discriminatory under all the circumstances. In making such a finding, the Board shall consider, among other relevant factors, the practices and customs of labor organizations in the particular industry, and the wages currently paid to the employees affected; and

(6) to cause or attempt to cause an employer to pay or deliver or agree to pay or deliver any money or other thing of value, in the nature of an exaction, for services which are not performed or not to be performed. . . .

The expressing of any views, argument, or opinion, or the dissemination thereof, whether in written, printed, graphic, or visual form, shall not constitute or be evidence of an unfair labor practice under any of the provisions of this Act, if such expression contains no threat of reprisal or force or promise of benefit. . . .

That where there is in effect a collective-bargaining contract covering employees in an industry affecting commerce, the duty to bargain collectively shall also mean that no party to such contract shall terminate or modify such contract, unless the party desiring such termination or modification—(1) serves a written notice upon the other party to the contract of the proposed termination or modification sixty days prior to the expiration date thereof, or in the event such contract contains no expiration date, sixty days prior to the time it is proposed to make such termination or modification; (2) offers to meet and confer with the other party for the purpose of negotiating a new contract . . . (3) notifies the Federal Mediation and Conciliation Service within thirty days after such notice of the existence of a dispute, and simultaneously . . . notifies any State or Territorial agency established to mediate and conciliate disputes . . . and (4) continues in full force and effect without resorting to strike or lockout, all the terms and conditions of the existing contract for a period of sixty days after such notice is given or until the expiration date of such contract, whichever occurs later. . . .

No investigation shall be made by the Board of any question affecting commerce concerning the representation of employees, raised by a labor organization . . . shall be entertained, and no complaint shall be issued pursuant to a charge made by a labor organization . . . unless there is on file with the Board an affidavit executed contemporaneously or within the preceding twelvemonth period by each officer of such labor organization and the officers of any national or international labor organization of which it is an affiliate or constituent unit that he is not a member of the Communist Party or affiliated with such party, and that he does not believe in, and is not a member of or supports any organization that believes in or teaches, the overthrow of the United States Government by force or by any illegal or unconstitutional methods. The provisions of section 35 A of the Criminal Code shall be applicable in respect to such affidavits. . . .

Section 301. . . . (b) Any labor organization which represents employees in an . . . industry affecting commerce . . . whose activities affect commerce . . . shall be bound by the acts of its agents. Any such labor organization may sue or be sued as an entity and in behalf of the employees whom it represents in the courts of the United States. Any money judgment against a labor organization in a district court of the United States shall be enforceable only against the organization as an entity and against its assets, and shall not be enforceable against any individual member or his assets. . . .

Section 303: (a) It shall be unlawful, for the purposes of this section . . . in an industry or activity affecting commerce, for; any labor organization to engage in, or to encourage the employees of any employer to engage in, a strike or a concerted refusal in the course of their employment to use, manufacture, process, transport, or otherwise handle or work on any goods, articles, materials, or commodities or to perform any services, where an object thereof is (1) forcing or requiring any employer or self-employed person to join any labor or employer organization or . . . to cease using selling, handling, transporting, or otherwise dealing in the products of any other producer, processor or manufacturer, or to cease doing business with any other person; (2) forcing . . . any other employer to recognize or bargain with a labor organization as the representative of his employees unless such labor organization has been certified as the representative of such employees . . . (3) forcing . . . any employer to recognize or bargain with a particular labor organization as the representative of his employees if another labor organization has been certified as the representative of such employees . . . (4) forcing . . . any employer to assign particular work to employees in a particular labor organization or in a particular trade, craft or class rather than to employees in another labor organization or in another trade, craft, or class unless such employer is failing to conform to an order of certification of the National Labor Relations Board. . . .

Section 305: It shall be unlawful for any individual employed by the United States or any agency thereof including wholly owned Government corporations to participate in any strike. Any individual employed by the United States or by any such agency who strikes shall be discharged immediately from employment, and shall forfeit his civil service status, if any, and shall not be eligible for re-employment for three years by the United States or any such agency. . . .

Section 313: It is unlawful for any national rank, or any corporation organized by authority of any law of Congress, to make a contribution or expenditure in connection with any election to any political office, or in connection with any primary election or political convention or caucus held to select candidates for any political office, or for any corporation whatever, or any labor organization to make a contribution or expenditure in connection with any election at which Presidential and Vice Presidential electors or a Senator or Representative in or a Delegate or Resident Commissioner to Congress are to be voted for, or in connection with any primary election or political convention or caucus held to select candidates for any of foregoing offices, or for any candidate, political committee, or other person to accept or receive any contribution prohibited by this section.

Source: "MultiEducator, Inc.," http://www.multied.com/documents/Tafthartley.html.

46. Terence V. Powderly: Excerpts from His Autobiography

Terence Powderly (1849–1924) led the **Knights of Labor (KOL)** *from 1879 to the end of 1893. He presided over the KOL's dramatic rise in the 1880s and its equally precipitous decline after 1888. In many respects, he was the first American labor leader to attract widespread national attention. At the height of his fame—roughly 1885 to 1890—Powderly's opinion on numerous matters was sought by journalists, clerics, politicians, and social reformers. He was a complex man, prone both to acts of admirable selflessness and self-seeking pettiness. Powderly seldom disappointed those seeking his opinion. By the mid-1880s, Powderly was so well known that his very name rallied some Gilded Age workers and repulsed others. His was such a strong personality that some workers and scholars mistakenly identified Powderly as synonymous with the KOL, though he himself was always careful to differentiate personal views from "official" statements on behalf of the Knights.*

In the passages below, Powderly explains the Knights of Labor's policies on **strikes** *and why both he and the Knights were against them. In other passages, he gives a powerful indictment of Gilded Age churches and explains why working people often distrusted them.*

It never was the intention of those who founded and built up the Knights of Labor to resort to the strike as first aid in the settlement of differences between employer and employed. Don't forget that the founders were all trade unionists who had seen the futility of ill-advised, hastily begun strikes. . . .

The public has been educated to believe that labor leaders . . . just glory in and fatten on strikes. Prior to my first election as G[eneral] Master Workman I declared my position on the strike question and stated I would never favor a strike until I became convinced:

First: That the cause was just.

Second: That every reasonable means had been resorted to to avert the strike.

Third: That the chances of winning were at least as good as the prospect of losing.

Fourth: That the means of defraying the expenses of the strike and assisting those in need were in the treasury or in sight of it.

. . . Our membership knew that I regarded the strike as a system of warfare, and that if I should be expected to make war the law should be complied with and the sinews of war provided prior to declaring war.

Whenever a strike was forced upon us, as it frequently was, the case would differ from one in which we, as an organization, declared a strike. . . . Not once did I, during my fourteen years' incumbency of the office of General Master Workman, order a strike. . . .

The world has been educated by a not overscrupulous press to believe that every "labor leader" . . . revels in strikes, and goes out of his way to order strikes. The reverse is true. I do not know . . . a labor officer who did not view the strike with gravest apprehension. Nothing can injure the conscientious officer . . . any more than to lose a strike unless it is to win one. If he loses he is sure to be charged with selling out, if he wins he'll be expected to keep on striking—and winning. . . .

While I never ordered a strike, I was directly responsible for the settlement of four hundred and eight cases of dispute between employer and employed . . . and was instrumental in the adjustment of some seven hundred other differences between workmen and employers. . . .

Precious lives were lost in strikes; homes were wrecked, and children deprived of education through strikes, millions of dollars were lost to labor through them, and in the main this great waste and loss could have been avoided. I could never rid my mind of the idea that in these avoidable strikes we were injuring posterity. . . .

Conditions change so rapidly that what we strike for and win this year may not be worth having next year. . . . Today's loss can seldom be replaced by tomorrow's gain.

Too many ministers today regard their calling as a profession or a trade to make a living by and not as a mission from on high . . . Churchianity, which largely supplanted Christianity and is often mistaken for it, has not stayed the hand of an individual trader, a national commercialist, or international murderer whose greed prompted him to reach out for the market of neighbor and enemy and gather in all that could be gained. . . .

The great power that came to Christianity through the teachings of Jesus Christ has been largely frittered away through the practice of Churchianity. . . . I can find little or no evidence to prove that the ordained teacher and preacher of Christianity has attempted to walk directly in the footsteps of the crucified One in driving the waterer of stocks, the gambler of life's necessities, the despoiler of children, the exploiter of labor, or the grabber of profits from the temple wherein the products of industry are exchanged.

Source: From *The Path I Trod: The Autobiography of Terence V. Powderly* by Harry Carman, Henry David and Paul Gutherie. © 1968 Columbia University Press. Reprinted with the permission of the publisher.

47. Textile Workers: Excerpt of Testimony before the U.S. Senate by John Hill, 1885

In the mid-1880s, at the height of the Gilded Age, when clashes between labor and capital seemed inevitable, the United States Senate held hearings on labor relations. The testimony of John Hill, a representative of a Georgia textile manufacturer, explained the natural advantages of the southern climate and defended the southern use of **child labor** *in the textile mills. Hill's 1885 comparison of southern workers with the immigrant workers of the Amoskeag Mills in Manchester, New Hampshire, suggests that southern workers were happy with child labor, long hours, and an inferior system of public education and that relations between the races were harmonious—at least in the workplace.*

Now as to the efficiency of labor in the two sections. The Southern operative is native born, while the average Northern operative is not. They have got more Canadian operatives in Manchester, N. H., than they have natives. Now, as it is a well-known fact to all who have studied the subject, the elements of mind, the general mental make-up and intelligence of the native American exceeds by far the average of like qualities in the lower classes of foreigners, the classes who immigrate into this country to work in mills. So in the same proportion are you likely to find the comparative intelligence of the Northern and the Southern operatives, the Southern being native and the Northern being a foreigner. There is more endurance in the constitution in a cold climate than in a warm one, and our advantage becomes a disadvantage in this respect, where it is a question of hard, heavy labor. Natural laws would therefore indicate that for heavy labor the Northern operative would be superior to the Southern, but while this is true, it is also true that a warm climate develops the human system earlier, and makes the action of both mind and body quicker than in a cold climate. The natives of warm climates are more impulsive, quicker to learn, and quicker in action, though not so enduring. This climate advances the period of manhood or womanhood fully a year and a half over the average climate of New England, so far as development is concerned. A man or a woman here in Columbus is as far advanced in physical development at fifteen years of age as a like person would be in Lowell at sixteen and a half years of age.

Now, for cotton manufacturing, capacity to endure hard labor is not a material point, because the labor is not hard. The motions required are quick rather than laborious, except in certain departments. In weaving there is probably about as much of one kind as the other, and, of course, weaving is a very important department. It may be stated as a general fact, therefore, that in this regard the advantages in the South are at least equal to those in the North.

In the matter of education the native American of the North averages superior to the native of the South, owing to the fact that for many years, covering the lives of all the operatives now in the mills of the North, the free-school system has been universal there, and the necessity of education has been generally and fully appreciated. In the South, while a free-school system does exist in this State, yet it is not so far advanced as the free-school system in New England; not so liberal; not so easy to be availed of. It furnishes less school accommodation in proportion to population, and there is less disposition on the part of the people to patronize it, and, generally speaking, owing to the very limited time it has been in existence, the advantages of our free school system here have not been reaped by our people to an extent that will at all compare with the benefits that the New England system has conferred upon the people there.

But again, as compared with foreign help, the probabilities are that even in the matter of education our Southern operatives have the advantage. In Alabama, South Carolina, and other States, where no attention has been paid to the free-school system, the operatives have not had the advantages that they have in Georgia.

The hours of labor in cotton manufacture in the Eagle and Phoenix mills average eleven per day, but in many mills they average twelve per day. In New England, in some of the States, the law prescribes ten hours as a day's work. That is so in Massachusetts, but not in New Hampshire. . . .

I might state that all mill operatives having to do with the process of cotton manufacturing involving quick perception and manipulation are white. In portions of the work, where it is only a question of muscle, and where intelligence is not a necessity, the laborers employed are either black or white, the preference, where it comes to a matter of mere muscle, being given to the colored laborer. I refer now to rolling a bale of cotton in, tearing it open, tumbling around boxes and bales, and such heavy work. It has been found, and is a fact patent to all who have studied the question, that the employment of colored labor in the finer processes of manufacturing is a question which is mooted only by those who know nothing about it. . . . It may be regarded as a fact about which those who understand the question can have no dispute, that it will be many years before the present condition of things can be changed. There are places to which each of these labor elements is specially adapted. The supply of both races is about equal to the demand, and there is an opportunity for support and for fair and reasonable prosperity open to one race as well as to the other.

There is a good feeling existing between the employers and the employed, both white and black, in the South, which is not equaled in any other section of this country, or in Europe either. There are no strikes here, no rebellions of the laborers, no disposition on the part of labor to combine against capital, and no disposition on the part of capital to oppress labor. Everything is in harmony, and a state of harmony and of prosperity in this respect exists which is to be found in no other place in the civilized world to the same extent as in the cotton States of the South. That is caused by the fact that there is a liberality upon the part of the employers which dispenses justice to the employed willingly and cheerfully, and without compulsion. This fact is recognized by the employees, and where there is justice between capital and labor, and no oppression, there is, of course, no necessity for collisions, strikes, or animosities. . . .

Now, I will make another statement which will probably be interesting to people who do not live here. The cotton States of the South are the only portion of the United States where whites and blacks work together upon the same work at the same pay and under the same regulations, the only part of this country where the two races will work side by side, justice being rendered to each, and the laborers of both races working in harmony and in unison, without rebellion and with mutual goodwill. I employed on mill No. 3 from fifty to seventy-five brick masons, and probably from fifteen to twenty rock masons. The men of both races were mixed, working side by side, black and white. They were paid equal wages, and there was perfect harmony between them and equal proficiency except in cases where special acquirements were necessary on special work, and, in one instance, for considerable length of time, a state of facts existed that could not exist in any other country in the world, viz, that the entire lot of laborers were superintended by a colored man. You can't see anything like that in New England, can you? But what I say of the harmonious relations between the laborers of the two races has particular reference to Georgia, and other States where the races have not been antagonized by violent political agitations in the past. . . .

I have been simply calling attention to the fact that we can do here what you cannot do there; that is, we can work the two races together on the same work in harmony, and I say again that you could not do that in the mines of Pennsylvania, in the rolling mills of Pittsburgh, in the manufacturing establishments of New York, or upon the buildings of New York, Boston, or Chicago. You could not find or get up in any of those places the same harmonious feeling which exists here between the races to-day.

The CHAIRMAN. Then it is not really the race question at all. It is simply this: that such a large part of your working population is colored that if you should undertake to exclude them from your labor market there would be nobody to do the work, and therefore, there being sufficient employment for both races, they work quietly alongside of each other, neither feeling that it is necessary to compete with the other for employment.

The WITNESS. Well, always, both before the war and since the war, there has been a better feeling between the two races here than at the North. The question of race, the question of the color of a man's face, does not arise at all in reference to this kind of labor, but in the North it does come in, and the consequence is that you find it impossible there to work the two races together harmoniously as we do here. I simply state this as a fact not generally known by parties at the North who have not investigated it. . . .

It is only in the proper place that the two races can come together harmoniously. They don't come together in the dining-room, they don't come together in society, but there is a place where they can come together harmoniously, and that is right down on this basis where it is a question of labor, and where the common sentiment of the people is that the two races are equal. So far as regards this question of such labor as can earn 60 or 70 cents a day, there is perfect equality between white and black labor here in the South. But that does not mean at all social equality. It has nothing to do with politics or with social equality or anything of the kind. It means just 75 cents a day for a day's work, whether the laborer is white or black, or $2.50 a day for a black mason, and $2.50 for a white mason. We have two blacksmiths at work at the Eagle and Phoenix mill, one of them being white and the other black, and they are on an equality in wages and in work. One of them is a very intelligent white man and the other is a very intelligent colored man. The question of equality does not come up with reference to those two men at all. They are both just blacksmiths working at $2.50 a day each, and drawing that amount of wages at the end of the week, and that is all there is to it. We do not mix the races in the machine shop. It is done only where there seems to be a certain suitableness in it. We do it on our rock walls and our brick walls, and among our carpenters, and we pay each one at the same rate for equal work.

Q. And give neither race the preference in selecting the men to be employed?

A. If I want a man to do certain things I want a colored man every time, while, on the other hand, if I want a man to do certain other things, I want a white man. I don't know that it hinges on the question of the whiteness or blackness of the man's skin; it hinges rather on the adaptability of the man to do the particular work that is required.

Q. Now, what have you to say to us in regard to child labor in factories?

A. Well, the child labor question is different here from what it is in the North, for sundry reasons. In the first place, it is a lamentable fact that parents here do not recognize the necessity of education to the extent that they do in the North. In the North all the people, including all the laboring classes, think it a duty to have their children educated, and the facilities which the free-school system gives them for that purpose are very largely used. Perhaps the laws of the Northern States regulate the matter somewhat; but laws are second to facts, and if the sentiment of the people did not justify such laws they would not be made. Then, too, a law that would be good in that regard in Massachusetts would not be good for anything in Alabama. You must adapt your laws to the State and conditions of society. Suppose you should pass a law in Alabama that, up to a certain age, children should not work because they must go to school, it wouldn't be good for anything; for the reason that, in the first place, even if they did not work, they would not go to school, because the parents would not want to send them, and also because if they did there are no schools to which they could send them generally. Again, on the other hand, that is not true of Georgia. Of course, I am now speaking only of the average. There are many people here who would be very apt and anxious to educate their children, and who would be very glad to send them to school. There are many who do send their children to school wherever they have the opportunity, but there are many others who do not; from want of thrift, or from the fact which does not exist elsewhere in this country, that the devastation produced by the war has swept away the material prosperity of the people and probably set them back fifty years in that respect, and as a consequence they are unable to educate their children as they would wish. For these reasons, and also because of the fact generally admitted, that economy is not one of the strongest points of the Southern people, there are a great many parents who would be glad to send their children to school, but who have not the opportunity or the means, being compelled to keep the children employed in procuring the necessaries of life.

In regard to the small children, more especially those in our spinning room, they are worth all they are paid, and the fact is that the wages they earn are a necessity for the support of the families from which the children come; so that if they were turned out there would be suffering upon the part of those families for want of that income. We do not really employ those children as a matter of preference, but as a matter of necessity. When a family comes here and a portion of them go to work in the mill they are sure to make application for employment for all their children who are of sufficient age to go to work in the mill, and they persist in those applications until those children are employed.

Q. At what ages are the children employed?

A. About ten years, I believe, is the youngest age at which we employ them.

Q. What do children of ten years and upward do?

A. They do this very light work, attending the spinning and winding machinery—very light work. There is no work that those children do that is sufficiently arduous to over-tax them or to interfere with their health or development. Their work is all light, and the only thing that can tax them is perhaps the hours of labor. . . .

Source: Report of the Committee of the Senate upon the Relation between Labor and Capital, 48th Congress, 4 (1885).

---

48. "There Is Power in a Union": A Song by Joe Hill, 1913

*Joseph Hillstrom (1879–1915) is the best known of the **Wobbly** songwriters. Known as **Joe Hill**, born as Joel Emmanuel Haggland, the Swedish immigrant was executed by firing squad in Utah after being convicted of murdering a store keeper. Hill joined the **Industrial Workers of the World (IWW)** in 1910 and, over the next five years, captured and articulated the meaning of the Wobbly cause in his songs, which, he argued were far more effective in promoting the union's cause than were pamphlets or posters, since the song would be repeated many times over. Hill set his lyrics to popular tunes of hymns, as he does in this selection.*

There Is Power in a Union
By Joe Hill
(Tune: "There Is Power in the Blood")

Would you have freedom from wage slavery,
Then join in the grand Industrial band;
Would you from mis'ry and hunger be free,
Then come! Do your share, like a man.

Chorus:

There is pow'r, there is pow'r
In a band of workingmen,
When they stand hand in hand,
That's a pow'r, that's a pow'r
That must rule in every land—
One Industrial Union Grand.

Would you have mansions of gold in the sky,
And live in a shack, way in the back?
Would you have wings up in heaven to fly,
And starve here with rags on your back?

If you've had "nuff" of "the blood of the lamb,"
Then join in the grand Industrial band;
If, for a change, you would have eggs and ham,
Then come, do your share, like a man.

If you like sluggers to beat off your head,
Then don't organize, all unions despise,
If you want nothing before you are dead,
Shake hands with your boss and look wise.

Come, all ye workers, from every land,
Come, join in the grand Industrial band,
Then we our share of this earth shall demand.
Come on! Do your share, like a man.

Source: I.W.W. Songs (Chicago: I.W.W. Publishing Bureau, 1916).

---

49. Thomas Geoghegan: Excerpt from *Which Side Are You On?*, 1991

Thomas Geoghegan, in the course of practicing labor law, represented workers at Wisconsin Steel. Here he gives an account of his efforts to recoup some of the pension funds due to his clients after the sale of Wisconsin Steel by International Harvester.

Geoghegan writes in the context of the decline of labor unions following the election of Ronald Reagan to the presidency and the emergence of a national climate of opinion that looked distrustfully upon unions.

For seven years (1981–88), I represented 2,500 former employees of Wisconsin Steel. We sued International Harvester, their former employer, for the benefits they lost when Harvester sold the mill to a tiny, undercapitalized company that quickly went bankrupt.

Wisconsin Steel was the first of the big Chicago mills to crash, and the crash was the most dramatic, because here, unlike most mills, the workers were cheated of their shutdown benefits. Even with the payments from the PBGC [Pension Benefit Guarantee Corporation], the workers still lost nearly $45 million. By 1988, if the interest on this money was added up, they had lost nearly $90 million. The benefits they lost, among others, include severance pay, supplemental unemployment benefits pay, extended vacation pay, "special payment," health insurance (for retirees). They even lost two weeks of wages because the paychecks bounced without warning when the mill suddenly closed in March, 1980.

But worst of all, 500 or so of them lost their pension benefits, often up to 60 percent, especially the "Rule of 65" pensions, which were the special shutdown benefits that went into effect only if the mill closed.

So not only did the workers lose their jobs; that would have been bad enough. But they also lost the $45 million, which was their "deindustrialization" money. The closing of Wisconsin Steel was, in many ways, like an earthquake. The first shock was that the mill closed. The second shock, like an aftershock, was that they would not get this money either. The money that would have cushioned the blow, that would have given them time to think, figure out what to do next, hold on to the car or the home a little longer: it was not much money, really, but it was enough, just enough, to make people lose their balance. Some of them could never get their balance back.

I spent all the Reagan years on this one case. It was endless. I felt like I was in prison. I used to think of that line from Richard II: "I wasted time, and now doth time waste me." I came to hate "deindustrialization." The mill had closed, but it seemed as if the litigation would never end, and I might have to clean up after this mill forever. I felt as the men must have felt: I was always living in the year 1980. I could not seem to leave 1980.

I wanted to move, go to New York, do anything else, but people told me, "You can't, you're stuck here," and they were right. I was stuck here. I was trapped in a way, just as the people in the neighborhood were trapped, trapped in homes they could not sell, like victims of an earthquake. Nobody was moving, nobody was going away. I was a labor lawyer, like it or not, until this damn case was done.

Here is how the case started:

In 1977, Harvester had owned Wisconsin Steel for seventy-five years, and the mill made the specially hardened steel for the trucks and machinery that Harvester manufactured. Gradually, Harvester had let the mill run down, and sometime in the mid-seventies, it began looking for a buyer. But no one in the business wanted to buy Wisconsin Steel. Not only was it run down, but there was an even bigger problem: the pension fund was short $65 million.

Wisconsin Steel, in short, was unsalable. Yet Harvester did not want to close it either. If it did so, it would owe the whole $65 million in pensions, plus another $20 million in special shutdown benefits, like severance pay. It almost seemed as if Harvester was trapped into keeping the mill open. Nor was Harvester the only steel company in the 1980s to have this problem. A union lawyer once told me, "The only reason half the steel mills in this country are still going is that they can't afford to pay the pensions." It was the revenge of the weak on the strong. "Shut us down, Mr. Employer, and you die, too."

So Harvester tried to close the mill indirectly. It transferred title to a dummy corporation. Then, when this corporate shell went bankrupt, Harvester could say, "Too bad, they're not our pensions now." But Harvester had to have an accomplice. It found one in a small engineering company, Envirodyne, Inc., which knew nothing about steel. Envirodyne was not much of a company, just two yuppies in a garage. But Envirodyne did not want to have to pay the pensions either. So Envirodyne transferred title to a subsidiary it created, EDC Holding Company. Then EDC transferred title to a subsidiary it created, WSC Corporation. One corporate shell came after another. It was like a game of Chinese boxes, and when you got to the last box, nothing was in it. Nobody would be paying the pensions.

Under our law, a subsidiary can go bankrupt and normally the parent company will not be liable for its debts. So when EDC or WSC went bankrupt, Harvester and even Envirodyne could say they owed nothing. Indeed, Harvester was not even the parent. But Harvester was the biggest creditor and held on through mortgages to everything of value. That was the malign beauty of it all, which I spent seven grudging years admiring. Harvester had dumped all the pension liabilities but kept control of all the assets. It could keep running the mill as if it still owned it. Envirodyne could conduct its little engineering experiments. And the workers, who may have been there twenty or thirty years, would lose their pensions, health insurance, severance pay, etc. Dumb, stupid organized labor would take the fall.

The deal was so mean, so vile, that even the investment bankers gagged. Lehman Brothers, the investment banking firm handling the sale, went to Harvester and objected on simple moral grounds. Peter Peterson, the president of Lehman, came out to a Harvester board meeting to express his distaste. He talked about the "appearance" and the "reality" of the transaction. He was ignored, but he made a record, at least, and it does show a certain honor: sometimes, even on Wall Street, someone may write a memo to the file.

Harvester kept the mill going for a decent interval (two years). Then, on March 28, 1980, with no warning to the workers, Harvester pulled the plug. It foreclosed on the mortgage, and the mill went down the drain. In minutes, WSC was in bankruptcy.

Everybody was stunned. They thought, "How could anything be wrong?"

Right before the mill closed, production almost cruelly began to go up. People were getting more overtime than ever. They were like old ladies, on their deathbeds, rougeing up their cheeks.

But no, it was something else: they never knew they were about to die, it was a total shock. They say people who die sudden, violent deaths are most likely to become ghosts and haunt the earth. On March 28, 1980, all the workers died a sudden, violent death, no time to say goodbye.

Men were obsessed with "the last day." Even seven years later, as we prepared for trial, they could not talk about anything else. Dozens of times, I asked potential witnesses, "Now what did you lose as a result of the closing of the mill?" And they answered with non sequiturs, their little stories about "the last day."

Mr. J. said, for example, "I'm walking off the shift, and my foreman comes over and says, 'Don't come back.'

"I said, 'What?'

"He said, 'Don't come back. It's over.'

"I said, 'What? What?'"

Another man said he was asleep, and someone phoned and woke him from a dream and said, "Don't come in, it's gone."

These stories might go on for fifteen, twenty minutes, just pointless stories. As witnesses, they worried me. They did not seem to care about the loss of pensions, etc. It was that phone call saying, "Don't come back." I was afraid that, as witnesses, they would talk about nothing else, and the jury would think, "What's the big deal about the last day?"

But maybe it was the day he died. The last day a man could remember himself as middle-class. The rest of his life began happening to someone else.

Over the years, I drove down to South Chicago to talk to the workers. I saw the neighborhood around Wisconsin Steel change. At first, in '81, '82, it was simply dead. By '85, it was beyond dead, and much more skeletal-looking: old tires, hubcaps, rusted human bones. Once, in the seventies, I used to dine in Slavic splendor at places like the Golden Shell. But nothing was that good now. Now I went hungry. Or I would drive twenty blocks north to the U of C and eat tunaburgers with biologists.

In the old days, driving down here, I used to see a sign: "Welcome to the Tenth Ward, Edward R. Vrdolyak, Alderman." Now I see a sign about a clinic for male impotence. This is how you know now you have entered the Tenth Ward.

Even the geography has begun to change. Now there is a whole mountain range of chemical waste rising to the south along I-80. What was once the Midwest has begun to look like the Adirondacks. There is even talk of ski lodges. Steelworkers from sex clinics could run the lifts.

When the mill crashed, so did the Union. Same week. Nobody ever saw it again.

It had never been much of a union anyway, just a small independent, not affiliated with the Steelworkers or the AFL-CIO. It did not even have a real labor lawyer: just Edward R. Vrdolyak (or ERV), the alderman, who wanted the worker-comp cases. ERV had a little office, and Tony Roque, the Union president, was an employee. Roque was an investigator or "runner," who brought in the injured men. Under Vrdolyak, the Union became a big, grinding worker-comp. machine, spitting out missing fingers, broken bones, all of it money in Eddie's pocket.

When the mill went down, ERV closed down the Union and walked away. He's got nothing against labor law. But there is no money in it, see? The money is in worker comp.

Poor Roque, the president, was in over his head. He was just a working guy, no genius, trying to figure out a Wall Street deal, with no one to help him, not even his boss, Vrdolyak. Even a good labor lawyer might not have been much help.

When Roque complained, Harvester handed him a sheet of paper. It said this document was a guarantee of the pensions. Roque signed it. Didn't really grasp it. In fact, the paper guaranteed just a tiny sliver of the pensions. By signing it, Roque unwittingly released Harvester from everything else: $65 million in pensions, $20 million in shutdown benefits.

Despite the shell, some lawyers at Harvester had thought the company could still be liable for the pensions. But now there was Roque's waiver. Harvester was delighted, amazed, that the Union could be so dumb.

When the mill went down, Tony Roque fled. Nobody saw him. He unlisted his phone number. People said he was in the hospital. Or he was dead. He was like a pilot who crashes a plane and 600 people die, the bodies lying all over South Chicago.

It was a mess.

Source: Thomas Geoghegan, *Which Side Are You On?: Trying to be for Labor When It's Flat on Its Back* (New York: Farrar, Strauss, Giroux: 1991).

---

50. Triangle Fire: Excerpts from the March 1911 *New York Times* Account of the Fire and from an April 1911 Speech by Rose Schneiderman

*The **Triangle Factory Fire of 1911** was not America's worst industrial accident, but it nonetheless captured the public imagination. Partly this was because it coincided with Progressive Era reform efforts to improve working conditions. The fire also served to underscore the dangers of **sweatshop** production against which labor unions had long warned. But a big part of Triangle's lurid appeal was also rooted in sexism. Prevailing views of women as fair, frail, and vulnerable enhanced the public's horror over the tragedy, as did graphic newspaper accounts like the one that appeared in the* New York Times *on March 26, 1911.*

*The Triangle Fire came on the heels of the **Uprising of the 20,000** and the two did much to bolster the recruitment efforts of the **International Ladies' Garment Workers' Union (ILGWU)**. The second document excerpts a famed speech from ILGWU organizer **Rose Schneiderman**, which she published in* The Survey *on April 8, 1911.*

New York Times, *March 26, 1911*

Three stories of a ten-floor building at the corner of Greene Street and Washington Place were burned yesterday, and while the fire was going on 141 young men and women at least 125 of them mere girls were burned to death or killed by jumping to the pavement below. . . .

Most of the victims were suffocated or burned to death within the building, but some who fought their way to the windows and leaped met death as surely, but perhaps more quickly, on the pavements below. . . .

The victims who are now lying at the Morgue waiting for some one to identify them by a tooth or the remains of a burned shoe were mostly girls from 16 to 23 years of age. They were employed at making shirtwaists by the Triangle Waist Company, the principal owners of which are Isaac Harris and Max Blanck. Most of them could barely speak English. Many of them came from Brooklyn. Almost all were the main support of their hard-working families. . . .

A heap of corpses lay on the sidewalk for more than an hour. The firemen were too busy dealing with the fire to pay any attention to people whom they supposed beyond their aid. When the excitement had subsided to such an extent that some of the firemen and policemen could pay attention to this mass of the supposedly dead they found about half way down in the pack a girl who was still breathing. She died two minutes after she was found. . . .

At 4:40 o'clock, nearly five hours after the employees in the rest of the building had gone home, the fire broke out. The one little fire escape in the interior was resorted to by many of the doomed victims. Some of them escaped by running down the stairs, but in a moment or two this avenue was cut off by flame. The girls rushed to the windows and looked down at Greene Street, 100 feet below them. Then one poor, little creature jumped. There was a plate glass protection over part of the sidewalk, but she crashed through it, wrecking it and breaking her body into a thousand pieces. Then they all began to drop. The crowd yelled "Don't jump!" but it was jump or be burned the proof of which is found in the fact that fifty burned bodies were taken from the ninth floor alone. They jumped, they crashed through broken glass, they crushed themselves to death on the sidewalk. . . .

[Fire] Chief Croker said it was an outrage. He spoke bitterly of the way in which the Manufacturers' Association had called a meeting in Wall Street to take measures against his proposal for enforcing better methods of protection for employees in cases of fire.

Four alarms were rung in fifteen minutes. The first five girls who jumped did so before the first engine could respond. . . . Thirty bodies clogged the elevator shaft. These dead were all girls. They had made their rush there blindly when they discovered that there was no chance to get out by the fire escape. Then they found that the elevator was as hopeless as anything else, and they fell there in their tracks and died.

The Triangle Waist Company employed about 600 women and less than 100 men. One of the saddest features of the thing is the fact that they had almost finished for the day. In five minutes more, if the fire had started then, probably not a life would have been lost.

How the fire started no one knows. On the three upper floors of the building were 600 employees of the waist company, 500 of whom were girls. The victims mostly Italians, Russians, Hungarians, and Germans were girls and men who had been employed by the firm of Harris & Blanck, owners of the Triangle Waist Company, after the strike in which the Jewish girls, formerly employed, had been become unionized and had demanded better working conditions. The building had experienced four recent fires and had been reported by the Fire Department to the Building Department as unsafe in account of the insufficiency of its exits.

The building itself was of the most modern construction and classed as fireproof. What burned so quickly and disastrously for the victims were shirtwaists, hanging on lines above tiers of workers, sewing machines placed so closely together that there was hardly aisle room for the girls between them, and shirtwaist trimmings and cuttings which littered the floors above the eighth and ninth stories.

Girls had begun leaping from the eighth story windows before firemen arrived. The firemen had trouble bringing their apparatus into position because of the bodies which strewed the pavement and sidewalks. While more bodies crashed down among them, they worked with desperation to run their ladders into position and to spread firenets. . . .

Thousands of people who had crushed in from Broadway and Washington Square and were screaming with horror at what they saw watched closely the work with the firenet. Three other girls who had leaped for it a moment after the first one, struck it on top of her, and all four rolled out and lay still upon the pavement.

Five girls who stood together at a window close [to] the Greene Street corner held their place while a fire ladder was worked toward them, but which stopped at its full length two stories lower down. They leaped together, clinging to each other, with fire streaming back from their hair and dresses. They struck a glass sidewalk cover and [into] the basement. There was no time to aid them. With water pouring in upon them from a dozen hose nozzles the bodies lay for two hours where they struck, as did the many others who leaped to their deaths. . . .

Source: "The Triangle Factory Fire," www.ilr.cornell.edu/trianglefire/texts/newspaper/nyt_032611_5.html.

"WE HAVE FOUND YOU WANTING"— ROSE SCHNEIDERMAN

I would be a traitor to these poor burned bodies if I came here to talk good fellowship. We have tried you good people of the public and we have found you wanting. The old Inquisition had its rack and its thumbscrews and its instruments of torture with iron teeth. We know what these things are today; the iron teeth are our necessities, the thumbscrews are the high-powered and swift machinery close to which we must work, and the rack is here in the firetrap structures that will destroy us the minute they catch on fire.

This is not the first time girls have been burned alive in the city. Every week I must learn of the untimely death of one of my sister workers. Every year thousands of us are maimed. The life of men and women is so cheap and property is so sacred. There are so many of us for one job it matters little if 146 of us are burned to death.

We have tried you citizens . . . you have a couple of dollars for the sorrowing mothers, brothers and sisters by way of a charity gift. But every time the workers come out in the only way they know to protest against conditions which are unbearable the strong hand of the law is allowed to press down heavily upon us. Public officials have only words of warning to us—warning that we must be intensely peaceable, and they have the workhouse just back of all their warnings. The strong hand of the law beats us back, when we rise, into the conditions that make life unbearable.

I can't talk fellowship to you who are gathered here. Too much blood has been spilled. I know from my experience it is up to the working people to save themselves. The only way they can save themselves is by a strong working-class movement.

Source: Rosalyn Baxandall and Linda Gordon, eds., America's Working Women: A Documentary History (New York: W. W. Norton, 1995), pp. 176–77.

---

51. Voluntarism: Excerpts from Samuel Gompers's Autobiography (1925)

American workers have often been ambivalent about the role of the State. Some workers have looked to government to alleviate injustice, legislate decent working conditions, eliminate class-based privilege, and otherwise level the playing field between employees and employers. Still others have feared the power of government, arguing that government is too often an arm of organized capital and is more likely to be a repressive agent than a progressive one.

*The early **American Federation of Labor (AFL)** fell into the latter category. AFL President **Samuel Gompers** embraced a labor version of laissez-faire in that he felt that capital and labor needed to resolve their disputes independent of government intervention. In Gompers's view, State intervention was dangerous on many levels, not the least of which was its tendency to undo what workers managed to win through their own efforts. But Gompers also feared benevolent government action, arguing that it weakened the labor movement by making workers beholden to the government rather than relying on their own organized might. (Some argue that those fears came to pass under the New Deal.)*

*Gompers and the AFL endorsed a rather elusive concept known as **voluntarism**. They saw both trade unions and political parties as noncoercive bodies that individuals could choose to join, or not. Thus, just as the AFL could not compel individual unions to join the federation or interfere in its personal affairs, neither should the State juxtapose itself between employees and employers. Gompers explains below:*

The methods and agencies for progress in the economic world must be evolved out of economic experience and life. It is a serious mistake to confuse the two fields or to carry the problems of one into the other. Trade unions or voluntary associations of wage-earners constitute one of the essential agencies for establishing procedure of control. The development of large-scale production, the increasing authority of science in determining processes, and the more recent investigations of management for the purpose of making it truly scientific, together with the marked tendency toward trade associations, are to me a most gratifying exemplification of my thought that discernment of the essential difference between the economic and the political clarifies the problem of progress.

Several times the plain question has been put to me by members of the Senate Committee on Judiciary: "Mr. Gompers, what can we do to allay the causes of strikes that bring discomfort and financial suffering to all alike?" I have had to answer, "Nothing." My answer has been interpreted as advocating a policy of drift. Quite the contrary to my real thought. Foremost in my mind is to tell the politicians to keep their hands off and thus preserve voluntary institutions and opportunity for individual and group initiative and leave the way open to deal with problems as the experience and facts of industry shall indicate. I have, with equal emphasis, opposed submitting determination of industrial policies to courts. But it is difficult for lawyers to understand that the most important human justice comes through other agencies than the political.

Source: Nick Salvatore, ed., *Seventy Years of Life and Labor: An Autobiography of Samuel Gompers* (1925; reprint Ithaca: ILR Press, 1984), pp. 134–35.

---

52. Women in the American Federation of Labor: Excerpt from Writings of Edward O'Donnell

*Women have always worked, but men have not always felt comfortable with that fact. For much of the nineteenth century, a Victorian ideal prevailed that held that male **wage** earners should be paid a **family wage** sufficient for them to provide for wives and children. This was only partially linked to the notion of a just wage; it also connected to the Victorian notion that the home was a woman's proper sphere, and that her natural realm of expertise and talent centered on the home and domestic duty.*

Social and economic reality clashed with hegemonic Victorian ideals. Millions of workingmen could not provide for their families adequately, forcing wives, sons, and daughters into the workplace. There, they often encountered hostility from the very organizations that sought to defend workers: labor unions. Although many unions organized women, quite a few labor advocates complained—not entirely without jus-tification—that the presence of women in the workplace undermined wages for men and threatened the very concept of the family wage. In their view, employers hired women (and children) at reduced rates as a way of curtailing union demands for higher wages.

Skilled craftsmen were among the most vocal in their opposition to women workers, and numerous unions affiliated with the early **American Federation of Labor (AFL)** *excluded women from membership. The views of Edward O'Donnell, of Boston's Central Labor Union, are typical of AFL attitudes about women in the pre-1920 period, though such views persisted well into the 1970s in some trades. Even today, some women complain they are not yet full partners in the labor union move-ment. This excerpt comes originally from Edward O'Donnell's "Women as Bread Winners—The Error of the Age," an article that appeared in October 1897 in the* American Federationist, *the official journal of the AFL.*

The invasion of the crafts by women has been developing for years amid irri-tation and injury to the workman. The right of the woman to win honest bread is accorded on all the sides, but with craftsmen it is an open question whether this manifestation is of a healthy social growth or not.

The rapid displacement of men by women in the factory and workshop has to be met sooner or later, and the question is forcing itself upon the leaders and thinkers among the labor organizations of the land.

Is it a pleasing indication of progress to see the father, the brother and the son displaced as the bread winner by the mother, sister and daughter?

Is not this revolutionary backslide, which certainly modernizes the present wage system in vogue, a menace to prosperity—a foe to our civilized preten-sions? . . .

The growing demand for female labor is not founded upon philanthropy, as those who encourage it would have sentimentalists believe; it does not spring from the milk of human kindness. It is an insidious assault upon the home; it is the knife of the assassin, aimed at the family circle—the divine injunction. It debars the man through financial embarrassment from family responsibility, and physically, mentally and socially excludes the woman equally from nature's dearest impulse. Is this the demand of civilized progress; is it the desire of Chris-tian dogma? . . .

The wholesale employment of women in the various handicrafts must grad-ually unsex them, as it most assuredly is demoralizing them, or stripping them of that modest demeanor that lends itself to the charm to their kind, while it numerically strengthens the multitudinous army of loafers, paupers, tramps and policemen, for no man who desires honest employment, and can secure it, cares to throw his life away upon such a wretched occupation as the latter.

The employment of women in the mechanical departments is encouraged because of its cheapness and easy manipulation, regardless of the consequent perils; and for no other reason. The generous sentiment enveloping this inducement is of criminal design, since it comes from a thirst to build riches upon the dismemberment of the family or the hearthstone cruelly dishonored. . . .

But somebody will say, would you have women pursue lives of shame rather than work? Certainly not; it is to the alarming introduction of women into the mechanical industries, hitherto enjoyed by the sterner sex, at a wage uncommandable by them, that leads so many into that deplorable pursuit. . . .

Source: Rosalyn Baxandall and Linda Gordon, eds., *America's Working Women: A Documentary History 1600 to the Present* (New York: W. W. Norton, 1995), pp. 162–64.

---

53. Women on the Breadlines During the Depression: An Account Published by Meridel Le Sueur in *New Masses,* 1932

*Meridel Le Sueur (1900–96) was the daughter of **socialist**-feminist parents, Marion Wharton and Alfred Le Sueur. She grew up in the Midwest amongst populist farmers and **Industrial Workers of the World (IWW)** activists. Le Sueur moved to the East Coast where she lived briefly with **Emma Goldman** and was friendly with John Reed and Edna St. Vincent Millay. She published her first article in 1927 and thereafter wrote numerous pieces on labor struggles; women's issues; and the plight of Native Americans, rural peoples, and the poor during the depression. With the women's movement of the 1970s, many of Le Sueur's works were given new life— several were published for the first time or reprinted. Below she gives an account of unemployed women in Minneapolis during the Great Depression. She continued writing progressive literature until close to her death, in St. Paul at age ninety-six. This account originally appeared in* New Masses *in 1932.*

I am sitting in the city free employment bureau. It's the woman's section. We have been sitting here now for four hours. We sit here every day, waiting for a job. There are no jobs. Most of us have had no breakfast. Some have had scant rations for over a year. Hunger makes a human being lapse into a state of lethargy, especially city hunger. Is there any place else in the world where a human being is supposed to go hungry amidst plenty without an outcry, without protest, where only the boldest steal or kill for bread, and the timid crawl the streets, hunger like the beak of a terrible bird at the vitals?

We sit looking at the floor. No one dares think of the coming winter. There are only a few more days of summer. Everyone is anxious to get work to lay up something for that long siege of bitter cold. But there is no work. Sitting in the room we all know it. That is why we don't talk much. We look at the floor dreading to see that knowledge in each other's eyes. There is a kind of humiliation in it. We look away from each other. We look at the floor. It's too terrible to see this animal terror in each other's eyes.

So we sit hour after hour, day after day, waiting for a job to come in. There are many women for a single job. A thin sharp woman sits inside the wire cage looking at the book. For four hours we have watched her looking at that book. She has a hard little eye. In the small bare room there are half a dozen women sitting on the benches waiting. Many come and go. Our faces are all familiar to each other, for we wait here everyday.

This is a domestic employment bureau. Most of the women who come here are middle aged, some have families, some raised their families and are now alone, some have men who are out of work. Hard times and the man leaves to hunt for work. He doesn't find it. He drifts on. The woman probably doesn't hear from him for a long time. She expects it. She isn't surprised. She struggles alone to feed the many mouths. Sometimes she gets help from the charities. If she's clever she can get herself a good living from the charities, if she's naturally a lick spittle, naturally a little docile and cunning. If she's proud then she starves silently, leaving her children to find work, coming home after a day's searching to wrestle with her house, her children.

Some such story is written on the faces of all these women. There are young girls too, fresh from the country. Some are made brazen too soon by the city. There is a great exodus of girls from the farms into the city now.

Thousands of farms have been vacated completely in Minnesota. The girls are trying to get work. The prettier ones can get jobs in the stores when there are any, or waiting on tables but these jobs are only for the attractive and the adroit, the others, the real peasants have a more difficult time. . . .

It's one of the great mysteries of the city where women go when they are out of work and hungry. There are not many women in the bread line. There are no flop houses for women as there are for men, where a bed can be had for a quarter or less. You don't see women lying on the floor at the mission in the free flops. They obviously don't sleep in the jungle or under newspapers in the park. There is no law I suppose against their being in these places but the fact is they rarely are.

Yet there must be as many women out of jobs in cities and suffering extreme poverty as there are men. What happens to them? Where do they go? Try to get into the Y.W.[C.A.] without any money or looking down at heel. Charities take care of very few and only those that are called "deserving." The lone girl is under suspicion by the virgin women who dispense charity.

I've lived in cities for many months broke, without help, too timid to get in bread lines. I've known many women to live like this until they simply faint on the street from privations, without saying a word to anyone. A woman will shut herself up in a room until it is taken away from her, and eat a cracker a day and be as quiet as a mouse so there are no social statistics concerning her.

I don't know why it is, but a woman will do this unless she has dependents, will go for weeks, verging on starvation, crawling in some hole, going through the streets ashamed, sitting in libraries, parks, going for days without speaking to a living soul like some exiled beast, keeping the runs mended in her stockings, shut up in terror in her own misery, until she becomes too super sensitive and timid to even ask for a job.

Bernice says even strange men she has met in the park have sometimes, that is in better days, given her a loan to pay her room rent. She has always paid them back.

In the afternoon the young girls, to forget the hunger and the deathly torture and fear of being jobless, try and pick up a man to take them to a ten cent show. They never go to more expensive ones, but they can always find a man willing to spend a dime to have the company of a girl for the afternoon.

Sometimes a girl facing the night without shelter will approach a man for lodging. A woman always asks a man for help. Rarely another woman. I have known girls to sleep in men's rooms for the night, on a pallet without molestation, and given breakfast in the morning.

It's no wonder these young girls refuse to marry, refuse to rear children. They are like certain savage tribes, who, when they have been conquered refuse to breed.

Not one of them but looks forward to starvation, for the coming winter. We are in a jungle and know it. We are beaten, entrapped. There is no way out. Even if there were a job, even if that thin acrid woman came and gave everyone in the room a job for a few days, a few hours, at thirty cents an hour, this would all be repeated tomorrow, the next day and the next.

Not one of these women but knows, that despite years of labour there is only starvation, humiliation in front of them. . . .

So we sit in this room like cattle, waiting for a non-existent job, willing to work to the farthest atom of energy, unable to work, unable to get food and lodging, unable to bear children; here we must sit in this shame looking at the floor, worse than beasts at a slaughter.

It is appalling to think that these women sitting so listless in the room may work as hard as it is possible for a human being to work, may labour night and day, like Mrs. Gray wash street cars from midnight to dawn and offices in the early evening, scrubbing for fourteen and fifteen hours a day, sleeping only five hours or so, doing this their whole lives, and never earn one day of security, having always before them the pit of the future. The endless labour, the bending back, the water soaked hands, earning never more than a week's wages, never having in their hands more life than that.

It's not the suffering, not birth, death, love that the young reject, but the suffering of endless labour without a dream, eating the spare bread in bitterness, a slave without the security of a slave.

Source: Meridel Le Sueur, *New Masses*, 1932.

---

54. Yellow-Dog Contract (1904)

*As more and more workers banded together in unions, fearful employers sought a variety of methods to deter organization. One of the most infamous of these was the **yellow-***

dog contract, *an agreement in which a worker swore not to join a labor union as a condition of employment. Although the term was not common until after 1902, the practice was common in the nineteenth century. The 1932* **Norris-LaGuardia Act** *and the 1935* **National Labor Relations Act** *abolished the practice, though many workers continue to complain that unwritten de facto yellow-dog contracts persist. The example below comes from a 1904 document required of Colorado miners seeking employment in the Cripple Creek region. It was usually accompanied by a housing lease agreement that reinforced the antiunion bias of the contract. The Colorado coalfield struggles convulsed the region from the 1890s through World War I. Although this document specifically mentions the Western Federation of Miners, its force was applied equally to other organizations, including the* **American Federation of Labor***.*

Mine No._____ Office No._____
APPLICATION FOR WORK
_____Mine.
_____ 190_.
Name, _____ _____.
Age, ____. Married? _____. Nationality, _____.
Residence, _____.
Occupation, _____.
Where last employed? _____.
For how long? _____.
In what capacity? _____.
Did you quit voluntarily, or were you discharged? _____.
If discharged, for what reason? _____.
How much experience have you had as _____? _____.
Where employed before coming to Cripple Creek district? _____.
Are you a member of the Western Federation of Miners? _____.
Have you ever been a member of the Western Federation of Miners? _____.
If so, when did you sever your connection with same? _____.
Do you belong to any labor organization; and if so, what? _____.
References: _____ _____.
_____,
Applicant.
Remarks: _____

Source: U.S. Congress, *A Report on Labor Disturbances in Colorado from 1880 to 1904, Inclusive* (1905), pp. 278–80.

---

55. Yellow-Dog Contract in the Coal Industry (1917)

The "yellow-dog contract" came to be so known because the popular saying was that it was so vile that no decent human being would even require an old yellow dog to sign such an agreement. The yellow-dog contract required workers, as a condition of employment, to agree not to join a union. The contract reproduced here was used by the Hitchman Coal and Coke Company. The majority of the Supreme Court, in Hitchman Coal and Coke v. Mitchell, *found the use of such contracts to be permissible under the Constitution.*

I am employed by and work for the Hitchman Coal & Coke Company with the express understanding that I am not a member of the United Mine Workers of America, and will not become so while an employee of the Hitchman Coal & Coke Company; that the Hitchman Coal & Coke Company is run non-union and agrees with me that it will run non-union while I am in its employ. If at any time I am employed by the Hitchman Coal & Coke Company I want to become connected with the United Mine Workers of America, or any affiliated organization, I agree to withdraw from the employment of said company, and agree that while I am in the employ of that company I will not make any efforts amongst its employees to bring about the unionizing of that mine against the company's wish. I have either read the above or heard the same read.

Source: Hitchman Coal and Coke Company v. Mitchell, 245 U.S. 229 (1917).

Bibliography

Compiling a bibliography of useful labor history books and sources is akin to trying to dam the ocean. Each year more superb works appear, and no one should construe the following list as definitive. These are mere starting points for deeper research. The books listed below are useful for the categories under which they appear. The editors in no way endorse *any* of these works in any sort of *best of* spirit. There are (literally) hundreds of stellar works that did not make it into the bibliography. The journal *Labor History* compiles a yearly list of titles published in the field of American history; we encourage researchers to consult the *Labor History* archive.

In keeping with the spirit of these volumes, we have largely avoided works on specialized topics. Readers are encouraged to see individual entries for suggestions on specialized topics. Our omission extends to individual trade unions. For the most part, we have listed works that deal with labor federations, but not individual unions. Many individual unions have histories that are easily located in databases. An excellent, though dated, guide to individual unions is Gary Fink, ed., *Labor Unions*, Westport, Conn.: Greenwood Press, 1977.

GENERAL SURVEYS

There are many fine labor-history-survey texts. Among the most thorough is Philip S. Foner's multivolume History of the American Labor Movement, *New York: International Publishers. Foner (1910–1994) was the preeminent labor historian of the twentieth century, and his survey encompasses nine volumes, all of which are now available in inexpensive paperback editions. Other good survey texts include the following:*

Babson, Steve. *The Unfinished Struggle: Turning Points in American Labor: 1877 to the Present*. New York: Rowman & Littlefield, 1999.

Brecher, Jeremy. *Strike!* Cambridge, Mass.: South End Press, 1997.

Dulles, Foster Rhea. *Labor in America: A History*. 6th ed. New York: Harlan Davidson, 1999.

Filipelli, Ronald. *Labor in the USA: A History*. New York: Alfred Knopf, 1984.

Green, James R. *The World of the Worker: Labor in Twentieth Century America*. New York: Hill and Wang, 1980.

Laurie, Bruce. *Artisans into Workers: Labor in Nineteenth-Century America*. New York: Hill and Wang, 1989.

Lens, Sidney. *The Labor Wars: From the Molly Maguires to the Sitdowns*. Garden City: Anchor Books, 1974.

Lichtenstein, Nelson. *State of the Union: A Century of American Labor*. Princeton, N.J.: Princeton University Press, 2002.

Meltzer, Milton. *Bread and Roses: The Struggle of American Labor 1865–1915*. New York: Mentor, 1967.

Rayback, Joseph G. *A History of American Labor*. New York: Free Press, 1966.

Zieger, Robert H. *American Workers: American Unions*. Baltimore: Johns Hopkins, 1994.

COLONIAL AMERICAN LABOR

Colonial labor is perhaps the least-studied aspect of American labor. Nonetheless, several very fine titles are available. Volume 1 of Philip Foner's History of the American Labor Movement *is a useful survey. Other good titles include the following:*

Applebaum, Herbert. *Colonial Americans at Work*. Lanham, Md.: University Press of America, 1996.

Innes, Stephen, ed., *Work and Labor in Early America*. Chapel Hill: University of North Carolina Press, 1988.

Jernegan, Marcus W. *Laboring and Dependent Classes in Colonial America, 1607–1783*. Westport, Conn.: Greenwood Press, 1980.

Morgan, Kenneth. *Slavery and Servitude in Colonial North America: A Short History*. New York: New York University Press, 2001.

EARLY REPUBLICAN AND ANTEBELLUM LABOR

We consciously chose not to list titles dealing with slavery, simply because said titles are too voluminous. More has been written about slavery than almost any other subject. Scholars researching slavery and slave work patterns would need to narrow their search parameters beyond those that make sense for us to list. We have included more general works on African American labor as a separate subsection.

Boydston, Jeanne. *Home and Work: Housework, Wages, and the Ideology of Labor in the Early Republic*. New York: Oxford Press, 1994.

Clark, Christopher. *The Roots of Rural Capitalism: Western Massachusetts, 1780–1860*. Ithaca, N.Y.: Cornell University Press, 1995.

Dawley, Alan. *Class and Community: The Industrial Revolution in Lynn*. Cambridge, Mass.: Harvard University Press, 1976.

Dublin, Thomas. *Women at Work: The Transformation of Work and Community in Lowell, Massachusetts, 1826–1860*. New York: Columbia University Press, 1979.

Glen, Robert. *Urban Workers in the Early Industrial Revolution*. New York: St. Martin's, 1984.

Hahn, Steven, and Jonathan Prude, eds. *The Countryside in the Age of Capitalist Transformation*. Chapel Hill: University of North Carolina Press, 1985.

Laurie, Bruce. *Working People of Philadelphia, 1800–1850*. Philadelphia: Temple University Press, 1980.

Pessen, Edward. *Most Uncommon Jacksonians: The Radical Leaders of the Early Labor Movement*. Albany: State University of New York Press, 1967.

Rock, Howard R., ed. *The New York City Artisan, 1789–1825: A Documentary History*. Albany: State University of New York Press, 1989.

Schultz, Ronald. *The Republic of Labor: Philadelphia Artisans and the Politics of Class, 1720–1840*. New York: Oxford Press, 1993.

Ware, Norman. *The Industrial Worker, 1840–1860*. 1924. Reprint, Chicago: Ivan R. Dee, 1990.

Wilentz, Sean. *Chants Democratic: New York City and the Rise of the American Working Class, 1788–1850*. New York: Oxford Press, 1984.

AMERICAN LABOR FROM THE CIVIL WAR TO 1900

Avrich, Paul. *The Haymarket Tragedy*. Princeton, N.J.: Princeton University Press, 1984.

Brundage, David. *The Making of Western Labor Radicalism: Denver's Organized Workers, 1878–1905*. Urbana: University of Illinois Press, 1994.

Fink, Leon. *Workingmen's Democracy: The Knights of Labor and American Politics*. Urbana: University of Illinois Press, 1983.

Foner, Philip. *The Great Labor Uprising of 1877*. New York: Monad Press, 1977.

Grob, Gerald. *Workers and Utopia: A Study of Ideological Conflict in the American Labor Movement, 1865–1900*. New York: Quadrangle Books, 1961.

Gutman, Herbert. *Power and Culture: Essays on the American Working Class*. New York: Pantheon, 1987.

———. *Work, Culture, and Society in Industrializing Society*. New York: Alfred A. Knopf, 1976.

Messer-Kruse, Timothy. *The Yankee International: Marxism and the American Reform Tradition*. Chapel Hill: University of North Carolina Press, 1998.

Montgomery, David. *Beyond Equality: Labor and the Radical Republicans 1862–1872*. Urbana: University of Illinois, 1981.

———. *Citizen Worker: The Experience of Workers in the United States with Democracy and the Free Market during the Nineteenth Century*. Cambridge: Cambridge University Press, 1993.

———. *Workers' Control in America*. Cambridge: Cambridge University Press, 1984.

Nelson, Bruce. *Beyond the Martyrs: A Social History of Chicago's Anarchists, 1870–1900*. New Brunswick, N.J.: Rutgers University Press, 1988.

Oestreicher, Richard. *Solidarity and Fragmentation: Working People and Class Consciousness in Detroit, 1875–1900*. Urbana: University of Illinois Press, 1986.

Rosenzweig, Roy. *Eight Hours for What We Will: Workers and Leisure in an Industrial City, 1870–1920*. Cambridge: Cambridge University Press, 1983.

Schneirov, Richard. *Labor and Urban Politics: Class Conflict and the Origins of Modern Liberalism in Chicago, 1864–97*. Urbana: University of Illinois Press, 1998.

Schneirov, Richard, Shelton Stromquist, and Nick Salvatore, eds., *The Pullman Strike and the Crisis of the 1890s*. Urbana: University of Illinois Press, 1999.

Stromquist, Shelton. *A Generation of Boomers: The Pattern of Railroad Labor Conflict in Nineteenth-Century America*. Urbana: University of Illinois Press, 1987.

Voss, Kim. *The Making of American Exceptionalism: The Knights of Labor and Class Formation in the Nineteenth Century*. Ithaca, N.Y.: Cornell University Press, 1993.

Ware, Norman. *The Labor Movement in the United States, 1860–1895: A Study in Democracy*. 1929. Reprint. Gloucester, Mass.: Peter Smith, 1959.

Weir, Robert E. *Beyond Labor's Veil: The Culture of the Knights of Labor*. University Park: Pennsylvania State University Press, 1996.

———. *Knights Unhorsed: Internal Conflict in a Gilded Age Social Movement*. Detroit: Wayne State University Press, 2000.

AMERICAN LABOR FROM 1900 TO 1929

Barrett, James R. *Work and Community in the Jungle: Chicago's Packinghouse Workers, 1894–1922*. Urbana: University of Illinois Press, 1987.

Bernstein, Irving. *The Lean Years: A History of the American Worker, 1920–1933*. Boston: Houghton Mifflin, 1960.

Brandes, Stuart. *American Welfare Capitalism, 1880–1940*. Chicago: University of Chicago Press, 1976.

Brody, David. *Labor in Crisis: The Steel Strike of 1919*. Urbana: University of Illinois Press, 1987.

———. *Steelworkers in America: The Non-Union Era*. Cambridge, Mass.: Harvard University Press, 1960.

Dubofsky, Melvyn. *Industrialism and the American Worker, 1865–1920*. 3rd ed. Arlington Heights, Ill.: AHM Publishing, 1996.

———. *We Shall Be All: A History of the Industrial Workers of the World*. Urbana: University of Illinois Press, 1988.

Ginger, Ray. *The Bending Cross: A Biography of Eugene Victor Debs*. New Brunswick: Rutgers University Press, 1949.

Goldberg, David. *A Tale of Three Cities: Labor Organization in Paterson, Passaic, and Lawrence, 1916–1921*. New Brunswick: Rutgers University Press, 1989.

Haydu, Jeffrey. *Making American Industry Safe for Democracy: Comparative Perspectives on the State and Employee Representation in the Era of World War I*. Urbana: University of Illinois Press, 1997.

Jacoby, Sanford. *Employing Bureaucracy: Managers, Unions, and the Transformation of Work in American Industry, 1900–1945*. New York: Columbia University Press, 1985.

Kazin, Michael. *Barons of Labor: The San Francisco Building Trades and Union Power in the Progressive Era*. Urbana: University of Illinois Press, 1987.

Keyssar, Alexander. *Out of Work: The First Century of Unemployment in Massachusetts*. New York: Cambridge University Press, 1986.

Lynd, Robert, and Helen Lynd. *Middletown: A Study in Contemporary American Culture*. New York: Harcourt Brace, 1929.

McCartin, Joseph. *Labor's Great War: The Struggle for Industrial Democracy and the Origins of Modern American Labor Relations, 1912–1921*. Chapel Hill: University of North Carolina Press, 1997.

Morris, James O. *Conflict Within the AFL: A Study of Craft versus Industrial Unionism, 1901–1938*. Ithaca: Cornell University Press, 1958.

Nelson, Daniel. *Frederick W. Taylor and Scientific Management*. Madison: University of Wisconsin Press, 1980.

————. *Managers and Workers: The Origins of the New Factory System in the United States, 1880–1920*. Madison: University of Wisconsin Press, 1975.

Russell, Francis. *A City in Terror: 1919, The Boston Police Strike*. New York: Viking Press, 1975.

Zieger, Robert. *Republicans and Labor, 1919–1929*. Lexington: University of Kentucky Press, 1969.

Zunz, Olivier. *The Changing Face of Inequality: Urbanization, Industrial Development, and Immigration in Detroit, 1880–1920*. Chicago: University of Chicago Press, 1983.

AMERICAN LABOR, THE DEPRESSION, THE NEW DEAL, AND WORLD WAR II

Alinsky, Saul. *John L. Lewis: An Unauthorized Biography*. New York: Putnam, 1949.

Atleson, James B. *Labor and the Wartime State: Labor Relations and Law During World War II*. Urbana: University of Illinois Press, 1998.

Auerbach, Jerold S. *Labor and Liberty: The LaFollette Committee and the New Deal*. Indianapolis: Bobbs-Merrill, 1966.

Bakke, E.W. *The Unemployed Worker: A Study of the Task of Making a Living Without a Job*. New Haven, Conn.: Yale University Press, 1940.

Bernstein, Irving. *A Caring Society: the New Deal, the Workers, and the Great Depression: A History of the American Worker, 1933–1941*. Boston: Houghton Mifflin, 1985.

————. *Turbulent Years: A History of the American Worker, 1933–1941*. Boston: Houghton Mifflin, 1969.

Cohen, Lizabeth. *Making a New Deal: Industrial Workers in Chicago, 1919–1939*. New York: Cambridge University Press, 1990.

Dubofsky, Melvin, and Warren Van Tine. *John L. Lewis: A Biography*. Ann Arbor: University of Michigan Press, 1969.

Fine, Sidney. *The Automobile Under the Blue Eagle: Labor, Management, and the Automobile Manufacturing Code*. Ann Arbor: University of Michigan Press, 1963.

————. *Sit-Down: The General Motors Strike of 1936–1937*. Ann Arbor: University of Michigan Press, 1969.

Friedlander, Peter. *The Emergence of a UAW Local, 1936–1939*. Pittsburgh: University of Pittsburgh Press, 1975.

Galenson, Walter. *The CIO Challenge to the AFL: A History of the American Labor Movement, 1935–1941*. Cambridge, Mass.: Harvard University Press, 1960.

Gerstle, Gary. *Working-Class Americanism: The Politics of Labor in a Textile City, 1914–1960*. New York: Cambridge University Press, 1989.

Gross, James A. *The Making of the National Labor Relations Board*. Albany: SUNY Press, 1974.

Hodges, James A. *New Deal Labor Policy and the Southern Cotton Textile Industry, 1933–1941*. Knoxville: University of Tennessee Press, 1986.

Horowitz, Roger. *"Negro and White, Unite and Fight": A Social History of Industrial Unionism in Meatpacking, 1930–1990*. Urbana: University of Illinois Press, 1997.

Leab, Daniel J. *A Union of Individuals: The Formation of the American Newspaper Guild, 1933–1936*. New York: Columbia University Press, 1970.

Lens, Sidney. *The Labor Wars: From the Molly Maguires to the Sitdowns*. Garden City: Doubleday, 1973.

Lichtenstein, Nelson. *Labor's War at Home: The CIO in World War II*. New York: Cambridge University Press, 1982.

Lynd, Robert, and Helen Lynd. *Middletown in Transition*. New York: Harcourt Brace, 1937.

Meier, August, and Elliott Rudwick. *Black Detroit and the Rise of the UAW*. New York: Oxford University Press, 1979.

Mortimer, Wyndham. *Organize!: My Life as a Union Man*. Boston: Beacon Press, 1971.

Nelson, Bruce. *Workers on the Waterfront: Seamen, Longshoremen, and Unionism in the 1930s*. Urbana: University of Illinois Press, 1988.

Plotke, David. *Building a Democratic Political Order: Reshaping American Liberalism in the 1930s and 1940s*. New York: Cambridge University Press, 1996.

Schatz, Ronald W. *The Electrical Workers: A History of Labor at General Electric and Westinghouse, 1923–1960*. Urbana: University of Illinois Press, 1983.

Zieger, Robert. *The CIO, 1935–1955*. Chapel Hill: University of North Carolina Press, 1995.

AMERICAN LABOR FROM 1945 TO 1980

Aronowitz, Stanley. *False Promises: The Making of American Working-Class Consciousness*. New York: McGraw Hill, 1973.

Berger, Bennett. *Working-Class Suburb: A Study of Autoworkers in Suburbia*. Berkeley: University of California Press, 1960.

Boyle, Kevin. *The UAW and the Heyday of American Liberalism, 1945–1968*. Ithaca: Cornell University Press, 1995.

Cochran, Bert. *Labor and Communism: The Conflict that Shaped American Unions*. Princeton: Princeton University Press, 1977.

Filipelli, Ronald L., and Mark D. McColloch. *Cold War in the Working Class: The Rise and Decline of the United Electrical Workers*. Albany: SUNY Press, 1995.

Fine, Sidney. *"Without Blare of Trumpets": Walter Drew, the National Erectors' Association, and the Open Shop Movement, 1903–1957*. Ann Arbor: University of Michigan Press, 1995.

Jacoby, Sanford. *Modern Manors: Welfare Capitalism Since the New Deal*. Princeton, N.J.: Princeton University Press, 1997.

Keeran, Roger. *The Communist Party and the Autoworkers Unions*. Bloomington: Indiana University Press, 1980.

Kornblum, William. *Blue-Collar Community*. Chicago: University of Chicago Press, 1974.

Levenstein, Harvey. *Communism, Anticommunism, and the CIO*. Westport: Greenwood Press, 1981.

Lichtenstein, Nelson. *State of the Union: A Century of American Labor*. Princeton, N.J.: Princeton University Press, 2002.

Meister, Dick, and Anne Loftis. *A Long Time Coming: The Struggle to Unionize America's Farm Workers*. New York: Macmillan, 1977.

Montgomery, David. *Workers' Control in America: Studies in the History of Work, Technology, and Labor Struggles*. Cambridge: Cambridge University Press, 1979.

Taft, Philip. *Organizing Dixie: Alabama Workers in the Industrial Era*. Westport: Greenwood Press, 1981.

Terkel, Studs. *Working*. New York: Pantheon Books, 1974.

AMERICAN LABOR 1980 TO THE PRESENT

Bensman, David, and Roberta Lynch. *Rusted Dreams: Hard Times in a Steel Community*. New York: McGraw-Hill, 1987.

Fink, Leon, and Brian Greenberg. *Upheaval in the Quiet Zone: A History of the Hospital Workers' Union, Local 1199*. Urbana: University of Illinois Press, 1989.

Geoghegan, Thomas. *Which Side Are You On?: Trying to Be For Labor When It's Flat on Its Back*. New York: Farrar, Strauss, Giroux, 1992.

Goldfield, Michael. *The Decline of Organized Labor in the United States*. Chicago: University of Chicago Press, 1987.

Gross, James. *Broken Promise: The Subversion of United States Labor Relations Policy, 1947–1995*. Philadelphia: Temple University Press, 1995.

Milkman, Ruth. *Farewell to the Factory: Auto Workers in the Late Twentieth Century*. Berkeley: University of California Press, 1997.

Moody, Kim. *An Injury to All: The Decline of American Unionism*. New York: Verso, 1988.

———. *Workers in a Lean World*. New York: Verso, 1997.

Parker, Mike, and Jane Slaughter. *Choosing Sides: Unions and the Team Concept*. Boston: South End Press, 1988.

Rosenblum, Jonathan D. *Copper Crucible: How the Arizona Miners' Strike of 1983 Recast Labor-Management Relations in America*. Ithaca: ILR Press, 1995.

Rosner, David. *Deadly Dust: Silicosis and the Politics of Occupational Disease in Twentieth-Century America*. Princeton, N.J.: Princeton University Press, 1991.

Sellers, Christopher C. *Hazards of the Job: From Industrial Disease to Environmental Health Science*. Chapel Hill: University of North Carolina Press, 1997.

Sugrue, Thomas J. *The Origins of the Urban Crisis: Race and Inequality in Postwar Detroit*. Princeton, N.J.: Princeton University Press, 1996.

Weiler, Paul C. *Governing the Workplace: The Future of Labor and Employment Law*. Cambridge, Mass.: Harvard University Press, 1990.

AFRICAN AMERICAN LABOR AND RACE

Arneson, Eric. *Brotherhoods of Color: Black Railroad Workers and the Struggle for Equality*. Cambridge, Mass.: Harvard University Press, 2001.

Asher, Robert, and Charles Stephenson, eds. *Labor Divided: Labor and Ethnicity in United States Labor Struggles, 1835–1960*. Albany: State University of New York Press, 1990.

Foner, Philip. *Organized Labor and the Black Worker, 1619–1973.* New York: Praeger Books, 1974.

Foner, Philip, and Ronald L. Lewis, eds. *Black Workers: A Documentary History From Colonial Times to the Present.* Philadelphia: Temple University Press, 1989.

Harris, William. *The Harder We Run: Black Workers Since the Civil War.* New York: Oxford Press, 1982.

————. *Keeping the Faith: A. Philip Randolph, Milton P. Webster, and the Brotherhood of Pullman Car Porters, 1925–1937.* Urbana: University of Illinois Press, 1997.

Hill, Herbert. "The Problem of Race in American Labor History." *Reviews in American History* 24 (1996): 189–208.

Honey, Michael K. *Southern Labor and Black Civil Rights: Organizing Memphis Workers.* Urbana: University of Illinois Press, 1993.

Letwin, Daniel. *The Challenge of Interracial Unionism: Alabama Coal Miners, 1878–1921.* Chapel Hill: University of North Carolina Press, 1998.

Mason, Patrick L., ed., *African Americans, Labor, and Society: Organizing for a New Agenda.* Detroit: Wayne State University Press, 2000.

Nelson, Bruce. *Divided We Stand: American Workers and the Struggle for Black Equality.* Princeton, N.J.: Princeton University Press, 2000.

Rachleff, Peter. *Black Labor in Richmond, 1865–1890.* Urbana: University of Illinois Press, 1989.

Roediger, David. *The Wages of Whiteness: Race and the Making of the American Working Class.* London: Verso, 1991.

Santino, Jack. *Miles of Smiles, Years of Struggle: Stories of Black Pullman Porters.* Urbana: University of Illinois Press, 1991.

Stromquist, Shelton, and Marvin Bergman, eds. *Unionizing the Jungles: Labor and Community in the Twentieth Century Meatpacking Industry.* Iowa City: University of Iowa Press, 1997.

ETHNICITY AND LABOR

Bodnar, John. *Immigration and Industrialization: Ethnicity in an American Milltown.* Pittsburgh: University of Pittsburgh Press, 1977.

————, et al. *Lives of Their Own: Blacks, Italians, and Poles in Pittsburgh, 1900–1960.* Urbana: University of Illinois Press, 1982.

Buhle, Paul, and Dan Georgakas, eds. *The Immigrant Left in the United States.* Albany: SUNY Press, 1996.

Chan, Sucheng. *This Bittersweet Soil: The Chinese in California Agriculture.* Berkeley: University of California Press, 1986.

Deutsch, Sarah. *No Separate Refuge: Culture, Class, and Gender on an Anglo-Hispanic Frontier in the American Southwest, 1880–1940.* New York: Oxford University Press, 1987.

Foley, Neil. *The White Scourge: Mexicans, Blacks, and Poor Whites in Texas Cotton Culture.* Berkeley: University of California Press, 1997.

Friday, Chris. *Organizing Asian American Labor: The Pacific Coast Salmon Industry, 1870–1942.* Philadelphia: Temple University Press, 1994.

Greene, Victor. *The Slavic Community on Strike: Immigrant Labor in Pennsylvania Anthracite.* South Bend: University of Notre Dame Press, 1968.

Griffen, Clyde, and Sally Griffen. *Natives and Newcomers: The Ordering of Opportunity in Mid-Nineteenth Century Pittsburgh*. Cambridge: Harvard University Press, 1978.

Guerin-Gonzalez, Camille. *Mexican Workers and American Dreams: Immigration, Repatriation, and California Farm Labor, 1900–1939*. New Brunswick: Rutgers University Press, 1994.

Haveven, Tamara. *Family Time and Industrial Time: The Relationship Between Family and Work in a New England Industrial Community*. New York: Cambridge University Press, 1982.

Ichioka, Yuji. *The Issei: The World of First-Generation Japanese Immigrants, 1885–1924*. Berkeley: University of California Press, 1988.

Kessner, Thomas. *The Golden Door: Italian and Jewish Immigrant Mobility in New York City, 1880–1915*. New York: Oxford University Press, 1977.

Korman, Gerd. *Industrialization, Immigrants and Americanizers: The View from Milwaukee*. Madison: State Historical Society of Wisconsin, 1967.

Morawska, Ewa T. *For Bread with Butter: The Life-Worlds of East Central Europeans in Johnstown, Pennsylvania, 1890–1940*. New York: Cambridge University Press, 1985.

Weber, Devra. *Dark Sweat, White Gold: California Farm Workers, Cotton, and the New Deal*. Berkeley: University of California Press, 1994.

GENDER AND LABOR

Baron, Ava. *Work Engendered: Toward a New History of American Labor*. Ithaca, N.Y.: Cornell University Press, 1991.

Baxandall, Rosalyn, and Linda Gordon, eds. *America's Working Women: A Documentary History 1600 to the Present*. New York: W. W. Norton, 1995.

Benson, Susan Porter. *Counter Cultures: Saleswomen, Managers, and Customers in American Department Stores, 1890–1940*. Urbana: University of Illinois Press, 1986.

Blewett, Mary H. *Men, Women, and Work: Class, Gender, and Protest in the New England Shoe Industry, 1780–1910*. Urbana: University of Illinois Press, 1990.

Buhle, Mari Jo. *Women and American Socialism 1870–1920*. Urbana: University of Illinois Press, 1983.

Foner, Philip S. *Women and the American Labor Movement: From the First Trade Unions to the Present*. New York: Free Press, 1982.

Gabin, Nancy. *Feminism and the Labor Movement: Women and the United Auto Workers, 1935–1975*. Ithaca, N.Y.: Cornell University Press, 1990.

Glenn, Susan A. *Daughters of the Shetl: Life and Labor in the Immigrant Generation*. Ithaca, N.Y.: Cornell University Press, 1990.

Groneman, Carol, and Mary Beth Norton. *"To Toil the Livelong Day": America's Women at Work, 1780–1980*. Ithaca, N.Y.: Cornell University Press, 1987.

Jones, Jaqueline. *Labor of Love, Labor of Sorrow: Black Women, Work and Family, from Slavery to the Present*. New York: Vintage Books, 1985.

Kesler-Harris, Alice. *Out to Work: A History of Wage-Earning Women in the United States*. Oxford: Oxford University Press, 1982.

Milkman, Ruth. *Women, Work, and Protest: A Century of U.S. Women's Labor History*. London: Routledge, 1987.

Strasser, Susan. *Never Done: A History of American Housework.* New York: Pantheon, 1982.

LAW, LABOR, AND THE STATE

Carrell, Michael R., and Christina Heavrin. *Labor Relations and Collective Bargaining: Cases, Practices, and Law.* Upper Saddle River, N.J.: Pearson Education, 2000.

Cihon, Patrick J., and James O. Castanega. *Employment and Labor Law.* Mason, Ohio: South-Western Publishing, 2001.

Dubofsky, Melvyn. *The State and Labor in Modern America.* Chapel Hill: University of North Carolina Press, 1994.

Feldpacker, Bruce. *Labor Guide to Labor Law.* Upper Saddle River, N.J.: Pearson Education, 1999.

Fick, Barbara J. *The American Bar Association Guide to Workplace Law: Everything You Need to Know about Your Rights as an Employee or Employer.* New York: Random House, 1997.

Sack, Steven M. *The Employee Rights Handbook.* New York: Warner, 2000.

Sexton, Patricia Cayo. *The War on Labor and the Left: Understanding America's Unique Conservatism.* Boulder, Colo.: Westview Press, 1991.

LEADERS OF LABOR

The single best source with which to begin a search on any American labor leader is Gary M. Fink, ed., Biographical Dictionary of American Labor Leaders, *Westport, Conn.: Greenwood Press, 1974. There are also fifteen insightful profiles in Melvyn Dubofsky and Warren Van Tine, eds.,* Labor Leaders in America, *Urbana: University of Illinois Press, 1987. Profiles of prominent radicals often appear in Mari Jo Buhle, Paul Buhle, and Dan Georgakas,* Encyclopedia of the American Left, *Urbana: University of Illinois Press, 1992. Below are biographies and autobiographies of some of the individuals who appear in these volumes.*

Anderson, Jervis A. *A. Philip Randolph: A Biographical Portrait.* Berkeley: University of California Press, 1990.

Atkinson, Linda. *Mother Jones: The Most Dangerous Woman in America.* New York: Crown, 1978.

Barnard, John. *Walter Reuther and the Rise of the Auto Workers.* Boston: Little, Brown, and Company, 1982.

Buhle, Paul. *Taking Care of Business: Samuel Gompers, George Meany, Lane Kirkland, and the Tragedy of American Labor.* New York: Monthly Review, 1999.

Camp, Helen. *Iron in Her Soul: Elizabeth Gurley Flynn and the American Left.* Pullman: Washington State University Press, 1995.

Ferris, Susan, Ricardo Sandoval, and Diana Hembree. *The Fight in the Fields: Cesar Chavez and the Farmworkers Movement.* New York: Harcourt, 1998.

Foner, Philip S., ed. *The Autobiographies of the Haymarket Martyrs.* New York: Monad, 1983.

Garrison, Dee. *Mary Heaton Vorse: The Life of an American Insurgent.* Philadelphia: Temple University Press, 1989.

Goldman, Emma. *Living My Life*. 2 vols. 1931. Reprint, New York: Dover, 1970.

Haywood, William. *The Autobiography of Big Bill Haywood*. 1929. Reprint, New York: International, 1966.

Jones, Mary. *The Autobiography of Mother Jones*. 1925. Reprint, Chicago: Charles Kerr Publishing, 1980.

Kaufman, Stuart, ed. *The Samuel Gompers Papers*. Vols. 1–9. Urbana: University of Illinois Press, 1986–.

Lichtenstein, Nelson. *Walter Reuther: The Most Dangerous Man in Detroit*. Urbana: University of Illinois Press, 1995.

Livesay, Harold. *Samuel Gompers and Organized Labor in America*. Boston: Little, Brown, and Company, 1978.

Phelan, Craig. *Grand Master Workman: Terence Powderly and the Knights of Labor*. Westport, Conn.: Greenwood Press, 2000.

———. *William Green: Biography of a Labor Leader*. Albany: State University of New York Press, 1989.

Powderly, Terence. *The Path I Trod: The Autobiography of Terence V. Powderly*. New York: Columbia University Press, 1940.

Reuther, Victor. *The Brothers Reuther and the Story of the UAW: A Memoir*. Boston: Houghton Mifflin, 1976.

Salvatore, Nick. *Eugene Debs: Citizen and Socialist*. Urbana: University of Illinois Press, 1982.

———, ed. *Seventy Years of Life and Labor: An Autobiography of Samuel Gompers*. Ithaca, N.Y.: Cornell University Press, 1984.

Seretan, L. Gene. *Daniel DeLeon: The Odyssey of an American Marxist*. Cambridge, Mass.: Harvard University Press, 1979.

Shulman, Alix Kates. *Red Emma Speaks: Selected Writings and Speeches by Emma Goldman*. New York: Random House, 1972.

Smith, Gibbs. *Joe Hill*. Salt Lake City: Peregrine Smith, 1984.

Wathen, Cindy, ed. *Remembering Cesar: The Legacy of Cesar Chavez*. Sanger, Calif.: Quill Driver Books, 2000.

Zipser, Arthur. *Workingclass Giant*. New York: International Publishers, 1981.

MEDIA, MUSIC, THE ARTS, AND LABOR

Boris, Eileen. *Art and Labor: Ruskin, Morris, and the Craftsman Ideal in America*. Philadelphia: Temple University Press, 1986.

Denisoff, R. Serge. *Great Day Coming: Folk Music and the American Left*. Baltimore: Penguin Books, 1973.

Foner, Philip S. *American Labor Songs of the 19th Century*. Urbana: University of Illinois Press, 1975.

Foner, Philip S., and Reinhard Schultz. *The Other America: Art and Labour [sic] in the United States*. West Nyack, N.Y.: Journeyman Press, 1985.

Godfried, Nathan. *WCFL: Chicago's Voice of Labor 1926–78*. Urbana: University of Illinois Press, 1997.

Greenway, John. *American Folksongs of Protest*. Philadelphia: University of Pennsylvania Press, 1953.

Halker, Clark D. *For Democracy, Workers, and God: Labor Song-Poems and Labor Protest, 1865–95*. Urbana: University of Illinois Press, 1991.

Lieberman, Robbie. *"My Song Is My Weapon": People's Songs, American Communism, and the Politics of Culture, 1930–50*. Urbana: University of Illinois Press, 1989.

O'Neill, William. *Echoes of Revolt: The Masses 1911–1917*. Chicago: Ivan Dee, 1966.

Ross, Steven J. *Working-Class Hollywood: Silent Film and the Shaping of Class in America*. Princeton, N.J.: Princeton University Press, 1998.

Schnapper, M. B. *American Labor: A Pictorial Social History*. Washington, D.C.: Public Affairs Press, 1972.

Seeger, Pete, and Bob Reiser. *Carry It On!: A History in Song and Picture of America's Working Men and Women*. New York: Simon and Schuster, 1985.

Stead, Peter. *Film and the Working Class: The Feature Film in British and American Society*. London: Routledge, 1991.

USEFUL LABOR WEB SITES

American Federation of Labor-Congress of Industrial Organizations (AFL-CIO) Labor History, www.aflcio.org.

American Federation of State, County and Municipal Employees (AFSCME) African American Labor History, www.afscme.org/about/aframlink.htm.

American Federation of State, County and Municipal Employees (AFSCME) Women's Labor History, www.afscme.org/otherlnk/whlinks.htm.

Child Labor Photographs of Lewis W. Hine, 1908–1912, www.boondocksnet.com/gallery/nclc/.

H-Net Bibliography of Comparative Labor History, www.h-net.msu.edu/~labor/threads/thrclhb.html.

Illinois Labor History Society, www.kentlaw.edu/ilhs.

Labor History Manuscripts in the Library of Congress, www.loc.gov/rr/mss/laborlc.html.

Mark Lause, American Labor History: An Online Study Guide, www.geocities.com/CollegePark/Quad/6460/AmLabHist/.

Organization of American Historians' Labor Bibliography, www/oah.org/pubs/magazine/labor/labor-bib.html.

Reference Source List Prepared by Andrew H. Lee, Tamiment Librarian, www.nyu.edu/library/bobst/research/tam/resources.

University of Illinois, Urbana-Champaign, Labor in Illinois, http:www.ilir.uiuc/edu/lii/.

U.S. Department of Labor, www.dol.gov/asp/programs/history/main.htm.

Wisconsin Labor History Society, www.wisconsinlaborhistory.org.

Index

Page numbers in bold indicate main discussion of entry.

List of Contributors

Carolyn Anderson
University of Rhode Island

Michael Bailey
University of Rhode Island

Lisa Barber
Bay Path College

Jaime Barnes
University of Rhode Island

John P. Beck
Michigan State University

Jon Bekken
Editor, *Industrial Worker*

Michele Bernier
Bay Path College

Don Binkowski
National Coalition of Independent
    Scholars

Mike Bonislawski
Boston College

Kevin Boyle
Ohio State University

Susan Roth Breitzer
University of Iowa

John W. Budd
University of Minnesota

Linnea Goodwin Burwood
State University of New York
    at Delhi

Stephen Burwood
State University of New York at
    Geneseo

Amanda Busjit
University of Rhode Island

Victor Caron
University of Rhode Island

John Cashman
Boston College

Bruce Cohen
Worcester State College

Cheryl Conley
Bay Path College

Alex Corlu
State University of New York at
    Binghamton

Yasmin Correa
Bay Path College

Evan Daniel
United Federation of Teachers

Howard Davis
University of Rhode Island

Dennis A. Deslippe
Australian National University

Timothy Draper
Waubonsee Community College

Babette Faehmel
University of Massachusetts at Amherst

Kenneth Ferus
University of Rhode Island

Pete Gingras
University of Rhode Island

Pauline Gladstone
Bay Path College

Tom Glynn
Rutgers University Libraries

Janet Greenlees
University of Exeter

James P. Hanlan
Worcester Polytechnic Institute

Simon Holzapfel
University of Massachusetts at Amherst

Walter Hourahan
University of Rhode Island

Shalynn Hunt
Bay Path College

Elizabeth Jozwiak
University of Wisconsin-Rock County

Leslie Juntunen
Bay Path College

Andrew E. Kersten
University of Wisconsin at Green Bay

Frank Koscielski
Wayne State University

Albert V. Lannon
Laney College

Penny Lewis
City University of New York

Erik Loomis
University of New Mexico

John F. Lyons
Joliet Junior College

Mark Marianek
University of Missouri

Dinah Mayo
University of Massachusetts at Amherst

Cornelia McAndrew
University of Rhode Island

Joseph A. McCartin
Georgetown University

Jeff McFadden
State University of New York at Binghamton

John McKerley
University of Iowa

Danielle McMullen
University of Rhode Island

Stephen Micelli
University of Toledo

Jay Miller
Wayne State University

Scott Molloy
University of Rhode Island

R. David Myers
The College of Santa Fe

Mitchell Newton-Matza
University of St. Francis

Mark Noon
Bloomsburg University

Kathleen Banks Nutter
Smith College

Chad Pearson
State University of New York at Albany

Sara Pleva
Bay Path College

Cristina Prochilo
National Trust for Historic Preservation

Margaret Raucher
Wayne State University

Jonathan Rees
University of Southern Colorado

Jim Riordan
University of Massachusetts at Amherst

Joseph F. Rodgers
University of Rhode Island

Maria Ruotolo
Bay Path College

Robert D. Sampson
University of Illinois at Urbana-
    Champaign

Patricia Shackleton
Michigan State University

Ralph Shaffer
California State University at Pomona

Robert Shaffer
Shippensburg University

Susan Sherwood
San Francisco State University

Anthony Silva
National Coalition of Independent
    Scholars

Edward Slavishak
University of North Carolina at Chapel
    Hill

T. Jason Soderstrum
Iowa State University

Joseph Turrini
Catholic University of America

Teri Voight
Bay Path College

Carl Weinberg
North Georgia College and State
    University

Emily Harrison Weir
Mount Holyoke College

Robert E. Weir
Bay Path College

Lisa J. Wells
Memorial University of Newfoundland

John Whitmer
Simpson College

James Wolfinger
Northwestern University

About the Editors

ROBERT E. WEIR is Associate Professor of History and Liberal Studies at Bay Path College. A 2001 Senior Fulbright Scholar, Weir is the author of *Knights Unhorsed: Internal Conflict in a Gilded Age Social Movement* and *Beyond Labor's Veil: the Culture of the Knights of Labor.*

JAMES P. HANLAN is Associate Professor of History and Secretary of the Faculty of Humanities and Arts at Worcester Polytechnic Institute. He is the author of *The Working Population of Manchester, New Hampshire, 1840–1866.*